third edition

Schools That Work

Where All Children Read and Write

Richard L. Allington

University of Tennessee at Knoxville

Patricia M. Cunningham

Wake Forest University

PEARSON

Boston • New York • San Francisco
Mexico City • Montreal • Toronto • London • Madrid • Munich • Paris
Hong Kong • Singapore • Tokyo • Cape Town • Sydney

Executive Editor: Aurora Martínez Ramos
Editorial Assistant: Mekea Harvey
Executive Marketing Manager: Krista Clark
Editorial Production Service: Omegatype Typography, Inc.
Composition Buyer: Linda Cox
Manufacturing Buyer: Linda Morris
Electronic Composition: Omegatype Typography, Inc.
Interior Design: Denise Hoffman
Cover Administrator: Kristina Mose-Libon

For related titles and support materials, visit our online catalog at www.ablongman.com.

Between the time website information is gathered and then published, it is not unusual for some sites to have closed. Also, the transcription of URLs can result in typographical errors. The publisher would appreciate notification where these errors occur so that they may be corrected in subsequent editions.

Library of Congress Cataloging-in-Publication Data

Allington, Richard L.
  Schools that work : where all children read and write / Richard L. Allington, Patricia M. Cunningham.—3rd ed.
    p. cm.
  Includes bibliographical references and index.
  ISBN 0-205-45635-9 (paperback)
  1. School management and organization. 2. Language arts (Elementary) 3. Reading (Elementary) I. Cunningham, Patricia Marr. II. Title.

  LB2805.A449 2007
  371.2—dc22

                                                                2005058600

Printed in the United States of America

10 9 8 7 6 5 4 3 2 1   11 10 09 08 07 06

Credits appear on page 342, which constitutes an extension of the copyright page.

contents

chapter **4** *The What of Reading:*
The Reading Curriculum   **74**

chapter **5** *Who Does What?*   **103**

chapter **9** *Family Involvement*   **220**

chapter **10** *Schools That Work for All Children*   **244**

chapter **11** *A Tour through a School: What to Look For*   **275** chapter **12** *Getting Started*   **299**

We have focused our professional careers on understanding how schools might organize instructional resources so that all children become readers and writers. In *Classrooms That Work: They Can All Read and Write,* fourth edition (Cunningham & Allington, 2007), we offer a framework for classroom instruction to achieve that end. In the closing chapter of that book, we note that forces outside the classroom can either foster or hinder progress in creating classrooms that work for all children. In this book, we primarily address factors that generally are beyond the control of classroom teachers.

We wrote this book because we see that many schools, despite the best of intentions, are organized in ways that thwart the creation of effective classrooms. Having worked with numerous schools, we find that many use the extraordinary financial resources offered by local, state, and federal education agencies—funds that support developmental kindergartens; bilingual, remedial, and special education programs; dropout prevention efforts; and family-involvement programs—in ways that cannot work to accelerate children's achievement.

Many schools are "stuck," unable to create more effective programs because historical policies and practices constrain their visions of how to implement change. Too often, schools add more of the "same old, same old," although increasing these efforts is often at odds with enhancing classroom effectiveness. For instance, 1992 was the year in which schools first employed more adults who were not classroom teachers than adults who were. Fifty-two percent of the people working in schools are not classroom teachers (National Commission on Teaching and America's Future, 1997)! The addition of these "special-program personnel"—resource-room teachers, speech therapists, counselors, psychologists, reading teachers, social workers, and others—has created in many schools an environment in which scheduling at-risk children for self-esteem workshops or articulation therapy takes precedence over ensuring access to intensive and effective classroom instruction. Special services squeezed into the school day often squeeze out effective instruction.

It is not just special programs that need restructuring. We need to rethink curriculum standards to meet the expanded literacy demands of a technological society. We need to rethink the very notion of the school day and school year as more and more children—now the majority—come from families in which parents are employed and often not at home until after 5:30, several hours after most children end their traditional school day. The compelling evidence that traditional in-service education offerings are largely ineffective should cause us to rethink the nature of professional development across the career-span for both teachers and administrators. Likewise, the way we assess students and evaluate programs must change; so, too, must family-involvement policies and initiatives.

Schools face new pressures and new mandates to close the achievement gaps that exist between more- and less-advantaged students, pupils with disabilities and those with none, and minority and majority students. Schools that are determined to develop all children as readers and writers will find that new ways of thinking are more important than increased funding. We are not suggesting that schools are well funded but rather that, with the money currently available, schools could achieve better outcomes than they do now.

As school systems attempt to meet the new challenges, there is a need for clear, effective resources. Principals, teachers, parents, and community members who are interested in school improvement need a source they all can read in which they will find not only research-based information but also a vision for creating schools that work.

This book provides practical information for those wanting to create elementary schools in which all children become readers and writers. We describe critical factors, such as professional roles, organization of time, curriculum, student assessment, professional development, and parental involvement, that can advance or impede the development of more effective educational settings. We draw on our combined 50-plus years of experience as teachers, curriculum coordinators, administrators, researchers, reformers, evaluators, and consultants in schools. Our ideas and recommendations are grounded in proven practices and current research. We describe exemplary efforts in real schools across the United States and offer a variety of activities for taking stock of the educational effort in your school. We offer you information on where to obtain specific materials that will support changing your school for the better—we even provide toll-free phone numbers and Web addresses in many instances.

In this new edition of *Schools That Work* we offer a clear view of how schools must change if they are to meet the new educational demands. The third edition summarizes recent research on reading development and instruction, on the importance and nature of effective classroom teaching, and on the use of technology for both teacher and student development. We have updated the entire book with a special emphasis on recent federal and state initiatives targeted at addressing the problems of struggling readers and writers. We have added what has recently been learned from studies of school change and teacher development. We continue to argue that because schools differ substantially, no single strategy will work in every location. Thus, we provide information and examples that we hope will help you develop your own vision of what your school might become—take a moment and scan the table of contents. In Chapters 2 and 11 we offer written snapshots and portraits of schools that really do work better for all children.

We know that schools where every child reads and writes can be created. We have seen these schools! Elementary schools have but one overriding mission: to foster the development of independent literacy in all students so that each person becomes literate for a lifetime. Our hope is that this book will move us a little closer to creating schools where all children are readers and writers.

We could not have written this book without the assistance of numerous school administrators, teachers, and university colleagues across the country. It is to these devoted and innovative professionals that we dedicate this book. We might have tried to list all the folks who invited us to schools to observe programs and talk with the professional staff and parents. However, the result would have been a very long list, and we would never have remembered everyone. We also want to thank the parents, children, and professional staffs of the Park Terrace School in Gloversville (New York), the Beall and Alta Vista Elementary Schools in the El Paso (Texas) Independent School District, the Montview Elementary School in Aurora (Colorado), the Moncure Elementary School in Chapel Hill (North Carolina), and the Cash and Clemmons Elementary Schools in Winston-Salem (North Carolina) for the use of the photographs we took while visiting; and the reviewers for this edition: Martha A. Adler, University of Michigan–Dearborn; Mariam Jean Dreher, University of Maryland–College Park; Helen Hoffner, Holy Family University; and Juan Lira, Texas A&M International University. Finally, both of us also are indebted to the many others—our colleagues, including especially our spouses, Anne McGill-Franzen and Jim Cunningham, and our students—who have helped us shape the ideas offered in our two books.

Richard L. Allington
Patricia M. Cunningham

chapter 1

The Schools We Have—
What We Must Change

No matter how smart or how cute or how wonderful a child might be, parents should hope that their child finds learning to read and write easy. For it is the children who have difficulty learning to read and write alongside their peers who most often struggle in school. Delays and difficulties in learning to read and write are the most common reasons given for retaining children, labeling them, placing them in a special track, group, class, or program. Too often, children who do not experience early school success experience no success at all. The longer children experience failure, the greater is the likelihood they will never be successful in school.

It is the children who arrive at kindergarten with a history of few home experiences with print, book, story, and pencil activities who are most likely to occupy the desks in the basic skills and special education classrooms in high school 10 years later. Early school

According to the U.S. Department of Commerce, soon nearly half of all U.S. workers will be employed in industries that produce or intensively use information technology products and services.

The congressionally appointed 21st Century Workforce Commission argues that too many adults entering the workforce lack the skills needed for such employment and warns that U.S. economic competitiveness will suffer unless schools change. To remedy persistent skills shortages in the workforce, the commission argues for "21st-century literacy" consisting of strong academic skills, thinking, reasoning, teamwork skills, and proficiency in using technology.

achievement, especially in reading and writing, is a terribly reliable predictor of later school achievement (Snow, Burns, & Griffin, 1998). It is these children who are least likely to experience success in kindergarten or first grade. These children often then continue to struggle throughout elementary, middle, and high school. The schools we have are better at sorting and labeling children than at accelerating their academic development (Allington, 1994b). Of course, some schools have created programs that work better than others. But, generally, the schools we have do not work well for all children.

In this book, we offer educators a vision of elementary schools where all children become successful, thoughtful readers and writers. U.S. society has changed, but our schools have remained largely static in their organization and predictable outcomes. The elementary school of today mirrors the basic design of the graded elementary school that was laid out in the early 1900s. Those schools were designed to sort children into three worker groups—laborers, craftspeople, and professionals—with most children sorted into the laborer group. But agriculture and factory work were the primary occupations of most workers during much of that century. Today, few people work in agriculture, and the number of factory workers and craftspeople is rapidly declining. Today, skills in information management in a technological workplace dominate the job market. Hardly anyone feels confident that schools are producing young adults with the knowledge, experiences, and skills they need to be successful in modern society. Federal projections indicate that the shifting U.S. economy will require a workforce in which the average worker, not only the bosses, will need some college or other postsecondary education simply to bring home a paycheck (Smith & Lincoln, 1988).

We need schools that educate children—not schools that simply sort children into worker groups. We need schools that help children exceed their destiny—schools where *all* children are successful, not just the lucky ones who find schooling easy. We need schools that develop in all children the knowledge, skills, and attitudes that have historically been reserved for a few. We need elementary schools that break the gridlock of low achievement that stymies later efforts to educate all children.

To accomplish this will require elementary schools to become quite different from most elementary schools today. In this book, we attempt to provide administrators, supervisors, and teachers with information and ideas that they will find useful when making decisions about organizing and delivering effective reading and writing instruction. We draw on what we have learned while working in elementary schools over the past 30-plus years.

We emphasize creating schools where all children become readers and writers because that has been the primary focus of our own work and because learning to read and write is essential to success in school and in society.

Too often, educational reformers have failed to learn from the past, and schools reform again and again and again—returning after a few years to practices found lacking in the past but seemingly lost from institutional memory (Cuban, 1990). If schools are to survive and succeed, the past cannot be forever repeated. It is possible to create elementary schools where all children become readers and writers alongside their friends.

In this book, we focus on the children who are struggling in current educational programs. We focus on these children because when schools work well for them, schools work better for all children.

Who Are the Struggling Readers and Writers?

The past 25 years have not been good years for many children in the United States. U.S. rates of childhood poverty are now higher than those in any of the nations viewed as our economic competitors (Berliner, 2005). As the new millenium began, 20 percent of children are living in poverty, a population that increased substantially despite one of the longest economic booms in U.S. history. The majority of these poor children are white, but minority children make up the greatest proportion. Today, 15 million children are being raised in single-parent households with incomes within $1,000 of the official poverty line. The average incomes of these single-parent families hover about the poverty line and at a level that is less than half of the average income for two-parent families. Eleven million workers are currently employed at or near minimum wage; the majority of these workers are women over age 25 with dependent children. Forty percent of all children will live in a household receiving Aid to Families with Dependent Children for at least one year before they reach age 18. Over half of all children are likely to have lived in a single-parent household during at least part of their childhood (Hodgkinson, 1993).

Children in Poverty

It is the children whose families are poor (including children of the working poor) whom our schools serve least well. School performance has been quite predictable from student social-class data. Schools that enroll large numbers of children from poor families rank among the lowest performing schools (Cooley, 1993). Conversely, when schools enroll few poor children, achievement typically ranks much higher. It is not only achievement that varies but also school attendance, high school completion rates, and college attendance after graduation. In fact, most measures of school quality vary as a function of poverty levels among the families in the community (Stipek, 2004). Education spending also varies along with student poverty. Ironically, U.S. society currently concentrates

Is Your School Biased?

In the ideal school, all children would have a similar opportunity to become liter-ate. But today, in many schools, the odds seem stacked against some children. It may be useful to examine the patterns of success and failure in your school. In the chart below we present information on first graders who were retained in one school.

	Poor	Male	Minority	ELL
Max		x		
Minh	x	x	x	x
Randy		x		
Miriam	x		x	
Jonah	x	x	x	
Harish	x	x	x	x
Candace	x		x	
Ereno		x	x	

In this school, 35 percent of the children were poor, 48 percent were male, and 20 percent were minority-group members. We found a bias, or overrepresentation, in this school on each characteristic: family poverty, gender, and minority-group membership. In other words, children retained were predominantly poor, male members of a minority group, or English language learners (ELL). We concluded that this school's programs did not work well for poor children, boys, or minorities.

This evaluation activity can be applied to any number of educational outcomes. For instance, schools might examine similar patterns in the identification of children who are gifted or children identified as learning disabled, or children selected for safety patrol. Crafting schools that work for all children begins with locating biases that exist in a school.

educational funds on those schools with the fewest children from poor families. More money is spent per student in relatively stable, relatively wealthy suburban schools than in schools that serve large numbers of poor children in rural or urban communities (Kozol, 1991). In addition, more is spent on high school educational programs than on elementary school educational efforts.

Poverty is not the only factor that places a child at risk of academic failure, but it is the most pervasive one. With childhood poverty on the rise, more of the children who ar-rive at school will be at risk for school failure. The central role of family poverty can be seen by examining the data on minority-student achievement. For example, the academic achievement of African American and Latino students from middle-class homes substan-tially exceeds the achievement of white and Asian students whose families are poor. Nearly a quarter of African American and Latino students from middle-class families achieved advanced levels of mathematics performance, compared with only 7 percent of the white students from poor families (Hodgkinson, 1993). This is not to suggest that minority status is unimportant but rather that family poverty, regardless of race, increases the likelihood that children will not be well served in school.

Parents' Education

Parental educational attainment is related to the success children experience in school. Parent educational attainment is related to family income. Better-educated parents generally earn more money than less-educated parents and, thus, are able to purchase various sorts of educational support for their children (e.g., tutorial assistance, home educational materials, or summer educational experiences). Parents who are better educated also have resources in addition to their larger incomes. They often have more time, energy, and schedule flexibility to assist their children in school-related activities. It is the minimum-wage worker who works the longest hours with the least flexibility for the smallest paycheck. It is the children of the working poor who are most likely to be latchkey children. These are the children whose parents can least afford after-school assistance or private tutors and are least able to provide their children with needed instructional support themselves.

All parents care about their children, but parents have different sorts of resources for acting on that caring and concern. All parents cannot help with homework. All parents cannot read to their children. All parents cannot attend parent conferences. Some parents struggle simply to feed, bathe, and get their children to school each day. Many parents feel that by regularly sending clean, healthy children to school they are fulfilling their parental obligations. Often, though, schools expect more.

Oddly, schools expect more from parents today, even though more children are living with only one parent or both parents are working (in the majority of families with school-age children). Schools are expecting more parent involvement when fewer parents are available and when many parents have less discretionary time than ever before. Besides, not all parents hold the same beliefs about parental responsibility. Parents' views of what parents should do often differ. Parents with white-collar jobs often have beliefs about their roles that match the beliefs of the white-collar teaching profession. Parents with blue-collar jobs often have different beliefs about the roles of parents and teachers. The differences seem related to differences in the careers of the different groups of parents (Lareau, 1989).

Imagine a widget manufacturing plant. As the factory whistle blows at 3:30 ending the workday, the foreman calls out to the assembly-line workers, "I'll go punch everyone out on the time clock. Let's all stay put for another hour to finish out this order of widgets." The workers quickly agree and continue building widgets until 4:30, donating the last hour without pay.

This image will strike anyone familiar with blue-collar work as rather ludicrous. Whether it is factory workers, day laborers, grocery store cashiers, or city public works employees, the workday is bounded by time, and extra time at work usually means extra wages. However, this is not typically the case for white-collar workers. Teachers, store managers, city department heads, lawyers, financial planners, and other white-collar workers earn a salary less often tied explicitly to how many hours they work. White-collar workers often stay late, take work home, and work on weekends, all without earning extra pay.

This difference in work patterns may explain why some parents see homework as useful and, indeed, necessary whereas others view it as an unwarranted intrusion on home life. Parents with white-collar occupations often support homework; other parents may believe schoolwork should be confined to the school day. White-collar parents view supporting children's homework as a parenting responsibility, but not all parents agree with this view. As long as such differences in beliefs exist, some children will be more likely to do their homework and receive parental assistance in completing it. We cannot simply assume all parents adhere to the same beliefs about school and parent roles.

Parents are important in children's school careers. Ideally, though, schools would be designed to be "family neutral"—neither rewarding nor penalizing children for differing levels of family involvement. Parents are better educated today than ever before; but only one in five is a college graduate, and one in five never completed high school. Schools cannot select their students' parents, but schools can change in ways that make parental educational resources less influential in determining children's success in school.

Gender

Gender also plays an important role in children's school careers. Boys, more often than girls, are retained in grade, placed in remedial classes, identified as having learning disabilities, and suspended from school. Regardless of other factors, boys seem to experience more difficulty than girls in elementary schools today. Boys' reading achievement, for instance, lags behind girls by a significant margin throughout K–12 schooling (Smith & Wilhelm, 2002). However, schools are more successful with some boys than with others. For instance, poor boys are much more likely to be retained than middle-class boys. Poor minority boys are most likely to be retained, identified as having a disability, placed in remedial classes, or suspended from school (Epstein, 1998). Schools cannot change children's gender, but schools can change in ways that make gender less important to school success.

"Immaturity" is a tag hung more often on boys. This supposed immaturity is viewed as one source of the difficulties boys experience. But boys in elementary schools today are older than elementary schoolboys of only a few years ago. There are several reasons for this change. First, and probably most important, is that middle-class parents are now more likely to hold younger boys out of school for an additional year (Mergendoller, Bellsimo, & Horan, 1990). These parents seem to recognize that schools are sometimes not well adapted to young boys. Second, the eligible entering age for kindergartners seems to be moving up. January 1 was a common birthdate cutoff for school entry 25 years ago, but today August/September/October cutoffs are more common.

Even though boys are now older, in many schools "immaturity" is the most common reason teachers give for the academic difficulties children experience. This is an odd situation for reasons beyond the fact that elementary schoolboys are now older. Reported indicators of immaturity include short attention spans, wigglyness, lack of small motor coordination, and hyperactivity. Studies, however, show that boys tend to favor activity over inactivity and large motor activity over small motor activity and are less likely to voluntarily engage in print and language play (especially when active alternatives are available). Boys, it seems to us, are often considered immature when they prefer the activities that most boys prefer.

Schools can have a balance of large motor and small motor activity—schools where dance and creative dramatics are as valued and as common as penmanship and coloring assignments. Schools can be developed where Lego and block activities are as common and as important as cutting, coloring, and pasting. Schools can be designed so that movement is encouraged and sitting passively in desks for long stretches is uncommon. Schools can dramatically expand their supply and use of informational books in reading lessons. Boys prefer informational texts, but narrative stories dominate during reading lessons (Duke, 2000). Schools where boys do as well as girls are possible. There is no need to perpetuate the current mythology that many boys are not ready for school. Instead, schools can be made more ready for boys. In our view when boys acting like boys have difficulty, it is the school that needs to change.

What Doesn't Work? Why Not?

Schools have typically offered a number of tired responses when children exhibit difficulty learning to read and write. These responses have long histories of offering little of benefit to children. Many common school responses do not accelerate literacy development, and struggling readers continue to struggle even after participating. Schools must respond more adequately to the difficulties some children experience and begin to respond as soon as children arrive.

The Gift of Time Is No Gift at All

When 5-year-olds come to school with little or no reading and writing experience, they often appear uninterested in learning to read and write. This disinterest may lead to the suggestion, "Perhaps we should wait for interest and readiness to develop."

Some schools set kindergarten entrance standards and denied limited-experiences children entry into kindergarten (or discouraged parents from enrolling their child). But leaving the limited-experience child in the home for another year did not seem to work very well. So some schools created "developmental" kindergartens. These were designed to be less academic and to provide the "gift of time"—a waiting period. Most children assigned to developmental kindergarten spend two years in kindergarten—one in the developmental kindergarten and one in the regular kindergarten. However, these programs often denied children involvement in the very literacy-learning experiences that fostered the development in more advantaged children. Too often these classrooms were not designed to immerse the children in a print-rich language and literacy environment. Too often these developmental programs had no story circles, no big books, no scribbling tables, no drawing and labeling activities, and none of a host of other activities that characterize the book, story, and print experiences of more advantaged preschool children (McGill-Franzen, Lanford, & Adams, 2002).

Children who arrive at school with few book, story, and print activity experiences are most likely to become candidates for "gift-of-time" projects, but waiting for development to occur rarely fosters development. To develop concepts about print, stories, and literacy, children need to be immersed in literate activity and literate environments. This does not mean that "unready" children need worksheets and drill. They need the chance to develop the same understandings that their more advantaged peers developed in their homes or in emergent literacy–oriented preschools. Their lack of experiences with books, stories, and print should signal the need for placement in literacy-rich classrooms with many books at hand, with markers, pencils, crayons, and paper, along with Legos, charts and labels, rhyme, rhythm, movement, and song (National Association for the Education of Young Children [NAEYC], 1998).

Retention in grade arrived with the advent of graded schools at the turn of the twentieth century. It was a hot topic in the 1930s and 1940s, and the research pointedly noted the lack of positive effects, either educational or social/emotional, on retained children. The 1950s and 1960s emphasized social promotion and ungraded schools. Educators talked about "teaching the whole child" and respecting "individual differences," and children moved from grade to grade along with their peers regardless of their academic development.

Accountability has been the watchword since the 1980s, and with the press for accountability retention has once again became a common response to the problem of failing to learn to read along with one's peers. States have passed laws mandating achievement of minimum standards to determine who will move to the next grade. In some schools, you can once again see 9-year-olds in the first grade. In fact, currently it is estimated that almost half the children in the United States are retained

The rise of high-stakes testing seems to have fostered an increase in both retention practice and special education placements. One study (Allington & McGill-Franzen, 1992) found that significantly more primary-grade children were being retained and/or placed in special education now than 35 years ago, before high-stakes testing was popular. Some schools seemed to use retention in grade and special education placement to artificially inflate the scores on state-mandated tests. As one principal said, "If they aren't likely to pass the state test, we'll flunk them or get them classified. . . . We used to try and do what was good for kids. Now, my neck is on the block" (McGill-Franzen & Allington, 1993a).

before grade 9 even though research evidence still indicates that positive effects of retention are hard to find (Allington & McGill-Franzen, 1995; Jimerson & Kaufman, 2003).

Many educators find it difficult to believe that nearly 50 percent of children have been retained. What is at work is the "cumulative effect" of years of retention practices. What happens in most schools is that small numbers add up over time. For instance, retaining only 5 percent of the children each year in grades K–8 results in 45 percent of all children retained by the end of eighth grade (5 percent × 9 years = 45 percent). If each teacher retains one child each year, almost half of all students will be retained before they arrive at high school.

Placement in a transitional-grade classroom (e.g., prefirst class) has the same negative effects as simple retention (Meisels, 1993; Shepard & Smith, 1990). The original concept of transitional classes was that through intensified instruction, low-achieving children could be "caught up" to their peers during the transitional-grade year. The notion was that smaller classes and more intensive teaching would accelerate learning and children would move from a transitional first grade into second grade. In practice, however, this intensive instruction did not occur. Without intensive instruction, learning acceleration did not occur. Instead, transitional-grade classes became much like repeating a grade with a different teacher.

Even if retention and transitional-grade classes were effective, and they are not, they would be expensive options for attempting to meet the needs of low-achieving children. The extra year of schooling adds the full cost of that year to the educational expenses. Currently, that cost will range from $4,500 to $11,000, depending on which district in which state the child attends school. Most remedial programs and summer-school programs cost less than $1,500 per child, and a semester of one-to-one daily tutorial instruction costs $2,500 to $3,500. Each of these options is not only less expensive but also more likely to actually serve the children well (Allington, 2004).

Ultimately, retained and transitioned children become older underachievers. In adolescence, two factors—being older than classmates and low achievement—are powerful predictors of who will drop out of school. Retained children are four times more likely than other students to drop out of high school. Obviously, the odds are stacked against any child who is retained (Denton, 2001).

The gap between research and policy and practice is currently quite large. We think that gap can best be explained by the fact that public polling data indicate most citizens

> Perhaps retention is popular because costs have been hidden in the general school budget and so it seems a no-cost option. A study of retention in California schools, however, estimated that current retention rates there created the need for an additional 60 elementary schools, each with 20 classrooms! Another study estimates the costs of grade retention in South Carolina at $30 million annually! We spend billions of educational dollars each year on retention, a failed solution. We spend that money on a symptom of the real problem: low achievement in reading. We spend the money on a response that does not address the root of the problem: inadequate instruction. Do we spend these billions on retention because retaining children is easier than creating more effective schools?

think children who have not mastered grade-level material should not be promoted (Allington, 1999). Politicians pay attention to the polls.

Retention practices not driven by state policies can best be explained by noting that retention effects are often examined quite differently by teachers (and administrators/supervisors) than they are by researchers. Basically, it seems, school personnel tend to examine short-term effects of retention while researchers examine longer-term effects (Allington & McGill-Franzen, 1995). School personnel often see modest improvement in performance in the year following retention. Researchers see retained children dropping out ten years later. The achievement of retained children gradually slips downward as they continue in school. Four or five years after retention, most retained children are again among the lowest-achieving students in their grade. Then they drop out.

In making the decision to retain, the appropriate question is, Will retention benefit the child more than the school? We think the evidence is so consistent and so powerful that we do not believe retention can be justified as benefiting children. The evidence gathered in study after study over 75 years (1930–2005) clearly indicates that the best policy keeps children with the peers they enter school with (Jimerson & Kaufman, 2003; Shepard & Smith, 1989).

Although we are quite convinced that retention does not benefit children, we need to note that the answer is not simply social promotion. Social promotion has fewer negative effects on children than retention, but social promotion alone does little to address the problem of low achievement. Low-achieving children who are simply promoted continue the pattern of low achievement, though they seem less likely to drop out.

Children who find learning to read difficult need some educational intervention that gives them access to sufficient instruction to accelerate their literacy learning (Allington, 2006). When social promotion is coupled with access to an extraordinary educational intervention, achievement is enhanced. The intervention might provide extended instructional time through an after-school program or a summer-school program. It might provide short-term tutorial assistance designed to accelerate development. Although few studies report on programs that combine social promotion with intensive intervention, those available suggest that increasing the intensity of instruction works far better than either retention or social promotion alone.

Tracking Does Not Get Children Back on Track

Tracking has been a common school response to the problem of children who do not progress as fast as average children. But tracking does not accelerate the development of children placed in the bottom tracks. Tracking occurs in the elementary school when children of similar achievement levels (achievement in reading, most commonly) are assigned to the same teacher. Such tracking began in the 1940s and was prevalent in most elementary schools through the 1960s. Its popularity waned but is currently on the rise in some school systems.

Tracking is based on flawed logic. The argument is made that not all children learn at the same rate and that if slow learners (or fast learners) are put together with one teacher, that teacher can teach them on their level and provide the instruction they need to progress to higher levels. Presented in this way, tracking seems reasonable. In practice, however, children placed in the bottom track achieve less than similar children placed in untracked classes (Denton, 2001; Gamoran, 1986; Wheelock, 1992). This occurs primarily because children placed in the low tracks are simply taught less; these children are offered a "slow it down" curriculum. The problem with tracking is that it purposely creates classrooms that produce low achievement. Tracking does not typically create for low-achieving students classroom environments that offer richer and more intensive instruction than that offered in the classrooms for the other students.

In addition, tracking models incorrectly assume an equal distribution of high-, middle-, and low-achieving children. If we recall the bell-shaped curve that is supposed to express the distribution of individual differences, we note a big hump in the middle range. There are simply far more middle-track students than either high- or low-track students. Thus, the low-track classes (and the high-track classes) invariably contain many children who would be more appropriately placed in the middle track. The end result of tracking is that both the low and the high tracks include many middle-track students. However, teachers tend to see each track as homogeneous and do not provide much differentiated instruction.

Tracking can take other forms. The most common arrangement is for teachers to have heterogeneous homeroom groups to whom they teach science, social studies, physical education, and so on, and then to track the children for math and reading. This is called the Joplin Plan, after Joplin, Missouri, where the plan originated in the 1950s. However, this plan didn't work very well then, and it cannot be recommended now—for two main reasons.

First, instructional time is lost whenever the children have to pack up and change classrooms (and even when the teachers change classrooms). It takes children a minimum of 10 to 15 minutes to pack up to leave one class, exit the room, get to the next class, unpack, and then get started at academic work again. If children switch for math and reading, this will take 30 to 60 minutes each day (or 2.5 to 5 hours weekly), which is 10 to 20 percent of the actual instructional time available in most elementary schools. Children must also adjust to perhaps three different teachers, and teachers could conceivably teach 75 to 90 different children each day. It is hard for teachers to maintain a level of commitment and concern for each child's education when each

The standard bell-shaped curve places about 70 percent of all students' achievement in the average range, leaving only 15 percent of students in the below-average and above-average ranges (or one standard deviation above or below the mean). Thus, with 100 third-grade students we would need high- and low-achievement classes each with 15 students and two average achievement classes with 35 students in each to distribute children appropriately (or we could add additional staff and create three average classes with 23 students or four such classes with 17 students). Any other system results in inappropriately placing average-achievement students in both the high- and low-achievement classes or tracks.

Seeing Time Lost to Transitions

I. Self-contained

Arrival | Homeroom | > | Reading | >> | Math | > | Science |

Lost |◄————| (12 minutes)

II. Departmentalized

Arrival | Homeroom | > > > > > |Reading | > > > > > | Science | > > > > > | Math |

Lost |◄————————————————| (45 minutes)

These two schematics depict typical transition time lost to regrouping in elementary school (each > represents 3 minutes). In scenario I, children arrive at school and settle in during attendance and lunch count periods, then have all classes in their homeroom. In this case some 12 minutes are lost for instruction as children stop work, put away one set of materials, take out other materials, and return to academic work (time shown between the vertical bars). In scenario II, 45 minutes are lost as children shift between reading, science, and math classrooms. If we add these transitions to those that already exist in schools (art, lunch, music, dismissal), we might lose as much as 2 hours of potential teaching time to transitions!

If these transition-time estimates seem uncommonly large, we suggest collecting transition-time information in several classes in any school. Do not forget to begin timing as soon as children end their academic work periods, and continue to time the transition until they return to work.

teacher has this many children to worry about. It is hard for teachers to know 75 to 90 children well—to know their strengths and weaknesses and individualities. It is also hard to schedule this many children into that many different sections according to achievement and maintain any sort of balanced class size—so again we get classes not nearly as homogeneous as first assumed.

Second, there are measurable benefits for increased integration of curriculum areas—for linking reading and writing strategies to social studies, math, and science to present a richer and more coherent course of study. But when children switch teachers for different classes, opportunities for the integration of instruction across curriculum areas, which might occur naturally in self-contained classrooms, are lost.

Twenty years ago, George (1988) summarized the research on tracking and concluded that "tracking is an idea whose time has passed." Regardless of the form it takes, tracking does not seem to enhance the academic learning of children.

Ability Grouping Has Little to Do with Ability

Related to tracking is the age-old practice of creating "ability groups" within classrooms. Of course, the groups created are really *achievement* groups, not ability groups, because children are placed in them based on some estimate of achievement, usually reading achievement.

Researchers have compared the reading instruction experienced by children in different reading groups in the same classrooms. In these studies researchers concluded that children placed in high groups received more and better instruction than children in low groups. This has been called the Matthew Effect after the Gospel of Matthew passage about the rich getting richer and the poor getting poorer (Stanovich, 2000).

More specifically, these studies report that higher-achievement groups have more opportunities to read (especially silent reading), more emphasis on skills-in-use, greater comprehension focus, more interactions that foster independence and self-monitoring, and so on. Children in lower-achievement groups do less reading and writing, more round-robin oral reading, more isolated skills and drills, and fewer comprehension activities, and they experience more dependency-creating instruction (Allington, 1983). In other words, the instruction traditionally offered in different groups literally created different kinds of readers. Children in top groups received instruction that facilitated developing independent, thoughtful readers. Children in low groups did not. Rigid reliance on achievement grouping is not an adequate response to the differences that children present us as learners.

Some schools have responded to the reported negative effects of *ability* grouping by mandating whole-class instruction with little or no modification of instruction for children who are finding learning to read difficult. However, real differences that children exhibit in literacy learning cannot simply be mandated away. Moving to whole-class instruction with little or no extraordinary support for children having academic learning difficulties will produce few benefits (McGill-Franzen, Zmach, Solic, & Love-Zeig, 2006).

Special Programs Aren't Special Enough

In the past 40 years, a proliferation of special programs has been created in an attempt to address the needs of children who find learning difficult (Allington, 2002a). These are the remedial reading and math classes, the resource room classes for individuals with learning disabilities, the speech and language therapy sessions, and the migrant and bilingual programs that operate in many schools. Unfortunately, there is little evidence that these efforts substantially alter the academic futures of the children served (Allington & McGill-Franzen, 1996; Puma et al., 1997). Simply put, most children who participate in these special programs do not become good readers. They do not catch up with their peers. And when the most common designs of these programs are examined, it becomes clear that such a disappointing outcome is exactly what one might reasonably expect. Several key features undermine the likelihood of obtaining positive effects on achievement.

Consider that each child who participates in these programs represents the failure of the classroom reading program to adapt to the instructional needs of all children. Adding these special programs has often led classroom teachers to believe that teaching all children is not their responsibility. In some schools we have studied, as many as three out of four classroom teachers told us that the reading instruction of remedial and special education students was not their responsibility! This is dismaying because these children spend

80 to 90 percent of their day in the regular classroom. Schools cannot solve the problems of struggling readers in programs that occupy 10–20 percent of the day. Struggling readers need classrooms that routinely provide instruction targeted at their immediate needs all day long (Allington, 2006).

A second common feature of these programs is that the "special" instruction replaces some part of the regular instruction offered. Because transitions from the classroom to the reading or resource room (or hallway) take time, children who participate have less time available to learn to read.

Struggling readers are more likely to experience curriculum fragmentation. All children benefit from a rich, organized, and consistent curriculum plan. In many cases struggling readers hop from material to material, from lesson to lesson, from teacher to teacher, across the school day. These are the children who find it difficult to keep up with their classwork but who are offered lessons from more different materials than anyone else in the school (Johnston & Allington, 1991).

Struggling readers are the children most likely to spend time with the least well-trained school personnel—teacher aides. The use of minimally trained paraprofessionals is one reason that children in these special programs are provided the lowest-quality instruction (Achilles, 1999; Gerber, Finn, Achilles, & Boyd-Zaharias, 2001). Heavy use of paraprofessional staff in special programs has been linked to limited effects on student learning. The schools relying most heavily on paraprofessional staff are the schools that enroll the largest numbers of poor children. Assigning relatively poorly trained paraprofessionals to work with children experiencing difficulty learning to read and write is unlikely to accelerate learning.

If special programs do not substantially expand children's opportunity to learn, if they do not substantially enhance the quality and intensity of instruction, then these programs are unlikely to benefit struggling readers and writers very much. If special programs do not routinely accelerate literacy development and allow children to experience classroom success, then the programs need restructuring. Finally, in our view, special programs must have a positive impact on the quality of classroom instruction to justify continuation. We argue this because no matter how good the special program, consistently high-quality regular classroom instruction is the key feature of schools where all children become readers and writers (Nye, Konstantopoulos, & Hedges, 2004).

Change Is Hard

The most sensible strategies for changing schools work gradually (although everyone wants instant improvement). It has taken a century to develop the school traditions of today, and these traditions cannot be undone easily or quickly. Creating schools that better respond to the difficulties that some children face when learning to read and write will require substantial institutional and individual learning. But that learning must begin with recognizing the mistakes already made. Change can be fostered, but the changes in classrooms matter most. Remember: Good schools are collections of good classrooms.

Fostering Change in the Classroom

We agree with Fullan and Hargreaves (1996): The primary problem in schools is that there is simply not enough opportunity or support for teachers to work together to improve instructional practices. Likewise, Elmore, Peterson, and McCarthy (1996) found that changes to "core instructional practices" were rarely achieved in the reform efforts they studied. When such changes did occur, they occurred in schools where professional conversations about specific instructional practices had been fostered, supported, and sustained.

Why Do Teachers Teach as They Do?

Why have so many school reform efforts been unsuccessful? We interpret the research available as indicating that the primary focus of instructional reform must be on developing the capacity of teachers to better address the instructional problems they confront

Researchers now suggest (finally) that the most promising solution to creating successful schools is to focus primarily on enhancing the expertise of classroom teachers. They found that all schools have some effective teachers. But some schools have larger numbers of more expert and more effective teachers and it was this variable that made a school "effective." These "teacher effects" were most important in higher-poverty schools.

The researchers concluded, "The finding that teacher effects are larger than school effects has interesting implications for improving student achievement. Many policies attempt to improve achievement by substituting one school for another (e.g., school choice) or changing the schools themselves (e.g., whole school reform). If teacher effects are larger than school effects, then policies focusing on teacher effects as a larger source of variation may be more promising than policies focusing on school effects" (Nye, Konstantopoulos, & Hedges, 2004, p. 254).

In order to create schools where all children learn to read and write, school districts must develop plans that support and sustain the development of teacher expertise and effectiveness. It seems there is no strategy as powerful as ensuring a school has large numbers of expert and effective teachers.

- How many expert teachers of reading and writing work in your school?
- How many expert teachers of reading and writing were hired this year? In the past three years?
- How many expert teachers of reading and writing has your professional development plan created this year? In the past three years?

daily. Too many reform efforts have targeted peripheral issues (funding, governance, accountability, inclusion, class size, curriculum frameworks, instructional materials, etc.). It isn't that these issues have no impacts on teaching but that none of them focuses on developing the instructional expertise of teachers.

Most teachers seem to teach as well as they know how. Imagine you observe a fourth-grade teacher conducting whole-class round-robin reading with a social studies textbook that most students cannot read accurately, fluently, and with comprehension. Is it usually the case that the teacher has the expertise to locate and organize a multisource, multilevel array of social studies curriculum materials that address the social studies standard or content that is the focus of that part of the text being read? Is the teacher ignoring his or her rich professional knowledge about

- How children develop historical thinking
- Selecting appropriate content texts for fourth graders
- Orchestrating a multilevel, multisource curriculum plan
- Creating integrated units of study
- Developing students' strategies for reading informational text
- The role of prior knowledge on comprehension, vocabulary, and word recognition

In our experience few teachers conducting round-robin reading of social studies texts are ignoring such expertise. Instead, they have developed little such expertise and simply are teaching in the best way they know. Perhaps they are teaching in the way they were taught.

Providing such teachers with rich curricular collections of multilevel informational books, historical fiction novels, biographies, and such to support the social studies text often leads to little change unless a substantial effort is made to enhance their expertise in how to use such texts to create a different sort of social studies instruction. Those efforts must focus not only on developing knowledge of each of the support texts and how it links to the social studies standards but also on developing pedagogical and classroom organizational expertise (McGill-Franzen, Ward, Goatley, & Machado, 2002).

Teachers who have the necessary expertise create powerful classroom lessons even when the school provides little organizational support. The most effective teachers we have studied often chose to spend their own money to buy the books they needed to teach the students they were assigned. They also begged, borrowed, and created curriculum materials. Our point is not to condone organizational shortcomings but to point out what has been long ignored: Expert teachers do whatever it takes to create the instructional environment they need to be effective. Imagine how many teachers might become more effective if schools made developing teacher instructional expertise their first organizational budget priority!

 Do classroom teachers and special staff share knowledge of each other's practice? If two teachers, each working with a child, know little of the other's instructional activities, it is unlikely that the instruction they offer the child is coherent and consistent. You may want to use a strategy employed in a classic study (Johnston, Allington, & Afflerbach, 1985) to examine shared knowledge in your school. Select a few children who participate in special programs. Interview both teachers who work with the children and ask each of them:

What work was _____ doing with you today?
What work did _____ do in his/her classroom (special program) today?

You might also ask which curriculum materials were used and what each teacher sees as the primary difficulty the children are having. In some schools little knowledge is shared; in others teachers not only share knowledge but share plans, goals, and instructional emphases. When classroom and support teachers exhibit higher levels of shared knowledge of each others' activities, we are likely to find higher levels of achievement.

The National Commission on Teaching and America's Future (1997) concluded:

"What teachers know and understand about content and students shapes how judiciously they select from texts and other materials and how effectively they present material in class. Their skill in assessing their students' progress also depends upon how deeply they understand learning, and how well they can interpret students' discussions and written work. No other intervention can make the difference that a knowledgeable, skillful teacher can make in the learning process." (p. 8) Investments in teacher development produced far greater student achievement gains than investments in new materials, reducing class size or increasing salaries, "spending on teacher education swamped other variables as the most productive investment for schools." (p. 9)

But the data they examined showed that fewer than 15 percent of American teachers had participated in even 9 hours of sustained professional development activity in a single curriculum area in the previous year. We know of no evidence that suggests how many hours it takes to develop the sorts of expertise we listed previously, but it is difficult to imagine that it could be accomplished in 9 hours of focused development work. And the vast majority of teachers didn't have the opportunity for even that.

Public Professional Conversation as Support for Change

Schools that are moving steadily toward becoming good schools—schools where all children become readers and writers—are schools where public professional conversations are fostered and supported. Professional conversations are those discussions of instructional

To paraphrase Fullan and Hargreaves (1996):

- Student achievement and teacher development are reciprocally related.
- When a school has one or two good teachers, it is usually a matter of individual initiative. But when a school has many good teachers, it is a result of leadership.

practices one holds with one's peers and coworkers. They are problem-exposing, problem-solving conversations. They are rare in many schools. They are largely private in many others. A school filled with public professional conversations has to be deliberately nurtured (Harwayne, 1999).

For public professional conversations to occur, the school has to be a place where professional trust is high—trust between teachers and between teachers and their administrator. Teaching has long been described as the "lonely profession" because most teachers work in professional isolation from one another. Although many teachers have private professional conversations with one or two trusted peers, these conversations are largely hidden from public view. Think about the conversations in your school. Think about the faculty meeting conversations. The staff room conversations. The hallway conversations. How often do these conversations involve specific, useful discussion of instructional problems and potential solutions? What venues are there during the school day for such conversations? What time is set aside each day for such conversations? Who is supposed to talk with whom every day about improving instructional practices?

The Current Policy Context and Creating Schools Where All Children Learn to Read and Write

The passage of the federal No Child Left Behind Act of 2001 (NCLB) introduced a more complex policy environment for U.S. schools. Central to the many provisions of NCLB is the focus on corrective actions when schools fail to achieve adequate yearly progress (AYP). Basically, demonstrating AYP requires that schools can demonstrate that various subgroups of students—economically disadvantaged, ethnic minority, pupils with disabilities, English language learners—are achieving reading and math proficiency (and soon science) at a rate comparable to the majority population. The NCLB legislation received broad bipartisan support perhaps because members of Congress were frustrated by the sizable gaps in achievement between members of the subgroups and the majority and because these gaps continue to exist some 40 years after the first federal legislation targeted to closing those gaps had been passed (the Elementary and Secondary Education Act of 1965).

In other words, NCLB was viewed by Congress as necessarily intrusive given the hundreds of millions of federal dollars that had been allocated to schools to better serve students in these subgroups and the still existing achievement gaps. Combine that with large-scale evaluation studies that suggested that federally funded programs such as Title 1 remedial reading, special education, and bilingual or English as a Second Language programs produced few longer-term positive academic outcomes and legislators had the basis for a tougher federal education policy. The basic premises underlying the NCLB were (1) that schools were not using the available federal funds in ways that research suggested would prove useful and (2) previous federal legislation had not held schools truly accountable for achieving the intended results of narrowing the achievement gap.

However, as Bracey (2003) has demonstrated, the achievement gap between minority and majority students and between advantaged and disadvantaged students had been narrowed, roughly cut in half between 1970 and 2000. Still the gap remained substantial such that by twelfth grade, students eligible for free school lunches performed at the same level as eighth-grade students who were not eligible. That four-year gap was smaller than it had been 30 years earlier but it was still a gap representing a large difference in reading proficiency.

Thus, Congress passed NCLB with its mandate that all children be reading proficiently by 2014. All children. Children in every subgroup.

Congress allowed states to determine the expected reading proficiency standards and to set the timetable for all children attaining that level of proficiency. This has created some significant differences in the targets and time lines in different states.

For instance, states have set very different proficiency standards. One way to examine the differences in state standards for reading development is to compare performances of children in different states on a single assessment. The Rand Corporation conducted just such a study. It compared the percentages of children that states reported meeting their standards to the percentage that achieved the proficient reading standard on the reading portion of the National Assessment of Educational Progress (NAEP). They found substantial differences among states in what seemed to constitute proficient reading at the fourth-grade level. In Texas, for example, 85 percent of children met the state standard while only 27 percent achieved the proficient reading standard on the NAEP. In South Carolina, on the other hand, 33 percent achieved the state standard and 26 percent achieved the NAEP proficient reading level. With similar percentages of fourth graders in these two states meeting the NAEP proficient standard (26 and 27 percent) one can only conclude that Texas reading standards are less demanding than those of South Carolina (85 versus 33 percent met state standards). Likewise, in Massachusetts 90 percent of students met the state reading standard and 40 percent achieved the NAEP proficient level while in Connecticut 43 percent achieved the NAEP proficient level but only 69 percent achieved the state standard. More Connecticut students achieved the NAEP proficient level but far fewer achieved the state standard than was the case in Massachusetts even though far more Massachusetts students achieved their state's reading standard. Obviously, Connecticut has adopted reading proficiency levels that extend beyond those established for students in Massachusetts.

These four states illustrate one problem with NCLB as it now stands. The law penalizes states more for setting high standards than it does for poor performance. Many more schools in South Carolina and Connecticut will fail to meet AYP goals than will schools in Texas and Massachusetts simply because of differences in state standards.

The law requires a series of corrective actions when schools fail to meet AYP goals year after year.

Year 1: Option for students to transfer to another school meeting AYP goals.

Year 2: Requirement of supplemental instructional services offered outside the school day (before or after school).

Year 3: Requirement of purchase of replacement proven reading program.

Year 4: Removal of school administration and targeted teaching staff.

Year 5: State takeover of school, turn to charter school status, outside agency assigned control (nonprofit or for-profit entity).

As a result of the differences in state standards we can expect that differences in the numbers of schools impacted by corrective actions will be substantial (unless the law is modified or federal standards are mandated for all states).

The corrective actions are potentially expensive, yet little research supports the effectiveness of bussing children to different schools, buying a new core reading program, replacing key staff, or state or corporate takeover of schools. Nonetheless, this is the law Congress passed almost unanimously. This is the law we will live with (until it is modified, repealed, or replaced).

NCLB Goals and Emphases

Regardless of the flaws in NCLB, we see no reason why reporting achievement by subgroups should not be supported, with or without NCLB mandates. In fact, our small-scale activity presented on page 4 of this text asks the same sorts of questions about whether a school's instructional program is positively (or negatively) impacting children from various subgroups. The several subgroups targeted in NCLB represent those children most often left behind.

What we are concerned with is the emphasis that NCLB, especially the Reading First component, places on the use of a core reading program as a solution to the underachievement of children who struggle. As we noted earlier, no core reading program currently has available independent, experimental research supporting its efficacy (Pressley, 2003). Few supplementary reading programs have such evidence. Instead, reading materials are currently judged on whether they seem to have incorporated findings from experimental research into their design. But that is not the same as evidence that such design features actually are incorporated in ways that improve reading instruction and enhance reading achievement.

Additionally, the most common sets of criteria for evaluating core programs often omit relevant findings from the research. Consider, for instance, that Guthrie and Humenick (2004) conducted a meta-analysis on experimental studies of classroom programs and found that when classroom instruction provided access to interesting texts, opportunities to work collaboratively, and choice of reading materials and work partners, significantly larger effects on achievement were observed than have been reported for having a systematic phonics program in place (National Reading Panel, 2001). None of the core reading program evaluation schemes that we have seen include these research-based components.

This is not to suggest that a core reading program is not useful. Rather it indicates that a core reading program can only be one aspect of an effective and evidence-based reading curriculum. It becomes problematic when schools attempt to implement a core reading program in a one-size-fits-all manner with a heavy emphasis on whole-group instruction—problematic because there is almost nothing so antiscientific as whole-class teaching.

Finally, we are concerned that NCLB undervalues the critical importance of teacher expertise in addressing the problem of underachieving students. Although NCLB provides funds for professional development, in too many cases the professional development seems to be targeted to use of the core program rather than to development of the broad expertise teachers need to adapt any commercial reading package in ways that most benefit students. As McGill-Franzen (2005) argues, it seems that the critical factor in any potential effects that might be observed is how effectively the teacher modifies, adapts, and supplements core program materials. No core program can work equally well in all classrooms or with all students. Expert teachers routinely modify curriculum materials and their accompanying lessons so that they work more effectively for more children than if the packaged plan and advice on teaching are strictly followed.

All Children Reading and Writing

As we argued earlier, there is good evidence that we can create schools where all children are readers and writers. We can even create schools where almost all children achieve traditional standards for their age level. Thus, the fundamental aim of NCLB complements our belief systems—beliefs based on evidence and experience.

Nonetheless, the NCLB is seriously flawed in many respects in our view. It is based on a theory of teaching, learning, and school change that simply cannot be supported by the evidence available, nor does the theory well match our experiences in successful school change. The focus on what the research says is narrowly targeted, and what the

Quoting from *USA Today,* "Although students in Texas, Georgia, and Mississippi scored among the bottom third of the states on the NAEP, they were among those with the highest pass rates on state tests" (p. 9D, December 16, 2004).

One interesting aspect of the Rand Corporation study of the differences in state standards is that there seemed to be little correlation between the difficulty of state standards and actual reading outcomes as assessed on the NAEP. In other words, some states (South Carolina, California) created higher levels for state reading proficiency and produced poor results on the NAEP. Other states (Massachusetts, Wisconsin) set lower standards and produced among the best NAEP performances. Still others (Texas, District of Columbia) set lower standards and had poor results on the NAEP.

Perhaps the rigor of state standards matters less than the quality of teaching and the levels of support states provide for developing teaching effectiveness. Although much hoopla has surrounded the setting of state standards and the testing of student attainment of those standards, we will suggest that little research has ever demonstrated that creating statewide standards was a reliable strategy for raising student achievement. Standards without support for developing teacher expertise is like setting fitness standards while eliminating recess and physical education classes.

research says is too often recast in a manner that suggests ideology has trumped evidence (Allington, 2002a).

But NCLB is the law we have to work with. By becoming more informed and more focused on closing the existing achievement gaps, schools can become places where all children learn to read and write (although writing and its relationship to reading is one of those research areas largely ignored in NCLB and its Reading First initiative).

Summary

We can create schools where all children become readers and writers. We can create good schools where every classroom is occupied by an expert and effective teacher. But such schools do not simply emerge. They have to be created.

Schools are being asked to shift their mission from sorting children into "ability" groups and then educating the easiest students well to supporting children so that all students achieve levels of academic performance historically attained by only a few. This is an enormous challenge.

We cannot achieve these new goals with the schools that we have. The schools we have were not designed to educate all children well. They were not designed to make readers and writers of every child who walks in the door. Creating schools where all children become readers and writers will require rethinking and restructuring the schools, particularly our efforts to address the problems presented by children who struggle to learn to read and write. Interventions designed to accelerate the literacy development of struggling readers and writers are simply quite different from traditional interventions that were more often designed to accommodate low achievement.

The only strategy we know for creating schools where all children become readers and writers involves creating schools where all teachers are more expert than most teachers are today. We need to create schools that make it easier for expert teachers to act on their expertise, but developing and refining the expertise of every teacher must become the primary focus of any elementary school hoping to become a good school—where all children become readers and writers.

In the next chapter, we transport you into some schools where all children become readers and writers. Once you have a vision of what can be accomplished, future chapters will provide the nitty-gritty details you need for "getting at it."

The Stories of Schools Where All Children Become Readers and Writers

I n this chapter, we tell you how one elementary school that serves many poor children has restructured so that all children become readers and writers. We also provide sketches of several larger efforts to restructure elementary schools—efforts to create schools that work for all children. The restructuring we describe did not come easily, and in fact, the folks in these schools would tell you they are "not done yet" but are still "becoming" schools that work.

The Story of a School in Trouble

Once upon a time in a small city in the southeastern United States, there was an elementary school that didn't work very well for children (Hall, Prevatte, & Cunningham, 1995). Approximately 75 percent of students were members of a minority group, mostly African American. About 80 percent of the children were poor, qualifying for free or reduced-price meals. Many of the students came from homes with limited book experiences. Before the restructuring, most students finished both first- and second-grade reading below grade level. Although the teachers were working hard, their instruction was often not developing children who were readers and writers. Behavior problems consumed valuable teaching time. Many students had tuned out learning and turned instead to disruptive behavior. The students consistently scored lower on achievement tests than those from other elementary schools in the district, and they had the worst attendance record. Parents did not actively participate in the school, and some viewed the school with hostility.

Even though the school's status seemed bleak and the needs too great, the faculty became determined to initiate change that would have an impact on the education of its children. The common instructional model used by classroom teachers had been quite traditional: a skills-driven basal reader with students assigned to one of three achievement groups. The bottom groups were usually the largest of the three groups, and students tended to maintain their place in these groups throughout the elementary grades. Grouping necessitated large quantities of seatwork, which turned into a discipline nightmare. Many students found it difficult to complete assigned seatwork independently, as expected. Worse yet, these students could not afford the luxury of nonproductive time even when they were working on this seatwork.

In addition to classroom instruction, many students also received support in a Title 1 remedial reading program. Students experiencing the least reading success were pulled out of the classroom for 30 minutes of remedial reading instruction each day. They were expected to assimilate back into the classroom on their return, but they rarely did. Many resented being singled out as problem readers and accounted for many of the discipline problems. Little growth in reading was measured for children in Title 1, and children remained in the remedial program as they progressed from grade to grade.

Upon looking closely at the instructional model in use, the school faculty determined that neither the use of reading groups nor the pull-out remedial programs were facilitating learning to read and the special programs were not having positive impacts on classroom performance or classroom instruction. At year's end, 40 percent of the first-grade students were struggling at the preprimer level and having little or no success. In second grade, 1 in 5 students was virtually a nonreader—unable to read anything but the very simplest text. Only 1 in 5 students was successful in the second-grade reading curriculum.

A team of several teachers and a curriculum coordinator newly assigned to the school decided to change the situation and began to explore alternatives. They read everything they could find on providing success-oriented instruction for struggling readers. They attended local professional meetings and picked the brains of presenters and others. When they heard about successful programs, they arranged to go see for themselves.

One visit led them to another local elementary school with a more heterogeneous population of children. This school had implemented the Four Blocks instructional program for reading/language arts instruction (Cunningham, Hall, & Defee, 1991). In this program, the 120–130 minutes of reading/language arts time was divided into four 30–35-minute blocks. These blocks—Writing, Self-Selected Reading, Guided Reading, and Working with Words—represented the four major competing approaches to reading instruction. All children were included in all four blocks and, thus, were provided with multiple "methods" through which they could learn to read and write.

The instruction in each block was multilevel, but the children were not placed in separate achievement-level groups. During the Writing block, children wrote at whatever level they could and all writing was accepted and encouraged. But minilessons on writing strategies were routinely offered to small, flexible groups of children. Books in the book baskets for Self-Selected Reading included easy, predictable books along with informational books and chapter books. Material read during the Guided Reading block included new and old reading series along with multiple copies of trade books on a variety of levels. Teachers made the Guided Reading block multilevel by varying the difficulty of the material read, and they ensured the success of all children by using a variety of partner and flexible small-group reading formats. Phonics and spelling activities included during the Working with Words block were also multilevel (Cunningham, 2000).

This multimethod, multilevel instruction achieved good success in the visited school, so the faculty in search of improvement decided to try to adapt the model. The staff committed to implement the new model fully until Christmas. If unsuccessful, the staff agreed they would not return to their previous model but would continue the search.

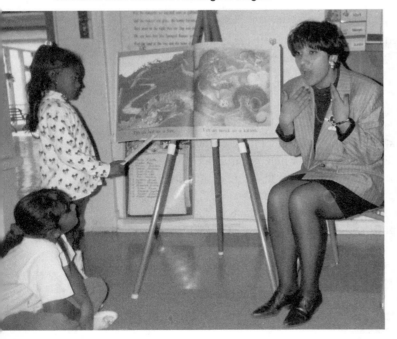

During the Guided Reading block, the teacher actively demonstrates effective reading strategies.

Professional development activities began the week before school started and continued all year long, as the curriculum coordinator supported the teachers in this change. The
teachers saw the need for multiple methods through which children could learn, as well as
the need to eliminate achievement groupings. They agreed that their pull-out programs
were not effective, but they still felt that their children needed some intensive small-group
instruction. The curriculum coordinator worked out a plan called FROG, *F*acilitating
*R*eading for *O*ptimum *G*rowth, which provided for additional daily small-group instruction for all first- and second-grade students.

FROG was designed to provide the intensive instruction needed to ensure the success
of all students. The role of existing personnel in the school was redefined. Remedial reading teachers and other special teachers formed FROG teams, which converged on each
classroom for 45 minutes each day. The students in each class were divided into small heterogeneous groups that included one higher-achieving student, two or three average students, and one low-achieving student. These groups received daily intensive instruction
with one of the FROG teachers or the classroom teacher. This instruction included the
components of the Four Blocks framework that the teachers felt could best be carried out
in small groups. Each FROG session included four 10- to 12-minute components.

All children participated in the Self-Selected Reading block as part of their classroom
multimethod, multilevel instruction. The FROG time began with a literary discussion
based on self-selected books. This discussion focused on a particular literary element,
such as author, character, plot, setting, mood, style, theme, or illustration. Children read
or discussed parts of their own book related to the literary element.

The second component of FROG, shared reading using predictable big books,
strengthened and supported the students' reading in the Guided Reading block. The students were taught to use a variety of reading strategies including semantic, syntactic, and
graphophonic cues. Punctuation, vocabulary, predictions—all teachable elements found in
a particular book—became part of the instruction as the teacher led the students to read a
predictable big book.

The third component included in each FROG session supported the Working with
Words block. Children were given letters and instruction on how to manipulate those letters to make a variety of words. The emphasis was on learning that words are made up of
predictable letter patterns.

The final component of FROG supported the Writing block. In the classroom, all
children wrote on self-selected topics. During the FROG time, the predictable big book
provided a model for teacher-directed writing instruction, allowing the children to make
the reading–writing connection. A prewriting activity was followed by writing, revision,
editing, and sharing.

When the 45-minute FROG time ended, the FROG teachers leaped to another
classroom, and the classroom teacher continued Four Blocks instruction with the whole
class.

Here is a typical classroom schedule showing how FROG time and the classroom four blocks worked together.

8:45	Opening activities
9:00	FROG
9:45	Guided Reading block
10:15	Self-Selected Reading block
10:45	Working with Words block
11:15	Lunch
11:45	Writing block
12:15	Math
12:45	Teacher read-aloud
1:00	Music/Library/Art
1:30	Integrated Science/Social Studies
2:00	Physical Education
2:30	Computer Technology
3:00	Dismissal

At the end of this first year of restructuring, informal reading inventories given to all children indicated that more than half the children were reading at or above grade level—a remarkable improvement over previous years. The combination of Four Blocks and the FROG model was making a difference. Other—as meaningful—changes also occurred at the school. Parents who had been reluctant to be part of the school began to trickle in. Membership in the parent–school association increased 120 percent. Parent volunteers increased dramatically, from 5 to 80. Behavior problems decreased dramatically, although they were not eliminated. The school no longer had the poorest attendance in the school system, with attendance rising to near average levels. But most significant was the change observed in the students. Formerly chaotic classrooms had become classrooms filled with excited children involved in reading and writing activity. Adding the FROG component to the Four Blocks instruction gave all students some small-group instruction. Making the FROG groups heterogeneous allowed struggling children to read, write, and share with others who were good models.

The first year of restructuring had begun with determination mixed with fear and uncertainty. The second year began with enthusiasm and positive anticipation. The teachers had a successful year behind them and were anticipating the implementation of several additional innovations. Students exhibited the same confidence and enthusiasm. This year, the school became a Title 1 Schoolwide Project. The building leadership team elected to use much of the federal Title 1 funding to reduce class sizes in the primary grades. Thus, school opened with fewer remedial reading teachers but with class sizes that averaged about 16 students (compared to the 25 students previously).

In another important and difficult decision, primary-grade teachers decided to stay with their classes for two years (grades 1 to 2). Teachers and parents felt this would contribute to a stronger "family" atmosphere (parents can request children be moved to another classroom in the second year). This shift moved classroom teachers away from thinking of themselves primarily as a particular grade-level teacher and gave them the responsibility for and the opportunity to provide the same children with high-quality lessons over a two-year period.

Classroom instruction in Four Blocks continued, as did FROG instruction. Smaller classes meant fewer interruptions during the day, and teachers who had developed more instructional expertise contributed to accelerated learning in the classroom. The students were on task and involved in reading and writing. Learning was their primary concern, leaving little time for discipline problems. Teachers had to work hard to keep the students supplied with books.

Results were indicative of the growth that occurred during the second year with Four Blocks multimethod, multilevel instruction and FROG and the first year with smaller classes. In May, 82 percent of first-grade students were reading on or above grade level and 18 percent read at the primer or preprimer level. There were no children who could not read at the preprimer level. In second grade, 83 percent of the students were reading on or above grade level—a dramatic increase from previous years. There were no nonreaders.

This story of change at one school shows how a faculty can alter the outcomes of education by rethinking the process of schooling. This is but a single example of the sorts of change that can be accomplished when a faculty and key administrators/supervisors decide it is time to change. The changes described were begun with no extra funding, but the school faculty soon found that various sorts of funds were available to assist them in their attempts to restructure the school. Such funding did not fall into their laps. Obtaining it required activism and initiative by the school staff.

The programs now in place largely resulted from reconsidering how to use the available funds to enhance classroom instruction to better benefit children. The changes made were the result of an honest examination of what was not working. When needed, the staff pursued extra funding sources and found many potential sources available for a school with a better plan. The school still has difficulties to address and to resolve, but it also has a faculty now well experienced in the process of change and determined to continue to improve on their efforts.

Reforming U.S. Elementary Schools

As elementary schools confront the challenge of developing thoughtful literacy as a trait demonstrated by all students, there has been a flurry of reform proposals for how to accomplish this goal along with funding opportunities for implementing elementary

Twenty-five years ago, Ron Edmonds (1981) made the following assertions:

1. We can, whenever and wherever we choose, successfully teach all children whose schooling is of interest to us.

2. We already know more than we need to do that.

3. Whether we do it finally depends on how we feel about the fact that we haven't done it so far.

educational reform. Much ado has been made about selecting "proven programs" in the quest for enhanced literacy proficiencies. Proven programs are said to be "research based," but often this means little more than the developer providing some sort of evaluation data indicating improved student achievement. There are two primary problems with the concept of "proven programs."

1 If we take the definition of "reliable, scientific research" offered in the federal No Child Left Behind Act (NCLB) as our measure of "provenness," then no current reform program could be implemented. The NCLB provides a rigorous test of "scientificness" that no model can presently sustain. The simple fact that most research on any intervention is done by the developers of that intervention contradicts the NCLB's emphasis on "non-biased" and "independent" research studies. Although nearly all educational reform efforts have some evidence of their impact on achievement, many have modest data on the impact of their intervention on the development of thoughtful literacy proficiencies. In fact, many of the so-called "proven" programs have only older, dated basic skills test data to support their claims of effectiveness. But as Knapp (1995) so aptly demonstrated, an emphasis on basic skills development is neither necessary nor sufficient for the development of thoughtful literacy.

2 The research on the implementation of various educational reform models suggests that nothing works everywhere but most ideas can be made to work somewhere (Berends, Bodilly, & Kirby, 2002). The researchers who conducted the recent large-scale study of effective classroom instruction (Taylor et al., 2000) noted that in their sample of schools few of the "proven programs" seemed to be having any substantive positive impact on achievement, in contrast to locally developed intervention efforts. Schools have invested in reform efforts such as Success for All, direct instruction, or Learning Styles only to be disappointed in the outcomes (Allington & Nowak, 2004) and then have ended their participation in that reform effort. In our view, unless the reform model is designed to enhance the instructional expertise of classroom teachers, there is little reason to expect the reform to produce substantive impacts on achievement over the longer term. Too few of the most popular models for reforming elementary schools have focused on the central reality of schools: It is developing the capacity of classroom teachers to offer high-quality instruction that will foster improved achievement.

In the remainder of this section we provide a brief review of several elementary school reform models. These are all "national" models in that they have been adopted in numerous schools across the United States. All are "proven" if making any one of the several lists of "proven" programs is considered to be evidence of their effectiveness in enhancing student achievement (see, for instance, the listings of "proven" programs at the following websites: www.ecs.org; www.nwrel.org; www.air.org).

These models vary enormously in scope, focus, and evidence. We include them because we visited one or more schools that implemented each one, and in each case we found aspects of the effort commendable. But a caution is in order: Nothing works everywhere. If your school is considering adopting one of these models (or one not listed here), we suggest that you gather as much information from as many sources as possible before you commit to any model. In fact, you might attempt to take what seems the strengths of various models and combine them into a hybrid reform model that best serves your community and context.

The Learning Network

The Learning Network (TLN) schools offer a climate of rich professional development that includes teacher research teams that analyze classroom reading instruction with the help of instructional coaches and the school principal. Continuous development of teacher expertise is a basic goal of TLN schools. A continuing questioning of current practices is the main strategy for promoting teacher learning (Backus, 2000). The primary vehicles for promoting questions about current practices are action plans, focused observations, and instructional dialogue.

These book baskets contain only a few of the books available in one Illinois classroom.

Action plans are developed by classroom teachers over time. For instance, one plan focused on developing a better understanding of the selection of books for independent reading baskets (Herzog, 1997). The teacher listed several professional resources she would read to deepen her understanding of the purpose for independent reading and for judging the complexity of texts that children might read. As she read, the teacher listed additional questions as they arose and noted the insights she gained from the various resources. The plan closed with a statement of how the teacher would judge the success of the plan. Three behaviors were listed, beginning with being able to explain to a colleague why certain books were selected.

Focused observations by a teacher–leader support the action plan. In the case above, the observations would focus on the independent reading selections, habits, and strategies observed by the teacher–leader in the classroom. After observing, the teacher–leader schedules a debriefing session in which the teacher–leader engages the classroom teacher

Resources for Further Information

Book: Herzog, M. (1997). *Inside Learning Network schools.* Katonah, NY: Richard C. Owen (www.rcowen.com).

Video: *Becoming a Community of Learners: The Learning Network in Easthampton (MA) public schools.* Katonah, NY: Richard C. Owen (www.rcowen.com).

Internet: www.rcowen.com

in an instructional dialogue about the focus of the observation (independent reading and book selection). The format is more one of professional conversation than of interrogation, but the observer's field notes provide the basis for the conversation. Changes in classroom instructional practices remain the primary goal of the process—changes that produce an improved instructional environment for students.

Classroom teachers use a similar process of observation/assessment, evaluation of the information, planning from the evaluation, and adjusting teaching processes based on the planning. Thus, planning is initiated for the week, but typically the plans must be adjusted day by day as student responses to the lessons are observed and evaluated.

In many TLN schools the number of specialist teachers is reduced substantially as children experiencing difficulty are integrated into the general education classrooms and provided quality instruction there. Central to the TLN is the belief that good instruction is simply good instruction for all learners regardless of social class, cultural background, age, or their proclivity for academic learning.

A weekly 90-minute, voluntary staff dialogue provides a setting for sharing problems and solutions as well as for addressing larger, schoolwide issues that impact on teacher capacity to design and deliver high-quality instruction. TLN fosters an "us/ours" attitude (as opposed to "me/mine"). The long-term goal for a TLN school is to become "self-winding" as each member of the instructional staff becomes able to move into and out of the teacher–leader role. In other words, the TLN process is never "done" or fully implemented because the model assumes that teaching can always be improved.

The Accelerated School Effort

The Accelerated Schools model was developed by Henry Levin and colleagues at Stanford University and has been implemented in a variety of schools (Hopfenberg & Levin, 1993; Knight & Stallings, 1995; Levin, 1987). The model calls for the collaboration of university and school personnel in a restructuring of the entire school. Faculty members at individual schools decide what their priorities are and implement day-to-day goals, but all Accelerated Schools have the following common broad goals: (1) the creation of a learning environment characterized by high expectations, (2) the elimination of any achievement gap by the end of elementary school, (3) the daily implementation of a fast-paced curriculum focusing on student engagement, and (4) involvement and empowerment of teachers and parents.

Teachers in Accelerated Schools are involved in professional development activities before implementation and then meet regularly to monitor their own progress toward their goals and to decide how their school can move toward realizing these goals. Parent education and involvement projects are implemented, and parents are included in decision-making teams. All participants in Accelerated Schools are asked to envision the education they would desire for their own children and then to work toward finding ways to provide that same level of excellence for all the children in their school.

Accelerated Schools move away from tracking and ability grouping and use a variety of cooperative groups and student tutor/partnership arrangements. They see language development as a real goal in every curriculum area, and they integrate curriculum around themes as much as possible. They optimize discovery learning, hands-on and real-world experiences, and the reading and writing of authentic texts whenever possible. They try to provide opportunities for all children to engage in the arts and to become part of extra-curricular activities. All school personnel feel responsible for helping the children develop social and critical thinking skills.

Accelerated Schools do not claim instant results. They acknowledge that it takes several years for a school to become the school that its staff and community envision. They acknowledge that children who come to school at risk will not all be on grade level the first year. They do, however, have high expectations (supported by their initial data) that, given a long-term schoolwide effort toward clearly defined goals, almost all children can leave elementary school with solid grade-level reading, writing, and thinking skills. The Accelerated Schools process is designed to be a six-year effort for reforming a traditional school into an Accelerated School. Each year, one grade level, beginning with kindergarten, is reorganized.

The Accelerated School process emphasizes a community inquiry to redesign elementary schools so that all children are successful. Over 100 Accelerated Schools now operate in a number of states. Henry Levin (1987) notes that many economically disadvantaged students begin school with experiential gaps in areas most valued by schools and that in our current schools these children often fall further behind more-advantaged peers each year. He argues it is critical that schools set a deadline for closing the achievement gap so that all children will be able to benefit from the regular instructional program by the time they leave for middle school. Without a deadline, some children will remain below level. Setting the end of fifth grade as the deadline gives schools six years (K–5) to accelerate the literacy development of children who started school with few book, story, or print activity experiences.

Accelerated Schools begin by restructuring programs with the funds available. Levin notes that it is more expensive to educate disadvantaged children and children who find learning more difficult.

Resources for Further Information

Book: Finman et al. (1996). *Accelerated Schools in action: Lessons from the field.* Thousand Oaks, CA: Corwin Press.

Video: *Accelerated Schools. Video Journal,* vol. 4 (www.schoolimprovement.com/products/index.jsp).

Internet: www.acceleratedschools.net

But extra-funding sources are routinely available in allocations for remedial, special, and bilingual education programs. In addition, those involved with the Accelerated Schools projects have generally found other willing donors when a well-conceived plan has been developed.

The Basic School Effort

Ernest Boyer (1995) conceptualized the Basic School during his tenure as president of the Carnegie Foundation for the Advancement of Teaching and shortly before his untimely death. Today the Basic School Network includes some 125 elementary schools in 26 states. Recent reports of improved student achievement (Bafumo,1998) suggest the Basic School design enhances performance on traditional accountability measures. However, the design of the school and especially the curricular design target many sorts of student learning not typically assessed in school accountability systems.

The Basic School is organized around four priorities, each with embedded themes:

1. *The School as Community:* shared vision, teachers as leaders, parents as partners
2. *A Curriculum with Coherence:* the centrality of language, core commonalities, measuring results
3. *A Climate for Learning:* patterns to fit purpose, resources to enrich, services to children
4. *A Commitment to Character:* core virtues, living with a purpose

Boyer's book *The Basic School* (1995) outlines in elegant detail how each of the priorities might be translated into specific proposals for how to organize and sustain a school. For instance, under the Coherent Curriculum priority Boyer suggests a curricular plan that encompasses eight core commonalities that comprise the integrated units of study that spiral through the grades. Each core commonality emphasizes experiences that all humans have in common:

1. The life cycle
2. The use of symbols
3. Producing and consuming
4. Membership in groups
5. A sense of time and space
6. Response to the aesthetic
7. Connections to nature
8. Living with a purpose

Thus, the Basic School design attempts to end the fragmentation of curriculum so prevalent in our schools (every 20 or 30 minutes change the book, change the topic, and change the assignment, rarely establishing links between the books, topics, or assignments that students complete). Instead of the traditional subject-matter organization, teachers teach integrated units around the core commonalities, often in multi-age classes in a vigorous attempt to foster three of the core virtues—responsibility, respect, and giving—through cooperative learning and cross-age mentoring. Multi-age groupings are not required but are examples of the design principle of "Patterns for a Purpose" under the Climate for Learning priority. In other words, Basic Schools are designed to employ a flexible view of grouping and regrouping while holding firm to the belief that caring relationships are not only critically important but typically built over extended periods of time (not typically, for instance, in a single school year). But grouping students should lead to purposeful groupings. Although a group of students might be organized generally as a multi-age grades 3–4–5 homeroom class, those same students would be regrouped throughout the week in focused groups (for intensive coaching), in individual groups (for independent study), in age-peer groups (for grade-level curricular work), and in a whole-school group (for community building).

Resources for Further Information

Book: Boyer, E. L. (1995). *The Basic School: A community for learning.* Princeton, NJ: Carnegie Foundation for the Advancement of Teaching; 800-777-4726.

Article: Elliot, I. (1998, September). A Basic School that's one happy family. *Teaching K–8,* 48–52. Also available at www.teachingK–8.com

Video: *The Basic School. Administrators Video Magazine,* vol. 2.2.

Internet: www.jmu.edu/.basicschools

Because the Basic School design is broadly conceived, no two designs look identical in organization, curriculum, or programs. Central to the Basic School model is adaptation to local constituencies—teachers, parents, children. This evolves from the belief that critical decisions about educating children should be made by the parents and teachers of those children. The centrality of language learning—reading, writing, speaking—is obvious in the broad curricular plan with attention to fostering language skills from phoneme awareness to analyzing the perspective of different characters in a novel, historical event, or social situation. The focus on teachers and teaching fits nicely with research on the importance of professional communities in improving teaching (Johnston, Allington, Guice, & Brooks, 1998) and on differentiated professional development opportunities across the career (Darling-Hammond, 1997).

Four Blocks Framework

The Four Blocks framework was developed by teachers who believed that to be successful in teaching *all* children to read and write, they were going to have to do it *all.* "Doing it all" means incorporating on a daily basis several different approaches to reading. The four blocks—Guided Reading, Self-Selected Reading, Writing, and Working with Words—represent four different approaches to teaching children to read (Cunningham & Allington, 2007). Daily instruction in all four blocks provides numerous and varied opportunities for all children to learn to read and write. Doing all four blocks acknowledges that all children do not learn in the same way and provides substantial instruction to support whatever learning personality a child comes with. The other big difference between children—their different literacy levels—is acknowledged by the use of a variety of during-reading formats and before-and-after reading activities to make each block as multilevel as possible. This provides additional support for children who struggle and additional challenges for children who catch on quickly.

In Four Blocks classrooms, the Self-Selected Reading block provides children with the opportunity to read from a variety of materials on their own level, including the widest possible range of topics, genres, and levels. While the children read, the teacher conferences with a fifth of the class each day. The block usually ends with one or two children sharing their book with the class in a "reader's chair" format. The goals of the Self-Selected Reading block are to

- Provide independent-level reading to consolidate skills and strategies
- Introduce children to all types of literature
- Encourage children's reading interests
- Build intrinsic motivation for reading

Self-selected reading is, by definition, multilevel. During the weekly conferences, teachers support children's choices and help children choose books that they can read and will enjoy.

The Writing block includes both self-selected writing in which children choose their topics and focused writing in which children learn how to write particular forms and on particular topics. The Writing block begins with a 10-minute minilesson, during which the teacher writes and models all the things writers do. Then the children go to their own writing. They are at different stages of the writing process—finishing a story, starting a new story, editing, illustrating, and so on. While the children write, the teacher conferences with individuals who are getting ready to publish. This block ends with the "author's chair" in which several students each day share work-in-progress or their published work. The goals of the Writing block are to

- Have children view writing as a way of telling about things
- Develop fluent writing for all children
- Teach students to apply grammar and mechanics in their own writing
- Teach particular writing forms
- Allow students to learn to read through writing
- Maintain the motivation and self-confidence of struggling writers

Writing is the most multilevel block because it is not limited by the availability of appropriate books. As teachers help children publish the piece they have chosen, they have the opportunity to truly individualize their teaching. Looking at the writing of the child usually reveals both what the child needs to move forward and what the child is ready to understand.

In the Working with Words block, children learn to read and spell high-frequency words and learn the patterns that allow them to decode and spell lots of words. The first 10 minutes of this block are usually given to reviewing Word Wall words. The remaining 15 to 25 minutes of words time is given to an activity that helps children learn to decode and spell. The goals of the Working with Words block are to

- Learn to read and spell the high-frequency words
- Learn how to decode and spell lots of other words using patterns from known words
- Automatically and fluently use phonics and spelling patterns while reading and writing

Activities in the Working with Words block are multilevel in a variety of ways. During the daily Word Wall practice, the children who have learned to read the words being practiced are learning to spell them. Other children who require lots of practice with words are learning to read them. Making Words, Reading Writing Rhymes, Using Words You Know, and other Working with Words block activities are also multilevel. Most lessons begin with short, easy words and progress to longer, more complex words. Children who still need to develop phonemic awareness can do this as they decide which words rhyme and stretch out words. Each lesson includes some sorting of words into patterns and then using those patterns to read and spell new words. Children whose word knowledge is at all different levels see how to use the patterns they see in words to read and spell other words.

Guided Reading lessons have a before-reading phase, a during-reading phase, and an after-reading phase. Before children read, teachers help them build and access prior knowledge, make connections to personal experiences, develop vocabulary essential for comprehension, make predictions, and set purposes for their reading. After reading, children connect new knowledge to what they knew before, follow up predictions, and discuss what they learned and how they are becoming better readers by using these reading strategies.

In Four Blocks classrooms, children read selections in various formats. On some days, the whole class reads together and the teacher uses shared reading, choral reading, echo reading, or ERT to encourage everyone's active participation. On other days, the children may read the selection with partners, or in playschool groups, book club groups, or think-aloud groups. Sometimes, teachers pull small coaching groups and read a selection with them while the other children read the selection with partners or individually. The goals of the Guided Reading block are to

- Teach comprehension skills and strategies
- Develop background knowledge, meaning vocabulary, and oral language
- Teach children how to read all types of literature
- Provide as much instructional-level reading as possible
- Maintain the motivation and self-confidence of struggling readers

Guided Reading is the hardest block to make multilevel. Any selection is going to be too hard for some children and too easy for others. Here are some of the most common multilevel tactics:

- Guided Reading time is not spent only in grade-level material. Rather, teachers alternate selections—one at the average reading level of the class and one at an easier level.

- In book club groups, teachers select four books tied together in some way, including one that is a little easier than average and one a little harder.

- Each selection—or parts of longer selections—is reread several times, each time for a different purpose in a different format. Rereading enables children who couldn't read the selection fluently the first time to achieve fluent reading by the last reading.

Successful Four Blocks High-Poverty Schools

Four Blocks has been implemented in a variety of schools throughout the United States and Canada. Some of these schools have large numbers of children who live in poverty. Here are some examples of successful schools with large numbers of poor children who have "beat the odds" using the Four Blocks framework.

- Ninety-eight percent of the children enrolled at Hall School in Grand Rapids, Michigan, qualify for free or reduced lunch. Ninety-eight percent of the children are Hispanic. After three years of full implementation of the Four Blocks framework, 68 percent of the students (fourth graders) met or exceeded the proficiency level on the Michigan Education Assessment Program (MEAP). Three years earlier, only 8 percent of Hall's students met or exceeded this standard.

- R. N. Wilentz School is a large urban school in Perth Amboy, New Jersey. Eighty-nine percent of Wilentz's students are Hispanic; 7 percent are African American; and 87 percent qualify for free or reduced lunch. After four years of Four Blocks implementation, 77 percent of third and fourth graders achieved proficient or advanced levels on the New Jersey state achievement tests.

- Monaview Elementary School in Greenville, South Carolina, is an urban school with high mobility, and 90 percent of its students are eligible for free or reduced lunch. Monaview had been designated by the state as a "corrective status" school when it began its implementation of Four Blocks. Five years later, the children were performing at better than expected levels and the school was no longer a "corrective status" school.

All three of these schools worked hard to implement the Four Blocks framework with fidelity. They had lots of opportunities for professional growth and persisted across several years to achieve the impressive results demonstrated by their students. Information about Four Blocks can be found at www.wfu.edu/fourblocks.

- On some days, some children read the selection by themselves and others read with partners while the teacher meets with a small group. These small coaching groups change regularly and do not include only the low readers.

- Extra easy reading time is allocated for children whose reading level is below even the easier selections read.

Literacy Collaborative

Literacy Collaborative (LC) is an American extension, or outgrowth, of the Reading Recovery intervention imported to the United States from New Zealand. While Reading Recovery is an effective early tutorial intervention focused on accelerating the development of the lowest achieving first-grade readers (D'Agostino & Murphy, 2004), LC is a whole-school process for reforming elementary literacy instruction. Each LC school is required to have Reading Recovery in place as a first-grade intervention.

As with Reading Recovery, LC focuses much effort on developing teacher expertise on teaching children to read using a teacher leader model. Teacher leaders attend one of the regional training sites around the nation to learn the theory and pedagogy of LC. They then return to their schools to support other teachers in developing this expertise in a year-long professional-development program of 40 hours. After the initial year, an additional 20 hours of LC professional development is required for all teachers. The teacher leaders offer coaching and provide a model classroom for other teachers to visit and observe LC in action.

Central to the Literacy Collaborative is the focus on ensuring children are matched with appropriate texts, so much emphasis is placed on the use of leveled texts rather than a single core series. Developing both substantial classroom collections of age-appropriate texts and school book rooms (see Chapter 4), so as to ensure an adequate supply of books of an appropriate level of complexity, is central to LC implementation. Teachers provide instructional scaffolding during guided reading lessons, word study practice, and project-focused writing. Teachers explicitly model and demonstrate composing, self-monitoring, comprehension, and decoding strategies while "following the lead of the child" to design the instructional support needed to advance children's reading and writing proficiencies.

The LC website (see Resources for Further Information box) provides a number of evaluation studies of LC. Also, Tivnan and Hemphill (2005) report on a comparative study of LC and three other early reading models. In this study, LC was found

Resources for Further Information

Articles: Tivnan, T., & Hemphill, L. (2005). Comparing four literacy reform models in high-poverty schools: Patterns of first-grade achievement. *Elementary School Journal, 105,* 419–441.

D'Agostino, J. V., & Murphy, J. A. (2004). A meta-analysis of Reading Recovery in United States schools. *Educational Evaluation and Policy Analysis, 26*(1): 23–38.

Internet: Literacy Collaborative, at www.lcosu.org

effective: low-income children who arrived with low levels of literacy development ended the first-grade year with reading achievement near or above (45th to 68th percentile) the national average in all areas except vocabulary (25th percentile, which was still above the average level of children across all four interventions studied). This comparative study may point to a primary problem that has received little attention thus far; poor children need lots of vocabulary development support in addition to lots of decoding support.

Comer School Development Program

James Comer (1988, 1996) developed and implemented a different sort of school change in the Martin Luther King Elementary School in New Haven, Connecticut. Comer argues that often school-change efforts focus too heavily on curricular and cognitive aspects of the school experience and fail to deal adequately with school–community relationships. Now implemented in a number of schools across the nation, the School Development program encourages student bonding with the school. But developing the bond involves substantially rethinking and restructuring traditional power relationships.

Comer argues that in many communities a substantial degree of mistrust exists between parents and school staff. Each group sees the other as a primary source for student failure to thrive. This mistrust fosters an alienation of students and their parents from the school and makes it unlikely that any sort of curricular change will resolve student learning difficulties. Thus, Comer and his colleagues set out to address the alienation first, realizing that most school personnel had neither the training in nor the past experience of working collaboratively alongside parents to resolve school issues.

A governance team of about a dozen members was established for the school. The team was led by the principal and included elected parents and teachers and a member of the nonprofessional staff. Each team also included a mental health professional. The team operated by consensus, not by majority rule, to foster cooperation rather than create a situation in which someone was a "loser." Teams focused their efforts on solution finding rather than blame placing. Team members acknowledged the legal authority of the principal, but the principal was expected to act in concert with team consensus. Issues ranging from academic programs to discipline to organization of the school day were all within the realm of team decision making.

Acknowledging that creating such teams and getting them up and running is not accomplished without difficulty, Comer (1988) maintains that the effort's success can be found in improved relations between parents and teachers, improved attendance, and improved academic achievement. The Martin Luther King School achievement test scores rose

Resources for Further Information

Book: Comer, J. P., Haynes, N., Joyner, E., & Ben Avie, N. (1999). *Child by child: The Comer process for change in education*. New York: Teachers College Press.

Video: *Community involvement: Working together to improve schools*. Video Journal, vol. 4 (www.schoolimprovement.com/products/index.jsp).

Internet: http://info.med.yale.edu/comer

across five years from the very bottom of New Haven school performance to third highest. More recent studies show improved attendance and social and psychological development among children enrolled in the schools along with evidence pointing to enhanced academic achievement (Comer et al., 1996).

The School Development programs were among the earliest attempts at implementing some form of shared decision making in school sites, and much can be learned from those efforts. But the focus on school–community relations and especially teacher–parent cooperation is what makes these efforts unique.

The Coalition of Essential Schools

The Coalition of Essential Schools (CES) has focused efforts primarily on middle school and high school education. Nonetheless, this educational restructuring effort is having an impact on the elementary school curriculum in many sites where CES schools now operate. The assumptions that guide change at CES sites are straightforward:

- *Intellectual focus.* Schools are to be designed to help students learn to use their minds well.
- *Simple goals.* The aphorism "Less is more" should dominate curriculum decisions. Teach fewer things better and more deeply.
- *Personalization.* Students learn best when instruction is more personal, involving more student choice and more teacher contact.
- *Universal goals.* "All means all" best summarizes the approach to goal setting. All goals apply to all students.
- *Student-as-worker.* Replacing the teacher-as-knowledge-deliverer with the student-as-worker metaphor allows teachers time to personalize instruction.
- *Diploma by exhibition.* The emphasis is on what students can do, not on the number of pages or units completed or on time spent in classes.
- *Attitude.* School climate should stress values of unanxious expectation, trust, and decency. Parents must be viewed as active, valued collaborators.
- *Staff.* Members are generalists first, specialists second. Thus, all staff have multiple roles and responsibilities (teacher, administrator, and counselor/advocate).
- *Budget.* Costs are not to exceed those of traditional schools by more than 10 percent; collaborative planning time is available; salaries are competitive.

The CES effort derives from the work of Ted Sizer (1988) and involves statewide efforts in a dozen states and local efforts across the United States. In addition, the CES projects have initiated collaborative efforts with the Education Commission of the States (Re: Learning), the Comer School Development Program, Harvard Project Zero, and other educational reform efforts. The CES change process involves reorganizing not only the curriculum and the school day and year but reorganizing decision making by "delayering" decisions about what to teach and how to teach. Participatory decision making includes parents and, often, students.

Resources for Further Information

Book: Wasley, P. (1998). *Stirring the chalkdust.* New York: Teachers College Press.

Article: Meier, D. (1996). Transforming schools into powerful communities. In W. Ayers & P. Ford (Eds.), *City kids, city teachers: Reports from the front row* (pp. 131–136). New York: New Press.

Internet: www.essentialschools.org

But what makes the CES schools unique is the elimination of subject-matter boundaries and rigid class schedules along with the emphasis on authentic assessment of authentic learning. The integration of mathematics and science, of literature and economics, and of civics and biology is indicative of the rethinking of the very nature of curriculum and instruction. Although this effort began with a focus on adolescent education, more and more frequently the basic principles are being applied to elementary schools. At New York City's Central Park East, for instance, the project began at the high school level but has been incorporated into the middle school and elementary school levels. The thoughtful curriculum combined with authentic assessment provides a powerful base for teaching and learning at any age.

Change Takes Time as Well as Good Intentions

One can pick up almost any educational journal (or even popular magazine) and find other stories of schools changing for the better. Likewise, a flood of professional and popular books describe school-change efforts (e.g., Allington & Walmsley, 1995; Harwayne, 1999; Sergiovanni, 2000). We suggest that it is *not* because of any lack of information that change is not more widespread.

What causes some schools to engage in rethinking what they are doing and how they are doing it? And what makes the status quo such a popular option? Undoubtedly, the answer is complex but in the end, we think that the beliefs education professionals hold about learners and learning are critical factors affecting the design of schools.

Professional Beliefs

Accelerating the learning of all children is an idea whose time has come. Given the large-scale evidence provided by the efforts discussed above, it is obviously not necessary to continue to slow down instruction or wait for children to develop. There is good research demonstrating that most children's reading and writing development can be accelerated if schools are reorganized and resources are used to create programs that provide children with access to instruction of sufficient quantity and quality (Vellutino et al., 1996). However, in too many schools the dominant belief is that inevitably there will be a bottom group of children who will never catch up with their peers. Adherence to this notion may be the most formidable barrier to creating schools where all children learn to read and write. Until teachers, administrators, and supervisors believe that all children can become

The Success for All (SFA) program was developed by Robert Slavin and colleagues at Johns Hopkins University (Slavin, Madden, Dolan, & Wasik, 1996). The model is currently in use in more than 1,000 schools across the nation.

SFA has been widely implemented, but the results for the SFA schools are in many ways disappointing (and perhaps for that reason a number of districts have pulled out of the program). Although more children are achieving grade-level reading at the end of first grade in SFA schools, Venezky (1998) reports that very few children actually read on level, or even very close to grade level, by the end of fifth grade. His reanalysis of the developers' research data indicated that the average end-of-year fifth grader read at the mid-third-grade level, a level only modestly better than that of students in the control schools without SFA.

As with many school reforms, the problem of "scaling up" SFA—implementing the model on a large scale—has proved to be an obstacle to maintaining the original high hopes of the intervention for enhancing academic achievement. Although the SFA design has a number of positive features and a fairly extensive research record documenting modest improvements in achievement, in our view it is hardly a "proven program" for accelerating the development of struggling readers as many supporters have claimed.

proficient readers and writers, efforts to create extraordinary instructional programs are unlikely to be sustained. Actually, as long as traditional beliefs dominate professional thinking in a school, it is unlikely that faculty will even consider changing instruction to speed the literacy development of early struggling readers.

Unfortunately, this belief issue often creates a chicken-or-egg dilemma. The nature of many current school programs reinforces the traditional professional belief system (Allington, McGill-Franzen, & Schick, 1997). When schools design and implement instructional programs that alter the status quo, long-standing beliefs are modified. For instance, implementing Reading Recovery in schools has caused a shift in the beliefs of classroom teachers about the literacy-learning capacities of struggling readers. As children are released from the program as successful grade-level readers, classroom teachers question the dominant belief that some children will never learn to read along with their peers. Similarly, reducing the stratification of children into various "ability" groups in Four Blocks, TLN, and CES sites has altered beliefs concerning the potential of many struggling readers. As teacher and administrator beliefs change, shifts in classroom practices become more likely.

However, because current instructional programs often maintain the status quo, it may be difficult to muster any intense interest in changing school programs dramatically without some strong and persuasive evidence. Even then, change proposals will often be greeted less than enthusiastically and with a somewhat skeptical eye. In our experience, reading about schools that work better for all children offers one potential approach for shifting beliefs, as do visits to such schools. Small demonstration projects initiated on a school site are also persuasive. In any event, long-standing professional beliefs support most school practices. For professional practice to change, professional beliefs must be addressed.

The difficulty of initiating change must be recognized. There is no quick fix. Maintaining the status quo is always easier than involving a school in changes. It is for this reason that changing school programs must be viewed as a long-term effort, not a shift that will miraculously emerge after a single workshop or staff-development session.

Change is necessary in most schools. In this chapter we provide examples of efforts that have dramatically enhanced the instructional programs in a number of schools. Although each effort was unique, several common themes emerge from these attempts to create schools where all children learn to read and write.

Ten Features of Successful Efforts

What do successful school-restructuring efforts have in common? We see ten features that emerge from the research on school change that has enhanced the academic achievement (e.g., thoughtful literacy) of students.

(1) School staff committed to the idea that all children could learn to read and write, and they worked to produce that outcome.

(2) Substantial investments were made in professional development. Few of the successful reform initiatives involved much of an outlay for specialized equipment or for trendy special materials. The major expenditure was in human capital, primarily investments to enhance teachers' instructional skills and to create teaching and learning environments that would support high-quality instruction.

(3) Planning was reorganized so that classroom teachers were more heavily involved in school decision making. In some schools, parents and community members also joined the school site-based management teams. Each of the restructuring efforts increased teacher and parent input and involvement.

(4) To implement new instructional approaches, the schools invested in classroom libraries, big books, magazine subscriptions, and student anthologies. In too many schools, especially those serving large numbers of poor children, children often have little to read. Putting books in classrooms and in school libraries makes it more likely that children will have books in their hands.

(5) The schools allocated larger amounts of classroom instructional time to actual reading and writing activities while using multiple approaches to literacy instruction. These schools emphasize real reading and writing activity during literacy lessons. Integration of reading and writing activities and integration of reading and writing with social studies and science lessons are also common. These sorts of integration reduce the fragmentation of both the school day and the curriculum.

(6) Special instructional programs were reorganized. Extra effort was made to connect special-program teachers with classroom instruction and classroom teachers. Even though some of the schools continue pull-out programs for special instructional support, attempts have been made to ease and facilitate collaboration among the various teachers working with the same children. Intensive instructional support is offered when needed, often using a tutorial model for children who most need their literacy development accelerated.

(7) Expanding instructional time by extending the normal school day for some children is another feature of many of the successful efforts. Strategies included using a before-school period, using part of the lunch period, and scheduling literacy support lessons after school. In some cases, summer programs were developed to extend the school year and to support or extend the gains made during the regular school year.

(8) The assessments of children's literacy development are tied more heavily to everyday reading and writing than to end-of-year standardized testing. Such annual testing has continued, but the frequent, authentic evaluation of reading and writing performances drives teaching. In some cases, the evaluation system was completely rewritten to focus on exhibitions and performances by students rather than maintaining an emphasis on daily homework and weekly test scores.

(9) Successful schools worked to involve families. They found that parents will become engaged because their children are succeeding and because they see a school community working in new ways to support their children. Parents are not simply expected to monitor homework. They are involved in making many of the tough decisions about the use of school resources, about curriculum, and about schedules. Often, family literacy programs were developed with family support services such as a homework hotline or a regular parent–teacher contact program.

(10) In most of the successful school reform efforts, change started small, not with a wholesale restructuring of the school. In some cases, change began in a single classroom. One classroom is only a beginning, but it *is* a beginning. Successful school-change efforts take time to accomplish, especially schoolwide change. It was not unusual to find a multi-year plan for changing current practice. But long-term plans call for long-term commitments to continuous improvement—commitments from the professional staff and from the district leaders who provide the resources that support the change effort.

Summary

Some schools change because the teachers push for change and initiate and carry much of the effort. Other schools change because a school district or building leader pushes change and creates an environment that encourages and supports it. This simplification illustrates the ideas of bottom-up (teachers initiate) and top-down (administrators initiate) approaches to reorganizing schools. Truth be told, we think that few pure examples of either approach exist. In our experience, change has occurred when teachers, administrators, and supervisors somehow come together around a common core of concerns.

Often, educational reformers have failed to understand that schools are collections of classrooms. Rather than attempting to restructure a school as a starting point, it will be more useful to begin by thinking about changing the instruction offered in classrooms (Nye, Konstantopoulos, & Hedges, 2004). The change needs to focus on more effective responses to the instructional needs of all children, but especially children who are struggling to become readers and writers. The change effort needs to focus on supporting classroom teachers in the process of improving their classroom literacy lessons. In working with schools, we try to begin by starting small while looking at the long term. We begin by asking school staff, "What would you like to see happening more often in the classrooms?" and "What would you like to see happening less frequently?"

After the development of some preliminary lists of things that teachers would like to see more and less of, it is time to begin to think about how to foster more of some activities and less of others. For instance, if more time spent reading in classrooms is a goal, then developing classroom libraries of 500 or more paperback titles is a good strategy to pursue. Enhancing access to books increases the amount of reading done in and out of school (Fielding, Wilson, & Anderson, 1986) and it increases student reading achievement (Guthrie & Humenick, 2004). At the same time, if we can provide classroom teachers with longer blocks of uninterrupted teaching time, we can support attempts to expand the time children spend actually reading and writing in the classroom.

If the goal is to see children spending less time filling in low-level skills sheets, the strategy might be to agree to limit the number of reams of paper available for reproducing these materials. We might then take the money saved through such reductions (paper costs, photocopying costs, costs of aides who copy the materials) and channel it into book purchases for classroom libraries. Time previously spent on seatwork activity can then be shifted to time spent reading, but only if children have access to a sufficient supply of comfortable, interesting reading materials. If off-task behavior is a central problem, we might work to ensure that classrooms have large supplies of books that children can read and are interested in reading (Allington, 2006). The point is that schools can be overwhelmed when they try to change everything at once. Go slow and take the long-term view. Don't forget: There is no quick fix and no one best way.

In the remainder of this book we explore the various aspects of school change in substantially greater depth. We attempt to offer clearer and more detailed descriptions of such efforts and to offer a clear rationale for why each is critical. In addition, each chapter offers examples from real schools engaged in change.

What Do We Now Know about Reading and Writing?

T he last 25 years have been exciting times for literacy researchers because so much has been learned about the processes of reading and writing. We now have a much clearer understanding of the mental processes that underlie both, and this new knowledge undercuts much conventional wisdom about how we learn to read and write. In addition, we know quite a bit about the kinds of schools and classrooms where all children become readers and writers.

Our goal in writing this book is to bring together all that we know about supporting successful literacy instruction and about accomplishing change in elementary schools. In this chapter we focus on what we know about the reading and writing processes and about

how to help children acquire literacy in our schools. We also point to some instances when common practice seems to run contrary to the best evidence on how we might foster reading and writing development in children. We attempt to provide a summary of important processes and principles but realize that our summaries risk oversimplifying complex issues. Thus, we hope that interested readers will locate and study the reports we cite in support of the generalizations, or principles, that we offer.

Reading and Writing Are *Thinking*

For much of the twentieth century it was assumed that once children learned to decode words, they could read. It was believed that when they could pronounce words, comprehension would follow, almost automatically. It was also assumed that writing was simply writing down words and that writing could not occur until children had mastered the decoding activity (which provided them with the skills to spell the words they were trying to write). Writing instruction was seen as primarily lessons in penmanship, spelling, punctuation, and the parts of speech. Reading and writing lessons focused more on developing the decoding and editing skills than on developing children's knowledge and thinking.

While the press and policy makers focus on America's literacy problems (e.g., the achievement gaps), we think it is useful also to celebrate the strengths of U.S. schools. In the area of literacy attainment, for instance, U.S. fourth graders performed above the international average in the last two international assessments and our ninth graders performed at the international average level of proficiency. Statistically, the fourth-grade students in only five nations performed better than U.S. students, and the students in only one nation (Sweden) outperformed U.S. fourth-grade students in literary reading. U.S. student performance in reading informational texts was somewhat lower with five nations performing better statistically, suggesting that is one area we might well focus on improving.

The highest-scoring nations tended to have much smaller and less diverse populations than the United States (e.g., Sweden, Netherlands, Latvia, Canada, Lithuania). But students enrolled in the schools of our major economic competitors—Germany, Japan, and Korea—all underperformed statistically compared to U.S. students.

We believe that we can, and need to, create schools that work better for all students. But, just once in awhile, everyone should praise the successes of U.S. schools today.

You can examine the international comparisons data yourself at www.nces.ed.gov/pubs2004/pirispub/3.asp.

This focus on low-level skills mastery resulted in an increased number of children who could perform low-level literacy activities. Today, more children achieve the "basic" literacy level as set on the National Assessment of Educational Progress (NAEP) than at any point in U.S. history (Perie, Grigg, & Donahue, 2005). But the number of students who achieve the "proficient" literacy level on the NAEP has barely changed over the past 35 years. The proficient level asks students to read, write, and think simultaneously. The tasks require students to summarize information read or to contrast two characters or to identify the primary argument in a persuasive essay (an editorial, for instance). Only about 25 percent of students satisfactorily complete such tasks. The focus on low-level skills that has been so popular politically—locating and remembering specific details, filling in the blanks, circling the answers, pronouncing the words, answering the factual questions, identifying the nouns and verbs, correctly spelling all the words—did not lead to much thoughtfulness by readers and writers. The result has been too many children who could read words accurately but who demonstrated little thinking while reading and little under-standing of what they had read, children who could write with few misspellings or punctu-ation errors but whose compositions showed little thought, persuasiveness, organization, or creativity.

Think for a moment about your own reading and writing. As you read a novel, you may find yourself transported into the scene. You find yourself liking some characters and despising others. You may notice a resemblance between a character and someone you know in real life. You may "see" the character. As you read a memo from a state education agency official, you may find yourself getting annoyed—wondering whether the author has any sense of the complexity of the directive issued. You may find yourself comparing the directive to previous directives, mentally noting changes in your responsibilities. In other words, you find yourself thinking. If you compose a memo in response, it matters whether the memo is going to the official who sent the directive or to colleagues who need the information about the new policy. It matters whether you write your memo to summa-rize the information or to criticize the directive. Both audience and purpose matter when you write. Someone who walks into your office immediately after you finish reading the memo may find you sitting and thinking. Someone who comes in while you are compos-ing your own memo may find you sitting in front of your computer screen, thinking. In fact, if your visitor asks what you are doing, you will likely reply, "I'm thinking [about this silly new policy . . ."]. The point is that whenever adults read and write they think. Reading or writing without thinking would be senseless.

Think about those reading and writing lessons that epitomize "basic skills" lessons. Many lessons require no text reading at all, only isolated word and sentence readings. Often, writing involves no composing, simply filling in blanks or copying sentences from a book or the board. *Recall, locate, list,* and *copy* are words that describe the central instructional tasks in basic skills lessons. Thinking is rarely required.

Fielding and Pearson (1994) contend "that a successful program of comprehension instruction" should include four components:

1. Large amounts of time for actual text reading
2. Teacher-directed instruction in comprehension strategies
3. Opportunities for peer and collaborative learning
4. Occasions for students to talk to a teacher and to one another about their responses to reading

We see reading lessons where remembering is confused with understanding. For instance, in many classroom lessons there is little focus on developing transferable strategies for understanding and much focus on guiding students to identify and remember specific information from the text being read (Duffy, 2001). In fact, much of the guidance in the traditional directed reading activity design of basal reader lessons and in the more recent guided reading lesson design seems bent on fostering recall of the story or information. Little in either design provides explicit strategy instruction that would foster the development of transferable strategies for comprehending while engaging in independent reading.

Taylor, Pearson, Peterson, and Rodriguez (2003) report on yearlong observational data from an intervention study of teachers in nine elementary schools from three regions of the United States. Their focus was on those factors that explain growth in reading fluency, comprehension, and writing in schools serving many children from low-income families. They found that the most consistent variable related to reading achievement growth was teacher emphasis on higher-order thinking either through the questions they asked or the sorts of tasks they assigned students. Although little comprehension instruction, higher-level questioning, or writing was actually observed at any grade level, more effective teachers asked more higher-level questions, engaged in discussion more often, and had kids do more writing. Interrogation was still overwhelmingly popular with 60–75 percent of lessons coded this way. Modeling of thinking processes was observed in only 3–5 percent of the lessons. Passive responding (round-robin reading, oral turn taking, listening to the teacher) accounted for two-thirds of the coded primary-grade lessons and three-quarters of lessons in grades 3–5. Taylor and colleagues found, however, that even modest increases in active responding, modeling, higher-level questions, and discussion proved effective at fostering reading growth.

It is important to understand that asking questions *after* reading—interrogation—does not typically foster the development of transferable strategies. After-reading questions serve two functions: assessment of student recall and fostering recall of specific information from the material read. Assessing student recall is often useful, but it is not the same as assessing understanding. Nor does it function to improve a student's comprehension processes. Recalling the phrase "slithery tove" in "Jabberwocky" does not mean you know what a slithery tove is. Likewise recalling the names of characters does not mean you understood their intentions or motivations. Accurately copying information from a text in order to respond to an end-of-chapter question does not indicate you understood what you read. Neither does filling in a worksheet blank with the correct word copied from the text.

Thoughtful Literacy

The notion of "thoughtful literacy" is almost always surrounded by terms such as *discussion, conversation, reflection,* and *revision.* Thoughtful literacy is what we demonstrate when we talk with someone else about an article we have read in a newsmagazine. Conversation is what we engage in when both of us have read the same article. Reflection is what we do when the conversation makes us rethink an earlier understanding. Revision is what happens when we say, "You could be right. I never thought of it that way."

We find letters written by an acquaintance interesting when they communicate something of interest to us. We rarely comment on the neatness of the handwriting and the spelling in such letters; instead we note the interestingness and usefulness of the content. It is the same with articles, editorials, directions, obituaries, and so on. In the real world, both reading and composing are meaning-focused activities. We may not recall a character's name, but we can still discuss the book. We may forget the town where the fire raged, but we will still discuss the tragedy.

Children are more likely to learn what they are taught than to learn things not taught. When reading lessons confuse remembering with understanding, children cannot be expected to see reading as thinking processes. When we emphasize editing accuracy (spelling, punctuation, capitalization) in writing lessons and neglect interestingness of the composition, children cannot be expected to see writing as a thinking process. When teachers emphasize pronouncing or spelling the words correctly and rarely focus on thoughtful applications of strategies and purposefulness, children not surprisingly become "basic" readers and writers and seldom display much thoughtfulness.

Consider how adults normally converse about materials they have read. Suppose you see a colleague carrying a popular novel into the teacher's lounge. Will you initiate a conversation about the book by interrogating your colleague about the names of characters, the cars they drive, their whereabouts on particular days, and so on (the kinds of questions that dominate classroom exchanges), or will you ask about your colleague's response to the book: "How do you like it?" Imagine asking your spouse about a newspaper or magazine story that you both read. Will you interrogate with questions about specific factual information: "What is the name of the commander of the Coast Guard cutter?" Or are your comments more likely to focus on response to the piece: "Can you believe that?" "Do you think she is guilty?" It might be useful to compare classroom talk after reading with the talk that normally occurs outside of school when folks read something. Think about the book or article conversations you have with adults outside of school. Think about how often you offer summaries, your personal point of view, comparisons to other information sources, and so on. Think how infrequently you focus on the sorts of details that too often dominate teacher questions after students have read something.

None of this is to argue that children do not need to be taught effective decoding strategies or the conventions of spelling and punctuation. What it does mean is that real readers and writers are constantly thinking while they read and write. It means if we want to create readers and writers, teachers must foster thinking from the beginning lesson. It means that lessons will need to focus on strategies and on selecting the strategy that fits the reading or writing activity. It means that discussion must replace much of the interrogation that now follows reading and writing activities.

Prior Knowledge Plays a Large Role in Reading Comprehension and Writing

The most important factor in determining how much readers will comprehend and how well writers will be able to communicate about a given topic is their level of knowledge about that topic (interest in the topic is also important but often is related to prior knowledge). The importance of prior knowledge to comprehension and communication is included in virtually all modern theories of reading (Anderson & Pearson, 1984; Pressley, Wood, & Woloshyn, 1992; Spivey, 1996). According to schema theory, prior knowledge provides a schema—a framework or structure—that helps thinking. Readers familiar with sports, for example, know that a baseball game has nine players on each side, that the players field different positions, and what players in each position are supposed to do. The writer considers these baseball basics to be "general knowledge" and, thus, does not explicitly explain them in a book or article about baseball. Readers who "know" baseball can listen to or read about a game and have little difficulty comprehending descriptions of games, plays, and so on. These readers literally carry in their heads a schema for baseball. They can envision the field, the baselines, the batter's box, and the dugout. They understand this technical vocabulary and much more. When they hear or read about a "double play," a "slider," a "blooping single to right," a "pick-off attempt," or a player "safe at first," these readers create mental images from the frameworks they possess. In contrast, readers whose prior knowledge of baseball is limited or nonexistent can read the same words and descriptions but not have the foggiest idea of what is going on.

Because comprehension and communication are so dependent on prior knowledge, children whose knowledge of a topic is limited have difficulty comprehending much of what they read and difficulty communicating in writing about that topic. And children who read little have the least opportunity to acquire new knowledge through reading.

Schools must be responsible for helping children learn about the world in which they live. When you think about what we teach children in schools, you can divide almost everything into two categories: knowledge and skills. The abilities to read, spell, write, do math, use the computer, sing a song, play the clarinet, throw a ball, and speak a foreign language are all skills—things you can do. The understandings that there are seven

In a demonstration of how influential prior knowledge can be, Beck and McKeown (1993) produced the passage below.

In 1367 Marain and the settlements ended a seven-year war with the Langurians and Pitoks. As a result of this war Languria was driven out of East Bacol. Marain would now rule Laman and other lands that once belonged to Languria. This brought peace to the Bacolian settlements. The settlers no longer had to worry about attacks from Laman. The Bacolians were happy to be part of Marain in 1367. Yet a dozen years later, these same people would be fighting the Marish for independence, or freedom from United Marain's rule.

That passage did not make much sense to most of the adults that read it. But read the next passage.

In 1763 Britain and the settlements ended a seven-year war with the French and Indians. As a result of this war France was driven out of North America. Britain would now rule Canada and other lands that once belonged to France. This brought peace to the American colonies. The settlers no longer had to worry about attacks from Canada. The Americans were happy to be part of Britain in 1763. Yet a dozen years later, these same people would be fighting the British for independence, or freedom from Great Britain's rule.

As you can see in the first passage, a few key words were changed (e.g., *Britain, France, Canada*). But changing those words was important because most adults were familiar with the original words but were not, of course, familiar with the fictional replacement vocabulary. Most children, however, were familiar with neither. The original passage made no more sense to them than the altered passage. The prior knowledge that we adults have often makes it hard for us to understand the difficulties children encounter in their reading.

continents, each state has two senators, the Civil War was fought in the 1860s, mammals are warm-blooded animals, and Martin Luther King, Jr., led the civil rights movement are all knowledge—things that you know. For many years, literacy instruction in elementary schools has focused on skills and largely ignored knowledge, particularly deep knowledge of topics. In many schools with large numbers of struggling readers, teachers are instructed to "teach the basics." The basics usually refer to the three R's—reading, 'riting, and 'rithmetic. The knowledge part of the curriculum, usually found in the subjects of science and social studies, are almost ignored in the primary grades of these schools.

Emphasizing the skill subjects and excluding the knowledge subjects often results in a short-term gain and a long-term deficit. Test scores in schools that emphasize skills in grades K–3 indicate that children do well through the second or third grade but test scores decline from fourth grade on. After third grade, teachers are supposed to, and do indeed try to, teach the knowledge subjects such as science and social studies. They often find, however, that even their average students can't read the textbooks or "can read them but not understand what they are reading." Children who can read the words but can't understand what they are reading are not really reading. These children who "have the skills" but who lack needed prior knowledge of critical school topics are a legacy of a primary grades curriculum that required teachers to spend all their time "on the basics."

This knowledge deficit, which usually rears its ugly head in third or fourth grade, does not disappear as children move through school. The Scholastic Achievement Test, which claims to predict how well students will do in college, is very dependent on prior knowledge. Our failure to raise SAT scores in spite of two decades of educational reform may be one of the clearest indicators that schools have focused more on skills development than on expanding children's knowledge of the world.

Children Benefit from Modeling, Demonstration, and Explanation

All children need instruction, but some children need substantial amounts of truly high-quality teaching to learn to read and write alongside their peers. What all children need, and some need more of, is models, explanations, and demonstrations of how reading is accomplished. What most do not need are more assignments without teacher-directed instruction, yet much of the work children do in school is not accompanied by any sort of instructional interaction or demonstration.

Children are routinely asked questions after reading but are infrequently provided with demonstrations of the comprehension strategies needed to answer the questions posed. In short, too often assigning and asking are confused with teaching. When the teacher-directed instructional component is left out of the lesson, it enormously reduces the potential of many activities (e.g., maps, webs, summary writing, response journals) for supporting the acquisition of complex comprehension strategies (Fielding & Pearson, 1994; Pressley, 2006). With no clear instruction, children are left to discover the strategies and processes so important to skillful readers and writers. Some children puzzle through the activities assigned but never discover the thinking patterns that proficient readers use.

Modeling, explaining, and demonstrating are essential teaching activities if all children are to learn to read and write. Teachers *model* the reading and writing processes by engaging in them while children observe. Reading aloud to children, for instance, provides a model of how reading sounds and how stories go. Composing a list of things needed for a project provides a model of one function of writing. Talking about how a newspaper story made us worry provides a model of response to text. Models are essential, but models do not give children much in the way of information about how proficient readers actually accomplish such feats.

Reading aloud to children is one way to model fluent reading and thoughtful talk about books, stories, and responses. While read-alouds have become increasingly popular, research indicates that nearly one-third of classroom teachers rarely read children's books aloud to their students (Hoffman, Roser, & Battle, 1993). They also offer guidelines for read-alouds:

- Designate a time each day for reading aloud, not a time-filler slot.
- Select quality literature to read.
- Discuss the books read with children.
- Create groups for children to share responses to books read.
- Reread selected pieces.

Explanation is probably the most common method teachers use to help children understand how one goes about reading and writing. Unfortunately, explanations can get wordy and often require a specialized language. We tell children that a good summary includes "the most important ideas," but some children are left wondering how to tell which ideas are most important. Unfortunately, explanations are often unhelpful. Children can define the main idea, for instance, but they still cannot construct an adequate summary reflecting the important information in a text. Explaining a process is an improvement compared to simply assigning students work, but many children do not acquire useful strategies from explanations alone.

Demonstration is teacher talk about the mental activities that occur during the reading and writing processes. Demonstration usually involves modeling and explaining along with demonstrating the thinking that occurs while reading and writing. For instance, a teacher might compose a summary of an informational passage on an overhead projector in front of the class (Cunningham & Allington, 2007). The teacher provides a model of the writing process and, ultimately, a model of a written summary. The teacher might work from a map or a web following an explanation of the essential summary elements. A demonstration would occur as the teacher thinks aloud during the composing, making visible the thinking that assembles the information for the summary, puts it into words, and finally creates a readable summary of the information presented. Similarly, the teacher demonstrates the

Writing in front of children while talking aloud demonstrates composing as a thinking process.

Children Benefit from Modeling, Demonstration, and Explanation

Resources for Further Information

Several small books provide substantial practical guidance for teachers interested in think-alouds and demonstrations of comprehension strategies and just how teacher talk influences children's learning. Any of these texts can be read in a weekend or less, and each would be a good choice for a Teachers as Professional Readers discussion group.

Duffy, G. G. (2003). *Explaining reading: A resource for teaching concepts, skills, and strategies*. New York: Guilford.

Johnston, P. H. (2004). *Choice words: How our language affects children's learning*. York, ME: Stenhouse.

Wilhelm, J. D. (2001). *Improving comprehension with think-aloud strategies*. New York: Scholastic Inc.

complex mental processes that readers engage in while reading when she talks children through a strategy for puzzling out an unfamiliar word while reading a story. For example, "I can try a couple of things: Read to the end of the sentence; look at the word and see if I know any other words that might help me figure it out; ask myself, 'What makes sense here?'; double-check what word makes sense against word structure; read the sentence using the word that makes sense and has the right letters." Demonstrating such thinking and how thinking shifts from incident to incident ("Here I can look at the picture to get a clue"; "I think the word will rhyme with *name* because it is spelled the same way"; and so on) gives children the chance to see that skillful strategy use is flexible and always requires thinking, not rote memory of rules.

Children only infrequently encounter such demonstrations in most classrooms. Children who find learning to read difficult often see the teacher and other children reading and writing, serving as models, but they wonder, "How do they do it?" All children benefit from instruction, but some children need incredible amounts of careful, personal instruction, with clear and repeated demonstrations of how readers and writers go about reading and writing (Duffy, 2003; Harvey & Goudvis, 2000). Left without adequate demonstrations, struggling readers are likely to continue trying to make sense out of lessons, but rarely will they accomplish this feat. Some of these children learn to score better on tests but never really learn to read and write.

If we are to teach all children to read and write, then models, explanations, and demonstrations of how we go about reading and writing will be essential elements of instructional programs. While some children may discover the effective strategies that proficient readers and writers use so easily and flexibly, other children require substantially more careful and personalized teaching to acquire the same strategies.

Fluency with Reading and Spelling Words Is Essential to Reading and Writing

Advances in technology have allowed researchers, mainly in the areas of psychology and artificial intelligence, to investigate brain functions, eye movements, and other basic reading processes. The focus of this research was not on how to teach reading or on comparisons of various approaches but rather on what happens internally when we read and how this changes as readers move from beginning stages to more sophisticated reading.

We know that readers look at nearly all the words and almost all the letters in those words. The amount of time spent processing each letter is incredibly small, only a few hundredths of a second in proficient readers. The astonishingly fast letter recognition for letters within familiar words and patterns is due to our brains expecting certain letters to occur in sequence with each other.

Readers usually recode printed words into sound. Although it is possible to read without any internal speech, we rarely do (Stanovich, 2000). Normally as we read, we think the words in our mind. We then check this phonological information with the visual information we received by analyzing the word for familiar spelling patterns. Saying the words

Although the National Reading Panel (NRP) report (2000) garnered much attention, there has been much debate among researchers and practitioners about what the NRP actually found in its meta-analysis of 38 studies on the effects of systematic phonics instruction in beginning reading programs. Here is a short synthesis of what was written in the full report produced by the NRP.

- Systematic phonics instruction in kindergarten and first grade produced a small positive effect on reading growth, most evident in tests assessing word and nonword pronunciation in isolation (p. 2–131).

- Comparisons among three methods of teaching decoding (analytic, analogy, other) demonstrated no significant difference. The NRP wrote, "The analysis showed that . . . the three categories of programs did not differ statistically from each other. The conclusion supported by these findings is that various types of phonics instruction are more effective than non-phonic approaches" (p. 2–132).

- "Phonics instruction failed to exert a significant impact on the reading performance of low-achieving readers in 2nd through 6th grade" (p. 2–133). This was the case, perhaps, because limited decoding skills are less often the problem than difficulties with fluency, vocabulary knowledge, and comprehension in older poor readers.

- The NRP also found no evidence supporting the use of decodable texts as a component of phonics instruction (p. 2–137).

Good readers are, invariably, good decoders. Children need effective decoding instruction. But, as the NRP so pointedly reminded us, effective decoding is but one of the many skills and proficiencies that effective reading instruction develops in beginning readers. Or, as Hammill and Swanson (in press) point out, even the NRP analyses indicated that 96 percent of the difference in reading achievement was accounted for by factors other than systematic phonics instruction.

aloud or thinking the words also seems to perform an important function in holding the words in auditory memory until enough words are read to create meaning.

Skilled readers recognize most words immediately and automatically without using context. Good readers use context to see if what they are reading makes sense. Context is also important for disambiguating the meaning of some words ("I had a *ball* throwing the *ball* at the *ball*."). Occasionally, readers use context to figure out what the word is. Most of the time, however, words are identified from their familiar spelling and the association of that spelling with a pronunciation. Context comes into play after, not before, the word is identified, as a result of the brain's processing of the letter-by-letter information it receives (Cunningham & Cunningham, 2002; Nicholson & Tan, 1999; Stanovich, 2000).

Skilled readers can accurately and quickly pronounce infrequent, phonetically regular words. When presented with unfamiliar but phonetically regular words—*nit, kirn, miracidium*—good readers immediately and seemingly effortlessly assign them a pronunciation (Daneman, 1991). This happens so quickly that readers are often unaware that they have not seen the word before and that they had to "figure it out." This effortless decoding involves the reader's accessing known spelling patterns or similar words (Cunningham & Cunningham, 2002).

There has been a long debate on whether to teach phonics by using a synthetic or an analytic approach. A *synthetic* approach generally teaches children to go letter by letter, assigning a pronunciation to each letter, and then blending the individual letters together. An *analytic* approach teaches rules (e.g., the *e* on the end makes the vowel long). Recent research, however, suggests that the brain is a pattern detector and that while we look at single letters we are considering all the letter patterns we know. Successful decoding of a word occurs when the brain recognizes a familiar spelling pattern or, if the pattern itself is not familiar, searches through its store of words with similar patterns (Adams, 1990; Cunningham et al., 1999; Goswami & Bryant, 1990). Skilled decoding, then, involves the use of an *analogy* strategy.

To decode an unfamiliar word—*knob,* for example—a child who knows many words that begin with *kn* would immediately assign to the *kn* the "n" sound. The initial *kn* would be stored in the brain as a spelling pattern. A child who knows only a few other words with *kn* and hasn't read those words very often would probably not have *kn* as a known spelling pattern and, thus, would have to do a quick search for known words that begin with *kn*. If the child found the words *know* and *knew* and then tried this same sound on the unknown word *knob,* that child would have used an analogy strategy. Likewise, the child might know the pronunciation for *ob* because of having correctly read so many words containing the *ob* pattern (*Bob, rob, cob, job, sob*). The child who had no stored spelling patterns for *kn* or *ob* and no known words to access and compare to would be unlikely to pronounce the unknown word *knob* successfully.

To summarize the cognitive activities involved in identifying words is to risk oversimplification, but that seems necessary if we want instructional practices to be compatible with what we know about how words are decoded. As we read, we look very quickly at almost all letters of each word. For most words, this visual information is recognized as a familiar pattern with which a spoken word is identified and pronounced (aloud or through internal speech). Words we have read before are instantly recognized as we see them. Words we have not read before are almost instantly pronounced based on spelling patterns encountered in other words. Meaning is accessed through visual word recognition, but the sound of the word supports the visual information and helps to hold the word in memory.

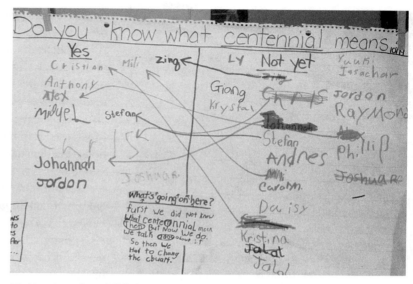

Making learning visible is a good way to develop more thoughtful readers and writers.

Reading and writing are meaning-constructing activities, but they are dependent on words. All good readers and writers have a store of high-frequency words that they read and spell instantly and automatically. Good readers and writers can also decode and spell most regular words. Decoding and spelling abilities increase in direct proportion to the amount of successful reading and writing children do. Word-fluency activities in classrooms should include lots of writing and easy reading as well as word manipulation and sorting activities designed to help children learn common spelling patterns (Cunningham, 2000; Cunningham & Allington, 2007; White, 2005).

Children Begin to Acquire Reading and Writing Processes Very Early

For much of the twentieth century, educators believed that reading instruction should be delayed until children reached a certain level of mental readiness. They believed that most children would achieve this level of readiness when they were about 6 years old. The most influential study (Morphett & Washburne, 1931) actually specified a mental age of 6½ years as the right age to begin reading instruction (but their methodology was enormously flawed). Some educators believed that writing should be delayed until reading abilities

In some areas, a rather rancorous debate focused around the term *developmentally appropriate.* Some people use the term to describe preschools and kindergartens without an academic emphasis. These often ardent professionals may assert that books, stories, and print activities in preschool or kindergarten classes are *developmentally inappropriate.* Many argue that, in one way or another, the "gift of time" is what these children need most. We believe that children who arrive at school with few book, story, and print experiences are the very children who need rich literacy environments and activities in their school (or preschool) day. In this we agree with McGill-Franzen (2006) and the National Association for the Education of Young Children (1998). Both offer advice for creating the classrooms we imagine as most appropriate. (The NAEYC guidelines are available at www.naeyc.org.)

were firmly in place and recommended that children begin writing when they were 8 or 9 years old.

To determine who was ready to read, most children were given readiness tests at the end of kindergarten or after a few weeks of first grade. These readiness tests assessed the skills then believed to be critical for success in beginning reading instruction. Most tests examined the skills of visual discrimination (find the shape that matches the first shape), phonological awareness (find the two pictures whose names begin with the same sound), letter naming, high-frequency word knowledge, and oral language vocabulary.

First graders who scored high on these readiness tests began reading instruction, usually with a basal reader. There were two schools of thought about how to proceed with poor scorers on the readiness tests. Some schools and teachers felt it best to "wait" for the readiness to develop. Other schools and teachers taught the skills—visual discrimination of shapes, phonemic segmentation of sounds in spoken words, letter names, and so on—in an attempt to develop readiness skills tested. But emergent literacy research found that reading development was more complicated than the readiness model assumed.

Emergent literacy research begins in the homes of young children, tracing their literacy development from birth until the time they read and write conventionally (Whitehurst & Lonigan, 2001). This observational research demonstrated that children in literate home environments engage in reading and writing long before beginning formal schooling. Children born into homes where someone reads and writes with them walk into school with an incredible foundation on which instruction can easily build. These children experience an average of over 1,000 hours of quality one-on-one reading and writing activities (Snow, Burns, & Griffin, 1998). They use reading and writing in a variety of ways and pass through a series of predictable stages on their journey from pretend reading and scribbling to conventional reading and writing. When parents read to children, interact with them about the print they see in the world—signs, cereal boxes, advertisements—and encourage and support their early writing efforts, reading and writing develop and grow with listening and speaking, concurrently rather than sequentially.

The emergent literacy research debunked the readiness/mental age theories. Rather than needing to learn all the skills—phonemic segmentation, letter names, right-to-left progression, and so on—before they began reading and writing, children with lots of print experiences learned these skills as they began reading and writing (McGill-Franzen, 2006). Readiness to read has more to do with book, story, and print experiences that occur before school entry than with drill on any subset of skills or achieving any particular mental age.

Emergent literacy research has shown us the kinds of literacy activity young children engage in that lead to developing the understandings essential to successful independent reading and writing. A great many important concepts and attitudes develop as children encounter print in various forms. Seven of these stand out and differentiate children who have had many print experiences from those who have not. Children who have had many print experiences

- Know why we read and write
- Have greater knowledge of the world
- Understand the conventions and jargon of print (e.g., book, page, title, letter)
- Have higher levels of phonological awareness (e.g., the ability to segment a spoken word, /hat/, into individual sounds, /h/a/t/)
- Can read some important-to-them words
- Know many letter names and sounds
- Are eager and confident in their fledgling reading and writing attempts (Pearson, 1993)

There has long been a debate over whether kindergartens should be primarily for play and socialization or offer a more academic orientation. Emergent literacy research supports neither kindergartens in which children play and socialize while we wait for literacy development nor kindergartens in which children work on isolated readiness skills (McGill-Franzen, 1992). Rather than wait or teach separate skills for children who have not had these early literacy experiences before coming to school, kindergartens and other early school experiences should simulate as closely as possible the "at-home" experiences of children who arrive at school with a familiarity with books and stories and who rather easily acquire fluency with reading and writing. We call these kindergartens "literate home simulation" kindergartens.

Children Need Enormous Opportunities to Read and Write Real Things

Peek into the homes of some children and you will see lots of real reading and writing activity. Parents write notes to each other about telephone calls taken and appointments to keep; they write lists and schedules that are posted on the refrigerator; they read newspapers (sometimes to each other), magazines, bills, letters from grandpa, and books. The parents read to the children and foster their writing (or scribbles and scratches). The parents talk to each other about the things they read and talk to their children about them too. Walk into the child's bedroom and you will find a bedroom library of personal children's books. When these children go to school, their parents encourage them to make purchases from school book clubs and often sit with them to discuss possible purchases and to hear about the books after they have arrived and have been read. In other words, some children see adults engaging in real reading and writing, talking about what they have read or written, and have adults who read and write with them and talk with them about what they read. These are the children who are likely to find learning to read in school relatively easy.

Imagine now that these already "lucky" children also attend a school where there is lots of real reading and writing activity. These children go to schools where teachers read to them from newspapers and magazines, as well as children's books, every day. Their teachers have bulletin boards and other displays where newspaper clippings, children's book reviews, and stories written by peers are routinely posted and discussed. The children write real things, and the teacher writes on an overhead projector as they watch her compose the morning message and listen to her "stretch" the words as she writes them. She supports their reading by modeling how good readers puzzle through difficult texts. These children write letters that they send, plays that they perform, reviews that they share, lists of questions for an interview that they will conduct, and lists of things that they need to buy for the class party. When lucky children attend these classrooms, their literacy is virtually assured.

But not all children are so lucky. Many children do not come from homes where they have seen adults constantly engaged in reading and writing and sharing and discussing what they have read or written. They arrive at school with no good idea of what reading and writing are for, much less any well-developed sense of even fundamental concepts about print and its relationship to talk.

Imagine that these children who haven't experienced these real reading and writing activities at home come to a school without classroom libraries and with a

Just before leaving for home, a student selects a book from the book bin.

school library inadequately stocked with books and other information resources, under-staffed (no one is readily available to help children find the perfect book), and largely inaccessible during and after the school day (only weekly class visits are allowed). In some of these schools children are not allowed to take the library books out of the school! Research shows that schools with many children from low-income families most likely fit the latter description (Duke, 2000; Guice, Allington, Johnston, Baker, & Michaelson, 1996; McGill-Franzen & Allington, 1993; Stipek, 2004). The children least likely to have books in their homes are the same children least likely to have books in their schools (McQuillan, 1998; Neuman & Celano, 2001).

Easy access to books, magazines, and other reading materials is an essential factor in schools where children become readers and writers (Allington, 2006). The classroom library is especially important for classrooms that work to create readers and writers. Well-designed classroom libraries work to increase the amount of reading that children do (Morrow, 1991). When classroom libraries are well designed and attractive and offer a wide range of appropriate books and magazines, children are more likely to use the libraries and read more books. This wider reading results in better readers (as measured on standardized tests). But most classroom libraries (90 percent) are not well designed nor well stocked (Fractor, Woodruff, Martinez, & Teale, 1993). Too often, classroom libraries have too few books, too little planning of the display, and little variety in either the difficulty or the types of books in the collections. In fact, by grade 5 only 25 percent of the classrooms have libraries!

Schools can create wonderful classroom libraries and school libraries, but doing so takes time and money. First, however, schools need a plan. Depending on the school and the community, the plan might be to develop better access to books over a 3-, 5-, or 10-year period. Until a plan is developed, access rarely improves. Without easy access to books, children are unlikely to become readers and writers.

Children Need to Read Lots of Easy Stuff

Before setting out for a weeklong vacation, few adults go to the local university bookstore or library and look for a really difficult book to read. Fewer look for a book on a topic they are uninterested in. Though adults know about the joys of learning, many more select an easy book on an interesting topic than select hard books on topics they care little about. Why is this so? Why do adults ignore the many difficult books available on arcane topics? Why do so many adults read easy, trashy novels? Why do even well-educated adults lean toward such books?

Children who find learning to read difficult are unlikely to find books in their classroom libraries that they can read comfortably (Johnston, Allington, Guice, & Brooks,

Easy access to engaging books of appropriate difficulty gets kids excited about reading.

1998). Classroom libraries are more often stocked with books too difficult for these children to handle. The content-area texts (e.g., science, social studies, math) are too difficult for them. Even the basal reader material is often beyond their reach. Yet enormous amounts of easy and interesting reading are absolutely essential to developing effective reading strategies, to say nothing of appropriate attitudes and responses. When children struggle with the material they are reading, they cannot apply the strategies that good readers use, and they do not develop the habits and attitudes that good readers do (Allington, 2004).

A variety of features influence the difficulty children experience in reading any given text. Most obvious, perhaps, is the complexity of the language and the familiarity (or unfamiliarity) of the topic. Traditionally, structural readability formulas were used to estimate a text's difficulty. These formulas typically used some measure of average sentence length and vocabulary familiarity to arrive at a designation of difficulty (usually provided in grade-level terms). But such formulas were never very accurate, even at estimating by grade level, much less predicting whether a text would be easy or difficult for a particular child. Although these formulas could provide rough distinctions between texts, most teachers could estimate text difficulty at least as well. More recent readability measures (e.g., Lexile) still provide only a ballpark estimate of the likelihood of a good fit between a child and a book.

If these formulas are of little value in matching children and books, what techniques can replace them? How can difficulty best be determined? One obvious technique is to try the book out on a child. In many instances, simply asking the child to read a few pages silently and then asking his or her opinion will suffice. Some teachers use a five-finger rule, asking children to count the number of unknown words they encounter. If a child cannot read five words on each page, the book is terribly difficult. We prefer a two- or three-finger rule for beginning readers. Of course, the problem with this approach is that it provides little leeway for texts that have 20 words per page compared with those that have 200 words per page.

A third method is also available. Several schemes for "leveling" books have been recently developed. The one we see most commonly used in schools is drawn from the work of Fountas and Pinnell. Their website (www.fountasandpinnellleveledbooks.com) provides a system and a bibliography of 15,000 children's books rated by difficulty.

Regardless of how book difficulty is determined, it is critical that all children in a classroom, including the least able readers, have easy "fingertip" access to books that they can read accurately, fluently, and with good comprehension. Ideally, all children would have books of an appropriate level of difficulty in their hands all day long and in their backpacks when they go home.

Easy reading material develops fluency and provides practice in using good reading strategies. Most reading, in fact, should be high-success reading. In developing classroom collections of books for children's self-selected reading, we recommend that about half the books be those that seem easy to read on engaging topics. These easy books should include a variety of genres and formats with our society's diversity well represented. There is no reason that classroom collections at different grade levels cannot have overlapping titles since not everyone will necessarily read all the titles each year. Besides, rereading a good book should be encouraged. Nevertheless, so many wonderful children's books are now available that collections can be created without overlapping titles.

Finally, it is important to remember that teachers can make books easier or more difficult (McGill-Franzen, 1993). Introducing books to children can involve developing specific knowledge that will ease reading demands. Encouraging children to read the popular series books (e.g., *Clifford, Junie B. Jones, Amber Brown, Hank the Cow Dog*) is another underutilized approach. Allowing children to discuss with each other the books they are reading is another potential strategy for easing reading demands. Similarly, working to develop background knowledge, perhaps by linking a historical novel to a current social studies unit, eases the reading demands made by books and stories. Reading part or all of the book to children eases the demands the book places on readers when they reread the material. Reading books to children often stimulates their interest in reading the book themselves (much like movies and TV miniseries stimulate adults to read the book version), while also reducing the difficulty for children.

John Guthrie and Nicole Humenick (2004) conducted a meta-analysis of 22 experimental or quasi-experimental studies of classroom reading instruction. They found that ensuring that students had access to an array of interesting texts produced reading achievement gains roughly four times as large ($d = 1.64$) as the small effect of providing systematic phonics instruction ($d = .41$) as reported by the National Reading Panel (2000). In addition, they found that providing students with choices about what to read, where, and with whom produced an impact on reading achievement more than three times as large ($d = 1.20$) as the effect size reported for systematic phonics instruction. This doesn't mean that systematic phonics instruction is not supported, just that there are other aspects of research-based reading instruction that are at least as important as phonics lessons.

There Is No One Best Way to Teach Children to Read and Write

Because reading and writing are complex and children and teachers are different, there can be no one best way to teach reading and writing. The complexity and variability found in every classroom mean there is not, and can never be, one best way to foster and develop reading and writing in all children.

Reading instruction began in the United States with an alphabetic approach. Children learned the letters and learned to spell and sound out the letters of words. This alphabetic method came to be called a *phonics approach* and has gone in and out of fashion but has always had advocates who insisted it was the only sensible approach to beginning reading instruction. A variety of instructional materials provide phonics activities for beginning readers, but those materials often do not reflect much of what we know about teaching decoding (Adams, 1990; Cunningham & Cunningham, 2000).

A second but common approach has been the *basal reader approach.* All basals include instruction in phonics of some kind. Some basals, offer heavier doses of phonics instruction. Most basal programs begin with sight words from predictable stories and place an emphasis on comprehension—although all basals include a phonics strand. Although basals differ in their emphasis, they all offer stories of gradually increasing difficulty and an emphasis on teacher-guided reading of generally shorter selections. Basals also provide workbooks and skill sheets, though of questionable value.

Throughout the years, many reading experts have advocated a *trade-book approach* for teaching reading. In the 1960s, Jeanette Veatch (1959) popularized what she called an "individualized reading" approach. This approach emphasizes children selecting books they want to read and teachers conferencing with them to provide individual help when needed. But teachers using this trade-book approach must be familiar with a broad range of children's books and must also be quite expert in the teaching of reading and writing.

A fourth approach, which has been more widely used in England, Australia, and other countries, has also returned to many U.S. classrooms. This *language experience/writing approach* is based on the premise that the easiest material for children to read is their own writing and that of their classmates. In this approach, then, the stories that children themselves compose, orally or in writing, provide the primary reading materials.

Throughout the years, these four major approaches—phonics, basal, trade book, language experience/writing—have been in and out of favor. Generally, once one approach has dominated long enough for educators to recognize its shortcomings, a different approach with different shortcomings replaces it. The question of which method is best cannot be answered because it is the wrong question. Each method has undeniable strengths.

Phonics instruction is clearly important because one big task of beginning readers is figuring out how our alphabetic language works. The National Reading Panel (2000) reviewed decades of research on beginning reading instruction and concluded that many children can decipher the letter–sound system with little direct instruction, but directly teaching this system seems to speed initial literacy acquisition for these children. The need for some explicit decoding strategies instruction was particularly clear for some children, especially those who have had limited exposure to reading and writing and have had fewer opportunities to figure out how our alphabetic system works.

Basal instruction gives teachers multiple copies of reading material that they can use to guide children's comprehension and strategy development. The reading selections found in basal readers are organized by estimating their difficulty with increasingly complex selections across the elementary grades. Because basals contain a wide variety of types of literature, children are exposed to many genres, authors, topics, and cultures they might miss if all their reading was self-selected. In addition, basals outline the major goals for each year and provide an organized curricular plan for accomplishing those goals with ways of evaluating whether students are meeting those goals.

The reading of real books is the ultimate aim of reading instruction, but that aim has often taken a backseat to phonics and basal instruction. Children have been expected to "read when they finished their work" or "read at home." Of course, children who came from homes where books were available and reading was valued were much more likely to engage in real reading than were children whose homes lacked these advantages. Better readers were also more likely to complete the assigned work and have time remaining to read self-selected trade books. The reemergence of the trade-book approach reminds us that the purpose of learning to read is to read real books. Children who read real books understand why they are learning to read and what reading really is.

Writing is an approach to reading that lets children figure out reading "from the inside out." As children write, they spell words they later see and recognize in their reading. Even when they can't spell a word perfectly, they try to "sound spell" it and actually put to

I Lik MAFNS,

The kindergarten student who wrote this ("I like muffins") demonstrates an emerging understanding of sounds and letters and how speech can be represented by print. The most common label for this emergent writing is *invented spelling*. However, we do not often use that terminology, preferring instead to label such efforts *sound spelling*. We think *sound spelling* better represents what children do when they first begin to develop an understanding of how talk gets written down—they try to represent the sounds they hear with the letters they know. Lots of writing activities in kindergarten, with encouragement to *sound spell* has been shown to develop both phonemic awareness and an understanding of the alphabetic principle.

use whatever letter–sound knowledge they have learned. Children who write are more avid and sensitive readers. Reading is a source of writing ideas and information. Reading also provides the writer with models of various writing styles. Like reading real books, writing is an authentic activity, and children who write become more fluent in reading (Tierney & Shanahan, 1991).

In the 1960s, the U.S. government spent hundreds of thousands of dollars to find out what the best approach to beginning reading really was. Data were collected from first- and second-grade classrooms around the country that used a variety of approaches to beginning reading. The study results were inconclusive. Every approach had some good results and some poor results. How well teachers carried out an approach seemed to be the major determinant of how well an approach worked. Some teachers used what the researchers called "combination approaches," such as language experience and basal or phonics and literature or literature and writing. The study concluded that, in general, combination approaches worked better than any single approach (Bond & Dykstra, 1967). Snow and her colleagues (1998) also concluded that children—especially children with limited preschool experiences with books, stories, and letters—need a rich variety of reading and writing experiences as well as some direct instruction in letter–sound patterns.

One major reason for providing a combination approach to literacy is the different personalities children bring to school. It is not possible to determine clearly which children will learn best with which approaches, but it is clear that when a teacher provides alternative routes to the goal of literacy, more children will find a route to take them there. Many children fail in school because their personalities and the approach taken to instruction do not match. Research, observation, and common sense tell us that no single approach will succeed in teaching all children (Pressley, 2006).

It Takes Time to Teach and Learn to Read

It should come as no surprise that children who start school behind their peers often do not catch up. It should not be surprising, especially if these children attend school for about the same number of hours, for the same number of days, and in the same size classes as the children who began school ahead of them. We can accelerate literacy learning, but teaching and learning take time. Children who come to school with hundreds or thousands of hours of home and preschool experiences with books, stories, and print are way ahead of many less fortunate children. We cannot expect these limited-experience children to catch up to those who arrive with substantially more experience without expanding the amount of instructional time we make available to them.

But most schools offer a standard schedule to all children and often actually organize instruction so that the lowest-achieving children are scheduled for the smallest amounts of reading and writing instruction and opportunity (Allington, 1991; Roth, Brooks-Dunn,

Linver, & Hofferth, 2002). It is important to reorganize schools, classrooms, and special programs in ways that expand children's opportunities to read and write to enhance their achievement. We know that increasing the amount of time children spend actually reading and writing in and out of school affects reading and writing development in positive ways. We know that increasing children's access to good books increases the time they spend reading in and out of school and accelerates reading development. In other words, when teachers have easy access to books, they allocate more time for reading those books. When children have easy access to books in classrooms, they are more likely to spend time reading in school and more likely to take those books home to read.

Even small amounts of time add up. Finding 12 additional minutes each day creates an additional hour each week of time for reading and writing activities. That weekly hour results in a day of reading each month and about two weeks' worth of reading and writing each year.

When books and magazines are not in ready supply in classrooms, teachers and students receive powerful messages about what is and is not important. When schools have no general guidelines about how much time to allocate to reading and writing instruction, allocations can be expected to vary from classroom to classroom. While time allocated to reading and writing lessons is a very crude benchmark for evaluating any instructional program, it is absolutely essential that teachers have time to teach and children have time to read and write during the school day. Fielding and Pearson (1994) recommend that classroom reading instructional blocks be organized so that children spend more time actually reading than they do learning about reading or talking and writing about completed reading assignments.

Expert Teachers Are Important

Just such a distribution of activities was reported to be characteristic of classrooms of exemplary elementary teachers (Pressley et al., 2001). In contrast to teachers in more typical classrooms, the exemplary classroom teachers organized their lessons so that students spent at least as much time reading and writing each day as they did on other reading/writing lesson activities. Both sets of teachers engaged students in before-, during-, and after-reading activities as well as in reading and writing activity. But the exemplary teachers introduced stories in half the time, demonstrated strategies in half the time, and engaged students in follow-up activities about half as lengthy as those offered in the typical classrooms. The end result was substantially better reading and writing achievement in the exemplary teachers' classrooms. At the end of the year, the poorest readers in those rooms read and wrote as well as the average readers in the typical classroom. And their phonics performance rivaled that of the best readers in the typical classrooms! This occurred even though these children spent far less time completing phonics worksheets and doing phonics drills and practice activities. In many senses this is an issue of balance. By balance, we mean how time for various instructional activities was allocated. In out-of-balance classrooms children spend too much time engaged in tasks that require little, if any, reading and writing. In balanced classrooms, on the other hand, students spend at least as much time actually reading and writing as they spend on others sorts of assignments.

Studies of enormously effective elementary classroom teachers provide us with the following characteristics of powerful classroom literacy teaching (Allington & Johnston, 2002; Ladson-Billings, 1994; Pressley et al., 2001; Taylor et al., 2000):

- *Much reading and writing activity.* Students in these classrooms read and wrote two or three times as much as students in classrooms of less effective teachers.
- *Multisourced curriculum.* Use of multiple curriculum materials better matched to student levels of development than can be accomplished with the use of a single curriculum material (e.g., a single basal or trade book that all students read). A multisourced curriculum also provides opportunities for ensuring more culturally relevant materials.
- *Multilevel curriculum.* The multiple curriculum materials reflect differing levels of complexity, levels that better reflect the observed student reading proficiencies.
- *Curriculum integration.* Reading and writing strategies taught with social studies materials, for instance. Spelling lessons were linked to phonics skills lessons, and both were linked to the books being read and the essays being written. In other words, the lessons offered across a day or a week were coherently linked together by skills, strategies, or content.
- *Small-group and side-by-side teaching.* Limited reliance on whole-group instruction.
- *Explicit teaching of useful strategies.* Modeling and demonstration of skills and strategy use occur regularly (a number of times each day). Teachers may introduce a skill or strategy in the context of a reading assignment, then offer explicit demonstrations of the use of that skill or strategy in isolation, and then return to the application of the skill or strategy in the context of reading or writing.
- *Managed choice.* Lessons have options for students, so not everyone reads the same book, writes the same essay, or does the same project. Teachers manage this choice, and the choices are not unlimited.
- *Open tasks.* The tasks students are assigned often have no single correct answer or method of completion. For instance, students may be asked to write about which character in the story they have read reminded them of themselves and why. Or in a social studies unit focusing on Native Americans they might develop a project that used a diorama or artwork or video or an oral presentation or an Internet-based tour of useful

websites. In other words, the "right" answer and the sorts of tasks completed vary from student to student.

- *Fostering self-monitoring.* Developing student capacity to be responsible for their own work and behavior. Both lesson design and classroom routines focus on increasing student independence in both academic and behavioral settings.
- *Focus on the child.* Awareness of individual students' social, emotional, and academic needs. Experts on the children in their classrooms. Sense of professional responsibility for each and every child's social, emotional, and academic growth.

It is important to note that the powerfully effective teachers also sometimes taught in "traditional" ways. Although the features noted previously differentiated the more effective from the less effective teachers, all lessons in the more effective teacher classrooms did not involve multiple texts (they used common texts for all students some of the time), and all lessons did not involve student choice in assignments (sometimes everyone did write on the same topic). But the more effective teachers routinely incorporated the features listed above into their lesson design, and the less effective teachers rarely, if ever, did so. In other words, the more effective teachers "balanced" their lessons differently than did the less effective teachers whose instruction was more unidimensional. The converging findings on the nature of powerful classroom instruction must become the basis for crafting both preservice and inservice professional development programs.

Unfortunately, many school district organizational plans (and, in many cases, state agency plans) have yet to reflect these key characteristics. Many schools still insist upon adopting a single text for all students—readers, core books, science and social studies texts, spellers, and so on. Special services (remedial support, special education) are designed so that all participants receive roughly the same amounts and sorts of services (three 30-minute sessions a week, daily 50-minute sessions) regardless of student needs. As more classrooms and intervention programs begin to reflect the research-based characteristics noted earlier, we can expect that more students will achieve thoughtful literacy.

We Can Help Every Child Become a Reader and Writer

One last research finding that permeates nearly every section of this book must be explored as we conclude this chapter: We can teach all children to read and write. For too long schools have operated from a belief that only some children would become readers and writers. In many cases, this belief system resulted in school programs that delivered exactly this result. But the new mandates that all children develop "on-grade-level" reading and writing proficiencies have forced schools to rethink their programs and their goals.

Recent research (McGill-Franzen, Allington, Yokoi, & Brooks, 1999; Pressley et al., 2001; Taylor et al., 2003; Vellutino et al., 1996) shows quite convincingly that our past does not have to dictate our future. These studies, and others, are powerful demonstrations that providing access to consistently high-quality instruction, especially in the classroom, can serve to literally eliminate the traditional "bottom group." Other convincing evidence shows that teachers, administrators, and supervisors find it almost impossible to plan educational programs that contradict their professional beliefs (Allington et al., 1997). Thus, the dilemma: As long as we believe that some children will never be readers and writers, we will fail to create schools that fulfill the potential of all children to become readers and writers.

Unfortunately, acceptance of the inevitability of student failure seems typically strongest in schools where many children currently fail. Children are least successful in schools where teachers lack confidence in their own efforts to help children become readers and writers. In these schools, initiating discussion about reorganizing so that all children are successful is often difficult. Of course, society also offers these schools the fewest resources in the face of the most compelling needs (Kozol, 1991).

The key point to be understood is that good evidence shows that schools can organize instruction so that nearly all children can learn to read and write alongside their peers. Children who begin school with few book, story, and print experiences can speed their literacy development and catch up with more advantaged peers. But to achieve such outcomes means providing some children with access to larger amounts of higher-quality instruction and supplying more actual opportunities to read and write each and every school day. Unfortunately, many traditional instructional programs simply slowed the instructional pace for children experiencing difficulty—practically ensuring they would always be behind. Thus, a central responsibility for today is rethinking those traditional efforts and redesigning school days and lessons so that all children become readers and writers.

Summary

Much has been learned about how children learn to read and write and about how to support successful classroom literacy instruction. Reading and writing are thoughtful, meaningful activities in the real world. Reading and writing in schools has, historically, not been best described as thoughtful. Instead, the words *trivial, routine,* and even *boring* have more often been used in discussing the reading and writing done in school. (Teachers always banned the one purposeful writing activity, writing notes to friends.) But the goals society has set for schools have changed, dramatically in some areas, and more thoughtful, or critical, literacy has been called for. Developing basic, or functional, literacy is no longer the charge given schools. Instead, the federal literacy standard is one that focuses on children's thinking before, during, and after reading and writing activities.

It is essential that children have many opportunities to read and write, especially school-day opportunities to read comfortable materials they have chosen and to discuss them with peers. To accomplish this requires greater access to a wider variety of appropriate reading material beyond the basal reader, the core trade book, or the common social studies textbook. It also requires substantial time be available every day in every classroom to engage in reading and writing activities. Many classrooms already offer more reading and writing opportunities than were available only a few years ago, but too often reading and writing opportunities remain enormously restricted, especially in the upper elementary grades.

Children also need models, explanations, and demonstrations of the powerful thinking strategies that skilled readers and writers use. It is not sufficient that teachers assign, interrogate, and correct students. The potential of teaching routines such as "think-alouds," "public writing/thinking," strategy lessons focused on self-monitoring, or personalized conferencing after reading or writing are enormous but generally underused.

For too long the quest has been focused on discovering the one best way to teach reading and writing. We believe that there can be no such approach. Learning to read and write is a complex activity. Children differ, teachers differ, and communities differ, and each works to preclude the discovery of any single best way to develop literacy. Different children, at different stages of development, at different times, in different schools, taught by different teachers, prosper and develop their literacy. Shift any one of these variables and the same children may flounder. What is needed are investments in developing each teacher's capacity to provide instruction that ensures all children acquire reading and writing proficiency. What is needed is a balanced instructional effort led by an expert teacher who takes advantage of the strengths of the four historically recurring patterns of classroom literacy instruction and the recent knowledge of how children learn to literate.

The literacy goals for elementary schools have changed, and classrooms must change to meet these new literacy standards. Thoughtful literacy as shown through children's selections of reading materials and discussions of their reading, their writing, and their responses to the reading and writing of their peers is the new literacy goal. If we expect children to achieve this thoughtful literacy, we must change classroom curriculum and instruction in many ways.

chapter 4

The What of Reading:
The Reading Curriculum

Educators debate curriculum endlessly. Particular curricular emphases come and go in what appear to be 30-year cycles (Langer & Allington, 1992). Curriculum materials can play an important role in shaping classroom instruction. This seems especially true in classrooms where the teacher has little expertise in teaching reading. In this chapter, we describe many of the most popular models and materials for organizing and engaging children in literacy learning. In our view, the classrooms that work best for all children are classrooms that offer curriculum alternatives in a balanced reading and language arts framework.

Curriculum Materials and Frameworks

Elementary school reading and language arts materials include a spectrum of different resources, including basal reader series, trade books, skills books, software, student-produced work, and everyday reading matter such as newspapers, magazines, directions, and lists. Curriculum materials can be placed in three broad categories: materials organized by others, materials organized by the teacher, and materials selected by children.

Most schools rely more heavily on materials organized by someone other than individual classroom teachers or by individual children. These "other organized" curriculum materials include commercial reading series, state-mandated grade-level core trade books, sets of big books, predictable book kits, trade-book sets with accompanying chapter questions and vocabulary lists, software, and skill packages produced and marketed by commercial publishers. Some of these sets of "other organized" materials are comprehensive, with an organizational plan spanning K–6 levels. Other sets are much more narrowly targeted—sets of predictable language books, for instance, organized into six levels of difficulty for first-grade classrooms, or computer software promoted as improving phonemic awareness skills. The primary advantage of "other organized" curriculum materials is the effort saved by not reinventing the wheel in every classroom. The greatest disadvantage of these materials is the lack of control and ownership that teachers experience when these materials form a mandated curriculum.

Commercial packages may offer a false sense of security by leading administrators and teachers to believe that "covering the curriculum" equates with "good teaching." We would argue for greater teacher involvement in curriculum selection and development. To us, the control that teachers exert in selecting and developing classroom curricula is the central issue to be concerned with. Local curriculum development and associated staff development, however, can seem expensive when compared with the purchase of commercial materials. In addition, materials created from scratch often fail to meet the standards of quality set by the commercial materials. But expertise about instructional design emerges from doing the development. Thus, we believe that teacher involvement with and ownership of the curriculum is an important concern. We also believe that few school districts or schools plan such development well enough or fund it sufficiently. Moving away from "other organized" curriculum needs to be recognized as a potentially powerful educational improvement activity—but

"For a long time we have been trying to train *stoplight readers.* We ask children to read a bit of a story, stop, and talk about it. But what we should be working for is *flashlight readers*—readers who take a book under the blanket with a flashlight, because they cannot bear to stop reading what may very well be the best book they have ever read. If you want illumination, friends, a flashlight will beat a stoplight every time" (Paterson, 1989, pp. 137–138).

one that requires substantial time and effort and funding to support. No commercial curriculum material can possibly meet the needs of all students in today's diverse classrooms.

Common Curriculum Frameworks

In studies of elementary school curriculum frameworks for reading and language arts instruction, Allington (1993) found three general patterns of materials:

- *Commercial reading series.* In some schools, the reading series was seen as the core curriculum. In schools using these readers, the curriculum provided reading materials through student anthologies or sets of leveled books. Generally, if trade books were used, they were assigned to an independent reading time and not integrated into the instructional curriculum.

- *Reading series and trade books.* Two patterns emerged. One was the use of trade books that came with or were recommended in one of the reading series; those trade books often were used to extend thematic reading. The other pattern was similar but the trade books were not linked to the lessons in the reading series in any discernible way. In some cases, a locally developed core-books curriculum accompanied the reading series. In others, individual teachers used favorite books they had chosen, or they allowed students to self-select books but insisted on trade-book reading along with reading series lessons.

- *Trade books.* In some schools, trade books were the curriculum. Several organizing frameworks were used, including teacher or committee selection of books, individual student selection of books, theme-based approaches, and commercially developed core-books plans.

Although schools could be described as best fitting one of these approaches, there was often much variation from classroom to classroom. Few schools were "pure" examples of any organizational approach. The amount of variation depended on the administrative pressure on teachers to implement a selected framework. Some schools had rigidly applied frameworks for following the reading series, and others had the same sort of rigid framework for adhering to a trade-book curriculum. In those schools we found less variation from classroom to classroom (but we still found a fair amount of variation in curricular use). In other schools teachers elected one of the three approaches, depending on their expertise in teaching reading. Regardless of which framework was used, teachers seemed more dissatisfied when administrators had pressed them to implement a particular framework. In schools where teachers had been more directly involved in the decision to implement whichever framework was in place in their classroom, they seemed more satisfied with and enthusiastic about the framework and the activities that flowed from it (Johnston et al., 1998).

Who Selects the Curriculum Framework?

All this points to several sources of tension in curricular planning. Who is in the best position to decide which framework will be adopted? Teachers have the most information about children in the schools and ultimately must implement the curriculum framework in their classrooms. School district officials are often far removed from the classroom. Nevertheless, historically, curricular planning decisions have been made at the district level by school district administrators with or without input from teachers (Allington & Guice, 1997). Involving teachers in such decision making is messier, more time-consuming, and may be more expensive than decision making at the district level. In addition, district administrators often have greater expertise in curriculum frameworks and more time to develop or review materials. Given the importance attached to teacher ownership of curriculum, however, it seems foolish to attempt to mandate a plan from a district office. Ideally, the curriculum framework adopted for a school would be the result of substantial teacher involvement.

Various state policies affect textbook adoption. About 40 percent of the states, mostly southern states, engage in some form of state textbook adoption. The majority of the states, however, leave textbook decisions up to individual school districts. School districts also vary in how textbooks are adopted. In the northeastern region, home of some of the best-performing states on the NAEP (Maine, Connecticut, Vermont), districtwide textbook adoptions are less common than in other regions of the United States. Instead, such decisions usually are made at the building level and in many cases are made by grade-level teams or individual teachers. Little research evidence supports state- or district-level adoptions of common textbooks although that pattern is so firmly entrenched in some regions that any shift away seems unlikely.

Relatedly, the research available does not provide strong evidence that any commercial program is routinely associated with proficient reading performance. Publishers of all sorts of materials can produce "evidence" of various sorts that their product improved reading achievement in some schools. But study after study, using all manner of research designs, suggests that district organizational support and classroom teacher quality are much more important factors than which materials are used (Allington & Nowak, 2004).

Involving teachers brings forward another sort of tension. How will the various preferences of different teachers be handled in adopting any curriculum framework? Should a simple majority rule? Should everyone "do their own thing"? In some schools the faculty is divided over what type of framework to put in place. Is there a need for a common curriculum framework across the various classrooms in an elementary school? Arguments for adopting such a plan focus primarily on the potential benefits to children. A coherent framework across the grades is seen as beneficial to children's literacy development. Detractors focus on benefits from teacher selection of classroom curriculum. Allowing each teacher to choose a framework might benefit students if such choices make teachers more effective.

Another factor is pressure from parents for standardizing curriculum experiences. In the absence of a common framework, parents often ask, "Why is the neighbor boy getting such a strong phonics emphasis and my child is just reading books?" or "Why did my son read a number of books last year in fourth grade and this year his sister hasn't read a single one?" Widely divergent classroom experiences, especially between classrooms at the same grade level, often stimulate parental and community concern. As one school board member asked, "Why can't we just figure out which books second graders will read each week? What is so hard about that?"

There is no simple answer to these commonly occurring questions. We can use the research (Guthrie & Humenick, 2004) to argue for child-centered frameworks in which children make more personal choices. But we can also argue that individual teachers know their students best and should select the framework for their own classrooms to ensure that children are reading and writing a variety of genres. The benefits of some common framework across the several years of an elementary school career are obviously arguable, as are the benefits of a common plan across all elementary schools, especially in districts having high student mobility. Pressure from parents and board members to standardize classroom experiences is also understandable. In these latter cases, one might also argue for selecting a commercial reading series to accomplish these goals and avoid the substantial time and cost of developing a local reading and writing curriculum. But then you may have a curriculum that is less flexible than needed.

What process of curriculum framework development and adoption is a school to use? We think the key is involving as many different stakeholders as possible in the development process. One reason that so few "pure" examples of the various frameworks exist in schools is the negotiation and compromise that occurred during the development phase. As discussions continued, persons with different perspectives and preferences came to better understand other points of view. Ultimately, a negotiated understanding, with concessions and shifts from all involved, is usually achieved. Unfortunately, these understandings rarely fit neatly into the various schemes that academics create for discussing curriculum development. But it is the involvement and the opportunity to openly express concerns and

There is much concern about "curriculum alignment" these days. This typically means that someone is worried about whether curriculum materials reflect the skills, strategies, and content of state standards or state assessments. Several problems are often encountered in attempts to "align" commercial curriculum materials.

- Because state standards vary substantially, no commercial material can possibly be aligned with the standards of every state.
- Commonly used checklist alignment strategies provide no indication of the emphasis or adequacy of the coverage of the various standards.
- Too many state tests are not currently aligned with the state's standards (Linn, 2000), and no national commercial test can be aligned with all states' standards.

We are suggesting not that curriculum alignment is a bad idea—although we would prefer to see the curriculum developed and the assessments then selected to evaluate the intended learning—but rather that the process is fraught with difficulties and no good evidence exists that alignment produces better teaching or learning.

feel that concerns have been recognized that allow the organization of curriculum plans to be achieved.

The broad categories of materials ultimately define children's curriculum experiences. Often, debates about curriculum frameworks are actually debates about materials. It seems important, then, to examine the most commonly used reading and language arts materials in more depth. Commercial reading series are widely used; trade books make regular appearances in reading and language arts curriculum. Likewise, spelling books, skills packages, and language arts basals routinely appear in schools. Also, we hear more about the potential for technology in developing literacy, especially for helping children become fluent writers.

Reading Series

The most commonly used reading materials are commercial reading series. Most adults grew up in an era when reading series *were* the reading curriculum in elementary schools. Their popularity has waxed and waned since their introduction over 150 years ago. The explosion in children's book publishing that began in the 1980s has created a climate in which many schools have reconsidered the role that reading series play in their reading and language arts curriculum. In addition, the reading series continually change to meet new market expectations and, at times, to reflect recent research on literacy learning.

- *Traditional, high-frequency word approach.* The number of new words introduced in each story is severely restricted. Stories are written so that a sight vocabulary of high-frequency words accumulates across stories. The Dick and Jane readers provide the benchmark with text like this: "Look. Look. Look at Dick. Look. Look at Jane." Soon children are reading sentences like this: "Look at Dick. Look at Dick run. Look at Jane jump. Jump Jane. Run Dick. Look at Dick and Jane."

- *Decodable text approach.* The basic vocabulary consists of decodable words—phonetically regular words. Thus, the stories read like this: "A rat sat. A rat sat on a mat. A rat had a hat. A rat had the hat on the mat." Soon children are reading sentences like this: "Dad had a fat hat. The lad had a bad hat. The cat had a glad hat. Dan and the lad and the rat had hats."

- *Predictable text approach.* Series using predictable texts take a very different approach to vocabulary control. Texts are constructed or selected based on topic familiarity, predictability of story line from language and artwork cues, and patterns of language repetition. In addition, this approach also involves the "shared reading experience" in which the teacher reads the story, often in big book format, to the children as they follow along. Thus, rather than teaching sets of high-frequency sight words or sets of letter–sound associations before children read, this approach attempts to ease the vocabulary demands on beginning readers through both the nature of the text and the shared reading experience. Children read texts like: "Black bug, black bug, what do you see? I see a baby looking at me" (our apologies to Bill Martin, Jr.).

Current reading series typically emphasize one form of vocabulary control or another, but some provide materials that reflect more than one approach. We think vocabulary control is important. However, we are dismayed when publishers get carried away. It seems obvious that beginning readers benefit from reading materials that restrict the number of new words that children encounter in a short period of time. Smaller sets of words make patterns more readily identifiable—patterns that help children understand the nature of the alphabetic principle that underlies printed English. But reading *is* thinking, and it is hard to imagine what children might be thinking about Dick and Jane or the rat with a hat.

A body of research supports each approach to vocabulary control, and the fact that so many children have learned to read while using the various materials suggests the flexibility children bring to learning to read. None of the approaches, however, has ever managed to teach all children to read—perhaps because children differ or perhaps because teachers differ in their enthusiasm for and expertise with the different approaches.

There seems to be much misinformation about the nature of beginning reading materials. For instance, misguided state policies mandate the use of beginning readers that provide decodable text as the reading diet for emerging readers. No research supports such mandates (Allington & Woodside-Jiron, 1998, 1999). What seems evident today is the same sort of promotionalism that followed the broader use of predictable texts and authentic literature a few years back. When predictable texts did not teach everyone to read, a different approach was touted, and legislators, state superintendents, and district administrators bought the exaggerated claims hook, line, and sinker, repeating the 1970s scenario after 30 years.

Hiebert (1999) makes the case for children reading texts that provide practice with high-frequency words, as well as opportunities to apply decoding skills and use meaning-based cues. She does not see such "multiple criterion" texts presently available, so she suggests that teachers may want to provide various kinds of texts—some more sight-word oriented, some more decoding oriented, and some more meaning-cue oriented—on a regular basis so that children learn to use all the word identification cues that fluent readers use.

We also favor the use of more natural language texts, more predictable texts that provide the opportunity to practice using decoding strategies. But the available texts vary enormously in how many words are introduced and how often words with common patterns appear within a single story (Hoffman, Roser, & Battle, 1993). Texts for beginning readers must help students understand three things:

- Reading is thinking. As we read we giggle, get goose bumps, worry, and get mad.
- English is an alphabetic language. Letters and clusters of letters are pronounced in predictable ways.
- Reading is an enjoyable and useful activity.

Generally speaking, we wish reading provided less emphasis on skill and drill worksheets and assessments and more emphasis on the integration of writing and spelling lessons, responses to and discussions of the stories read, and the use of more authentic evaluation strategies. However, most publishers also offer lots of ancillary skills materials, especially in states with skills-based testing programs, that are not central to the lesson plan. Most series also offer trade-book packages or classroom sets of trade books—children's books selected to link to the stories in the readers by theme, by genre, by topic, by author, or in some other way.

Historically, reading-series lessons were organized around specific skill instruction. More recently, most series have offered different organizational plans while retaining an instructional strand for developing various skills and strategies associated with developing literacy proficiency. Today, thematic organization seems popular. You will find reading series with science and social studies themes, for instance. Some series offer genre units, providing several mysteries, myths, tall tales, or biographies to familiarize the student with the selected genre.

The developers and publishers of any commercial curriculum materials often claim that "research" supports the use of their product. The problem with such claims lies in evaluating the veracity of such claims. If we use the guidelines offered in the federal NCLB Act (Allington, 2006), virtually none of the many claims would be considered verified. The primary sticking point is the NCLB standard that requires independent, nonbiased verification studies. This criteria suggest that only programs with substantial positive effects as demonstrated in studies conducted by researchers with no ties to the program should be considered legitimate. The reality of the current situation is that most claims are based on developer-conducted studies, not studies conducted by independent researchers.

For instance, if we look carefully at the effectiveness claims made for almost any commercial phonics or comprehension curriculum we find that independent research evidence is sadly lacking. Instead, the publisher may provide data drawn from a single school or district that used their product. Often those data are presented in ways to make the impact look impressive. But publisher-generated data are not independent evidence of positive effects.

Publishers' assertions about effectiveness may also include general statements that suggest that their product design reflects important research findings. Again, this is not evidence that the product actually reflects those findings nor that the product has demonstrated effects on achievement. Promoters and publishers may also stack the deck by selectively reporting studies that reported positive effects while excluding studies that found no positive effects. Stahl, Duffy-Hester, and Stahl (1998) drew this conclusion about a widely distributed monograph that reported on the effects of direct instruction. Caveat emptor!

One other positive feature of newer basal reader series is the attention paid to representing the diversity of American culture in the stories selected for inclusion. Children's books written by minority authors or featuring authentic depictions of minority cultures or characters are becoming more common. Unfortunately, many school and classroom libraries have few books that truly reflect the diversity of the U.S. population. The current situation in elementary schools seems to mirror what Applebee (1991) found in his study of high school literature curricula: Reading anthologies provide a much more diverse selection of authors and characters than do the books most frequently selected by teachers for their students to read.

We believe that the flexible use of good reading series can play a useful role in the elementary school curriculum. The role we see is different from their historical role. No series can be the whole reading and language arts curriculum. Perhaps planning to allocate two or three days each week to lessons in the reading series is a good place to begin. Then fill the remaining days with lots of reading and writing opportunities. No series provides enough reading for anyone to become a good reader. None provides sufficient writing activity to develop proficient writing skills. In addition, heavy reliance on these series severely limits the development of reading stamina and important student book selection strategies. To fulfill their potential, reading series must be viewed as nothing more than another useful resource for teachers to draw on while planning and delivering instruction. When they become *the* curriculum and dominate instructional decisions, children cannot be well served.

Other Language Arts Textbooks

In many schools it is common practice to use a commercial reading series, a spelling book, and a language art textbook. To this array, some schools even add a handwriting book and a phonics workbook. Typically, neither schools nor publishers pay attention to integrating language arts instruction. Thus even when a school purchases these materials from the same publisher, the several daily language arts lessons offered are typically fragmented and incoherent. If we wanted to make learning to read and write as difficult as possible, fragmenting language learning into several unrelated lessons each day would be a good way to do it. In contrast, integrating the language arts produces the potential for building on the reciprocal processes inherent in learning to read, write, speak, and spell.

We see little benefit from purchasing some of these commercial materials. The benefits of integration are so obvious that today many of the new reading series offer an integrated framework (usually integrating reading, writing, and spelling at the minimum). It only makes sense to design instructional activities that link reading and writing. Well-crafted prose provides a useful model for creating author's craft lessons, for instance, in which children study how the story or report is organized, how authors begin, how they close, how they create "pictures in a reader's mind," and so on. Learning how stories or persuasive arguments or information is organized is important for comprehension and for composition. As Tierney and Shanahan (1991) point out, integration of reading and writing fosters growth in both.

Linking decoding lessons with spelling and with writing and reading also makes sense. Children benefit from reading and writing the same words and from using those words in oral and written language activities. Spelling becomes more than rote memorization when the target words are used in writing activities, studied in decoding lessons, and read in the texts they encounter. Phonics strategies become more obviously useful when children actually encounter decodable words in their reading and when the strategies are linked to spelling.

Handwriting series do not seem very useful. Their heavy emphasis on transcription, letter formation, neatness, punctuation, and spelling may actually inhibit children's exploration of writing as a learning activity. Children do need to learn the conventions of written language, but these are far better taught in the course of real writing. Besides, in our experience, no matter what the system, some children (like both of us) know how to write more

Teachers and administrators often think of children's books as the primary reading materials in literature-based classrooms, but we argue for the use of magazines and newspapers as well. An ever-increasing supply of children's magazines is available (at least 25 with a national circulation), and every classroom needs a magazine rack for focusing attention on current issues. If we wish to make school reading more authentic, we need to reconsider the role of magazines in the reading and language arts curriculum.

A useful resource for identifying magazines to order for a school or classroom library is *Magazines for Kids and Teens,* edited by D. Stoll (Newark, DE: International Reading Association, 1997. To order, call 1-800-336-READ or visit www.reading.org).

legibly than one would guess from their writing samples. The time that children might spend attempting to copy neatly will be better spent actually writing and learning that writing is a powerful system for putting your words, your ideas, on paper.

Trade Books as Curriculum

A strong, balanced literacy curriculum requires children's access to a large supply of books. Three common approaches are used for organizing literacy instruction around trade-book reading: self-selected reading, core-books curriculum, and thematic plans. In many schools, these approaches are combined in various ways, and in many cases, one of them accompanies the use of a reading series. We discuss each approach separately and then present a few models of combination approaches.

Self-Selected Reading

Self-selected reading was popularized by Veatch (1959) and focuses primarily on motivation for reading. Arguing that personal motive is the most powerful force in learning, advocates of self-selected reading recommend a very student-centered approach to literacy teaching and learning. Well-stocked classroom and school libraries are crucial and individual book conferences are the primary means of instructional support. Many advocates of the "engagement" approach to reading instruction have resurrected self-selection and argued for a literacy curriculum based on "authentic" reading and writing experiences (Guthrie, 2004).

Authentic experiences are shaped by individual purpose and motivation. When teachers select materials for students to read and topics for students to write about, the reading and writing experiences can be considered *inauthentic.* In real-world reading and writing, adults typically decide what they themselves will read and write. As adults we decide which sections of the newspaper to read, which paperbacks to purchase, which manuals we need, and so on. In addition, adults decide whether to skim a text or read it thoroughly. They decide whether to take notes, to write a summary, or to discuss the material with peers. Most reading outside school is driven by personal motives and preferences, and the evidence available indicates that literacy events in school should be similarly driven. (Guthrie & Humenick, 2004).

Self-selected reading is not part of the traditional curriculum. Teachers using this approach respond to children's interests. During book conferences teachers might discuss the book read, respond to journal entries that students elected to create, offer a strategy lesson that seems appropriate to a problem the child encountered while reading, or direct the child to other books. At the heart of this approach is the teacher as a source of support when children find support is needed.

Core Books

The use of core books in elementary school reading and language arts program is popular in some schools, especially in the upper grades. Turn-of-the-century curriculum guides often listed core books to be read at different grade levels (Langer & Allington, 1992), and William Bennett, former U.S. secretary of education, compiled a core reading list for elementary schools. Core lists often represent one of three quite different thrusts.

Bennett's list featured "classic" children's books. Thus, many of the texts on his list present a Eurocentric view of U.S. society. Such a list fits reasonably well with the "cultural literacy" notions some have offered. Works such as *Treasure Island, Hansel and Gretel, The Adventures of Tom Sawyer, The Swiss Family Robinson, Little Women, Ivanhoe,* and *Alice's Adventures in Wonderland* are likely candidates for such a list.

A second approach to core books emphasizes portraying U.S. diversity and selecting books that seem to match children's intellectual and moral development. The 1987 California English Language Arts Framework, for instance, noted that "with a rich and diverse background in literature, students can begin to discover both the remarkable wholeness in the intricately woven tapestry of American society and the unique variety brought by many cultures to that intriguing fabric" (p. 7). Culturally relevant literacy instruction necessarily involves children in reading stories and books that reflect their culture, not just texts reflecting the dominant culture. Because the United States is a glorious melting pot of diversity, all children benefit from reading about the diversity of American experiences.

The third approach to core books emphasizes award-winning titles and books that adults believe have substantial appeal to children (or books that teachers studied in their college courses on children's literature). The problem with award-winning books is that it is adults who give the awards. These books are those that adults saw as having special merit. Book sales indicate, however, that the most popular children's books are series books, such as *Junie B. Jones, Ramona Quimby, Harry Potter,* or *Animorphs*. Many of the best-selling children's

In an odd turn of events we have found schools where use of core books dramatically restricts the amount of reading that children do. In some schools as few as six core books were to be read each year, and some teachers managed to make six books last all year! We have been in schools where three weeks were spent on John Gardiner's *Stone Fox,* and eight weeks were spent on Gary Paulsen's *Hatchet,* even though it takes the typical fourth grader a little over an hour to read *Stone Fox* and the typical sixth grader perhaps five hours to read *Hatchet*.

books never make a core-books list, and very few ever receive awards from the adults who select the "best" children's literature.

No matter how a core list is developed, certain books seem to become the exclusive property of certain grade levels. In many schools, grade-level teams develop core lists to identify which books "belong" to which teachers. In the absence of such a list, questions such as whether to use E. B. White's *Charlotte's Web* in third or fourth grade or Scott O'Dell's *Island of the Blue Dolphin* in fifth or sixth grade often arise. We saw a fourth-grade teacher walk into a second-grade classroom and snatch a copy of *Charlotte's Web* off the shelf, saying that it is "a fourth-grade book." In our experience, the most common type of core-books list in elementary schools is this protective core list.

Any of the core-books approaches seems at odds with self-selected reading and authentic approaches and at odds with the research when every student is expected to read the same books. Core-books lists indicate what adults think children should read at different grade levels. As in the secondary school literature curriculum, some general notions about what children should read and why literature is important determine the makeup of the lists, and children's personal preferences and personal motives in selecting reading materials are ignored.

Thematic Plans

Thematic plans are yet another way to organize reading lessons and activity. One potential benefit of this approach is the possibilities it offers for integrating social studies and science topics into the reading curriculum. Always popular as an organizing framework in kindergarten, thematic organization of literature units is the hallmark of integrated approaches to the elementary school curriculum. Themes with a focus on social studies topics, science content, or health and development are common, as are literary themes.

No matter how trade books are used, it seems necessary to evaluate the literature that children will read. Attempts to foster a balance in what children read during six or seven years of elementary school might raise several questions about the materials being used:

1. Is there a balance of fiction and informational reading? A balance in the types of writing children do? A balance of genres within the broad categories of reading materials and writing products?

2. Is there adequate representation of ethnic, linguistic, and cultural groups and experiences? Do the works fairly depict the contributions of various groups?

3. Do children encounter significant works and ideas that broaden their views of themselves and society?

4. Is there a clear indication of where students will be offered instructional support for developing the strategies all children need to become richly literate? Does the approach provide teachers with evaluation tools to determine children's instructional needs?

5. Does the approach provide teachers with sufficient support for developing the instructional component?

6. Does the approach enhance teacher instructional expertise over time?

7. Does the approach foster depth of knowing and thoughtfulness?

8. Can all of the children actually read the recommended books?

For schools interested in a theme-based approach to integrating the elementary curriculum, *BookLinks* (434 West Downer Place, Aurora, IL 60506), an award-winning magazine published by the American Library Association, provides easy-to-follow bibliographies (e.g., coastal ecosystems, African American illustrators, Native Americans of the Great Plains) and essays organized by theme. The essays review the texts selected for each theme and usually offer several book-linked activities for students. Back issues of *BookLinks* are available at www.ala.org/booklinks.

No matter which approach to trade-book curriculum is selected, the books must come from somewhere. The purchase of book sets for thematic units or core books may be handled through a book vendor or a catalog order. Classroom libraries might include a wide range of books selected to meet a variety of criteria. These collections may evolve and expand across time. Books for independent self-selected reading might come from a classroom library, a school library, a public library, a bookstore, or a book club. Each of these book sources fits some situations better than others, but each is important to children's literacy development.

School and Classroom Libraries

In U.S. elementary schools, the school library is a relatively recent addition. Before the passage of the Elementary and Secondary Education Act (ESEA) of 1965, most schools did not have libraries or librarians. After much federal funding (check how many titles in your library now have an ESEA stamp inside), nearly all elementary schools had central library collections, and most had at least part-time librarian support. When many of the ESEA programs were merged into block-grant programs in the 1980s, federal funds for libraries vanished, and the quality and quantity of holdings in many libraries, especially those in schools serving large numbers of children from low-income families, began to deteriorate.

In a recent survey of an urban school library collection, we found that almost two-thirds of the books available had been purchased prior to 1975. Two-thirds of the books were more than 30 years old, including most of the informational and reference texts. The only atlas available was published in the 1960s (when Ceylon, British Honduras, and East Germany were still shown on maps). Even though this school enrolled primarily minority children, fewer than 5 percent of the books were written by minority authors or included minority characters. In addition, this library had fewer than half the recommended number of books, even counting all the outdated ones on the shelves.

The National Library Power Program presents an excellent opportunity for schools and communities to work collaboratively to improve school libraries. Funded by the Dewitt Wallace–Reader's Digest Fund, this program provides both resources and funding opportunities. For further information write The National Library Power Program, American Library Association, 50 East Huron Street, Chicago, IL 60611.

The library collection at this school reflected a larger and distressing trend in library facilities in schools with many poor children and schools with few poor children. One comparative study (Guice et al., 1996) reported that schools enrolling many poor children had 50 percent fewer books than did schools enrolling primarily more advantaged students. Children from poor families not only have fewer books to read in their homes but have fewer books in their schools and classrooms as well. In 1975, the American Library Association set minimum standards for elementary school library collections (about 20 volumes per child so that a school with 500 students would need a library of 10,000 to 12,000 books plus media, magazines, and software). These standards were created before literature-based curriculum or thematic units were popular, so their adequacy for today's schools is questionable. Still, very few schools with many poor children met even those standards (although half the schools serving mostly advantaged children did).

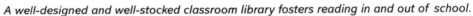

A well-designed and well-stocked classroom library fosters reading in and out of school.

Even more alarming is that in California over half of all school libraries closed in the past 30 years (McQuillan, 1998). Oddly, in this era of increasing evidence on the importance of children's access to a wide variety of interesting texts in elementary schools (Guthrie & Humenick, 2004), the national trend is for library funding to be shrinking and, in some cases, vanishing completely. Libraries in low-income neighborhood schools are typically the hardest hit.

School libraries need to offer children lots of choices, which is why the recommended numbers of volumes seem so high. Libraries need also to have a substantial supply of informational books that would not be necessary in every classroom. Many school libraries have woefully inadequate informational collections. Often the few books available are outdated and not accurate or useful.

All schools need wonderful school library collections as well as substantial classroom libraries. Schools serving many poor children need especially good collections in both settings simply because these children have less access to books and magazines outside of school (Neuman & Celano, 2001). Library collections also need to be easily accessible to children. This means that the traditional once-a-week trip cannot be sustained. Libraries need to be available before and after school, especially for children with few books at home. Libraries need to be available across the school day to children who need access to informational books, atlases, and specialized materials for thematic projects. In other words, most school library collections and services need to expand.

We would also argue for expanding school library services into the summer months. It makes little sense to have a community's largest (we hope) collection of children's books locked up for three months each year. Access during the summer months need not be a daily feature. But if the library were open two evenings a week, children could be assured of a steady supply of summer reading materials. This is critically important in lower-income communities, where children generally do not have their own "bedroom library" collections. It seems especially important in rural areas where no substantial public library system exists (Allington & McGill-Franzen, 2003).

The adequacy of the school library access and collections may also be related to the size and adequacy of classroom libraries, though the two have important but different functions. Classroom libraries put books at the fingertips of children and, thus, are likely to increase the amount of reading children do in and out of school (Fractor, Woodruff, Martinez, & Teale, 1993). Determining the appropriate size of a classroom library, then, is no easy

Schools might consider flextime for librarians to extend library access beyond the school day. For instance, librarians might begin their workday two hours later than other instructional staff and work two hours later. This type of scheduling is especially important in schools where many children do not have access to books and informational materials at home. In addition, the library might be open only four days a week but remain open year-round for the same costs as a five-days-a-week schedule during the school year. Some schools use volunteers from the community or from the student body to assist the librarian during the extended hours.

matter. In fact, such libraries need more titles in the primary grades, for children might read three or four little books during a single reading block. Nonetheless, we hazard recommending some minimum-size standards.

Basically, different classroom collections of 700 to 750 different books for primary-grade classrooms and 400 books for upper-grade classrooms are the goals to strive for. In addition, each classroom might also have multiple copies of some books so that children might pair up, or cluster up, and read the same book simultaneously. Regardless of number, the collection should include a broad array of easier and harder books representing a variety of genres and topics.

When creating classroom libraries, remember that every classroom needs a supply of books that struggling readers can read comfortably. Too often, in our experience, the third-grade classroom collection has no books that children experiencing difficulty with reading can read easily and independently. All children benefit from high-success reading, making an occasional foray into more difficult reading, but children experiencing difficulty benefit most of all from a classroom collection that includes a number of less difficult, interesting books (perhaps a third of the books).

Building Classroom Libraries

There are strategies that schools might use to significantly expand the choices that classroom libraries provide without buying all the books at once. For instance, three third-grade teachers could work together to select books for their classroom libraries. If each had $200 allocated for such purchases each year, they could pool their money and with the $600 purchase 100 to 200 titles each year. In that way they could create three rotating collections of 35 to 70 titles. Each teacher would get one of the collections for a three-month period and then exchange that collection for one of the others. Across the school year, the third graders would have the opportunity to select from each of the three collections. In the second year, the collections would be expanded and teachers would rotate six sets of 35 to 70 books.

Another strategy for developing the initial classroom library collection is to ask for donations from parents, especially parents of older children. Using this scheme, one school managed to collect an average of 100 titles each year for each classroom. Book clubs' bonus-book plans offer another strategy for developing or expanding collections.

"Because engaged readers spend 500% more time reading than disengaged students, educators should attempt to increase engaged reading time by 200%–500%. This may require substantial reconfigurations of curriculum" (Guthrie, 2004, p. 1).

Requesting parent–teacher organization assistance or business support is another possibility. Also, old basal reading anthologies can be cut apart and some of the selections bound between cardboard covers to create little books. This strategy works especially well in primary-grade classrooms, where the most books are needed. Many basal stories are not very different from the stories in books found in the various collections of easy-reading little books.

Every school's budget should contain ample funds for such purchases each year. One way to find the money to buy books for school or classroom libraries is to save the funds from some other category. In a study of the costs of seatwork, Jachym, Allington, and Broikou (1989) found that some schools were spending upwards of $100 per child per year for seatwork. Most of the money was spent on duplicating materials (photocopying, dittos, etc.). Reducing the average cost (about $50 per student) of seatwork by half would have freed up about $25 per child per year, and that would amount to at least $500 per classroom for the purchase of books—or $250 per classroom and at least $5,000 additional for school library acquisitions.

One other budgeting consideration must be addressed. In an odd state of affairs, there seems to be an inverse relationship between the numbers of classroom aides employed and the sufficiency of school and classroom libraries (Allington, 2006). It is high-poverty schools that employ the largest numbers of aides. It is also high-poverty schools that have the least adequate school and classroom libraries. In this case it isn't so much a matter of basic funding differences (although that, too, typically comes into play) as it is a matter of funding priorities. But given a high-poverty school with an inadequate supply of books, a $30,000 annual investment in books to improve both school and classroom library collections seems a wiser investment than the same amount spent to fund two classroom aide positions.

The United States is wealthy enough that no child should ever leave school without a book in his or her backpack. Every child who wants a book should have one to read every night. School and classroom libraries are critical resources for children from lower-income families. If we want children to read outside of school—and we do if we want them to become proficient readers—then we must ensure easy, fingertip access to a wide range of interesting books that can be read with comprehension.

Displaying Classroom Collections

Once books have been acquired for classroom collections, it is time to think about organizing the classroom reading corner and displaying them. Morrow (1991) summarized the research on characteristics of classroom library centers that promoted children's voluntary reading. Such libraries:

- Provided physical accessibility and attractiveness
- Partitioned off the rest of the classroom on at least two sides to give a feeling of privacy
- Allowed for an area large enough to hold about five children at a time
- Offered comfortable seating such as a rocking chair, pillows, and a rug
- Held a wide variety of literature, including picture books, informational books, magazines, and newspapers

- Circulated new books regularly
- Displayed featured books on open-faced shelves
- Displayed attractive posters and a literature-related bulletin board
- Offered taped stories with headsets
- Checked books in and out using a simple procedure

Morrow's review also notes that children in classrooms with library centers read about 50 percent more books than did children in classrooms without such centers. Unattractive shelves of books with their spines displayed were not popular classroom locations with children. Well-designed library areas were popular and used far more frequently. Real-world reading materials, magazines, and newspapers make these centers attractive and foster the reading of a wide variety of texts. Merely putting books into classrooms is not enough. Classroom collections need some wonderful coffee-table books—those large, richly illustrated conversation pieces—for children to browse through. In addition, magazines and a daily newspaper for the upper grades should be added.

All of this may seem a tall order given current budget situations. At the same time, we too often visit schools with few books but with lots of commercial test preparation materials—materials no research supports. Every school needs a vision of what school and classroom libraries need to become. Without such visions, there will be no plan of action. Without some plan of action, nothing will change. If we are to create thoughtful schools where all children become literate, we need school and classroom libraries that provide all children access to the books they will need to accomplish that end.

Fountas and Pinnell (1999) produced a guide, *Matching Books to Readers,* for developing book rooms for grades K–4. Their book also provides a listing of children's books by level of difficulty. In many book rooms, books are arranged by difficulty (in some they are organized by topic, theme, genre, and author as well as by difficulty).

Leveling books by difficulty has become a hot topic in recent years. Nearly every publisher provides some sort of leveling system (numbers, letters, stages, etc.), but almost no publishers use any common standard. The limits of traditional readability formulas for estimating the difficulty of books below grade 3 has long been known. But it is precisely at the below-grade-3 level that most publishers now provide some sort of leveling system. The good news is that the Fountas and Pinnell leveling system seems to be emerging as an industry standard. (www.fountasandpinnellleveledbooks.com)

Book Rooms

One of the most innovative ideas, traveling to the United States here from New Zealand, for expanding the number of books available without busting the budget is the school book room, or instructional resource room (Mace, 1997). A book room is simply a site where a collection of instructional materials is stored for use by the whole school faculty. In an odd tradition, classroom teachers in the United States often think of the books in their classrooms as *their* books. Some of this possessiveness is due, undoubtedly, to another odd tradition—the expectation that teachers will be willing to spend their own funds to purchase the books they need to teach the children they were assigned. This notion is odd because one might think that the school, as a basic organizational responsibility, should provide needed instructional materials. When teachers do buy books with their own funds, perhaps it is natural for them to consider the books *their* books.

This tendency to assume ownership of all the books and other instructional materials in a classroom becomes very expensive. If we must buy each of the four third-grade teachers 25 copies of a trade book, we buy 100 books but purchase only one title. For the same money we could buy 100 different books, or five copies of 20 books, or 25 copies of four books. Any strategy other than buying 100 copies of the same book enhances the book supply. Even if we want all fourth-grade students to read the same books (though one would wonder why that was the case), buying 25 copies of four titles and rotating those titles around the fourth-grade classrooms makes more sense.

This Texas elementary school's book room provides teachers with easy access to an array of books organized by difficulty.

A school book room operates on much the same principle. We can purchase a substantial collection of books at different levels of difficulty, on different themes, of different genres, and by different authors and make them available for schoolwide use. Teachers at P.S. 191 in New York City were traditionally allocated $100 each per year to purchase books for their classrooms. By combining their funds, these teachers were able, over a period of several years, to stock a magnificent book room (Mace, 1997). Gradually, other funds were located and used to add to that initial supply. In addition, the development of the book room stimulated much collaboration among teachers in sharing and developing lessons using those books.

Book Clubs

Another strategy for putting books into the hands of children is participation in a commercial book club. For almost a half-century book clubs have offered low-cost paperback editions of children's books by mail order. Children's book clubs operate almost exclusively through schools. Classroom teachers distribute the flyers listing the monthly offerings.

Tools for Estimating the Reading Level of Texts

Recently updated, the *Dale–Chall Readability Formula* has been around for 50 years. It works best on upper elementary materials and above, and it provides a two-year difficulty band estimate that nicely emphasizes the notion of an "estimated" level of difficulty. The procedure is available on *Readability Master 2000* software (1-800-666-BOOK). When you use this software, you type in samples of text and the calculations are completed automatically.

Also available for 50 years, the *Flesch–Kincaid Formula* was revised in the 1970s. Microsoft Word uses this formula for estimating the difficulty of documents (go to the Grammar feature under Preferences and click on Document Statistics). By typing in text samples (or scanning them in), you can get an estimate, in grade-level terms, of difficulty.

The *Degrees of Reading Power* (DRP) procedure estimates text difficulty on a unique scale that is linked to achievement levels on the DRP standardized reading achievement test. According to the developers, the scores on the DRP test and the DRP estimates of text difficulty together provide a generally reliable match between texts and students. Support for this argument centers on the integration of the DRP measurement technique into the formula and test-item development. The publishers (www.tasaliteracy.org) also offer software with over 12,000 textbooks and trade books rated by difficulty. This software allows searches for texts on particular topics within a specified difficulty range. Also provided is a conversion table for converting DRP difficulty levels into grade-level equivalents.

The *Lexile Framework* (www.lexile.com) also estimates difficulty on a unique scale (although, again, conversion to grade-level equivalents is possible). The developers, however, have negotiated agreements with some publishers of textbooks and trade books and publishers of achievement tests so that they might offer services for matching children with books.

Then classroom teachers, paraprofessionals, or parent volunteers typically collect the order forms and the money for children's book orders, which are usually mailed out for the whole school at one time. Several weeks later, the shipment of books arrives, and each order is distributed to classroom teachers who, in turn, distribute the selections to children. Paraprofessionals or parent volunteers could conduct this activity in most cases, but teacher encouragement and support for book purchases remains an important factor.

Each of the major book club companies offers free books or other merchandise credits to teachers based on the number of books children order. Each also offers an array of books selected for particular grade levels and representing a variety of children's interests.

In a study of book clubs, the first of its kind, Strickland and Walmsley (1994) reported on a number of facets of book club participation. The study found that participation in book clubs was widespread and that classroom teachers overwhelmingly made the decisions about whether to participate and which club or clubs to join. Almost two-thirds of the teachers using book clubs participated in two or more companies' book clubs. None of the teachers required children to participate, though about half of the teachers reported encouraging participation. In these teachers' classrooms, 60 percent of the children ordered books at least some of the time, and 40 percent never or rarely ordered books. The teachers felt that parental interest and family incomes were the primary determinants of who ordered books. Participation influenced children's literacy development in a variety of ways:

Major Book Club Companies

Scholastic, 555 Broadway, New York, NY 10012 (1-800-325-6149)

Troll, 100 Corporate Drive, Mahwah, NJ 07430 (1-800-541-1097)

Trumpet, 666 Fifth Avenue, New York, NY 10003 (1-800-826-0110)

- Students exercised a personal choice in making selections.
- Selecting books required personal involvement and an investment of time.
- Students experienced ownership of books, both physically and intellectually.
- Shared literacy values were demonstrated among children, parents, and teachers.

Book clubs offer many children their best chance to have a book of their own. Book clubs provide easy access to inexpensive paperbacks (each club offered about 40 titles every month at an average cost of $2.00 each). Book club selections are substantially discounted from the normal retail price, even for paperback editions. In addition, book clubs provide access to books for children who live far from a children's bookstore or from a public library.

Book club participation seems to offer a wholly appropriate way to increase the number of books children have to read and discuss. But it does cost money, and not all children live in families that have the discretionary funds to purchase children's books, even low-cost books. The teachers whom Strickland and Walmsley (1994) studied were concerned about children from poor families and employed several strategies in an attempt to ensure that all children who wanted to order books were able to. These strategies included

- Using the credits from other children's orders to purchase books
- Purchasing books with funds from a parent or community organization
- Spending their own funds to purchase books

We think that schools should be concerned with this issue and develop schoolwide policies for providing all children the opportunity to participate in book clubs. Perhaps all children could be assured of receiving at least one book for each order sent in by the school. Children who receive free or reduced-price meals might simply be given the forms and told to rank order their book preferences. Using school or community-generated funds, each child would then receive his or her first choice.

Book Fairs

A wonderful strategy for putting trade books into classrooms and children's hands is organizing a book fair. As children's literature has risen in popularity, the use of school book fairs has become increasingly common. Similar in some respects to book club participation—for example, most book fairs also earn bonus books for the schools—the book fair offers a number of advantages. Children can handle and preview the books before they purchase them, and teachers can usually request that particular titles, authors, genres, or topics be made available at the fair.

Scheduling the book fair to extend during parent–teacher conference hours is one way to foster parent participation, as is scheduling the fair during the September open-house period. Posting notices of the book fair in public places and businesses in the neighborhood will attract parents of preschool children. This seems especially important if few bookstores are available in the area for young parents to shop in. Providing some selections for preschool-age children can encourage more parent reading before school entry.

Scheduling the book fair to extend beyond normal school hours and inviting community members to drop in—creating a community book fair rather than a school book fair—can foster not only more purchases but also community support for reading.

School Bookstores

Another strategy for increasing children's access to books is organizing a school bookstore. Many elementary schools run small stores to sell school supplies (and snacks), and such stores might add children's books to their stock. By regularly ordering a few titles, the store can keep books at children's fingertips. If no school store exists, consider setting up a bookstore that also sells some school supplies. Such a store does not have to take up much space. We have seen bookstores operating out of a former broom closet and operating from a mobile cart (much like the carts commonly found in malls and airports).

Books can be purchased for the store through a book distributor or a local trade bookstore, in most cases. One school ordered books from book clubs and resold them to children through the bookstore at no profit. The store might be open only one or two days each week and staffed by older children, paraprofessional staff, or community volunteers.

Displays that show off book covers are absolutely necessary, and ordering multiple copies of a few titles, selected to be of interest to a range of children, seems to work better than ordering lots of single copies. Reviews of books ordered might be inserted in the school newspaper or in newsletters sent home to parents (with directions to share with children). Reviews can be written by children (ideally) or by teachers, librarians, or other staff (including administrators).

At P.S. 121 in New York City the teachers organized a school bookstore run by the fourth-grade students. Because of a space shortage, the bookstore was set up two days a week on tables in the hallway. It was open for about a half-hour each day. Students worked as booksellers, cashiers, security, and advertising personnel. Each staffer received coupons for two books each month if they appeared at work each time the store was open. All books were priced at $1.50, and books were purchased in bulk from a variety of low-cost sources including publishers' clearance catalogs, book clubs, and wholesalers. With practice, setting up and taking down the bookstore took less than 10 minutes. The store was so successful that as the Christmas holidays neared, the store had to be opened each day. Parents began coming to shop for Christmas presents at the bookstore!

In a rural school we found a "books for a buck" program. It was much like the used-paperback stores doing business in many suburban strip malls. The titles were all used books in good condition. When children finished a book, they could trade it in for another book for only a quarter. The small cash flow was used to buy book collections at yard sales, a project of the PTA. Parents and children also donated books. When donating a new book, children could work and even swap for a book already in the collection. In this school, aides and parent volunteers ran the bookstore both before and after school (and during summer school) every day of the week.

The neighborhood near P.S. 121 had no bookstores. Neither did the neighborhood near the rural school. The limited availability of bookstores, especially bookstores with a large collection of affordable children's books, is a reality in many communities (Neuman & Celano, 2001). In such situations, a school bookstore can provide access to inexpensive but wonderful children's books.

The Reading Is Fundamental Program

The U.S. government has an inexpensive book distribution program targeted to putting books in the hands of disadvantaged children: the Reading Is Fundamental (RIF) program. There are 23,000 local RIF sites across the country today, and the vast majority are associated with schools. In most projects, 75 percent of the costs of the books given to disadvantaged children comes from federal monies, and 25 percent is raised from local efforts. Roughly 1,000 RIF projects are wholly funded from local monies, usually funds from corporate partners and local fund-raising efforts. RIF projects are staffed by volunteers because administrative and operating costs are not reimbursable. Almost 15 million books are distributed annually to five million children in all

For information about RIF, contact RIF, Smithsonian Institution, Room 500, 600 Maryland Avenue, S.W., Washington, DC 20024 (1-800-RIF-READ or www.rif.org).

50 states (www.rif.org). Still, RIF served only about 5 percent of all school-age children (about one of every five poor children).

Unfortunately, obtaining federal funding for new RIF projects is currently very difficult. Recently, more than 1,000 applications for new projects were declined because of lack of available federal funds. This could change if Congress decided to expand the RIF program. Still, schools can develop a locally funded RIF effort and thereby gain access to the inexpensive book list that has been the raison d'être for RIF. In addition, the national RIF office provides guidance and support materials to locally funded projects.

The first task is obtaining local funding. Most RIF programs are staffed by parent volunteers, and we suggest that the search for one or more local sponsors is best handled by these volunteers. RIF requires that at least three free books be distributed to each child, so you must determine the approximate number of children to be served. All children in a school must be served. RIF offers, for instance, Braille books for children with vision loss. Because RIF limits book costs to a maximum of $5.00, the upper limit is fairly easy to establish. However, few books on the RIF lists cost that much, so you could easily use an average price of $2.50 and set a base estimate of $7.50 per child. You should be sure to develop a plan for recognizing local sponsors before the search for local support begins. Youth athletic teams are so successful in gaining local funding from business because they invariably print the sponsor's name on team jerseys. That sort of visibility ensures that everyone knows who is supporting the effort. RIF projects need to make the same links just as visible.

Technology as a Source of Curriculum Materials

Most schools have invested in technology of various sorts. Why, then, do most classrooms make rather limited use of technology to develop literacy skills? For three reasons:

1. Many schools provide teachers with little actual training in using the tools purchased.
2. Many schools provide little time for teachers to develop new lessons or to review new curriculum products.
3. Many schools relied heavily on one-time grants for purchases, and both the hardware and software they bought are now dated.

We typically see little technology in use during our visits to classrooms, and the most common uses are very low-level drill and practice activities—the electronic skill worksheet. One reason is the abundance of old equipment in most schools. Computerized worksheets and drills are no more useful than the traditional paper–pencil or flashcard activities, and we cannot recommend them as solutions to the problems that struggling readers face.

There are many expensive reading software programs now being heavily marketed to schools, especially schools that have received federal funding under Reading First. Each of these products typically is advertised as being "scientific" and having a substantial research base. Truth be told, the "research" most often provided is little more than testimonials with some graphs and charts depicting huge gains in reading achievement. When published studies are cited or distributed, almost invariably the authors are the developers of the software. Here we provide just two examples of independent research studies conducted in real schools using two hotly marketed and expensive software products. Other similar studies exist but these two examples are a bit of what sales representatives will never provide you.

Rouse, C. E., & Krueger, A. B. (2004). "Putting computerized instruction to the test: A randomized evaluation of a 'scientifically-based' reading program." *Economics of Education Review, 23*(4): 323–338.

Half of 500 students from grades 3 through 6 were randomly assigned to participate in Fast-ForWord training. The remaining students served as a no-treatment control group. All students in both groups were drawn from a student population scoring in the bottom 20 percent on state reading tests. Students in both groups had improved reading scores with no significant difference in gains by the FastForWord group. The same pattern was found on other measures of language performance.

Patterson, W. A., Henry, J. J., et al. (2003). "Investigating the effectiveness of an integrated learning system on early emergent readers." *Reading Research Quarterly, 38*(2): 172–207.

A one-year, multiple-methods study of the effectiveness of the Waterford Early Literacy Program on kindergarten and first-grade children was conducted in an urban school district. Eight Waterford and eight comparable control classrooms participated in this quasi-experimental study. The main effect for the Waterford Early Literacy Program was not significant, indicating no benefits for participation. Only the univariate analysis for reading achievement was significant, showing Waterford less effective than control classrooms offering traditional reading instruction.

"It is clear from the present results that the Waterford Early Literacy Program had relatively little overall effect on the participants' literacy development. To the extent there was an effect, it was in a negative direction. On the other hand, teacher variables had a consistently strong effect on reading success" (p. 198).

The data showed that children "were happily engaged" with Waterford software but also that this engagement did not enhance literacy development.

As we said, although there are more such independent studies available in the research literature, you probably cannot expect that marketers will steer you in their direction.

However, powerful technological tools are available, and costs are rapidly dropping. We see an enormous potential for technology in instructional and assessment activities, but, as the National Reading Panel (2000) pointed out, there is little research now available that documents that potential. We believe that to achieve that potential, schools must develop far better long-term planning for technology acquisition and implementation than most have today.

A good first step in thinking about technology-based curriculum is to sort through the roles we expect technology to play in some or all classrooms. For instance, do we see technology as a potential source of instructional support for literacy? The old electronic worksheets were seen this way (even though they offered little real support for students). Now, early literacy software can display a children's book on the color monitor and provide a variety of supportive activities. The computer reads the story aloud, highlighting each word as it is read. When children touch objects in the illustrations, the computer provides a label and a voice reads the label. In some cases, children can type in their own extension of the story, select from the original artwork to illustrate their addition, and then ask the computer to read back what they have written. New software products are interactive and instructional. But, of course, such software requires the newer, more powerful computers to operate.

A number of simulation software packages also expand opportunities for reading and thinking as children learn about geography, biology, life cycles of ants, rain forests, oceans, colonial North America, or city management. Other software programs allow children to compose music for lyrics they have written and to support artistic expression for illustrating their stories.

A second role that technology might play is to expand opportunities to engage in reading and writing real things. Using the computer as a word processor or desktop publishing center are two examples. For many children, the computer solves some difficulties associated with composing, revising, editing, and publishing their work (it also makes the final product wonderfully professional looking with very little computer expertise). Going one step further and linking into a computer network allows children to become electronic pen pals with children around the world, and also links children with similar interests or with a shared problem-solving activity. Participating in one of these networks increases the amount of reading and writing that children do.

We cannot sing the praises of some websites loudly enough—such as the Discovery Channel site (www.discovery.com) or the Smithsonian Institution site (www.smithsonian.org). These and thousands of other sites (including elementary school websites) offer instantaneous access to a wealth of educational resources important to elementary schools.

Access to the Internet provides access to an enormous set of informational resources that no single school could ever afford to collect. Internet access poses some risks, even when blocking software

(software to block access to certain websites) is in place. But the potential for improved reports and other assignments is enhanced as children explore cyberspace. Our own children are now Internet experts, and they helped us locate resources as we wrote this book. Learning to use the "crawler" search engines dramatically enhances the likelihood of locating information on specific topics. There are now millions of links between educational websites, so finding one good website simply leads directly to other related websites.

Also, adaptive hardware and software facilitate learning by children with disabilities. There is word processing software that "learns" an individual's writing style and vocabulary and then finishes words and sentences for the writer. This reduces the number of keystrokes that children need to type in a response or to compose a story. Word processing packages that check spelling, grammar, and style for adherence to conventions are a real boon for all children. Voice-recognition software has reached such a level of sophistication that simply "talking" a paper into the computer is possible.

In short, the variety of software is enormous and growing every day. We mention only a few examples because technology is changing so rapidly and new product development has exploded. The best software available today, however, requires more powerful computers than those that many schools now have, which is why a long-term plan is a necessity. So begin to plan by exploring possibilities and visiting schools and conferences that highlight educational technology. Find out what sort of technology teachers envision as a necessity. Involve parents. At the Elsmere Elementary School in Bethlehem, New York, three parents provided the primary stimulus for developing network access capabilities and securing donated equipment and a commitment from the school district to provide an annual acquisition, training, and maintenance budget for the school's technology effort. These parents provided the expertise and familiarized staff with technology and fostered the development of a clearer vision of the roles that technology could play in educating students.

It is important to develop a five-year plan and a realistic budget that includes expenses for training as well as for equipment. Remember that all teachers must become technology literate for the greatest impact. Merely hiring a computer teacher and stocking a computer lab does not typically enhance classroom instruction. Do not overlook community resources when developing the plan. Local colleges and community colleges often can provide "techies" as resources, at times "on loan" or as part of an internship. Parents, retirees, and other community members as well as students, can often offer useful services and guidance as technology is upgraded and implemented into the school day.

We close this section by noting that schools might consider acquiring donated equipment or purchasing rehabilitated hardware. Computers, hard drives, modems, and even software that are being replaced in business and industry are likely to be superior to the equipment and programs available in many schools. The purchase of used but rehabilitated computers offers the potential for real savings while upgrading a school's technology. Of course, such efforts need to fit into the larger overall plan.

Summary

Materials and activities for children are at the heart of any instructional program. Textbooks and other commercial curriculum materials can play a vital role in efforts to fashion a school where all children are readers and writers. Teaching is a time-consuming occupation, and teachers do not have time to reinvent the wheel. But before we can achieve our goals, the quality of commercial materials and the quality of their use in classrooms must improve.

One way to evaluate any commercial reading material is to estimate its "educative potential" (McGill-Franzen, Zmach, Love, & Solic, in press). As McGill-Franzen and her colleagues noted, after an analysis of several "proven" reading programs, current commercial programs gave few suggestions on how a teacher might adapt a lesson to better meet the needs of struggling readers. In other words, the programs largely left it up to the teacher to decide what modifications would be useful in adapting lessons for students who just didn't "get it" after the standard lesson had been offered. Commercial curriculum products could help teachers acquire new knowledge and new teaching skills but, currently, most products seem not to include such support.

There are several frameworks for organizing reading and language arts instruction. Little good evidence suggests that any particular framework reliably produces superior results. Instead, in study after study, the classroom teacher is the critical factor (McGill-Franzen, 2000). What does seem important is who selects the framework that is to be used. Teacher and community involvement in developing curriculum frameworks and selecting curriculum materials seems crucial. Mandated frameworks and curriculum foster resistance and dissatisfaction. It is important for school staff to engage in ongoing discussions about what curriculum framework and which curriculum materials to select.

Most schools have a framework in place. The more flexibly that framework works to accommodate teacher preferences, the more effective the framework appears to be. All teachers seem to teach better when they are teaching in ways that are compatible with their personal perspectives on teaching and learning. Children differ, and so do teachers. We realize that no curriculum framework will be acceptable to all teachers, but we think that children benefit from coherent curricular experiences across their elementary school careers. Of course, they benefit most from constant exposure to excellent teachers. The challenge is to find the middle ground that allows teachers flexibility and adaptability and affords children coherence and consistency. Creating schools where all children become readers and writers requires that teachers teach effectively and that children are offered a rich, coherent instructional program with abundant opportunities to select, read, and discuss wonderful books.

Who Does What?

ccording to the National Center for Educational Statistics (NCES), the pupil/teacher ratio has shrunk considerably since 1960. At the same time, class size has not changed dramatically. These contradictory trends can be explained by understanding the substantial growth in the specialists' roles in schools today (Allington, 1994b). In 1960, few schools employed reading teachers, teachers of students with learning disabilities, speech and language teachers, art teachers, physical education teachers, bilingual teachers, teachers of students who are gifted and talented, and so on. In addition, few schools had librarians (because few had libraries), psychologists, counselors, or social workers on staff. Few schools had assistant principals. Few had A/V or technology specialists. As curricular goals expanded, elementary schools added more special content-area teachers. As state and federal

programs for struggling readers expanded, schools added more special teachers and more paraprofessionals. In special education programs alone, the number of aides has increased tenfold in the past 30 years.

Today, in many elementary schools with high concentrations of low-income children, there are as many special teachers and special staff members as there are classroom teachers. When the paraprofessional staff is considered, there are often more adults who are not classroom teachers than there are classroom teachers! According to recent NCES data, more than half the adults working in the average school today are not classroom teachers. Whenever a school begins to consider reorganizing to better meet the needs of all children, the roles and responsibilities of all professional and paraprofessional staff must be considered.

In this chapter, we explore the roles and responsibilities of the various professional and paraprofessional staff members typically found in elementary schools today. We begin with classroom teachers because recent research has confirmed that classroom teachers play the critical role in developing the literacy of all children (Nye et al., 2004). Although parents, special teachers, and paraprofessionals can play important roles, the classroom teacher ultimately has the greatest opportunity to develop readers and writers. In actuality, the roles that other adults play are simply supporting roles to classroom instruction. The traditional roles of the other adults involved with children must also change in many schools. We discuss some potentially new roles for these adults as we help you reconsider instructional programs.

The Critical Nature of Classroom Teachers

Some children come to schools at high risk for failure yet succeed. Every teacher knows children who succeeded despite little background knowledge or home support. Some schools and teachers have an astonishingly high number of these "unexpected" successes (Ladson-Billings, 1994; Nye et al., 2004). Although we must recognize that children's homes and backgrounds influence failure or success, we must also realize that what happens in classrooms minute by minute, day after day, determines how much will be learned by how many children.

As classroom and remedial reading teachers, college professors, and teacher consultants, we have observed, researched, discussed, and worried about children at high risk for reading failure for a combined 60-plus years. Over those years, we have observed schools where, year after year, children at high risk for failure beat the odds and learned to read and write. At first, we thought some strange, mysterious, even mystical variable must be at work in these sites. Ultimately, we concluded that schools with success in teaching all children had enormously effective classroom instruction. In these schools, it was not the "super specialist" teacher who was producing the excellent results, nor was it only a new curriculum or a new parent-training component. In these schools, classroom teachers provided large amounts of high-quality literacy instruction. Although special staff members often supported classroom teachers, the high-quality classroom instruction primarily produced the high levels of student achievement. Research supports our observations about schools that achieve success with all children. High-quality classroom instruction is the critical variable in literacy development.

Most past attempts to change less effective schools into more effective ones have been disappointing. Evidence that the "effective schools" movement actually created many effective schools is limited (Rowan, 1990). It seems that the "effective schools" effort may have overlooked a critical and central aspect of schools, especially elementary schools—namely, that schools are collections of classrooms where, usually, a single teacher and stable group of children meet and interact for five or six hours each day. No school can be effective unless the instruction offered in these classrooms is effective. In our own work, we have found many more effective classroom teachers than effective schools. Some schools, however, have a larger number of effective classroom teachers than do others. When most classroom teachers are effective, the school appears effective. When many classroom teachers are ineffective, the school appears ineffective.

Though this may seem obvious, we think the implications are important. For too long, efforts in improving school effectiveness have been focused everywhere but on the classroom teacher. Schools have hired specialist teachers; purchased new curriculum materials; added social workers; created discipline, attendance, and homework policies; attempted to entice parental involvement; and mandated more and more testing. In most schools it is difficult to find any major effort or expenditure targeted at directly improving specific features of the instruction offered by classroom teachers.

What we are thinking of here are substantial targeted professional development strands that provide teachers with a means of more effectively knowing their students. There is no evidence that buying a new basal reader provides teachers with better information on how to offer explicit strategy lessons that improve student self-monitoring. But developing self-monitoring is critical, and teachers

Al Shanker, the late president of the American Federation of Teachers, once commented on how General Motors managed to restructure its traditional factory model to produce the award-winning Saturn automobile (*The New York Times,* January 24, 1993, p. 7). GM offered 136 workers from its plants about 400 hours of training within a few months of the opening of the new Saturn manufacturing plant, splitting their hours between classroom and on-the-job training. Every other employee received, and continues to receive, 92 hours of training each year. Over 600 training courses are available, and new courses are developed as the product or the manufacturing process changes. Shanker noted, "Imagine what a training program like this would do for people trying to restructure schools. . . . It is ironic that a bunch of people whose business is building cars understand so well the importance of educating their employees whereas people in education seem to assume that teachers will be able to step right into a new way of doing things with little or no help."

can develop the necessary skills with targeted and longer-term support (Duffy, 1993; Pressley, Wood, & Woloshyn, 1992). Adding an achievement test, especially when the results arrive five months later, does nothing to improve teachers' knowledge of their children's instructional needs. But providing 10 hours of targeted professional development and in-class coaching on using running records to assess the appropriateness of the texts that students are reading would provide such expertise.

Classroom teachers have the opportunity to know children better than any other member of a school staff, but often classroom teachers' expertise about the children they teach has not been valued. Much lack of recognition of the importance of classroom teachers' role can be traced to a distinct federal policy of creating an ever-expanding "second system" of specialist teachers and professional staff. Before 1960, and the Great Society programs, including the Elementary and Secondary Education Act of 1965 (ESEA), most elementary schools had few specialist teachers, paraprofessionals, or specialized staff. Beginning with ESEA and the hiring of remedial reading specialists, through the Education of Handicapped Children Act of 1975 and the hiring of more special education teachers, to the more recent reading coaches movement, an era evolved in which most new education dollars went to fund the "second system." Studies show the impact most dramatically in urban school systems where today only about one-quarter to one-half of the

Catherine Snow and her colleagues (1990) provided dramatic evidence of the importance of classroom teachers in developing the literacy proficiencies of struggling readers. In their book, *Unfulfilled Expectations,* they report on a naturalistic study of schools serving children from low-income families. The research team studied the impact of classrooms and home environments on children's learning. The table below summarizes the impact of two or more years of consistent high classroom support, mixed classroom support, and low classroom support.

Percentage of Children Who Are Successful with Varying Levels of Home and Classroom Support

	High Home Support	Low Home Support
Consistent high classroom support	100%	100%
Mixed classroom support	100%	25%
Consistent low classroom support	60%	0%

The findings illustrate the enormous impact of access to consistently high-quality classroom instruction. Anything less had dramatically negative impacts on the achievement of children from homes where parents did not provide high levels of home literacy support.

educational funds go to support classroom instruction—half to three-quarters of the money now supports administration, supervision, and special programs (Fischer, 1990; Harp, 1993).

Most educational reform efforts have also been marked by a search for "the one best way" to teach. Curriculum is debated endlessly while what seem to be even more critical elements of schools are largely ignored. The evidence indicates that there is no one best way to teach and that investments in curriculum plans and materials are typically less cost-effective than comparable investments in teacher professional development (Darling-Hammond, 1997).

Classroom teachers are important, and effective classroom literacy instruction cannot be produced from a single master plan that all teachers are mandated to follow (Duffy & Hoffmann, 1999). As we noted in Chapter 3, researchers have identified a number of characteristics of classrooms where all children become readers and writers. But to foster the development of such sorts of teaching, classroom teachers need support more often than mandates. Classroom teachers need the opportunity to work and talk collaboratively about their work with their peers. But powerless teachers—teachers who have little authority over their teaching—do not talk about their work and working conditions, if only because such talk is either fruitless (because no one in power is listening) or dangerous (because someone in power is eavesdropping). The point that needs to be understood is that many efforts to change schools fail because teachers are important if change is to occur and few teachers actually change simply because change is mandated. In Chapter 8 we explore in depth the issues of how effective change in classroom instruction can be accomplished.

Rethinking the "Second System"

Over the past 35 years, U.S. elementary schools have added and expanded the "second system" of special programs, primarily to try to meet the needs of limited-experience children—those children who arrived at school with few experiences with books, stories, or print. However, the development of the second system has consumed enormous amounts of money that could have been used to fund other efforts or programs. But not just the fiscal costs need examination (Allington, 1994, 2002).

Currently, "second system" programs may undermine the critical role classroom teachers play in the futures of struggling readers. For 40 years, classroom teachers have been led to believe that they were ill equipped to teach these children. For almost as long, classroom teachers and specialist teachers have been educated in different strands of teacher education programs and attended different professional-development sessions. Is it any wonder then that many classroom teachers feel a limited sense of professional responsibility for teaching struggling readers in their classroom?

Concerns about the continuing expansion of the "second system," reports of fragmentation, interference, reduced accountability, and limited effects of these efforts on academic achievement have forced federal education officials to begin to rethink the roles that federal funds might play in addressing the educational needs of disadvantaged students and students with disabilities (LeTendre, 1991). These two shifts are summed up in the words *collaboration* and *inclusion.* In the federal Title 1 program, this push for collaboration began in the mid-1980s with the call for program coordination with the core curriculum and an emphasis on delivery of Title 1 remediation in the classroom (Johnston, Allington, & Afflerbach, 1985). In special education there has been a more recent emphasis on providing services in the regular classroom environment and a shift to consulting with classroom teachers in an attempt to support modifications to classroom instruction. This "inclusionary" education emphasis is buttressed by increasing evidence that the achievement of children with disabilities rises with increased integration, with no negative effects on other children's achievement (Sharpe, York, & Knight, 1994). In addition, the Americans with Disabilities Act of 1990 requires that all individuals with disabilities, including children, have the right to participate fully in all aspects of U.S. society without discrimination (including, it is argued, instruction in regular classrooms in the neighborhood school).

More recently, Congress mandated all pupils with disabilities be included in all district, state, and national assessments of academic achievement. The assessment results for these pupils are to be included in the calculation of AYP, and the performances are to be reported to the parents of these children. Clearly, Congress was disturbed that, in too many cases, the low achievement of many special needs pupils was being "hidden" from public view when these students were exempted from the achievement testing done in schools.

In addition, according to guidelines for implementing the new requirements of the Individuals with Disabilities Education Act (IDEA), the development of individualized educational plans (IEPs) for pupils with disabilities is now to be guided by the state academic standards. The classroom teacher must be substantively involved in the development of the IEP and in IEP development meetings. Both annual and triennial reviews of the academic progress of pupils with disabilities are to be benchmarked against the the relevant state standards. In other words, the new goal of special education services is to accelerate the academic development of pupils with disabilities so that they meet state academic achievement standards—thus the emphasis on supporting the child and his or her teacher in the classroom.

We expect that federal education programs will continue these trends over the next few years. In fact, there is every reason to believe that the future will see fewer specialist teachers and staff in schools and greater popularity for alternatives to the traditional models. In the meantime, serious issues need to be addressed about the design and delivery of instruction for children who participate in one or more of these programs (Allington, 2006).

 If classroom teachers are to be expected to teach inclusion students, they must be involved in the design of each student's individualized educational plan (IEP). In too many schools, classroom teachers fall at the 1 or 2 level on the scale below. The less involved the classroom teacher is in the IEP process, the less likely classroom instruction is adapted to meet the needs of pupils with disabilities. This is a primary reason the new special education regulations require the involvement of the child's classroom teacher in IEP development.

Please rate your participation in the development of the IEP for the pupils with disabilities in your classroom.

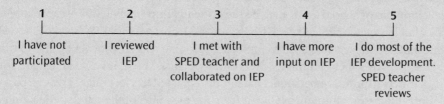

1	2	3	4	5
I have not participated	I reviewed IEP	I met with SPED teacher and collaborated on IEP	I have more input on IEP	I do most of the IEP development. SPED teacher reviews

If classroom teachers are to accept professional responsibility for teaching struggling readers in their classrooms, school and district policies and practices must support their involvement and their efforts. The focus on inclusive education does not mean simply dumping students with special educational needs back into the general education classroom. Schools now must produce documented improvements in academic achievement. The assessment of this achievement occurs primarily with the same tests that general education students take. The achievement target is satisfactory performance on the state's general education academic assessments.

With these new goals, schools need to create a general sense that special programs are part of a unified plan of action addressing the needs of struggling readers. Too often, special teachers and special programs have simply existed in a school but were not really part of the school. Often these special personnel were not supervised by a building administrator. Often, it was neither the building administrator nor the classroom teachers who scheduled special teachers' work with children but someone at a district special-programs office. In some cases, special-program personnel did not attend building staff meetings nor did they participate in staff development activities with classroom teachers. In too many cases, school districts seemed to have engaged in planning classroom and special-program curriculum and instruction as wholly separate entities. In these situations, it is not surprising that classroom teachers felt little involvement with special programs and reduced responsibility for teaching the students who participated in them. Similarly, it is not surprising that specialist teachers too often were little involved in improving classroom instruction.

Sharing and Collaborating

To create schools that work for all children, we need to create a stronger sense of shared responsibility. Shared responsibility is unlikely in schools where classroom and special-program teachers share little knowledge of each other's instructional practices. When two teachers working with the same children have little shared knowledge of each other's instruction, it is unlikely that the children are participating in the most coherent and supportive instructional environment.

Developing shared knowledge of instructional practices in classroom and specialist teachers is a good starting point for enhancing a sense of shared responsibility. Collaborative development of shared goals may be the critically important activity, especially in schools with large numbers of special-program students (Allington & Broikou, 1988).

Several activities can be used to initiate developing shared knowledge and to foster collaboration between classroom teachers and specialists. First, involve all teachers in staff meetings. Special-program personnel cannot be expected to view themselves as part of a team effort if they are routinely excluded from the meetings of the regular education staff. Second, schedule shared staff-development sessions. Although there will be times when special-program staff need to gather for sessions particularly targeted to their needs, generally staff development must include all professional staff members at the school. It may be useful to schedule special-program staff presentations of their programs during staff meetings or staff-development days. Similarly, special-program staff often benefit from sessions offered by classroom teachers describing their classroom instructional programs.

When the classroom teachers meet to work on general curriculum development issues, special-program staff must be involved. Too many reading teachers, speech therapists, school psychologists, and special education teachers remain largely uninformed

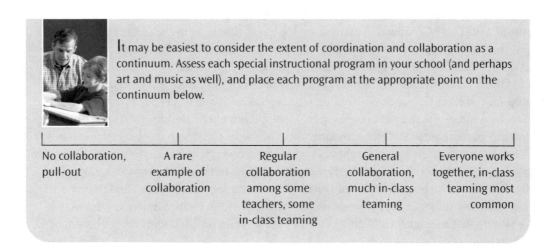

It may be easiest to consider the extent of coordination and collaboration as a continuum. Assess each special instructional program in your school (and perhaps art and music as well), and place each program at the appropriate point on the continuum below.

No collaboration, pull-out	A rare example of collaboration	Regular collaboration among some teachers, some in-class teaming	General collaboration, much in-class teaming	Everyone works together, in-class teaming most common

about existing state academic standards and even naive about the nature of the many new state assessments of these standards. In order to design appropriate instruction for special needs students, all professional staff must be familiar with the state curriculum standards.

A second set of activities involves getting special-program staff into classrooms often, even if for brief periods. For instance, when special-program staff come to the classroom to pick up children that participate in their pull-out instruction, two immediate benefits are gained. First, special-program teachers acquire more information about the classroom instruction even from brief visits (30 seconds twice a day). Just coming into the room offers the chance to get a sense of the common kinds of reading and language arts activities. Likewise, these visits provide glimpses of the classroom environment and organization. Second, this strategy of picking children up at their classrooms tends to reduce the amount of transition time spent in the special-program classroom. We find children are engaged in academic work more quickly after their walk with the specialist to the classroom, perhaps because some social talk occurs during this time. Thus, picking up children at their classroom provides double benefits.

Another activity that fosters shared knowledge is a traveling notebook. The notebook can be a simple spiral-bound pad with a string run through the spiral binding and looped over a child's neck when the child is leaving for special-program instruction. The classroom teacher simply writes in the notebook the classroom material and pages being used during the lesson that day. In addition, the classroom teacher might jot a comment about the child's performance (e.g., "Tim had difficulty following the story line") or a particular skill or strategy the teacher feels needs additional attention ("Tim has difficulty with long words"). The special-program teacher jots notes back to the classroom teacher ("We worked on a Making Big Words activity today") and returns the notebook with the child after their instructional session. The point is that the notes do not have to be long or complicated to enhance shared knowledge, especially if they are written regularly.

A fourth activity is shared development of lesson plans. In this case, the classroom teacher shares a copy of his or her lesson plan for reading and language arts with the special program teacher, who uses that as one source of information in planning support instruction. Even better than simply sharing the plans is to sit together and create jointly the lessons to be offered by both teachers. Of course, this requires time for both teachers to meet, but in most schools such time is available before and after the school day. However, if special-program teachers work with children from many classrooms, the task becomes more complicated.

A fifth strategy to foster collaboration is creating grade-level or grade-cluster teams made up of classroom teachers and specialists. For instance, if the K–2 teachers were a single team that met regularly to share instructional planning and small-group discussions of strategies for better addressing the needs of struggling readers, then assigning several special teachers to the team serves a number of purposes. Specialist teachers have the opportunity to listen and learn from classroom teachers and vice versa. As they listen, both groups develop greater shared knowledge and an expanded repertoire of instructional modifications. The specialists assigned to the team would work with children from the classrooms of other team members.

At one rural New York school, teams of classroom teachers meet every morning for about 35 minutes before children arrive. Specialist teachers attend these meetings (as well as other team meetings focused only on targeted children) at least once each week and work with classroom teachers to address how best to modify instruction to meet the needs of struggling readers. The design of remedial and special education services is constantly changing at the school as both classroom and specialist teachers work continually to adapt the intervention to best meet the needs of the students served. None of this could happen without the collaboration that team membership provides.

A final strategy is having special-program teachers provide all of their instructional support in the regular classroom rather than in a location down the hall. One goal of "in-class" instructional support is to improve classroom instruction through developing shared knowledge and creating more coherent instructional interventions. In addition, participating students should lose less instructional time in transition from one setting to another.

In-class instructional support, whether remediation or special education, produces achievement gains at least as large as the gains from pull-out instruction without having a

Although special services for struggling readers can offer powerful instructional support, we cannot forget that these children still spend 90 to 95 percent of their school day in the general education classroom. That is why the quality of classroom instruction is so important. But for classroom teachers to teach well, they must have daily schedules that limit the number of disruptions to their lessons.

To provide instruction that is well coordinated with the instructional support, classroom teachers must have a reasonable number of specialist teachers to work and plan with. In many schools special-program schedules are not coordinated with the classroom schedules. In many schools a half-dozen or more special teachers work with children from a single classroom. In such cases, one should not be surprised that neither the classroom instruction nor the support instruction provides struggling readers with needed support.

Answer the following questions about each classroom in your building. If more than two special teachers work with children and more than 20 percent of the children leave the room for these lessons, then you may find that classroom teachers simply cannot provide the sorts of instruction necessary. If all students are not in the classroom together for at least 4 hours every day, then the classroom teachers' jobs are made most difficult. Rethink the special-program schedules so that classroom teachers have all their children together for most of the day.

How many special teachers work with children from this room? _____

How many children leave the room for part of the day? _____

How many hours each day are *all* children in the room? _____

negative impact on the achievement of other students in the room (Gelzheiser et al., 1992; Sharpe et al., 1994). But proponents argue more often from a moral perspective: Segregating some children from their peers is wrong unless large benefits to the children can be demonstrated, but such benefits have not usually been reported.

In our view, the critical issue is providing children with access to high-quality instruction rather than the issue of location. But in-class, collaborative instructional models focused on enhancing achievement in the core curriculum of the classroom do, in fact, seem to offer the greatest promise for providing high-quality instruction. Nonetheless, we see variety in the design of instructional support for struggling readers as a simple necessity. We would have schools offer instructional support that provided flexibility in intensity, location, schedule, emphasis, and so on. No single program design can possibly be expected to meet the needs of all children. That said, we emphasize creating responsive, in-class support, collaboratively planned and offered by classroom and special teachers.

Reading Teachers, Reading Specialists, and Reading Coaches

Recently the National Center for Educational Statistics (2004) reported that some 30,000 reading specialists were employed in U.S. elementary schools and another 30,000 teachers taught at least one period of remedial reading daily. Most of the specialized reading instruction (75%) was offered in a setting other than the student's regular classroom. It seems the pull-out model initiated some 40 years ago is still alive in our nation's schools today.

Perhaps surprisingly, only about one-third of the reading specialists had earned a degree that included an emphasis on preparation for teaching reading! Although two-thirds of the reading specialists held a graduate degree, only half earned that degree in reading education. Most of the remaining graduate degrees earned were general elementary education degrees. These data suggest a primary focus for reform efforts—strengthening and expanding the preparation of teachers, especially teachers employed as reading specialists, in the area of reading education. It seems that although many states issue a reading specialist credential, few states actually require reading specialists, reading supervisors, or reading coaches to have earned such credentials.

We begin this section with this discouraging information because we have been convinced that most schools would be more effective if they employed more teachers with advanced credentials in reading education. In some schools we visit, almost half of the staff have earned a graduate degree in reading. In other schools, no one has earned such credentials. In some districts central office personnel responsible for directing the reading/language area have all earned such credentials and in other districts none have. In some districts half of all elementary school principals have reading credentials, whereas in other districts none do. Over the years it has become apparent how tightly linked the level of reading expertise (as indicated by the number of advanced reading credentials) is to the level of student performance in schools and districts. Also tightly linked to the expertise that is available is the quality of the plan for developing reading and writing proficiencies. In other words, as a general rule, when districts have larger numbers of teachers and administrators with graduate-level preparation in reading, we find districts where student reading proficiency is higher.

So what sort of experiences seem most common for obtaining credentials as a special teacher of reading, reading teacher, or reading specialist? The International Reading Association's Standards for Reading Professionals indicate 18–21 credit hours of graduate education coursework including supervised practicum and other features. Most states that offer reading specialist credentials follow these standards, though several offer such credentials based on a similar amount of undergraduate coursework. It seems odd to us, in this era of an emphasis on highly qualified teachers, that more schools and districts have not targeted the hiring of additional staff with reading specialist credentials (for positions as classroom teachers, reading specialists, principals, supervisors, etc.).

Both of us came of age during the last big federal reading initiative—the Right to Read era. We both earned graduate degrees in reading literally free of cost through federal programs that provided tuition scholarships for interested teachers or provided loan forgiveness for those who earned advanced credentials in reading and then worked for five or more years in a high-poverty school. This may be one important aspect of federal policy missing from the NCLB and from state initiatives for improving reading outcomes.

What Do Reading Specialists Do in Elementary Schools?

The best evidence for what reading specialists might do comes from the data from schools with exemplary reading programs, schools that are beating the odds, gathered by the International Reading Association's (IRA) Commission (Bean, Swan, & Knaub, 2003). They found that reading specialists spend most of their time providing supplementary reading instruction to struggling readers. They may also mentor new teachers, assess children experiencing reading difficulties, and provide building-level reading program leadership. The Figure 5.1 illustrates the several roles these reading specialists report as part of their responsibilities.

In this sample of reading specialists from schools recognized for the success of their reading instructional efforts, all specialists held advanced reading credentials. It is unclear why so many schools (according to the NCES data cited previously) have failed to employ credentialed reading specialists in large numbers. Perhaps it is a problem of supply and demand with too few reading specialists available to fill all the positions. But it may also be the case that too few districts have sought out professional staff with advanced reading credentials. Whatever the reason, it seems to us that ensuring that every school has an adequate supply of teachers with advanced reading credentials should be a primary priority for district officials and for state policy makers.

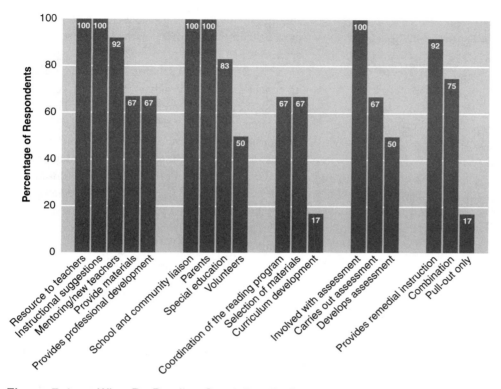

Figure 5.1 ● What Do Reading Specialists Do?

Source: Bean, Rita M., Swan, Allison L., Knaub, Rebecca B. (2003, February). Reading specialists in schools with exemplary reading programs: Functional, versatile, and prepared. *The Reading Teacher, 56*(5), 446–455. Copyright © 2003 International Reading Association.

What's the Difference between a Reading Specialist and a Reading Coach?

If we follow the guidelines set forth in the IRA position statement, *The Role and Qualifications for the Reading Coach in the United States* (www.reading.org/resources/issues/positioncoach.html), all reading coaches would be credentialed reading specialists. But the evidence suggests that most reading coaches today fail to meet that criterion. As illustrated in Figure 5.1, showing the duties of reading specialists, many already function as reading coaches, that is, when reading specialists mentor teachers. By providing teachers with needed instructional materials, offering professional development, and providing reading leadership for the school, they seem to be accomplishing what most people assign as the responsibilities of reading coaches. The big difference in roles, it seems, is how much time is spent working with teachers versus how much time is spent providing instruction to struggling readers. In most schools we have observed, reading coaches only work

Resources for Further Information

Books: Toll, C. A. (2005). *The literacy coach's survival guide: Essential questions and practical answers.* International Reading Association.

Bean, R. M. (2004). *Reading specialist: Leadership for the classroom, school and community.* New York: Guilford.

Walpole, S., & McKenna, M. (2004). *The literacy coach's handbook: A guide to research-based practices.* New York: Guilford.

sparingly with struggling readers and instead spend most of their time involved in the teacher support activities.

The IRA position statement argues the reasons all coaches should have advanced reading credentials but they actually seem obvious to us. How can someone with little expertise in reading development, assessment, curriculum, and such provide useful advice as a reading coach? This statement does recognize that people with those credentials may be scarce and so suggests that some coaches might be hired and then supervised by a credentialed reading specialist while they work toward earning the credentials themselves.

Coaching involves more than simply having expertise about the reading process. Reading coaches should have a record as an effective classroom teacher of reading and should have participated in professional development or graduate work targeted to building coaching skills (e.g., supporting teachers' reflections and development, facilitator of adult professional learning, participant/observer).

Although there is less evidence than we would like illustrating the impact of reading coaches on classroom reading instruction and student reading achievement, the reading coach model is being widely implemented today, especially in schools eligible for federal Reading First funds. However, there is an evidence base for coaching as a strategy for enhancing the quality of instruction (Joyce & Showers, 2002). But when coaches have little or no expertise in reading, it seems likely that the coaching model will prove untenable as a path to improving reading lessons and reading achievement.

Special Education Teachers

The largest number of special educators work with students considered to have "mild or moderate" disabilities. These are students who have typically been identified as pupils with a learning disability, language disability, behavioral or emotional disability, and/or an attention deficit disorder with or without hyperactivity. Students in these categories represent about 80 percent of pupils with disabilities. The learning disability category has grown the fastest over the past 30 years and now accounts for about half of all pupils with disabilities. It has been estimated that 80 percent of pupils with learning disabilities exhibit a reading disability (Lyon, 1996).

In the decades following the passage of the Education of Handicapped Children's Act of 1975, learning disabilities became a recognized and reimbursable category of pupils with disabilities. In fact, during the 10 years following passage of that act, one could observe a shift of several hundred thousand children from remedial reading programs into special education programs (McGill-Franzen, 1987). Perhaps this shift occurred because federal funding also shifted away from Title 1 remedial reading programs to funding special education programs. A similar shift occurred in federal training funds as funding supporting earning advanced reading credentials was replaced with funding supporting earning special education credentials. Then there were the new high-stakes testing policies. One could link increases in the identification of students with disabilities to the introduction of high-stakes testing (Allington & McGill-Franzen, 1992). One potential explanation for this phenomenon was that pupils with disabilities were, at that time, typically excused from high-stakes testing. Thus, removing lower-achieving students from remedial classes and assigning them, instead, to special education classes allowed schools to report higher levels of achievement.

Regardless, the point is that many struggling readers were shifted from one federally funded support program to another. The problem is that few states require special education teachers to complete more than a single course in reading education. Thus, many struggling readers now had all of their reading instruction provided by someone with little preparation for teaching reading. When the federal government required pupils with disabilities to begin participating in state testing programs (1998–1999) the poor performance of pupils with disabilities prompted Congress to include those students in the requirement for demonstrating AYP. From a policy maker's perspective, improved, if not normalized, reading achievement was the reason why special education had been provided excess funding for individualized education. But the testing evidence indicated that most pupils with disabilities continued to struggle with reading and many demonstrated little improvement from year to year, even with special education services.

Suddenly, special educators were given a new charge: Accelerate the reading (and math) development of pupils with disabilities or risk the corrective actions required under NCLB—corrective actions that could cost educators their jobs. Congress originally allowed 1 percent of the total school population to not be tested on the standard state assessments. That has now risen to 2 percent of the total population. That 2 percent represents the proportion of the school population they feel is unable to meet state standards even with special education participation.

It was special education students who were least likely to make AYP in the first rounds of assessment required by NCLB. Suddenly, many schools are working hard to improve the quality and intensity of reading instruction provided to pupils with disabilities. Special education teachers are revising their instructional programs and, in many cases, looking for additional support from classroom reading programs or from reading specialists.

The evidence available to date (Allington, 2002a, 2006; Foorman & Torgeson, 2001) indicates that pupils with learning disabilities benefit most from the same evidence-based reading lessons that other children benefit from. What these struggling readers need are more lessons and more expert and intensive lessons (tutorials and very small-group lessons). There is little evidence supporting the notion that these students need some different sort of reading curriculum or reading lessons. When effective classroom instruction is combined with additional very small-group (two or three students) or tutorial instruction, almost all pupils with learning disabilities can demonstrate not just improved reading proficiencies but also reading proficiencies that begin to mirror those of their classroom peers. In fact, Mathes, Denton, Fletcher, Anthony, Francis, and Schatschneider (2005) found no significant differences in reading outcomes when pupils exhibiting reading and learning disabilities were provided with two quite different reading interventions in combination with enhanced classroom reading instruction. In other words, it seems that providing these students with expert, intensive small-group reading instruction is more important than the exact nature of the curriculum materials used.

Special education teachers will be under continuing pressure to accelerate their students' reading development. Working with classroom teachers to ensure high-quality classroom reading instruction and perhaps working with the reading specialist to design and deliver intensive, high-quality reading lessons seem the most promising path for developing the reading proficiencies of pupils with disabilities.

Other Professional Staff in Elementary Schools

The usefulness of other professional staff in an elementary school is best measured by the impact they have on enhancing the quality of classroom instruction. Examining the roles of other staff from this premise provides a substantially different view of their functions and utility.

Teachers of English Language Learners

Providing instructional support, especially for literacy learning, is critical when children are acquiring English-language proficiency. The fundamental goal of such support is to develop English proficiency as quickly as possible so that the child can prosper in the classroom where English is spoken. Developing native language literacy proficiency (e.g., reading and writing in Spanish) is the initial goal in some programs. Even in these programs, however, developing English language literacy is an ultimate goal (developing bilingual proficiency in English and the native language is a very desirable goal).

So how might teachers of English language learners (ELL) improve the instruction offered in elementary school classrooms? First, they need to be in those classrooms. Similar to the situation of other specialist teachers, ELL teachers simply cannot operate solely from separate classrooms. Ideally, they, too, become classroom-based consulting teachers who work with classroom teachers to improve their teaching of second language or bilingual children and work with the children on their classroom tasks.

At one elementary school in El Paso, Texas, the ELL teachers operate as classroom teachers and teach in Spanish and English, and children learn to read in both languages almost simultaneously. Some classroom teachers are not proficiently bilingual themselves and offer most instruction in English (to students who exhibit dominant English-language proficiency or whose parents wish an English-dominant program). However, the teachers meet as grade-level teams without regard to classroom language. Bilingual teachers have translated English big books into Spanish and translated Spanish big books into English. Both versions of these books are shared in all classes. The bilingual teachers share their expertise concerning problems that appear for Spanish-speakers in the planned curriculum. They offer advice and support for the monolingual teachers in the grade-level team meetings.

At an elementary magnet school in Fairfax County, Virginia, a large percentage of the children do not speak English as their first language; the largest proportion of children speak Spanish. Instruction there is arranged around conceptual units. Units of instruction

Resources for Further Information

Roughly 10 percent of all schoolchildren have been identified as English language learners (ELLs). The percentage of ELLs has risen dramatically, doubling between 1992 and 2002, primarily as a result of expanded immigration. Two out of three Hispanic students and nine out of ten Asian students have at least one immigrant parent. The NCLB rules require that schools demonstrate that ELL students are making reading progress comparable to their English-speaking peers. As with other struggling readers, ELL students who struggle with reading will need high-quality classroom reading lessons, even if specialist-teacher ELL support is available. The good news is that effective reading and content lessons for ELLS share many of the features of effective reading lessons for English language students (e.g., using multisource/multilevel curriculum materials, engaging in instructionally useful conversations with the teacher and with peers, promoting activities that foster active involvement and engagement, focusing on strategies' instruction and use, and building core curriculum background knowledge).

One primary distinguishing feature of research-based lessons involving ELLs is attention to "comprehensible input." This isn't simply slowing and simplifying teacher talk but also may feature a small bit of both along with many other accommodations that assist students in understanding. To learn more about an effective lesson design for supporting ELL reading and writing, use the following resources.

Video: Hudec, J., & Short, D. (n.d.). *The SIOP model: Sheltered instruction for academic achievement.* Washington, DC: Center for Applied Linguistics.

Training Guide: Echevarria, J., Vogt, E., & Short, D. (2002). *Making content comprehensible for English learners: The SIOP model.* New York: Pearson/Allyn & Bacon.

Internet: www.siopinstitute.net

are organized around large concepts such as change, communication, or habitats. Within each unit, children explore a variety of topics depending on the curriculum demands and the children's interests. In the change unit, for example, second graders pursued the science topic of dinosaurs and fossils along with the social studies topic of families, communities, and family histories.

For half of each day, the classroom teacher teaches the language arts to the class, integrating as much as possible around the unit topic. This instruction is carried out in English. For the other half of the day, the classroom teacher offers instruction in science, health, and math, again integrating as much as possible. During the science, health, and math half of the day, a bilingual teacher takes six to seven children from each of three second-grade classrooms and does the same science, health, and math content with them in Spanish. This Spanish immersion group includes some native Spanish-speakers as well as some native English-speakers whose parents want them to become bilingual and choose to have them participate in the half-day Spanish instruction.

This two-way immersion arrangement has many advantages (and is now used in over 200 schools). The unit–topic integration is one of the major curriculum adaptations recommended for schools containing a large portion of children whose first language is not English (Chamot & O'Malley, 1994; Christian & Genesee, 1998). Children appear to develop fluency in English speaking, listening, reading, and writing when their instruction is intensively focused on one topic through which they can learn vocabulary and increase their background knowledge. By focusing on the same topic in both Spanish and English, children from both native languages can transfer whatever prior knowledge they have. Including native English-speakers in the Spanish half of the day allows the native Spanish-speaking children to help translate as needed. These native English-speaking friends can return the favor for the native Spanish-speakers in the English immersion half of the day. Using science, health, and math as the content of instruction during the Spanish half of the day ensures that children whose native language is Spanish do not fall behind in this content as they acquire English.

We think these schools offer incredibly powerful models for providing high-quality instruction and using the talents of all children regardless of the language they come to school with. In both cases, the bilingual education teachers enhance the quality of classroom instruction and enhance the learning of many children beyond those targeted for special assistance. (For further information on two-way immersion programs contact the Center for Research on Diversity and Excellence at the Center for Applied Linguistics, www.cal.org/crede.)

Teachers of the Gifted and Talented

Many schools created gifted and talented programs in the same model as the special education and remedial programs—hiring a special teacher who pulled selected children from their classrooms a few times each week to work on projects wholly unrelated to classroom lessons. The popularity of this model has declined, but the model is still in use in some locales. A more powerful alternative that has become popular shifts the focus away from working with a small group of children identified on the basis of some standardized test score to a consultative model with a more invitational approach to participation.

It is becoming more common today to find teachers of the gifted and talented working with classroom teachers to develop and extend study of a core curriculum topic for interested students. Gardner's (1993) notion of "multiple intelligences" has also been influential in reshaping the nature of such programs. In this case the focus has shifted away from narrowly defined academic skills to a broader view of intelligence that includes artistic, musical, movement, athletic, verbal, and performance skills as components of intellectual competence. When the gifted and talented teacher works alongside the classroom teacher to tailor curriculum demands and activities to extend the learning of selected students, improved classroom instruction is more likely to occur.

Some schools, however, have elected to invest funds in strengthening the classroom instruction so that all students, but especially those identified as gifted, are better served. For instance, in lieu of investing in another specialist teacher salary (and associated fringe benefits and supplies), a school might take the roughly $50,000 annual cost and invest in both additional materials and professional development activities. In an elementary school with 20 classroom teachers, that would result in an annual fund of $2,500 per classroom per year. These funds might go to purchase more and better text resources (e.g., encyclopedias, atlases, magazines, children's books) and improved computer equipment (with telecommunications and CD-ROM capabilities, or simulation games such as SimCity) or to fund a teacher's attendance and participation in a conference on adapting instruction for academically talented children or visit to another school with a classroom-based model already in place. Over five years this design would result in an investment of a quarter-million dollars in enhancing the school capacity for better meeting the needs of academically talented children. Each classroom teacher would have had the opportunity to invest over $10,000 toward the goal of improving the quality of classroom instruction. All the money invested continues to pay dividends to all children.

School Librarians

How does a librarian work to enhance the quality of classroom instruction? Not by checking books in and out of the library according to the guidelines published by American Library Association (1998) in its monograph, *Information Power*. That is a task better assigned to a paraprofessional clerk or to parent volunteers. Librarians can support and improve classroom instruction when they spend much of their time locating resource materials to support classroom teachers' topic-centered units or classroom interest areas. Librarians improve classroom instruction when they support students in developing improved problem formation strategies and search strategies for research projects. Librarians improve classroom instruction by keeping the library open for extended hours so that students (and their parents) might use the resources when completing classroom projects and assignments. Librarians can and should play potentially powerful roles in shaping and supporting improved classroom instruction.

Social Workers

There has been a recent interest in adding social workers to the school professional staff. Social workers might improve classroom instruction by working with families to improve their capacity to support their children's development of academic and social skills. They might help children and their families gain access to needed health and social services so that children who need eyeglasses, for instance, are assured of getting them as quickly as possible. Social workers might work with children outside the regular school day in either individual or small-group sessions. However, if children are pulled out of classes to meet with the social worker, the situation is more likely to interfere with classroom learning opportunities than expand them. To avoid this, school social workers could work from early afternoon until mid-evening. This arrangement would allow contact with teachers at the end of their workday and create the opportunity for family interventions that are more accommodating to most family schedules and are more powerful than student-based interventions.

School Psychologists

Currently, many school psychologists have narrowly defined job responsibilities consisting primarily of completing individualized assessments of students' achievements and aptitudes as part of the process of completing referrals for identifying students with disabilities. This is unfortunate, and the National Association of School Psychologists is working to end this narrow role definition (www.naspweb.org). The more appropriate role, in the association's view, would be primarily consultative and classroom based. In other words, school psychologists would focus more time and effort on assisting classroom teachers in modifying the classroom environment or improving student performance in the classroom.

This recommended role seems to better fit the premise that support staff in a school should be primarily concerned with improving classroom instruction. The shift away from simply testing children and preparing assessment reports is also supported by research on the limited validity of the testing for classifying students and the limited role the testing actually plays in the special education referral and placement process (Allington & McGill-Franzen, 1996; Mehan, Hartweck, & Meihls, 1986). Reducing the reliance on standardized testing while shifting to more classroom-based evaluations of student performance creates a powerful alternative to the simple labeling of children. The shift to a consulting model for working with teachers in adapting their practices and modifying student behavior substantially improves the likelihood that classroom instruction will be enhanced.

Speech and Language Teachers

Mostly primary-grade children receive speech and language services in schools. The most frequently used program design has children leaving the classroom individually or in small groups to work with a speech and language teacher several times a week. This model, however, shows little promise for improving classroom instruction. An improved model places the speech and language teacher in the classroom for most services and targets much heavier reliance on collaborating with the classroom teacher in planning interventions linked to classroom literacy lessons and strategies that support the child's monitoring of appropriate language production.

At the very least, the intervention emphasis must be split between classroom support and individual or small-group lessons. When the strategies developed in such lessons are linked to the classroom lessons and supported and extended by the classroom teacher, children can be expected to make better progress. Only small and slow improvements can be expected when language lessons are offered in isolation from the classroom and unsupported during the many hours of classroom instruction.

Paraprofessionals and Volunteers

Most schools make use of paraprofessionals; most have at least a few peer tutors and adult volunteers. Each of these roles can provide useful support for classroom instruction, but each needs to be handled somewhat judiciously to ensure that classroom instruction is improved.

Paraprofessionals

There are a number of good reasons for schools to employ community residents as paraprofessionals. They include

- Ensuring community members' active involvement in the school
- Increasing ethnic and language diversity in the school
- Freeing teachers to focus on academic, rather than clerical or management, tasks
- Increasing employment opportunities in low-income neighborhoods
- Reducing costs compared with hiring more teachers

Little evidence suggests, however, that actually using paraprofessionals to instruct children, even under a teacher's supervision, benefits the children served (Anderson & Pellicier, 1990; Gerber, Finn, Achilles, & Boyd-Zaharias, 2001; Rowan & Guthrie, 1989). Consider that most paraprofessionals are employed in remedial or special education

The Ten Best Jobs for Aides

1. Binding children's stories into books
2. Running the school bookstore
3. Reshelving library books
4. Collecting and distributing book club orders
5. Using a word processor to prepare "galley proofs" of student work
6. Assisting students publishing a school newspaper
7. Reading to students
8. Rehearsing students in Reader's Theater performances
9. Monitoring students in the classroom to free the teacher to work individually
10. Taking attendance, lunch counts, medical slips, and setting up and cleaning up after projects while the teacher teaches

programs. Using the least well-trained adults to instruct children with the most complex learning difficulties simply does not make sense. Few schools employ paraprofessionals to work with children who are gifted or to work in advanced-placement classes. Consider that schools with fewer poor children employ fewer paraprofessionals. Why is it that paraprofessionals are most likely employed in schools with many poor and special needs children, in schools with patterns of low achievement?

Paraprofessionals are a relatively recent addition to the educational workforce. In the late 1950s, the Fund for the Advancement of Education (Stoddard, 1957) created a blueprint for "the schools of tomorrow." Professionalization of teaching was set as a major goal, and the report decried the substantial time that teachers spent in nonacademic activity. Paraprofessionals were offered as one reasonable solution to altering that situation. Teacher aides, the report declared, would allow the redeployment of teacher time so as to provide more teaching service to each pupil and make it possible for teachers to meet children's individual needs better. Aides would be assigned the duties that occupied roughly one-fourth of teachers' time (attendance, bathroom, lunch, recess, cleanup, preparing to leave, clerical work, and so on). The report noted, "Careful lines are to be drawn between those teaching functions to be performed by the teacher and those chores and other non-professional duties that could be performed by an aide."

The Five Worst Jobs for Aides

1. Tutoring low-achieving children
2. Drilling and practicing skills in isolation with low-achieving children
3. Providing seatwork assistance to low-achieving children
4. Guiding oral reading of low-achieving children
5. Providing small-group lessons for low-achieving children

However, in an odd turn of events, at least for struggling readers, many schools have come to rely on aides to replace the teacher and to function as tutors, albeit usually with some minimal supervision. Today this seems more often true when aides are funded from special-program funds. Title 1 remedial reading aides, for instance, report spending 60 percent of their time working with small groups and 30 percent in a tutorial setting serving an average of 31 students each day. Schools enrolling many poor children are twice as likely to employ aides as other schools (Millsap, Moss, & Gamse, 1993; Stullich, 2000). The situation seems not especially different with special education aides. The instruction that aides offer is typically focused on low-level tasks and often seems more likely to foster dependence on adults than independent achievement.

Currently, then, paraprofessionals are routinely deployed to work with struggling readers, which is unlikely to enhance the quality of instruction these children receive. If aides were well trained, the situation might be less dismal, but most aides receive little training before or after they begin their job (Downing, Ryndak, & Clark, 2000). A few studies have shown that training in specific instructional roles and routines can enhance the quality of the educational intervention offered and improve the outcomes for children working with those aides (Brown, Morris, et al., 2005). But such training is relatively rare.

Paraprofessionals might enhance the instruction offered in the classroom for some children while not enhancing the instruction offered other children. For instance, one common use of paraprofessionals is to have them work with the lowest-achieving children while the teacher works with higher-achieving children. This design enhances the likelihood that the instruction for the teacher's group will be improved because the teacher does not have to monitor the low-achievement children. However, the design offers little chance of improving the instruction offered low-achieving children.

The Tennessee STAR study has received much attention because of the rich and powerful evidence it provided on the benefits of class size reduction (Achilles, 1999; Gerber, Finn, Achilles, & Boyd-Zaharias, 2001). Largely unnoticed were the data on the impact of putting teacher aides in every classroom. The study compared large classes (25+), small classes (15–18), and large classes with a full-time aide. Achievement patterns demonstrated highest achievement in small classes, next in order were large classes, and trailing both others were the large classes with full-time aides. Activity logs suggest that struggling readers in the classrooms with aides received the smallest amount of high-quality instruction, mostly because the aides spent more time working with them than did the classroom teachers. The data from this study are producing a shift in federal program rules away from using aides and paraprofessionals in instructional roles.

The "time replacement" model allowed under federal program guidelines is one alternative that can actually improve the instruction for low-achieving children. In this case, the paraprofessional works with the higher-achieving students and frees the classroom teacher to work with low-achieving students. Of course, this results in a reduced likelihood that instruction is improved for the higher-achieving students. Nonetheless, this model seems preferable because it enhances the instruction of the children most in need of more and better teaching.

Paraprofessionals can be employed in ways that improve classroom instruction, but both program design and paraprofessional training need to be focused on that goal if it is to occur. Likewise, classroom teachers need clear understanding of how paraprofessionals might be most profitably used. Too often, neither the paraprofessional staff nor the classroom teachers have received adequate training in the most effective roles that paraprofessionals might play.

The NCLB and IDEA regulations require that paraprofessionals be directly supervised by certified teachers if they are involved in any instructional role. This means that the teacher develops the lesson, including selection of the materials, and provides guidance in the lesson delivery. In addition, the certified teacher is responsible for regular monitoring of student progress in the lessons delivered by paraprofessionals.

We believe that schools should develop career ladders for teacher aides. It is difficult to recommend that aides be allowed in instructional roles without some substantial training (and only then with supervision). Untrained paraprofessional staff might do some of the clerical work and "chores" of teachers and might even be allowed to monitor hallways and playgrounds (although the potential liability problems in such cases seem enormous). The following illustrates a formal delineation of paraprofessional roles that schools might create:

Level 1. Office clerical, classroom chores, AV equipment setup, hallway/entrance monitoring. No specific training in child development but some in communication with staff and parents, general training in educational procedures, and so on. Aides assist teachers in duplicating materials, binding books, helping with classroom cleanup after project time, locating and setting up audiovisual equipment, and performing a variety of other tasks that do not require direct work with children.

Level 2. General classroom support with some direct instructional contact with children. Initial training in child development, human learning, principles of effective instruction, general classroom procedures, and so on, with a one-year supervised internship (paid). At this level, aides would continue with some Level 1 assignments but would also have some direct contact with children. Aides might monitor the classroom, for instance, while the teacher worked with individual or small groups of students. They might read to children or assist in organizing a Reader's Theater project or a book publishing. Of course, aides would receive substantial training on how to effectively accomplish those instructional activities.

Level 3. Instructional responsibilities under direct supervision of certified personnel. Aides earn a two-year postsecondary degree with emphasis on human development and educational processes and satisfactory completion of a two-year internship (paid). They would learn how to observe and record student behavior, as well as strategies for monitoring students while working independently, interviewing students, supporting students during reading and writing, and searching for books and information generally. These responsibilities would require good verbal skills and familiarity with curriculum materials and classroom instructional contexts. Ongoing training would be regularly provided. Level 3 aides would become potential candidates for progressing to a bachelor's degree and teacher certification.

This proposal is not unlike some proposals already in existence in several states and those supported generally by the American Federation of Teachers (www.aft.org/psrp). Ongoing staff development would be provided for aides in all categories (most aides now receive less than 9 hours a year of training). Training for classroom teachers is also needed if they are to make most effective use of aides. In many cases, Level 3 aides and teachers might often share the same training sessions.

We would evaluate the use of teacher aides in the same way we evaluate other staff: Does their presence positively affect the quality of classroom instruction? We have no doubt that aides can be trained and employed in ways that routinely lead to an affirmative response, but aides are not teachers and cannot be expected to expertly address the educational needs of struggling readers and writers.

Volunteers

Adult volunteers also work in most schools. The nature of the volunteers' work is wide ranging, from clerical work in the school library to actual tutorial assistance in some schools. Volunteers work in both before- and after-school programs as well as during the school day. Some work for only short periods, to help construct a new playground or to put on a Christmas pageant, for instance. Others work for longer terms, in some cases for nearly a lifetime.

The guest reader format is one short-term, usually single-visit, volunteer opportunity that seems to have the potential for enormous payoffs. The guest reader might be a parent or another community member who comes into the school or a classroom to read from a favorite book. Usually the guest reader talks about the book and why it was selected. He or she may also stay and respond to children's questions about the book or the reader's reading habits more generally. In many cases, bringing in adult males as guest readers has been emphasized. For instance, one school invited male firefighters, police officers, college athletes, construction workers, barbers, and other men to read once a month or so in various classrooms. This program was designed to provide adult male reader role models for the boys in the school, some of whom were from single-parent families and had had few opportunities to see men reading and writing.

One volunteer tutoring model is offered in *Book Buddies: Guidelines for Volunteer Tutors of Emergent and Early Readers* by Johnston, Invernizzi, and Juel (1998). Certified reading teachers are tapped as a site coordinator for each school. The site coordinator trains the tutors, monitors their tutoring, and provides feedback and support for improved lesson designs. Each school also has a volunteer who works as a volunteer recruiter and coordinator to match schedules of tutors and children. Some tutors do work with students during the school day, but the emphasis is on before- and after-school tutoring. Tutors meet twice a week with their student and follow a structured lesson model that involves lots of reading of appropriate books as well as word work that integrates phonics, spelling, and reading. The research evidence on the Book Buddies effect on reading achievement is quite impressive.

A school has a wonderful opportunity to immediately affect the quality of its instruction when new personnel are considered for employment. To ensure that new personnel fit the new roles described, it is important to design the application and interview process so that experience with and enthusiasm for collaboration, integrated curriculum, inclusion, and authentic assessment—to name a few—are addressed. For instance, the job posting for several positions at South Lake Middle School in Irvine, California, listed the following common elements necessary for all positions:

- Knowledge, understanding, and successful exhibition of integrating curriculum and providing connectedness for all learners
- Knowledge, understanding, and successful exhibition of authentic assessment
- Successful demonstration of working as a flexible, contributing member of a team of professionals
- Understanding of the use of technology to support learning
- Active pursuit of continual professional growth and commitment to supporting colleagues' growth

When the opportunity to employ new staff arises, take advantage of that opportunity. Ask about previous collaborative teaching experience, about experiences with inclusionary education, about past work with paraprofessionals and the librarian or art teacher. Involve other instructional staff in the interview and decision-making process. These are the people who will have to work with the new staff member. Most important, do not forget to ask what the candidate has read lately. If we want teachers who develop readers and writers, we need teachers who read and write themselves.

We have visited schools where volunteer parents and high school students work with children to create their own dramatic performances of children's literature. In another school, college students majoring in dance work with children to create interpretations of poetry, song lyrics, and fairy tales they have read. In another case, college athletes tutor low-achieving children, resulting in improved academic achievement for both groups. In some instances, tutors are awarded released time from their regular jobs to tutor children. Some schools make use of retirees as tutors. In many cases, the volunteers work with children outside regular school hours so as to not interrupt classroom instruction. In the most fruitful efforts, the volunteers are provided substantial training before they work with children (Wasik, 1998).

The use of volunteers should also be evaluated by asking whether their presence improves the quality of classroom instruction for struggling readers. Volunteers can play potentially powerful roles in schools seeking to improve the responsiveness of programs to children's needs. But volunteers who are not well trained cannot routinely be expected to offer high-quality support. Also, if volunteers work during the school day (as opposed to working in before- or after-school programs), we must ask whether their activities are so powerful that they can replace effective classroom instruction.

Administrators Matter

This chapter began with a rationale for refocusing school improvement efforts on classroom teachers. To close the chapter, a focus on the importance of school administrators seems appropriate. The primary work of the school administrator is the improvement of classroom instruction in the school. Accomplishing this goal requires substantial familiarity with classrooms in the school and with all those other adults that work there. Working to improve literacy instruction, specifically, requires a fair amount of expertise about fostering literacy development and substantial skills in fostering collaborative relationships. Both areas of expertise have become more important to the role of the administrator as the nature of literacy demands change and as research points to the benefits of more teacher involvement in the administration of a school (Leithwood & Jantzi, 1999).

Various terms reflect the changing nature of literacy demands and the changed expectations for school outcomes. Some refer to the *new literacy,* others *thoughtful literacy,* and still others *higher-order literacy.* Regardless of the label, emphasis has shifted away from the achievement of minimum literacy competencies and toward fostering thinking through problem solving, application, and discussion. Likewise, whether the term is *teacher empowerment, site-based management, building leadership councils, shared decision making,* or something else, the evidence available suggests a need to move away from central-office decision making and toward building-level decision making with decision-making teams that involve teachers and parents, not just administrators (Johnston et al., 1998).

Both shifts demand administrators with additional skills, knowledge, and aptitudes for working with people. Both involve negotiating new procedures, processes, and program emphases. We have argued that the classroom teacher and classroom instruction must necessarily be the focus of efforts to reformulate schools. Thus, the primary task of both district and school administrators becomes one of orchestrating resources and collaborative efforts toward improving classroom instruction.

In many schools, change has been the result of much effort, leadership, and support from district or building administrators. In other schools, change has been more difficult because administrators hindered progress more often than they fostered it.

Twenty-seven centuries ago the Chinese philosopher Lao Tzu wrote about effective leaders: When their task is accomplished, their work done, the people all remark, "We have done it ourselves."

Administrators have critically important roles in reculturing and restructuring elementary schools. However, not every school will have an administrator who can or is willing to lead the change process. In such cases, it is most often the teachers who take the lead and who support each other.

But for teachers to take the lead requires supportive administrators at both district and building levels. Ideally, leadership and support are available from school district administrators, especially for building administrators' efforts in supporting teachers. In other words, not only teachers need support—building administrators do also. Sometimes the best support is advice and information. In other cases it is help in accessing needed resources, or it may be providing an "outsider" evaluation documenting progress. To experiment, to take risks, building administrators need support from the central office.

It is not the case that elementary school administrators must have all the answers before the change process can begin (Barth, 1990). If that were so, change would never get started. It is also not the case that administrators have to take charge and lay out detailed plans for everyone. The ideal elementary principal is an experienced elementary educator who focuses on the quality of classroom instruction, facilitates collecting information on school programs, advocates for teachers and for children, and fosters reflection and collaboration on the part of those involved in the change process (Taylor, Pearson, Peterson, & Rodriguez, 2005).

Administrators also need to foster support for change in the community. Often parents are quite comfortable with the existing arrangements, especially the parents we are most likely to hear from—the parents of the achieving children. Administrators need to foster both parent confidence and community confidence, usually by inviting parent and community participation in planning changes. In some cases, simply keeping the community well informed will be sufficient. As schools experiment with various forms of site-based management, administrators must develop the skills needed to organize effectively and to support teacher and parent management teams.

Still, it remains essential that administrators have some good sense of what high-quality schools for all children might look like. Administrators must be able to find information needed to weigh the options available. Administrators need to know how to gather, organize, and present information on the effects of decisions about school programs. Administrators need to ask not "Are we doing things right?" but "Are we doing the right things?"

Summary

Effective classroom teachers are the only absolutely essential element of an effective school. Everyone else in the school is employed simply to enhance the quality of classroom instruction. One can imagine an effective school without a group of remedial teachers, without a school psychologist, without a gifted and talented teacher, without a social worker, and even without an administrator. Improving schools requires that classroom instruction improve.

However, there is little evidence that support staff roles are currently defined as primarily focused on improving classroom instruction. If schools are to become more effective, either those roles require redefinition or the support staff positions should be considered for elimination. The questions that need to be asked are these: What could we purchase with the special-program funds that will be most likely to enhance the quality of classroom instruction for struggling readers? What sorts of expenditures will benefit these children most? When there is limited evidence that special-program staff are routinely improving classroom instruction, it is time to consider other ways the funds might be spent.

For too long educational policy in the United States has simply been to add more and more specialists to the staff of the elementary school, especially elementary schools serving large concentrations of low-income children. Little attention has been paid to the potential interrelationships or conflicts that might arise from this milieu of additional personnel. In some cases these additions have resulted in school days that are so fragmented and classrooms where so many children come and go so often that running an effective classroom instructional program has become almost impossible.

In rethinking how elementary schools might better serve all children, it will be essential to begin by clearly examining who does what. A first step in restructuring the elementary school will be to redefine the roles that everyone plays. Classroom teachers will necessarily have to take more responsibility for teaching all children. Specialist staff roles must be reshaped to clearly indicate that their primary purpose is to improve classroom instruction. The administrator's role will also change to supporter of classroom instruction, negotiator of collaborative efforts, and resource seeker.

chapter 6

Time:
Minutes, Hours, Days, Weeks, Years

Time matters in teaching and learning. Time is truly important for struggling learners. These children have no time to waste. There has been much discussion of the quantity of the time children in the United States spend in school, usually in relation to the amount of time children in other nations spend there. Classroom research has often reported on time allocations in teaching and the use of the time that is available. Teachers are often heard to complain that there is not enough time to do all that needs to be done. Legislators are now mandating (and sometimes funding) extended instructional time programs such as after-school and

summer-school programs. In this chapter we explore ways in which instructional time might be found or created in elementary schools. We begin with a brief review of the importance of time allocations for teaching.

Time Is Important in Teaching and Learning

Across virtually every study of classroom effectiveness in elementary schools, one finding stands out: Teachers who allocate more time to reading and language arts instruction are the teachers whose children show the greatest gains in literacy development. Another finding of those studies is that the amount of time allocated to teaching reading and writing varies substantially from school to school. Often, much variation can be found within a school as different teachers schedule more or less reading and writing time (Denham & Lieberman, 1980; Knapp, 1995).

Surprisingly, though, schools with many children from lower-income families routinely seem to schedule less instructional time for classroom reading and language arts than do schools with few poor children (Birman, 1988; Roth, Brooks-Dunn, Linver, & Hofferth, 2002). In these national studies teachers in schools with the fewest low-income children routinely allocated substantially longer periods of time for teaching reading and writing than did schools with many poor children—about 25 percent more time each day. Another way of looking at those findings is that schools with lower reading achievement routinely allocated less time for reading instruction than did schools with higher achievement.

Another large-scale study of high-achieving, higher-poverty schools found that in low-income schools that exceeded expected achievement levels substantial blocks of time were allocated for literacy teaching and learning (Knapp, 1995). Children attending these high-achieving, higher-poverty schools also spent more time actually reading and writing than did children attending lower-achieving schools. Both the time allocated for reading instruction and the time students actually spent reading and writing were substantially higher in the high-achieving schools than in the lower-achieving schools.

In a study using teacher-reported time from a large national sample of elementary school teachers, Roth and her colleagues (2002) found that the typical school day was 6 hours and 35 minutes. But three clusters of time scheduled emerged: 6-hour, 6½-hour, and 7-hour days. Students attending schools with the shortest days (6 hours) attended school for 180 fewer hours a year than the 7-hour-day students. Students in the longest-day schools spent an average of an additional 30 minutes daily on traditional academic subjects (reading/language arts, math, science, social studies) than students attending the schools with the shortest day. They also found that teachers in classrooms enrolling predominantly white students were significantly more likely to work in schools with longer school days than were teachers whose classrooms were comprised of primarily minority students. This difference in scheduled time represents roughly a half-day of additional academic time each week or two days per month or roughly an additional month of instruction each school year. Overall 2 hours and 10 minutes of each day were devoted to nonacademic activities (e.g., routines, snack, lunch, recess, enrichment). In the areas of enrichment and recess the school days of minority and majority students also differed. Whereas only 15 percent of the teachers of white children reported no recess period, 40 percent of teachers of African American students reported no recess as part of the daily schedule.

This study suggests that some states and school districts have developed school day schedules that offer teachers substantially more opportunities to teach and provide students with more time to learn. The data from this study did not explain why such wide differences in time scheduled existed. Perhaps it is state or local traditions that would explain the variation. No matter what the reason, such variation in time scheduled would seem to be one source of the variation in achievement between schools serving different communities.

Cameron, Connor, and Morrison (2005) report an observational study of first-grade classrooms. They found that, on average, teachers spent 54 minutes per day in transitional, nonacademic activities (line up, wait for start of lesson, distribute materials, take attendance, clean up, have snack, manage disruptions). They also found wide variation (from 14–129 minutes) between the classrooms. They also found that an average of 22 minutes per day were spent on orient/organize activities (discussion of what is coming next, how to plan time, options available, etc.). Again wide variation (from 2–59 minutes) existed from classroom to classroom. Even without accounting for time spent in lunch, recess, and other nonacademic periods, over an hour each day was lost to academic instruction in the typical classroom and almost 3 hours a day were lost in the least well-organized classrooms.

These studies suggest that two factors, school district schedule and teacher use of scheduled time, account for much of the variation in how much time is used for academic instruction during the school day. One might wonder why so much variation exists in both daily time scheduled and how teachers choose to use that time.

One possible explanation for a common finding—less time for literacy lessons in schools with high concentrations of poor children—may be linked to the beliefs of the professional staff in the school. If poor children are seen as slow, unmotivated, or unlikely to ever achieve grade-level proficiency, then teachers and administrators would be acting contrary to their beliefs if they designed programs that attempted to accelerate literacy learning (Allington et al., 1997). A key finding from a number of studies of effective schools and classrooms has been the high expectations for learning. Another way of looking at those data is that teachers and administrators in those schools and classrooms believed they could teach all children effectively.

More effective teachers see themselves as powerful agents of change. They believe their efforts are at the roots of the success their children have. Less effective teachers often reported feeling ineffective in dealing with the struggling readers in their classrooms. They opted to assign much of the responsibility for struggling readers' achievement to special programs. One result of such differences in beliefs was readily observed in the classroom. The more effective teachers worked more often and more intensively with the struggling readers in their classrooms than did the less effective teachers (Day, 2001; Pressley et al., 2001).

Teachers' beliefs develop within a school's organizational context. Several years ago, we were asked to work with an urban elementary school where reading achievement was substantially below both national and district averages and ranked near the bottom of all city schools. After we spent one day in the building, a fundamental issue concerning instructional time surfaced. In this school, following an administrative directive, all classroom teachers offered 45 minutes of reading instruction daily. Contrast that three-quarters of an hour with the nearly two hours allocated in the suburban elementary schools our own children attended! Teachers in both schools had certain beliefs, shaped by administrative directives and expectations, about how much instruction was needed. How the 45-minute allocation came to be and how it was ultimately increased (substantially improved achievement was one result) is a long story, but the terrible fact remains that many children in the urban school were not acquiring literacy simply because they were not being taught very much. Because most teachers in the building had taught there for some time, they were unaware of how limited their time allocations for instruction were.

Time is important in elementary schools. Teachers who view developing children's literacy as among their most important tasks typically allocate larger amounts of time to literacy instruction than do teachers who rank literacy development lower on their list of priorities. Teachers who believe that all children can learn to read and write allocate more time than do teachers who believe that some children are unlikely to become literate. Teachers who see themselves as powerful influences on the reading development of their children work more often and more closely with their struggling readers (McGill-Franzen, 1994). But many of the teachers we talk with have no good idea of how much time they should be allocating to reading and writing instruction, and few have any good information on how much time other teachers allocate. Consider these common findings:

- Teachers in lower-achieving schools allocate less time for reading than do teachers in higher-achieving schools.
- In most schools, some teachers allocate twice as much time to reading instruction as other teachers.
- More effective teachers allocate more time for reading instruction and have their children read and write more than do less effective teachers.
- Most intervention programs for struggling readers do not increase the amount of time struggling students spend reading and writing.

Time Is Important in Teaching and Learning

Some Kids Need More Instruction and That Takes More Time

One way to think of the differences children bring with them as literacy learners is to view these differences as primarily differences in how much instruction and how much practice they will need to develop reading and writing proficiencies comparable to their peers'. Children exhibit real differences in the ease with which they acquire almost any skill, strategy, or understanding. Children also differ in the ease with which they acquire literacy. But understanding that some children will need more instruction or more opportunities to see a strategy modeled for them is quite different from viewing those children as unlikely literacy learners. Understanding the importance of providing more instruction and more reading and writing opportunities to children who find learning to read difficult forces us to consider how time to accomplish these increases might be captured or created.

The differences children exhibit in their proclivity for literacy learning may stem from several sources. Some of these differences may be explained by the experiences children have in their homes and communities. When children see adults reading and writing, they usually become interested in learning to read and write themselves. Of course, children who have many experiences with reading and writing before they come to school often arrive at school with a head start on literacy learning. Often their literacy has already "emerged," and they can recognize some words and many letters. They may arrive doing a fair approximation of writing. Children with far fewer of these experiences—the limited-experience children—start school behind their more advantaged peers. These children have invested less time in literacy activities, and usually their development lags behind that of those peers who have invested more time. Spending more time in school developing their literacy will undoubtedly be necessary, at least initially, until these children catch up with their peers.

Expanded preschool experiences rich in literacy learning might provide this extra time. The time might come by enrolling such children in summer-school programs before they enter kindergarten and between kindergarten and first grade. Parent training might be another possibility if started early enough and parents are supported adequately. But if children with few home experiences with print and stories, with little in the way of preschool experiences with print and stories, are just plunked down in kindergarten with more advantaged peers, then schools are placing these children at risk of never catching up. Children who have spent little time with books and print before they begin school will necessarily need more instructional time allocated to them when they arrive at school (McGill-Franzen, 2006).

Imagine this eager learner: Willie. Willie has been read to since he was able to focus on a book (about 6 months of age). Willie had his own magnetic letters and scribble pad with colored markers, but he never played much with those things. He preferred his Legos. Willie may be an engineer in the making—he was playing with the "eight-year-old-and-up" Lego kits before he started school. When Willie arrived at school, he did not do as well as his peers on letter naming and letter formation, coloring within lines, or tracing dot-to-dot figures. Willie preferred to play in the block area (the classroom had no Lego area). He was attentive during story-reading sessions—he loved a good story—but he liked building, stacking, and imaginative play with the small toy cars in his desk.

As the year wore on, Willie's teacher grew worried. During a parent conference, she mentioned her concerns to his parents. She also suggested that Willie seemed "developmentally unready" for promotion to first grade. Her comments spurred Willie's parents into action. They began to spend some time each evening working with Willie on letters and words. They reviewed schoolwork with Willie. They worked on proper letter formation with Willie. They played, making word games with the magnetic letters on the refrigerator. Willie got a strong dose of individual attention, especially from his mother, who had been a primary teacher before she went into educational sales.

Willie was promoted, but his parents hired a wonderful tutor to work with him during the summer and sent him to a summer day care program with an academic component. Willie entered first grade and never looked back. His parents continued their involvement throughout elementary school, and Willie thrived. He still liked Legos best of all, but he loved reading informational books (usually about cars, trucks, trains, and planes) and mystery books (he ultimately owned and read the complete *Encyclopedia Brown* series).

Willie's story is a middle-class kid story that recurs hundreds of thousands of times each year. His parents did what most middle-class parents do—they gave their child substantial amounts of high-quality literacy lessons to catch him up. If Willie had not had such well-educated and financially successful parents, his story might have turned out quite differently. We tell Willie's tale because it shows the effects of added instructional

It may be useful to gather a small bit of data on the use of time in your classroom or your school. The simplest procedure is to use an inexpensive stopwatch that allows you to collect cumulative time. Use a watch that allows you to turn it on when time is being used for nonacademic activities (e.g., attendance, announcement, directions, snacks, lining up, cleaning up, transitions, etc.) and to turn it off when the activity becomes focused on academic teaching and learning. Ideally the watch will simply keep track of the nonacademic time so that at the end of the day or the period you can jot down how much cumulative time was spent in nonacademic activity.

- You might track nonacademic time at the beginning of each day for one week to estimate how efficient the beginning-of-the-day school procedures are.
- You could collect the same sort of evidence for the end-of-the-school-day routines.

We mention these because our experience suggests that it is the beginning- and end-of-day routines that can most easily be made more efficient (use less time).

Some Kids Need More Instruction and That Takes More Time

time and individual instructional attention. Willie needed extra instructional time, and, luckily for him, his parents had the time, educational backgrounds, and financial resources to provide it. But when children are not as lucky as Willie, where will the additional time and individual instruction come from?

Children differ in how much instructional support they will need to become readers and writers. Some children, like Willie, are lucky to have parents with substantial educational, financial, and attitudinal resources. Other children need extraordinary instruction but must rely on the school to provide it. Whenever such support is needed, extra time must be found to schedule the extraordinary instruction. Both teaching and learning take time. Whenever children need more teaching, schools must find or create more time. Unfortunately, few schools organize instructional programs in ways that offer additional time for teaching children who need extraordinary support. Why? Perhaps because the differences in children's literacy learning are not viewed primarily as differences in the amount of instruction they will need to develop into readers and writers alongside their peers.

Creating Time to Teach and Learn

Most elementary schools in the United States are open for instruction for 180 to 190 days each year. Most children spend between five and seven hours a day in these schools. However, in many schools, one-third to one-half of the school day is scheduled for nonacademic activities (Roth et al., 2002). Routine activities such as arriving in the building and hanging up coats in cubbies or closets, taking attendance, making announcements, and gathering lunch money often take 15 to 30 minutes at the beginning of each school day. Recess and lunch periods combine to occupy another 45 to 60 minutes. Snack time, bathroom, safety patrol, birthday celebrations, holiday festivities, testing, and a host of other nonacademic activities may eat away another 30 to 50 minutes. Packing-up activities at the end of the day as children prepare to leave on different buses or as walkers and bus riders prepare to leave at spaced intervals take 15 to 20 minutes. Suddenly, the six and one-half hour school day offers only four hours of academic instructional time!

Over the past 40 years, most elementary schools have hired special-subject teachers to offer weekly art, music, and physical education classes for children. As libraries were developed in elementary schools, children were scheduled for weekly library visits. Thus, another 45 to 60 minutes each day are now typically scheduled for participation in these beneficial but non-core-curriculum activities. At the same time, in most states, additional topics have been added to the elementary school curriculum. Is it any wonder, then, that so many elementary school teachers report that the lack of time needed to get everything done that has to be done is one of the most pressing problems they face?

Consider that, to this point, we have not even addressed the issue of participation in special programs during the elementary school day. Children who participate in Title 1 or resource-room special education classes or in speech-therapy or gifted classes are usually scheduled out of their classrooms during the three or so hours that remain after the routine activities and the special subject classes are completed. Struggling readers often have no long blocks of uninterrupted literacy instruction; instead, they move from room to room, program to program, teacher to teacher, for their instruction (Johnston & Allington, 1991). This "planned fragmentation" of the elementary school day creates difficulties for classroom teachers as well. Some have no academic period in which all students are present! Often only relatively short blocks of time are available for classroom teachers in many elementary schools. However, coherent, high-quality classroom literacy instruction— essential for struggling readers—is most easily achieved when classroom teachers have large blocks of uninterrupted time.

"Safe" Blocks of Classroom Instructional Time

Teachers need time to teach. In some schools this basic truth seems, somehow, to have been forgotten. Most states mandate between 300 and 360 minutes a day of academic instructional time for elementary schools. In too many cases, however, one-third, or more, of the available academic time is consumed by a variety of nonacademic functions. In our experience, the higher the achievement in a school, the more academic learning time is honored and protected. In many of the lower-achieving schools that we have visited, the beginning of academic learning time does not coincide with the beginning of the school day. "Settling in" takes 15 to 20 minutes each morning. "Packing up" takes another 10 to 20 minutes each afternoon. Public address announcements, assemblies, snack breaks, and so on, consume another 20 to 30 minutes each day. We regularly find an hour of potential academic learning time lost to poor organizational planning.

The creation of "safe" blocks provides time for reading whole books.

What is most troubling is that in too many schools where achievement is low, we find no sense of urgency about instructional time. None. Academic learning is important. Altering a few organizational procedures could have a major impact in many schools. Such changes would provide 10 to 20 percent more time for teaching. Imagine that every child is at her or his desk reading within a minute of the beginning of the school day. Imagine that every child is writing when the final bell rings. Imagine how much more instructional time there could be if "settling in" tasks (attendance, Pledge of Allegiance, announcements, lunch counts, etc.) were completed before the first bell signaling the start of academic learning time. Imagine if "packing up" activities (afternoon announcements, room cleanup, jackets and boots, etc.) were done after the final bell. Just by changing beginning- and ending-of-the-day routines, we could recapture more time than many children now have to read and write all day. Schools must become more efficient in their use of instructional time. Teachers need time to teach. Children need time to learn.

Once the beginning- and ending-of-the-day routines are improved, a good next step would be the creation of "safe" periods or "safe" days in all classrooms. Safe periods would provide uninterrupted blocks of instructional time. For instance, primary-grade classrooms have the entire morning as a "safe" block in which no special subjects would intrude and no children would be scheduled for participation in special programs. Primary-grade classes would have art, music, physical education, and library only in the afternoons. Children who receive speech and language therapy and children who participate in Title 1, bilingual, or special education programs away from the classroom would be scheduled for those services in the afternoon. Thus, primary-grade teachers could plan to have the whole morning for instructing all children. Upper-grade classes would have the afternoon protected from intrusions. The special-subject classes and the special instructional programs would serve children in the upper grades during the morning time block.

Providing extended "safe" periods for classroom academic instruction would require little real restructuring of teachers' roles and responsibilities. In many cases, however, it would require that the schedules of special-subject teachers, special-program teachers, and special-program paraprofessionals be developed at the building level rather than at the district level. These schedules would need to be centrally developed in the building if "safe" periods were created. This change might require a revision in special-program applications to state and federal agencies. Nonetheless, creating "safe" periods is a good idea that seems easily achievable in most schools. What is required is a commitment to focus attention on the availability of classroom instructional time as the top priority in schedule making.

Extended-Day Plans

Another restructuring of school schedules can complement the creation of "safe" periods in the classroom. The basic notion is to extend the school day by a little or a lot for some or all children. We will describe a plan that extends the day a little for some children. But first it is critical to note that before teachers and administrators begin planning programs that keep children in the school building for more hours each day or more months each year, they must feel confident that they have already strengthened and expanded the instructional program during the regular school day.

Students who participate in special instructional programs during the school day receive no additional instructional time. In fact, good evidence suggests that these students actually experience a reduction in instructional time (Allington & McGill-Franzen, 1993).

Why should Ronald lose 20 to 25 minutes of instruction each day (1½ to 2 hours every week) just to go down the hall to complete workbook activities with an untrained teacher aide? By the time Ronald packs up and leaves his classroom, travels down the hall, greets the aide, waits for other children to arrive, and finally gets his vocabulary workbook from the aide, 10 to 12 minutes have passed since he put away his classroom work. The vocabulary workbook is the least effective way to develop vocabulary, and the aide offers no instruction; she is not allowed to "teach." Ronald works on some words that are not in his reader, his library book, or even his science book. When his pull-out session ends, it will take him another 10 to 12 minutes to pack up, say good-bye, travel back, and get re-engaged in classroom instruction. Ronald is scheduled for a half-hour of remediation, but he is actually "unavailable" for classroom instruction for 40 to 45 minutes each day, and he typically works about 20 of the 30 minutes for which he is scheduled. Given these time realities, the activities monitored by the aide need to be a lot more effective than his classroom lessons just to keep Ronald from falling farther behind. But they won't be, and Ronald won't get better at reading this year.

This reduction happens because it takes time to leave the classroom, travel to a special-program room, and settle in for instruction (and to leave that room, return to the class-room, and settle in). This lost time is called *transition time,* and it steals minutes every day. Even if transition time amounts to only 10 minutes a day (most studies indicate a 20- to 25-minute daily loss), nearly an hour each week is lost to children who participate daily. The loss of 10 minutes from a 30-minute special-program period means the special teacher has to be at least 50 percent more effective than the classroom teacher just to produce the same amount of progress children would make if they did not participate. In other words, time lost to transition means special-program teachers must teach more in less time to accomplish any improvement in achievement.

In addition, children who leave the classroom during the school day miss the instruction offered while they are absent. Currently, children who find learning to read difficult are likely to be scheduled for special instructional programs during some part of the classroom reading and language arts time. Thus, participation typically provides them not with more instruction but with different instruction. Without real increases in instructional time or intensity, special programs cannot be expected to accelerate children's literacy learning. Without a collaboratively planned, coherent curriculum focus, we can expect more often to confuse children than to assist them.

Using Flextime to Extend Struggling Readers' School Day   The problems of interrupted classroom instruction and decreased instructional time for struggling readers can be addressed in several ways. First, special-program teachers might be shifted onto flextime schedules. They would not work the same hours as classroom teachers. Depending on the school and the community, they might come to school an hour earlier than classroom teachers, or they might arrive an hour or more later. Some of the children who participate in the special instructional programs would then work with these teachers either before or after the regular school day. One school we visited used flextime to provide professional staff for an extensive after-school program—at no additional cost! In this case the remedial reading and special education teachers began their work day 90 minutes later than other teachers. Their work day was extended, then, by that period at the end of the day. These special-program teachers organized and supervised a 90-minute daily after-school volunteer tutoring program as well as providing small-group remediation to groups of targeted children who attended the after-school program.

In nearly all schools, some children walk to school and thus pose no transportation problems should their school day be extended. Even in schools where many children ride buses, bus transportation is often available after the regular school day as buses make several runs to transport children from different schools in the system. Even if special transportation must be arranged, the idea of working outside the regular school day has much to recommend it. Of course, flextime scheduling of special-program teachers would not allow all participating children to be served in an extended-day program, but moving even some of that instructional support into an extended-day program would expand the potential opportunity to learn for those children served.

One elementary school's faculty is scheduled in the building from 8:00 until 4:30 each day, and children attend from 8:45 until 3:00. Each teacher and administrator (and librarian, nurse, secretary, and janitor) works with one child for 20 minutes each day before school. Classroom teachers usually work with a child from their classrooms while others work with whichever children seem particularly well matched to their strengths and interests. In addition, a few other adults, usually parents of children who attend the school, also work before or after school with children. These adults typically work with kindergarten and first-grade children and simply sit with them while they read and reread simple predictable books. The children read or reread four or five of these little books each day.

These before-school efforts are so successful that only a few children participate in any remedial or special education program beyond second grade (although a few upper-grade children do come to the extended-day program when they need extra assistance). The children who participate vary as their need for extraordinary instructional support varies. Some children come regularly; others are scheduled only after an illness or when a brief review or reteaching is necessary.

Summer Programs

Summer-school programs offer the potential to expand children's opportunity to learn. Access to summer school seems especially important for struggling readers. Research suggests that disadvantaged children acquire literacy at approximately the same rate as their more advantaged peers during the school year. During the summer, advantaged children continue to develop literacy abilities (though not as rapidly as during the school year), while disadvantaged children actually lose literacy abilities (Allington & McGill-Franzen, 2003; Entwisle, Alexander, & Olson, 1997). This "summer reading loss" is critical because these children begin school with fewer literacy experiences than their more advantaged peers and thus are behind them in literacy development from the start of school. Although school experiences develop literacy in all children, economically disadvantaged children and struggling readers most often lose ground over the summer. Thus, even when the school is doing a good job, these children often cannot match their more advantaged peers' rate of literacy development year after year because the lack of summer reading experiences leads to an overall loss of some of the gains made in school.

Stemming Summer Reading Loss   If we want poor children to read during the summer, we might work to ensure children access to reading materials of appropriate difficulty and interest during the summer months. We could accomplish this by allowing library books to be checked out for the summer, through a summer reading book-loan program, or through simply giving children several books for summer reading. This approach is designed to promote summer reading by providing children with reading materials. It is a low-effort, low-cost model that will benefit only some children. But it seems particularly important when many students come from lower-income families, because they are the children who have the most limited access to books at home.

Another idea is to enhance community-based access to books, stories, and print activities during the summer months. Many towns and cities offer summer recreational activities for children, many quite educational though rarely book oriented. We think schools need to become much better partners with other community agencies, especially for the summer months. The basic notion is to work with these agencies to develop ways to improve children's opportunities to read and write during the summer.

For instance, in one town an honor library of children's books, mostly paperbacks, was set up at the town recreational park where children came to swim, play in Little League and soccer games, and participate in other forms of recreation. Children took home books they wanted to read, and everyone hoped they remembered to bring them back. The book collections were a bit ragtag to begin with and more so at the end of the summer, but hundreds of books were taken home each week and only a few were lost forever. Some of the recreation staff found that story-time activities were a wonderful way to occupy children during rest periods and waiting-for-parent periods at the end of the day. Such activities increased parental awareness of the honor library and increased the use of books by children.

These strategies are inexpensive because they involve no summer professional staff time. We offer this model because of its simplicity and potential for increasing the time children spend reading. Such plans could be easily expanded to other summer venues such as YMCA/YWCA camps and centers or even to neighborhood commercial establishments

The Arbor Hill Elementary School in Albany, New York, represents one example of the development of extended-day programs. Using a combination of local, state, and federal funding, Arbor Hill Elementary operates from 7:30 in the morning until well into the evening and offers Saturday-school and summer-school programs. An Early Bird Story Hour is staffed by paraprofessionals each morning before the school day officially begins. Then a breakfast program feeds most of the students before classes start at 8:45. After 3:00, when many urban elementary schools are emptying of children for the day, Arbor Hill Elementary begins a schedule of homework support sessions, piano lessons, drama club activities, karate, ballet, gymnastics, science projects, craft projects, and a Police Athletic League sports program. Nearly three-quarters of the 750 students participate in one or more of the scheduled activities. After 5:00, other activities are offered for students and their parents, including aerobics classes, adult and parent education sessions, and computer classes.

such as grocery stores or ice cream shops. The basic goal is to put books into the community and stimulate community interest in reading to and with children.

Schools might go a step further by opening the school library and, perhaps, arranging "reading clubs"—groups of children reading the same books or books on similar topics. Such activities might also be coordinated with community agencies. Most schools could move a bit more aggressively, but with a modest investment, to stem summer reading loss. Consider the Friday summer drop-in center. In this case, few staff members are needed and most activities are group oriented, often as cooperative learning groups. Most activities are scheduled in a single large-group area or outdoors, but the school library remains open. In some cases, bookstores, book fairs, and sleepy-time read-ins (everyone sleeps over in the gym) are also scheduled. Story-hour sessions are a regular feature, and older children are available to read selected books to small groups of preschoolers or primary students. Either morning hours or an evening schedule seems most popular. Parents are more often available in the evening for joint children and parent activities. This model emphasizes increasing the access children have to books but provides little in the way of instructional intervention. Thus, enhanced achievement results from additional independent reading more than from additional instruction. The need for only one or two staff members along with several volunteers (perhaps high school students or folks who are school-year volunteers) makes this an inexpensive option.

Extending Instructional Time   Many children, however, need more than opportunities to engage in reading to stem summer reading loss. Some need more instruction as well as more opportunities to practice reading and writing. In these cases, schools may need to rethink the school year. For instance, in some Philadelphia elementary schools that serve many economically disadvantaged children, the faculty decided to use federal Title 1 program funds to extend the school year for a month. Remedial services during the regular school year were substantially reduced to fund the summer-school effort. Teachers were interested in shifting to this extended-time model because the number of children participating in one or more special instructional programs during the school year had grown so large that classroom teachers felt they themselves had been rendered ineffective. So many children were coming from and going to special programs all day long that it was difficult to carry out effective classroom instruction. Moving to the summer-school design not only worked to reduce the children's summer reading losses but also enhanced classroom instructional efforts (Winfield, 1991).

Another school's summer program was redesigned so that all children participated in a daily half-hour tutorial focused on reading and writing strategy development, spent another hour and a half in independent and small-group literacy learning and practice, and spent a final hour in art, music, or creative dramatics linked to the books they were reading. The school also opened its library for the summer. This is an important consideration, for the books most elementary children read come from their schools (Lamme, 1976). Also, funds were allocated to give each child a paperback book each week for his or her bedroom library. This is important because many children have no books at home (Smith, Constantino, & Krashen, 1997).

A third school selected the Foxfire model for their summer-school effort. Children engaged in authentic literacy activities that included collecting and illustrating (with artwork and Polaroid photos) oral histories of buildings, companies, and people in the neighborhood. The summer school took the shape of collaborative work teams and probably looked more like a newsroom than an elementary school. But children were almost constantly reading, writing, editing, summarizing, transcribing, discussing, and illustrating real stories about real places and people. Using desktop publishing software, the students created reports of their work that were bound into books by paraprofessional staff in the fall and added to the school library collection.

Summer schools work when they expand children's opportunities to actually read and write and to receive instructional assistance and support. It is possible to design summer-school programs that do *not* work very well. In one program we studied, children attended

How Much Summer Reading?

It seems that older elementary school students don't actually have to read a lot to stem summer reading loss but they do have to read. Kim (2004) found that when sixth-grade students read four or five books over the summer no decline in reading achievement was found. When fewer books or no books were read over the summer, student reading achievement upon return to school had slipped. The students fell into three roughly equal groups: heavy readers, four or more books; moderate readers, one to three books; and nonreaders. In this study the school district required students to read over the summer and provided parents with a list of 120 appropriate titles. But fewer than half the parents returned the signed verification form and even fewer students turned in the required book reports. Students from more advantaged families were more likely to do both and ease of access to books was related to book reading behavior.

summer school in the morning for five weeks. But the only reading or writing instruction they received was during a daily half-hour instructional block. Even though instructional groups were small (three to four children), the daily half-hour resulted in only an additional 10 to 12 hours of reading instruction (or roughly equivalent to the reading time available during one and one-half weeks during the school year). No one should expect large gains from 10 to 12 hours of small-group instruction. In an attempt to make this summer program "fun," the planners included much playground time, much arts and craft time, and much breakfast, snack, and lunch time. Not much time was left for teaching children to read and, predictably, participation generally fostered little reading or writing development.

Support for summer-school and year-round programs is growing among parents as the number of work-outside-the-home mothers increases. The United States is no longer an agricultural society in which children are needed to work in the fields during the summer months. It may be that all schools need to consider expanding the school year, not so much to catch up with our international competitors but to catch up with the rest of U.S. society.

Making Sense of Time

Having tried hard to convince you that time is a critical issue in planning and organizing literacy-learning programs, we need to sort out a few of the bugaboos that enmesh issues of time in school. We first note that spending twice as much time engaging in ineffective instructional practices will hardly produce any desired result. Time matters, but how time is used matters more. Setting aside large blocks of uninterrupted time or extending the school day or year are good beginnings, but only beginning steps.

Scheduled Time

Much of what we have discussed concerning time falls into the category *scheduled time allocations*. In fact, much of what policy makers and educational planners usually discuss (and sometimes regulate) falls into this category. For instance, most state education agencies mandate the length of both the school day and the school year. Although these vary from state to state, the differences can be important. School districts also regulate time, most, but not all, usually elect to follow the minimum-length school day and year. Across a state, then, most kids go to school the same number of hours each day and the same number of days each year. This is so even though it is obvious to practically everyone that some districts have substantial numbers of children who are at risk of school failure and other districts have but few.

This situation may be changing, however. Recently, one state legislature considered revising the traditional compulsory attendance laws. Rather than setting a single standard of attendance for all students (say, 180 days), the proposed law sets attendance standards based, in large part, on student achievement. Schools would be required to offer year-round classes for children who were lagging behind peers academically (and were candidates for retention in grade or special education placement). The fundamental rationale for redefining compulsory attendance lies in the notion of expanding instructional opportunity for some children.

Perhaps it would be reasonable to have the length of the school day and school year differentiated by the characteristics of children who attend each school. Schools that enroll large numbers of children who have had few book and print experiences or children whose parents lack most of the educational and financial resources to provide extraordinary instruction for their children might be open year-round and routinely offer extended-day and Saturday school sessions. But that policy would only address the issue of planned time allocations. It would be a good first step, but how teachers and children use that time is even more important.

Sometimes even well-intentioned principals create interruptions during instructional blocks. During a recent morning observation in an elementary classroom, we listened to nine intercom interruptions. None of the announcements was particularly important—reminders about a school roller-skating party, a Cub Scout den meeting, a special soccer club program, a cafeteria menu change, an upcoming bake sale, and so on. Each announcement was made separately, and though each took less than a minute, it effectively stopped all classroom work while everyone stared up at the box on the wall. If schools use public address systems, use should be sharply limited to one or two brief periods at the very beginning or end of each day and in the case of real emergencies.

Allocated Time

Nearly all elementary schools in every state operate for the same number of hours each day, but these schools differ in *allocated academic learning time*. The school bell rings to start the school day but does not signal the beginning of time actually allocated to academic learning. Wander into almost any elementary school classroom and look at the schedule on the chalkboard or glance at the teacher's plan book. If the school bell rings at 9:00 to signal the official start of the day, in most classrooms academic learning time begins between 9:15 and 9:30, after the morning setting-up routines (attendance, lunch counts, announcements, flag, etc.) are completed. The length of setting-up time varies by school and by classroom within schools, depending on how efficiently organized the school is (Cameron et al., 2005). Within classrooms, routines vary; some teachers use less than half the time that others need to accomplish the daily setting-up activities because some teachers are better organized than others. In any event, in too many schools the start of the school day rarely signals the start of allocated learning time.

In addition to "settling in" activities, other scheduled activities reduce academic learning time. For instance, when lunch is scheduled for the period from 11:30 to 12:15, the actual loss of academic learning time usually extends from 11:20 to 12:30 because children and their teachers end an academic activity early to pass in papers, clean off desktops, and begin to line up to make an orderly exit to lunch. Similar losses of academic time

The amount of time allocated to reading instruction in the early grades seems to have declined over the years while the amount of time spent on other things has increased across the elementary school grades. The table below (derived from Borg, 1980) presents the average number of minutes allocated to reading instruction and to management, transition, and wait periods in second- and fifth-grade classrooms in three eras.

	Grade 2		Grade 5	
	Reading	*Nonacademic*	*Reading*	*Nonacademic*
1904	157	7	119	7
1926	137	11	108	10
1980	88	44	110	47

In addition, the amount of time spent in art, music, and physical education has increased, nearly doubling from 35 minutes to 65 minutes each day.

occur when children go to and return from recess periods and special classes or library visits. Whole-class bathroom breaks, snack periods, and unscheduled interruptions such as announcements over the intercom or visitors at the door also increase the loss of allocated learning time.

In our ideal elementary school, virtually all of the scheduled instructional time would be allocated to instruction. The school day would be restructured so that "settling in," "transitioning," and "packing up" activities were completed outside scheduled instructional time, before or after the official instructional day.

Available Time

Scheduled academic learning time always exceeds *available academic learning time.* Not all the time actually available for academic learning is necessarily used for academic activities by each classroom teacher. Even if it were, there would likely be substantial differences in how different teachers elected to use it. Consider, for instance, that in one study of 100 classrooms (Fisher & Berliner, 1985) second-grade teachers spent from 60 to 140 minutes a day on reading instruction; or that over a school year, one fifth-grade class had less than 1,000 minutes of comprehension instruction (less than 10 minutes daily), while other classes offered more than 5,000 minutes; or that one second-grade class spent 9 minutes of instructional time on money concepts, while other classes averaged 315 minutes. Such differences can sometimes be explained by noting that different teachers emphasize different subjects and different content within a subject. In other cases, the differences are explained by noting substantially different uses of available academic learning time; some teachers simply get to teaching more quickly and more often than do others.

We have found that teachers often do not have a clear sense of how much of the available academic learning time should be allocated to reading and language arts instruction. In many schools, teachers seemed to have worked out a consensus on this issue, but in others, no one seems very much aware of what others are doing or how much time they allocate for different subjects. At times, teachers are surprised to find out that they allocate only half as much time to reading and language arts activities as other teachers at the same grade level in their building. We are not suggesting that such issues be mandated but rather that time allocations be discussed and considered.

In our ideal elementary school, the administration and staff would have engaged in serious discussions concerning how much time would be made available for reading and writing instruction. Based on the best research available, we would expect that 120 to 150 minutes each day would be available for literacy lessons in grades K–6.

Engaged Time

Even when similar amounts of time are allocated to reading and language arts activities in classrooms, major differences in literacy-learning outcomes can occur, because attention to learning is normally a prerequisite to actual learning. Again, classrooms differ in student engagement in the learning activities. The amount of *time engaged in learning* is the most potent predictor of literacy learning (and most other sorts of learning). In the study of 100 teachers mentioned above, it was noted that in some classrooms about half the children were actually engaged in the learning activities in front of them, while in other classrooms about 90 percent were engaged. Children who are engaged in academic work learn more than those children who are simply sitting at their desks waiting for the next activity to begin. And waiting seems to be what most off-task children are doing in the least engaged and least effective classrooms (Pressley et al., 2001; Taylor et al., 2000). Students who finish their work early wait for the next activity. Students who experience a problem wait for assistance. Students who have papers to be checked stand in line at the teacher's desk, waiting to have the paper graded. In the least effective classrooms, waiting occupied many minutes of every allocated instructional hour.

Engagement in learning is important, and two factors—task difficulty and task interest—have a bearing on the likelihood that students are engaged in the learning activity. Most of us work assiduously to avoid tasks that are impossible for us to do. Most of us even try to avoid tasks that are very hard, unless we have a tremendous interest in the activity. Most adults, for instance, avoid difficult books (they hire accountants to avoid reading the tax manuals) unless the book covers a topic they are extremely interested in (and even then they more often search for easy books on the topic). Most adults try to avoid uninteresting books. The worst-case scenario is being required to read a difficult book on something we have no interest in (perhaps a scholarly text presenting economic analyses of educational productivity). Children are not very much different from adults in this respect. Too often we point to the "distractability" of the child who is off-task during a lesson or activity, rather than considering alternative explanations such as task difficulty and task interest. In such situations it is important to evaluate the "holding power" of the activity by assessing the difficulty of the task and the interest it generates (Allington, 2006).

Much has been written about students' on-task and off-task behavior. We know that off-task behavior is associated with lower-achieving students (though hardly exclusive to them), but the reason children are off-task is often not understood. During reading and language arts activities, on-task behavior is associated with access to comfortable reading materials—materials that can be read accurately, fluently, and with good comprehension. Gambrell, Wilson, and Gannt (1981) observed differences in on-task behavior when good and poor readers were reading materials of varying degrees of difficulty. Poor readers were generally off-task more often, but they were also more often confronted with reading materials that were quite difficult for them. When poor readers had access to reading materials they could read comfortably, their off-task behavior became comparable to the good readers'. But in classrooms, poor readers are far more likely to be given materials to read that are difficult for them. Schemes using the same material for all students often create difficulties for lower-achieving readers. In these cases one might expect increased off-task behavior from children who find the reading difficult.

A major finding of teacher effectiveness studies (Allington & Johnston, 2001; Keene, 2002; Pressley et al., 2001; Taylor et al., 2000) was that lower-achieving children with more effective teachers more often had appropriate texts and tasks to complete and were more likely to be engaged in their work. Because they were more often engaged in reading and writing activity, lower-achieving students in the more effective classrooms demonstrated substantially more growth on achievement tests.

In our ideal elementary school, all children would have books they can read accurately, fluently, and with comprehension in their hands, their desks, and their backpacks when they go home at the end of the day. If we want to design schools that work better for struggling readers, then we need to ensure that every minute of every school day is well spent—that every minute of every day every child will be working on appropriate texts and tasks. This brings us to a final point.

Tasks Are Important

The *type of literacy activity* that children are engaged in during the available academic learning time is important. It *does* matter what kinds of work children spend their time doing. In fact, the nature of the academic work that children do is probably the best predictor of what they will learn. On the one hand, word-search puzzles seem to have a fairly substantial holding power for most children, but children can do word searches without being able to even read the words! So we might enter a classroom and see all children hard at work, or engaged, in completing a word-search activity, but it would be hard to say what, if anything, they were learning.

On the other hand, we might enter a classroom where many children are quietly chatting to each other and assume they are not engaged in learning. But a closer look would indicate that they are discussing what they have just read. This type of activity encourages the authentic conversations that all literate people have with one another about books. In another classroom we might see children lolling about all over the room, engaged in silent reading of self-selected children's books. This scene does not look very much like a traditional classroom or very much like a traditional reading lesson. But the time that children actually spend reading and writing and engaged in conversations about that activity is the most powerful factor in developing children's reading and writing.

Classrooms differ enormously in the amount of time children spend engaged in actual reading and writing activities. One federal study of schools in three states that served many low-income children (Knapp, 1995) noted that in some classrooms children actually read only 5 minutes daily while in other classrooms children averaged 48 minutes of actual reading each day. In some classrooms, children spent only about 15 percent of the time allocated for reading instruction actually reading. In other classrooms, children spent over 75 percent of that time reading. A similar pattern of variation existed in writing activity. In some classrooms, children averaged only 8 minutes a day of writing, and in others they averaged 48 minutes. In some classrooms, children did less than one extended writing activity each week, and in other classrooms children averaged eight. Schools with higher achievement levels had more teachers offering longer blocks of time for both reading and writing. Classrooms with higher achievement were classrooms where students engaged in substantially more actual reading and writing activity. Still, the extent of variation was surprising and was found to be related to teachers' beliefs about the children they taught, school and district curricular policies, and school and district provisions for staff development. These variations were not random occurrences but were largely predictable from district factors, school factors, and teacher factors.

This finding was replicated in the teacher effectiveness studies (Allington & Johnston, 2001; Keene, 2002; Pressley et al., 2001; Taylor et al., 2000). Although there were wide variations in how much time children in less effective classrooms spent reading and writing each day, children in more effective classrooms read and wrote two or three times as much every day, all year. While first graders in the less effective classrooms read from 3 to 5 little books each week, those in the more effective classrooms read between 20 and 30. While fourth graders in the less effective classrooms read their reading, science, and social studies textbooks and one or two other books, those in the more effective classrooms read between 20 and 50 books in addition to their textbooks.

Given that most children are in school about 6½ hours each day and about 5½ hours of that time are scheduled for instruction, it is surprising that so many children spend so little time actually reading or writing in school. In many schools, teachers (and often administrators) seem uncomfortable when children are *only* reading! These teachers seem to view reading more as a leisure activity than as real educational work. Similarly, they seem uncomfortable when children are *only* writing or sharing their stories with classmates. Often, traditional seatwork assignments make these teachers more comfortable. Some teachers and principals see seatwork as the real work of the school literacy program and assign only small amounts of reading and writing. Unfortunately, such a view is sadly out-of-date given what we know about how children might best spend their time to become readers and writers.

Traditional seatwork is relatively useless as a developer of reading and writing proficiency (Leinhardt, Zigmond, & Cooley, 1981; Taylor, Frye, & Maruyama, 1990). It is not that all seatwork tasks are largely irrelevant to effective strategy development, but rather that seatwork often does not focus on strategy use (Cunningham, 1982). Instead, much seatwork requires only that children be able to locate information and copy it onto a worksheet. Most seatwork presents low-level tasks and consumes time that might better be used to expand the opportunity to read and write. Far more powerful are occasions in which children spend large blocks of time reading and writing and interacting with their teachers about the books they are reading and the stories they are writing. A better balance between real reading and writing and skills-oriented seatwork is needed in many classrooms.

Struggling readers, especially, benefit from both increased opportunities to read and write and increased instructional guidance. Of course, for reading to replace seatwork, we will need to make access to interesting, comfortable reading material as easy as access to worksheets (Guthrie & Humenick, 2004). Too many schools make workbooks, worksheets, and dittos far more accessible than books, magazines, and newspapers. Many schools spend far more on seatwork supplies than on books and magazines for the classroom. The basic question that needs to be asked is, Why do teachers often find it easier to access 25 workbooks than 25 trade books or 25 copies of a magazine?

In our ideal elementary school, thoughtful literacy development would be the goal. To achieve this goal, instructional time would be honored and protected every day, all day. Teachers would have large blocks of uninterrupted time to teach reading and writing. Classrooms would be stocked with a wide array of reading materials so that all children have easy access to texts and books they can read accurately, fluently, and with good comprehension. Lessons would be designed so that actual reading and writing activities dominate the day. There would, of course, be lots of occasions for participating in powerful strategy lessons, but in this school everyone would realize that strategies must be well practiced to become independently useful to children.

Is Time a Problem in Your School?

Should providing more time for children to read and write and more time for teachers to teach reading and writing become an immediate priority in your school? To answer this question, information about what is *really* happening is needed. Here are some possible ways to gather that information.

- *Ask people.* The direct route is so obvious that it is often ignored. Ask classroom teachers to keep track of the time they spend in all activities for one week and then figure out how many minutes were spent in teaching reading and writing and how long children were actually reading and writing. Ask special teachers to keep track of their time, too. Also ask children to log their activities for a day and then figure out how many minutes they spent reading and writing.

- *Observe in classrooms,* paying attention to how much reading and writing instruction and actual reading and writing are occurring. After visiting classrooms, note what is actually happening during the time allocated for reading and language arts. Is there a good balance between reading and writing and the other activities that have long dominated the school day? After a few weeks, estimate how much of the allocated time children are engaged in actual reading and writing activities.

- *Shadow some children* whose literacy development is of concern. Focus in on three or four children who are struggling with their literacy development, and see how much time they are engaged in literacy-promoting activities. If a child goes to a special class, determine how much time that child spends traveling to and from and getting started. Determine what the child misses while out of the classroom. When the child is engaged in classroom activities, observe carefully with the "What is this child really doing?" question in mind. If the class is engaged in self-selected reading, does this child spend most of his or her time traveling back and forth to the bookshelf? Slide alongside the child and ask him or her to quietly read a bit of the book to you (a section the child has already read). Is the reading fluent? Is it accurate? Ask the child to tell you a bit about the book. Does comprehension seem strong? If the class is writing, how many words does this child actually write? If the teacher is working with the class or with a group that includes this child, does this child appear to be attending to and able to profit from the instruction? As you observe, estimate the number of children who have appropriate reading materials in front of them.

Prisoners of Time is the title of the report from the National Education Commission on Time and Learning (2000), a legislatively established independent commission charged with providing a comprehensive review of the relationship between time and learning in U.S. schools. After reviewing the limitations of schooling defined by the same minimum time requirements for all students the commission noted:

Learning in America is a prisoner of time. For the past 150 years, American schools have held time constant and let learning vary. . . . It should surprise no one that some bright, hard-working students do reasonably well. Everyone else—from the typical student to the dropout—runs into trouble. . . . In the school of the future, learning—in the form of high measurable standards of student performance—must become the fixed goal. Time must become an adjustable resource.

Summary

Time matters in teaching and learning literacy. Some children require extra opportunities to engage in reading and writing and need greater access to their teacher and to instructional guidance and support. Schools can organize the instructional day in ways that increase or decrease the amount of time allocated to classroom instruction. Too often, current school policies deny teachers large blocks of instructional time. We propose the creation of "safe" periods for each classroom—periods in which all children are available to participate in classroom instruction. Extended-day programs and summer programs offer real opportunities to increase the instructional time available to both teachers and children. But before asking children to stay around the school longer, we need to ensure that the time they spend during the regular school day is time well spent.

Classroom organization and management affect the instructional time children have each day. In the schools we study, we invariably find two classrooms, at the same grade level, where opportunities to read and write differ enormously. Part of the difference is attributable to differences in the value the teachers assign to teaching reading or differences in the teachers' understandings about what time allocations are considered appropriate. Often these differences in beliefs and understandings are linked to differences in professional-development opportunities in different schools. But they can also reflect differences in the structure of the school day and in the efficiency with which teachers accomplish routine tasks such as opening and closing activities and moving from one activity to another.

Just as important as time allocation is the way children spend allocated time. Increasing the time that children spend on tasks that offer little potential for fostering literacy development does not make sense. Thus, when addressing the issue of time, schools must consider how children spend the time now allocated. In some cases, the best first step would be to improve the quality of the tasks that children do during the time currently available.

Time is important, and struggling readers have no time to lose during the school day. Even small amounts of time lost daily can accumulate to large amounts across a year or across an elementary school career. Creating schools where all children become readers and writers requires careful consideration of how the available time is used and how additional instructional time for children who find learning to read difficult might be found or created.

Tests, Assessments, and Report Cards

Probably no other educational topic generates as much conversation as testing. Some folks argue that tests play an essential role in advancing educational reform, while others argue that tests inhibit the most needed reforms. Like talk about many other educational issues, the talk about testing often presents the situation as dichotomous—either supporting more and better testing or rejecting all traditional testing in favor of alternative assessment procedures. We believe there is a middle ground that offers a balanced alternative. Obviously, current testing programs have limitations and unintended effects, but so do the alternatives proposed to replace them. Traditional large-group testing can play a useful role in creating schools

where all children become readers and writers, but many common testing practices will need to be reconsidered to achieve that potential. Likewise, many alternative evaluation procedures have the potential for improving instructional efforts, but public confidence in these procedures and professional expertise in their use will need to be fostered before that potential can be fulfilled.

In this chapter, we discuss norm-referenced and performance-referenced tests and briefly review the limitations of large-group achievement tests. Then we offer ideas for an improved assessment plan that incorporates large-group tests and alternative strategies for evaluating both individual literacy development and the effectiveness of instructional programs.

Large-Group Achievement Testing

A national study (Barton & Coley, 1994) reported that the most common testing programs in elementary schools use group-administered paper–pencil tests consisting primarily of multiple-choice questions. This format has dominated school testing for reading achievement (though not writing assessment) for the past 40 years. Two types of tests—national norm-referenced group achievement tests and state-sponsored performance-referenced tests—are used to assess achievement in most schools. These tests have a number of design formats in common, but some significant differences can be found in their construction and most common uses.

Norm-Referenced Reading Achievement Tests

The use of norm-referenced achievement tests has grown substantially in the last 35 years. Some of this growth was fueled by the accountability movement as states imposed annual testing programs on schools. Before 1970, only a few states mandated testing, but by 1990, 47 states required schools to test students (Coley & Goertz, 1990), and today every state is to test every child in grades 3 through 8 annually to comply with the provisions of the NCLB act.

Norm-referenced tests are constructed so that the results can be placed on a number of comparative scales. For instance, scores can be reported as a percentile rank, a stanine range, a normal curve equivalent, a lexile level, and a grade equivalent. Because tests were administered to a large sample of students in a variety of schools across the nation, the scores provide comparisons to the performances of students in the norming population.

Norm-referenced achievement test data have two basic uses. Test scores are often used to rank-order school performance and, inappropriately, to rank-order individual children's performance. Administrators can find out how their school's performance compares with other schools' and, in most cases, how performance compares with performance in other schools with similar students. Thus, in an ideal world, norm-referenced achievement tests might provide a reasonably efficient and cheap means of estimating how well instructional programs at a school are doing in comparison to programs at other schools nationally.

Unfortunately, it is not an ideal world, and there are routine reports of the widespread use of unethical and ethically questionable practices affecting the administration and scoring of norm-referenced achievement tests, and the reporting of test results. In short, test preparation and administration activities that are designed to raise test scores without actually improving the ability being assessed are unethical. Too many schools, in our experience, are focused more on improving student performances

In discussing the development of commercial group achievement tests, James Popham (2001), former director of the National Research Center on Educational Assessment, notes: "Items covering the most important things that teachers teach tend to be excluded from standardized achievement tests. Thus, the more important the content, the more likely that teachers are to stress it. The more teachers stress important content, the better students will do on an item measuring that content. But the better students do on such an item, the more likely it is that the item will disappear from the test" (p. 48).

on reading tests than on improving students' reading proficiencies. Many common test preparation activities are not only unethical but also ineffective. There is no reliable evidence, for instance, that hours of work in test-preparation workbooks (or on test-preparation software) improves either test scores or students' actual reading proficiency. When students spend more than three hours in test-preparation activity, valuable instructional time is being wasted.

In many schools test scores are used inappropriately to make decisions about individual students. Probably the most important change schools could make would be to end the use of norm-referenced achievement test results to rank students and to place them in groups or programs. Very simply, performances on norm-referenced achievement tests do not lead to very reliable predictions of individual children's reading development. A look in the technical manual of most tests quickly confirms the inappropriateness of using such scores as measures of who reads best (or worst). Norm-referenced group achievement tests work reasonably well for comparing the performances of groups of children (e.g., classes, grade levels, schools, or district aggregate performances), but they are not reliable measures of individual achievement and should not be used to promote or retain children or to assign them to reading groups, special programs, or particular levels of basal readers (Heubert & Hauser, 1999).

Norm-referenced tests rest on probability theory (remember the coin-flip analogy from your tests and measurements class?). The basic premise is: No test performance is ever a wholly reliable measure of individual reading development because the test scores that some children achieve overestimate their actual reading development, and the test scores that other children achieve underestimate their actual development. Theoretically, all this error is balanced when the performances of a number of children are aggregated.

Test publishers work hard to illustrate the lack of reliability in individual performances. Figure 7.1 is an illustration of a test publisher's report of the scores of one child on a norm-referenced achievement test. Notice how the test scores are represented as bands in the display to the right of the reported national percentile ranking (PR) and national stanine (S) columns. These bands indicate the range of scores that best represent this child's academic development. The bands in the illustration better communicate the meaning of the test results by graphically illustrating the lack of precision inherent in the specific test scores reported (the "word reading" percentile ranking of 52 actually is better represented as a score falling into a range of scores somewhere between the percentile ranks 39 and 63). In a footnote on this report, the test publisher indicates that overlapping test bands denote no "meaningful difference" in the scores reported. Notice that only the "listening comprehension" measure does not overlap other scores—even though the percentile rankings from 52 to 70 are reported on the other five measures. The five sub-test scores are considered equivalent. This student's word reading skills are not weaker than his vocabulary skills, even though the percentile ranks differ substantially. The key point is

Haladyna, Nolan, and Haas (1991) offer a listing of common test preparation practices and their judgment of the ethics of such practices. Their ethical judgments are based on their answer to the question "Will the practice artificially raise test scores without actually enhancing children's reading development?" In other words, will the practice simply make the school look as though it is doing a better job than it actually is? Below is the researchers' listing of practices with their ethical-value rating (E = ethical, U = unethical, HU = highly unethical).

E	Training general test-wiseness
E	Increasing motivation through appeals to parents and students
U	Developing curriculum based on test
U	Presenting children with items similar to those on test
U	Using *Scoring High* or other score-boosting workbooks or software
U	Altering test administration procedures (e.g., adding time)
HU	Excluding low-achieving students (including children with disabilities) from taking the test
HU	Presenting students with items verbatim from tests prior to administration
HU	Altering answer sheets or discarding some tests

Nearly every practice listed was in use somewhere. Some, such as use of special workbooks, were used widely even though deemed unethical (because although scores may rise, the children do not actually read any better). The question that remains is whether the problem is the tests themselves or the practices of educators involved with the testing programs.

Tests	National PR	S	National Percentile Bands
			Below Average Average Above Average
			1 5 10 20 30 40 50 60 70 80 90 95 99
Word Study Skills	65	6	
Word Reading	52	5	
Reading Comprehension	68	6	
Vocabulary	70	6	
Listening Comprehension	95	8	
Spelling	52	5	

Figure 7.1 ● A Sample Pupil Profile from a Popular Norm-Referenced Achievement Test

that norm-referenced achievement tests, though offering an illusion of precision, are not reliable estimates of individual reading development.

The National Academy of Education (Heubert & Hauser, 1999) concluded that the research available indicates that norm-referenced tests are simply not technically reliable enough to use in making high-stakes decisions (grade promotion, graduation). Nonetheless, there are districts, even states, where failure to achieve a specified level on a norm-referenced group test means children will be retained in grade. So much for research as a guide to policy making.

It is also important to note that even if norm-referenced group achievement tests were much more reliable indicators of individual reading development, they would still suffer some problems of validity. Such tests do not measure everything that children might know or be able to achieve. In fact, norm-referenced achievement tests assess only a narrow range of the reading processes that children are expected to develop. Such tests do not measure, for instance, whether children read widely across a variety of genres, authors, and topics. They do not tell us whether children can discuss what they have read or synthesize across texts or compare one author with another. The tests do not really tell us much about reading habits or strategies that children might use. They do not provide much information about comprehension processes, since the tests measure primarily the lowest-level cognitive processes operating on short pieces of text. They do not tell us whether children have refined strategies for selecting books or for locating materials to pursue developing expertise on a topic. In short, current tests measure only a few aspects of reading development.

We note that as new norm-referenced assessments have come to the market (e.g., Terranova, Stanford9), there is a trend to include both longer "authentic" texts and "extended response" items. Both changes represent improvements. Using texts that were not

● . . . .

160

In a review of the research on test preparation, Guthrie (2002) provides Figure 7.2 illustrating that almost all of the differences in test scores are accounted for by three factors:

• Reading ability

• World knowledge

• Motivation

Guthrie indicates that substantial amounts of test preparation can produce lower test scores because (1) these materials and activities fail to develop any of the three important factors in test performance and (2) test preparation can actually lead students to become less careful as they take the test because they feel they know what they are supposed to do and don't need to read the directions.

specially written for the test and providing items in which children actually compose an answer are improvements over the traditional artificial paragraph and sole use of multiple-choice tasks. But neither improvement provides much in the way of broader, richer, deeper information on the literacy development of children.

For an assessment to be valid, it needs to measure not only what is taught but also what is important. Today most norm-referenced group reading tests measure neither very well, although, as just noted, test developers have made some important improvements in recent years. Still, an analysis of state reading proficiency tests indicates that few test the acquisition of the higher-order reading proficiencies targeted for instruction (Valencia & Wixson, 2001). Nonetheless, norm-referenced tests can provide snapshots of the reading development of groups of children and, we believe, can play a useful role as part of a broader and more comprehensive program evaluation effort.

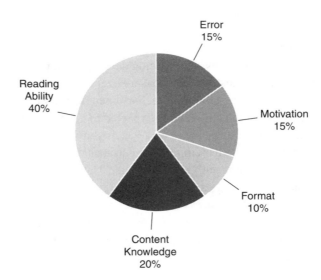

Figure 7.2 ● Components of Reading Test Performance

Source: Guthrie, John T. (2002). Preparing students for high-stress test taking in reading. In A. E. Farstrup & S. J. Samuels (Eds.), *What research has to say about instruction* (pp. 370–391). Newark, DE: International Reading Association. Copyright © 2002 International Reading Association.

Value-added assessment has become a hot topic, especially in political circles. Developed by Bill Sanders (1998) of the University of Tennessee, value-added assessment uses students' gains to estimate instructional productivity. In other words, each student's achievement growth is measured using the previous year's test scores as the base. Instructional productivity as estimated by achievement growth is determined by subtracting last year's score from the current test score. This method goes a long way toward leveling the playing field, compared with the simple recording of which class meets a state test performance benchmark, because it factors in each student's previous achievement. But the value-added process does not account for summer reading loss (see Chapter 6 for more details), which primarily impacts poor children and lower-achieving students (Cooper et al., 1996). Nor does it account for different levels of parental support (private tutoring, academic summer camps, educational computer software, etc.). Thus, schools that enroll more advantaged children and who have fewer struggling readers are awarded credit that is undeserved. Even if current tests were valid and reliable measures of student achievement, value-added assessment strategies still undeservedly penalize teachers who work in some schools while giving an advantage to those who work in others.

We suggest that schools need to be clear about how they will use norm-referenced reading achievement test results. Keep in mind that such results cannot be used to sort individual children accurately or to rank-order children on literacy development. Neither can they be used to inform instructional practices specifically, although they might play a general role in this realm. We think that norm-referenced achievement tests are best used to monitor basic reading achievement patterns in a school. Every child does not need to be tested every year to accomplish this, however.

Buly and Valencia (2002) administered a series of norm-referenced individually administered diagnostic tests to fourth-grade students whose reading performance fell below the state benchmark. Using a statistical technique, cluster analysis, they found six clusters of reading performances:

- Automatic word callers (18%) read accurately but with poor comprehension
- Struggling word callers (15%) better at reading word lists than connected text
- Word stumblers (18%) made many self-corrections when reading text, much decoding persistence but slow
- Slow word callers (17%), not automatic decoders but can do it slowly
- Slow, steady comprehenders (24%) who perform on level but read slowly and do not complete test
- Readers with disabilities (9%) with word recognition, because of severe decoding problems they perform poorly in all areas

Having second- and fifth-grade achievement data available (even anonymous data) across a three-to-five-year period allows school personnel to broadly examine the effects of changes made in various aspects of the program. For instance, a school staff might collect (or recover from older school records) the achievement test scores for a three-year period when the instructional programs were relatively stable before implementing a new program design (shifting to whole-day kindergarten, adding Reading Recovery as an intervention for struggling first-grade students, shifting to a multilevel, nonability-grouped primary-grade reading program, or increasing the number of trade books available and the time spent in school actually reading). Continuing to collect the second- and fifth-grade test scores over the next three years would allow school staff to examine the effects of such changes. There are two questions to be asked of the data:

- Has the average reading achievement level of second and fifth graders increased since the intervention?
- Are fewer children exhibiting substantially delayed reading development?

The two questions focus on longer-term effects of interventions, but it is the longer-term effects that are important. Short-term improvement, which is the usual focus of evaluations, is fine, but if those effects are not maintained across the elementary years, the intervention's usefulness is questionable (or the intervention needs more long-term supportive efforts). Continuing to collect annual achievement data at second and fifth grade will allow school staff to examine continuing effects of two sorts. What intervention effects appear some five years later at fifth grade? Is the original effect sustained or enhanced as the intervention ages?

Their analysis illustrates one reason no single intervention design could ever hope to be successful with all struggling readers. The study also illustrates just how little instructionally useful information many state tests (and group achievement tests) provide. Diagnostic testing found students with word reading difficulties fell into four groups with different intervention needs. Perhaps if we had more sensitive assessments of comprehension we could identify whether students with poor comprehension were primarily lacking effective strategies, or lacking in background knowledge and vocabulary, or whether lack of fluency or some other factor best explained their poor comprehension.

In any event, knowing that a student has not met a state standard or a norm-referenced cutoff (e.g., 35th percentile) offers little useful information to guide what we might do to improve reading performance. It should indicate that something must be done, but the limited reliability of such assessments to accurately estimate reading achievement coupled with the lack of useful information, even assuming the accuracy of the test scores, means that we might consider these tests the "canary in the coal mine." We will need to do more assessment—more instructionally useful assessment—in order to have a better idea about what sort of intervention to implement.

Given the limited instructional usefulness of group achievement tests, it might be best if schools gave such tests anonymously to students—that is, with no names recorded on the tests. While providing information on how well school programs were fostering basic literacy achievement, anonymous testing would ensure that schools did not use test scores inappropriately to make decisions about individual students. Norm-referenced tests measure only some of the many things children need to learn. Nonetheless, an anonymous achievement-testing program would allow school personnel to monitor the overall effectiveness of instruction and provide one basis for making decisions about the need for program improvements.

Performance-Referenced Achievement Testing

Passage of the Improving America's Schools Act (IASA) of 1994 produced a new breed of large-group assessments. The IASA required states to adopt challenging new content and performance standards for all students and new assessments that measure the progress of all children in attaining the level of performance specified in the content standards. Federally funded Title 1 programs were to report states' progress, as measured by the new tests, in assisting economically disadvantaged students in meeting those same standards. Thus, a flurry of standards-development activities took place, and within a couple of years the majority of states had curriculum-content standards and group achievement tests to estimate progress in meeting those standards in reading and the other language arts. Much has been written about the new standards documents, and in many cases the documents have been graded or rated by one group or another. However, the same state standards were given grades that ranged from A to D, depending on who did the rating (Olson, 1998).

The different state content and performance standards differed in substantial ways. Some states provided a grade-by-grade listing of specific skills reminiscent of the 1970s' skills hierarchies. Other states provided broad content standards for attainment across several grades (K–4, 5–8, 9–12). Some state performance standards hinged on demonstrating mastery of specific skills; others required demonstrations of higher-order reading and writing proficiencies. If there was any observable trend, it was that states where NAEP performance ranked below the national average (these also tend to be textbook adoption states) seemed more likely to elect to create a skills-testing framework and states achieving above the NAEP national average elected demonstrations of higher-order literacy proficiencies.

Most states contracted development of the new state tests to commercial test publishers. Theoretically the new tests were to be linked to the new content standards. But many times the standards indicated stances, strategies, or skills that were not very amenable to large-group assessment. Nonetheless, some cut-off performance level was then set as the state standard. Some states simply purchased an "off-the-shelf" norm-referenced test and set their performance standard at some national percentile rank. Thus, in many respects, the performance-referenced tests looked very much like the traditional large-group norm-referenced tests that test publishers market. In too many cases there was little alignment between the state tests and the state standards (Linn, 2000). There are, of course, exceptions, but the general situation is that all third- through eighth-grade students are now assessed statewide. In some states every child at every grade level is assessed annually and most states also test at ninth or tenth grade. Lots of time and money are invested in testing.

As was the case for norm-referenced tests, the National Academy of Science (Heubert & Hauser, 1999) report on high-stakes testing recommends against using state test scores as the sole criterion for retention or graduation decisions. Perhaps more importantly, Heubert and Hauser note that the process of setting performance standards has serious flaws. The failure of most children to achieve an established performance level, they suggest, is evidence not so much of challenging standards as of a flawed process for developing performance benchmarks. The report goes on to suggest that performance levels indicating rampant failures of schools to educate children well are better evidence of political manipulation than evidence of actual achievement trends.

One issue that has been little discussed is the process of setting performance standards at the state or federal level. NCLB allows states to establish the minimum performance levels on their state assessments. Progress toward meeting the goal of everyone reading on level by 2014 is tied then to those standards. It is evident that different states have set quite different levels of reading proficiency as their standard (see Chapter 1 for examples). Given these differences one might wonder how state and federal standards were established. It is an interesting story (see Smith, 2004, for a detailed analysis).

Basically, standard setting is far more a political process than a scientific process. The key question in standard setting seems to be: What level is politically tolerable? In one state a group of teachers and a group of businesspersons were asked to identify the sorts of items on a state test that they thought would be the sort of task a high school graduate should be able to do. The state officials compared the decisions of the two groups and estimated what percentage of students would have failed the state test administered that year using each group's recommended standard. Ultimately the state officials decided to use the business group's recommended performance level because 36 percent of students were estimated to fail using that criterion. That was seen as politically tolerable even though more difficult than the previous state standard. The teachers' recommendation was ignored primarily because it was substantially higher than the business group's recommendation. Using the teacher standard would have meant that two-thirds of the students would have failed to meet the standard and would, thus, be denied a diploma. That was likely to cause too much political pain.

Who's to say how well a third grader should read? Historically, we set the third-grade reading level at the average level of achievement of third graders. Thus, half of the students were below average and half were above average. But if 98 percent of students are to meet the standard, will states lower their minimum performance to something below the traditional third-grade level? Recently there have been such murmurings.

When the federal NAEP reading standards were initially set, 49 percent of students failed to achieve the "basic" level of proficiency (in 2005, 35 percent failed to meet that level). Thus, the original fourth-grade NAEP basic reading standard seems to have been set at what was historically considered grade level—that point where half of the students score above and half below. But even the federal proficiency levels have been sorely criticized with the General Accounting Office, the National Academy of Science, and the Center for Research on Educational Standards and Student Testing all cautioning that the NAEP standards were misleading and that the reporting on those standards should be terminated (Bracey, 2003).

None of this is meant to deny the political reality of standards for reading proficiency. There are now standards for reading in every state as well as minimum performance levels for reading proficiency. But this does not mean that there is anything "scientific" about such standards or about performance levels. That is one reason the state proficiency levels vary so widely. Neither the states with the hardest-to-meet standards (SC, CT, LA, CA) nor the states with the easiest-to-meet standards (TX, MA, MS, CO) have evidence to suggest that their standards are the appropriate ones. What we do know is that there is little relationship between the standards the states have set for reading and the standards the federal government has set.

The Appeal of Tests to Policy Makers

Why all this testing? There is a notion of "standards-driven" reform activity. The basic assumption is that schools in the United States have not provided a rigorous curriculum and the development of new "challenging" academic standards and tests that measure progress toward attaining those standards will turn the education system around and get it headed in the right direction. At the same time, the reading proficiency of U.S. students has reached an all-time high on the NAEP (www.nces.ed.gov/naep), and U.S. fourth-grade students' reading achievement was exceeded by students in only a few nations (www.nces.ed.gov/pubs2004/pirlspubl) in the most recent international comparisons. Nonetheless, politicians of every stripe at every level (national, state, mayoral) have jumped on education reform as a campaign theme.

Obviously schools can do better. But we doubt that the proliferation of testing provides any real solution—or even direction—to the problems that schools face. Although large-scale assessments can serve a potentially useful role in monitoring the progress of schools in fulfilling the aspiration of educating all children well, they may also have negative impacts such as narrowing the curriculum and reducing the autonomy of teachers and schools in decisions about how best to meet the instructional needs of the children they serve (Murphy, 1998). In our view, traditionally, the literacy curriculum has been too narrowly focused, and narrowing it further will be disastrous. We believe the professional

 Robert Linn (2000), Distinguished Professor at the Center for Research on Evaluation, Standards, and Student Testing at the University of Colorado, in his address accepting the AERA Career Contribution Award, noted four reasons why tests appeal to policy makers:

1. They are relatively inexpensive in comparison with professional development, attracting good teachers, reducing class size, or increasing instructional time.
2. Testing can be externally mandated. It is much more difficult to mandate policies that actually affect what happens in classrooms.
3. Tests can be quickly implemented, before the next election.
4. Test results are visible. They are reported to the press. Poor results are desirable for policy makers who, before the next election, want to show they have made an impact.

closest to the children is more likely than policy makers hundreds of miles away from the school to understand the critical needs of students.

Assessment that provides immediate feedback on instructional needs is what will improve the quality of classroom teaching. Thus, in the next section we discuss alternatives to annual large-group assessments.

Observational Strategies: Alternatives to Large-Group Assessments

Educators are interested in alternatives because they recognize the several common limitations of norm- and performance-referenced testing:

- The tests typically separate reading and writing.
- The tests assess components of reading in isolation from the curriculum.
- The tests assess only narrow aspects of reading and writing processes.
- The tests reduce a complex array of learnings to a single number or criterion.
- Parents, teachers, and administrators often misinterpret the tests.
- The tests lead few teachers to ownership of results.
- The information from tests is too general and often too dated to be useful for improving teaching.

Because of those concerns, much has been written about the potential of alternative forms of assessment for improving educational practices. Much of the impetus for change has come from implementing more naturalistic assessments of students' writing; the new writing assessments seem to foster an increased emphasis on students' actually writing during the school day (Koretz, Stecher, Klein, & McCaffrey, 1994). Proponents of replacing traditional achievement tests with alternative assessments argue that the new assessments will foster changes in instruction—primarily a shift toward more thoughtful teaching and learning.

Some proponents use the term *instructionally useful assessment* to describe the assessment processes that schools might implement to improve instruction. The possibilities range from wholly personal practices to externally imposed practices. Assessments can be done in the context of daily work or isolated from daily activities. Assessments can be individual or group focused. Assessment results can be diagnostic or simply summative, offering little feedback on how performance might be improved.

The idea behind developing more instructionally useful assessments is that the most common limitations of traditional assessment practices can be overcome by more personal and more integrated evaluations drawn from the daily work that children do in the classroom. Virtually all instructionally useful assessment alternatives rely on teacher observation of literacy development.

Teachers continually observe children in their classrooms, but many teachers are hard-pressed to discuss the development that is occurring right in front of them. For instance, when asked to describe children as writers, many teachers focus on neatness, punctuation, and spelling and have little to say about the genres of writing that children use. Many teachers have difficulty discussing critical features of writing, such as cohesion, plot and character development, organization of information, and argument. Many do not seem to know how children gather information, develop stories, or revise and edit their work. A similar situation exists for reading development. Many teachers are unable to describe children's reading development much beyond noting their rank in the classroom (in the low group) or their "reading level" (in the 3/1 reader, still reading easy books) or offering some comment about skills development ("has difficulty with short vowels"). Impoverished observations such as these usually stem from (1) limited skills for observing children's literacy processes and (2) limited knowledge of how reading and writing competence develops in children.

The big question is this: Do teachers develop expertise that results in better observation, or do they enhance expertise by learning observational strategies? The answer, we believe, is yes! Acquiring more complex understandings of how children learn to read and write improves observational skills. And acquiring observational strategies helps develop understanding of children's literacy learning. But what observational strategies might teachers need to better understand learning to read and write?

For a detailed presentation of the range of assessment strategies we recommend, see *Put to the Test: Tools and Techniques for Classroom Assessment* (Kuhs, Johnson, Agruso, & Monrad, 2001). This book covers each of the assessment strategies we have recommended for improving instruction as well as providing guidelines for developing assessment rubrics for both reading and writing.

A first step in learning to observe is learning to record what one observes. The human brain can hold only limited amounts of information in an active bin, and the constantly active classroom environment provides millions of bits of information every day. At the end of the average school day, children and activities blur together in the absence of some sort of record keeping. Stopping by after school to ask about the specific performances of a single child during the morning reading lesson usually results in generalities rather than insights as to specific strategy use. For instance, teachers may talk generally about a child's engagement or lack of it, but they will usually be unable to link engagement and disengagement to specific activities, tasks, or student interest in or facility with assignments given. Only by more closely observing children and recording what has been observed can teachers begin to provide more specific information about children's learning.

Observing Children's Reading

The time-tested observational stalwart is recording oral reading errors and behaviors. There are several forms for such recording, but all generally provide the teacher with a record of how accurately children read the material. Even if the record provides only an accuracy rating (92 percent of words accurately identified), the record is more useful than the very general information available from teachers who do not make oral reading records. Children need much exposure to materials that they can read nearly error-free, 97 to 100 percent accuracy. When children receive a steady diet of reading material that they read with lower accuracy, reading development is inhibited. Hence, the need for classroom teachers to observe and record reading accuracy regularly.

An oral reading record that is a bit more detailed—indicating, for instance, which words the child had difficulty with—provides better information for instructional planning. A child who has consistent difficulty with words of three or more syllables

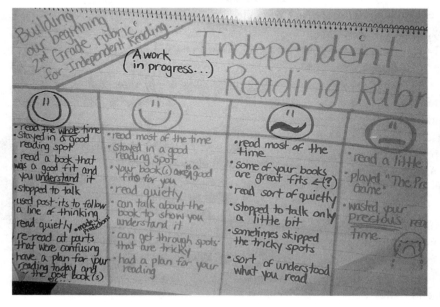

This New York City classroom provides students with criteria for evaluating their own independent reading performance.

provides evidence of the need for better strategies for dealing with longer words (often the strategies that work on short words do not work on long ones). Similarly, an oral reading record that contains information about a child's phrasing and fluency when reading aloud provides yet more information on the sorts of instructional interventions to consider (opportunities to reread, taped read-alongs modeling fluent reading). A classroom teacher, reading teacher, or special education teacher might use the records from one day's classroom reading lesson to offer a personalized strategy lesson immediately, thereby making it more likely that such lessons actually address current instructional needs.

The particular form of the oral reading record is less important than the existence of some record. Whenever children read aloud in classrooms, teachers should be recording that performance in some manner. Our favorite recording technique is the "running record" scheme devised by Marie Clay (1993) and developed by Peter Johnston (2000) in his small, practical guide, *Running Records*.

The running record technique requires only lined paper and a pencil for recording the reading performance. As children read, the teacher makes a check for every word pronounced correctly. Each line on the recording sheet corresponds to a line in the text being read. When a child mispronounces a word, the teacher writes down the mispronunciation instead of recording a check. Noting page numbers on the recording sheets makes it easy to later compare the child's reading to the text. Establishing reading accuracy is quite easy—teachers count the checks for the correctly pronounced words and count the mispronunciations. We strongly recommend Johnston's little book to educators interested in developing useful records of children's oral performance (the book is accompanied by audiotapes for training in the procedures).

Even more basic is simply recording oral reading fluency as *good, fair,* and *poor* (Allington, 2006). As simple as this might seem, fluency or the lack of it provides good evidence of the ease or difficulty the child is having with any given text. Teachers simply listen, usually with the book closed, as the child reads aloud a part of a text that he or she has had the opportunity to read previously. Regularly recording the fluency level of children's reading provides good information for planning instruction and for evaluating its effects. If oral reading remains a struggle, the difficulty of the materials, the procedures for introducing the materials, and the child's strategies for predicting and self-monitoring need to be evaluated.

Many schools use the Dynamic Indicators of Basic Early Literacy Skills (DIBELS) to track reading fluency. Two recent studies suggests caution should be observed when using DIBELS indicators. Carlisle, Schilling, Scott, and Zeng (2004) found that nearly half of the second- and third-grade struggling readers had been misidentified—although their DIBELS performances suggested on-level reading proficiency, these students' performance on the state reading assessment fell in the below-average range. They also note that the DIBELS subtests are highly intercorrelated, suggesting that administering each of the subtests provided little more information than administering just the oral reading fluency subtest. Pressley, Hilden, and Shankland (2005) concluded that "DIBELS mispredicts reading performance on other assessments much of the time, and at best is a measure of who reads quickly without regard to whether the reader comprehends what is read" (p. 1).

Oral reading, however, is only a small part of the reading activity in any classroom. How can teachers observe silent reading? Consider how we observe other adults when they read. In an airport, for instance, it is easy to observe the different materials (newspapers, magazines, popular novels, technical materials, memos, children's books, etc.) that people are reading. Formally collecting information on these different materials could be considered research. If we were interested in what reading went on at airports, we could routinely collect this observational data. Depending on the fundamental purpose of our observation, we might collect detailed records on titles and authors or on types of materials or on the readers' gender. We might even chat briefly with readers to gather information on motivation, response, habits, and plans. Teachers (and administrators) could collect similar information from observing silent reading activity in classrooms.

We might also want to note general reading speed or observe and note the discussions that follow a reader's completion of a book. We could collect information on partner roles during paired-reading activities. By conferencing with or interviewing children, we could add information on response to books, reasons for selecting certain books, and so on. Outside of school we rarely interrogate people to find out whether they are really reading that newspaper in front of them! We rarely quiz friends or loved ones to ensure they understand the novel they are reading. Instead, we watch, we discuss, and we share. Such activities are also useful and powerful in school and can provide wonderfully rich assessment opportunities if we simply record what we see and hear.

Brenda Power (1996) provides a straightforward discussion of techniques for observing children in her small book, *Taking Note.* There is no one right way to observe children learning. But exemplary teachers know their children's current status as readers and writers both more thoroughly and differently than do less effective teachers (Johnston, 2000). One reason for the differences is that exemplary teachers have a broader view of literacy accomplishments and better strategies for observing and recording the development of their students.

Observing Children's Writing

Reading is only a small part of the literacy work that goes on in classrooms and only a small part of any good observational scheme. Schools need records of children's writing development. Evaluating a student's essay by assigning a grade provides little information for instructional planning. Grades tell writers little about how the piece might be improved. Grades offer little information for support teachers about which aspects of writing need attention. Grades offer little information to parents about how a child's writing is developing.

In contrast, written observations about what development was noticed in each child's work provide enormously useful information that can be communicated to children, to support teachers, to parents. Observations of spelling development or attention to writing conventions (capitalization, punctuation) provide useful information about lessons needed and which students to include. Although samples of children's writing can be saved in a portfolio, the interpretation of a child's writing development on a particular assignment is needed for the next day's lesson. So saving writing is not sufficient. Teachers also need to record their observations of children's writing development regularly.

Because writing results in a visible, external product, assessing and evaluating children's writing development seems easier than monitoring their reading development. Children's writing development can be looked at in a variety of ways. Many teachers and parents keep samples of writing, including first-draft writing and published pieces. Looking at papers written several months apart should provide information about whether the writing is becoming better organized and clearer and whether the child is moving toward proficiency with expected punctuation and other editing considerations, including more conventional spelling of words. It is also helpful to look at the first and final drafts of the same piece. This snapshot of the writing process will tell you whether children are becoming better able to revise, edit, and polish their writing.

Figure 7.3 shows a portion of the K–2 writing fluency scale developed by one school to help teachers focus on writing development from kindergarten through second grade. In this school, teachers collected five writing samples from each child—end of kindergarten, middle of first grade, end of first grade, middle of second grade, and end of second grade. These writing samples were all focused on the same topic—a topic such as "Things I Like to Do" or "A Day in Our Classroom," which most children knew a lot about. The writing samples were scored by two persons using the *K–2 Writing Fluency Scale* and were placed in the child's cumulative portfolio. The growth and development of writing fluency was clearly documented by comparing the five writing samples focused on the same topic across two and a half years of school.

Some states have mandated end-of-grade-level writing tests for children from third grade on. Certain types of writing—descriptive, narrative, persuasive, and so on—are expected at certain grade levels, and on a designated day, all children at a particular grade level write to the same writing prompts. These writing samples are then scored. Often they are scored "holistically" by teachers trained to use a writing scale. Children's writing is evaluated against some common standard sample.

Of course, there are always problems with any kind of one-shot, one-day assessment. Certain children do not perform well on any kind of tests. Everyone has "bad days." Certain prompts are more relevant to some children than to others. Although the scorers are trained to achieve reliability, there is sometimes a very fine line between a sample scored 2 and another scored 3. Despite these problems, we believe that such writing tests provide

---

Primary Writing Fluency Scale

1. Emerging

___ Expresses ideas mainly through pictures or letter strings.

___ Uses some sound spelling according to beginning sounds heard.

___ Focuses on topic.

___ Writes one or two bare ideas.

2. Developing

___ Relates sentences to topic.

___ Writes sentences that may be short or repetitive.

___ Uses some detail that may be presented in list-like form.

___ Uses sound spelling that can generally be read by others.

___ Uses some punctuation and capitalization but may be inconsistent.

3. Early Fluent

___ Focuses on topic.

___ Uses sentences in logical order.

___ Uses varied sentence patterns.

___ Uses some evidence of detail or elaboration.

___ Uses sound spelling, if needed, to express ideas.

___ Uses clear or vivid language.

___ Shows growing ability to handle mechanics.

4. Fluent

___ Shows organization or sense of story.

___ Has clear beginning, middle, end.

___ Connects related ideas smoothly.

___ Expresses several ideas with detail or elaboration.

___ Shows originality in word choice.

___ Shows growing control of writing through generally correct mechanics.

___ Shows excitement, humor, suspense, or some creative element.

___ Spells most words correctly.

Figure 7.3 ● A Sample of a Primary Writing Fluency Scale

more useful information than does most other norm-referenced testing. Children cannot "guess" their way through the test, and the test closely matches the terminal writing behavior expected from an educated person. For evaluating an individual child's development, we get more information by looking at many samples written across time and some first- to final-draft companion pieces. For deciding how well a school is meeting the challenge of producing clear, fluent writers, state writing assessments typically provide useful information.

One effect of the increase in mandated testing of writing is that children now spend more school time writing. For years, various groups tried to convince teachers of the clear research finding (Hillocks, 2002) that time spent on worksheet activities emphasizing written language mechanics—punctuation, capitalization, grammar, usage—was largely wasted time because children did not transfer these skills to their own writing. As long as the mandated tests tested these skills in a multiple-choice format, teachers continued to teach them in an isolated-from-writing worksheet way. Now that some assessments focus more on how clearly children communicate ideas in writing, composing has replaced grammar and contractions worksheets in many elementary classrooms.

Writing assessments usually include evaluative criteria for spelling accuracy, punctuation, and grammar, but the evaluation of children's writing goes well beyond these features. Teachers do need to monitor children's adherence to such conventions, especially in pieces that are being revised and, perhaps, published. Children do need instruction on these conventions, but these lessons need to draw from children's own writing, not from some arbitrary skills hierarchy. Teaching the conventions of writing is most powerfully done in the context of children's writing activities—their attempts to communicate their ideas in print. Proficiency in writing is fostered when teachers write in front of students and demonstrate how they think as they compose, revise, and edit.

Teachers can gain high-quality information about the acquisition of literacy by observing children's writing. Composing opens a window to the thinking processes children use. Whether observations focus on the development of control over print and composition conventions such as spelling, punctuation, and grammar, or focus more on issues such as topic selection, argumentation, clarity, or fluency of writing, children's compositions provide a rich record of literacy development.

Many of the state writing assessments use a form of holistic scoring that draws heavily on the original work of Richard Lloyd-Jones (1977). He called the procedure "primary trait" scoring and offered rubrics for evaluating persuasive essays on a 0 to 4 scale:

0   No response, fragment

1   Does not take a clear position or offers no reasons for position taken

2   Takes a position and offers one unelaborated reason

3   Takes a position and gives one elaborated reason, one elaborated and one unelaborated reason, or two or three unelaborated reasons

4   Takes a position and offers two or more elaborated reasons, one elaborated and two or more unelaborated reasons, or four or more unelaborated reasons.

This scoring, with its focus on meaning making, has become known as holistic assessment.

One lesson learned from the exemplary teacher studies (Allington & Johnston, 2002) was that high achievement is linked to turning over to the students themselves much of the evaluation of their writing. As one exemplary teacher pointed out, "My basic job is to teach them how to edit their own writing. If I do all the correcting, I become their editor and they don't develop the editing skills they need going into middle school." Thus, he used differentiated editing guides reflecting the features individuals were focusing their improvement efforts on. The rubrics he provided were developed from those used in scoring the state writing examination. Children came to writing conferences with their editing checklists already completed and verified by a peer. This allowed him to focus his attention (and time) on extending writing skills rather than on editing work for students. Another exemplary teacher noted, "I'd never have time to actually teach writing if I had to edit every draft and revision for them."

Observing Book Selection

Teachers may observe how capable children are at selecting books for independent reading. Some children, usually struggling readers, seem to spend much of the time allocated for independent classroom reading "wandering" around the book display area, and they spend more time considering selections than actually reading (Michelson, 1993). Reasons for this wandering may include the limited supply of books that struggling readers can actually read and a lack of motivation stemming from unsuccessful prior experiences with books and reading. Also many struggling readers find selecting a comfortable book difficult because they have not developed any good sense of what books they might like or any strategies for determining what books are manageable for them. Failing to observe and record during book-selection periods and failing to observe and record the appropriateness of the books children select lead to a sort of "blindness" in teachers. Without good records, the teacher has little information to interpret and little basis for instructional intervention. Without such records, support teachers have little information to guide the instruction they offer.

Records of which books children have read are also useful. Too often, schools lack adequate information on students' reading habits and so find it difficult to plan programs to increase the amount or breadth of reading. Several possibilities might be considered. The first is to have each child keep a reading log and at the end of each year place the log in the student's cumulative file. The student log can be easily photocopied so that both the school and the child have copies.

For reading logs or lists to be useful, a school needs a way to organize the information. Information on individual reading habits is most useful when the records of individual children are pulled together and summarized at least annually. Such summaries can be accomplished on computers. Older children can enter their reading log data into a computer database and bypass the traditional paper–pencil log. Teacher aides can enter data for younger students. Computerized logs make generating summaries relatively painless.

In his column on assessment that appears in *Reading Teacher,* Peter A. Johnston (2005) asks: What kind of literacy should assessments reflect?

He suggests that currently in short supply are assessments that:

- Socialize children into monitoring their own literacy learning.
- Foster resilient learners who believe effort is more than ability.
- Develop reciprocity, a willingness to engage in joint learning activities.

Johnston uses an example from the New Zealand Educational Monitoring Project in which a small group of children is given a supply of books and then, in a limited time framework, must evaluate the books individually and collectively decide which titles to include in their classroom library. Performance is evaluated by listening to the arguments for which books to include, noting the evaluative criteria children use and the negotiation and persuasion that occur.

Imagine the sorts of responses that might be given by students from different classrooms or school systems. Imagine what classrooms that prepare children well for this task might look like.

Such summaries might be largely quantitative and indicate the number of titles read. Schools with access to even this information can judge the adequacy of the volume and range of reading children are experiencing. Such information also provides at least a crude basis for judging whether targeted interventions (e.g., adding books to classroom libraries, adding a Reading Is Fundamental project, or expanding book club participation) have an impact on children's reading volume.

Information on volume and range of reading is important. Does anyone know how many books the typical child with a learning disability read last year? Does anyone know whether most fifth-grade students have read one or more biographies? Does anyone know what books of what sorts all third graders have read? Answers to questions such as these are important for better addressing the impacts of a school reading program. Gathering better information on what books children read and whether they read them in or out of school provides a stronger basis for planning instructional, curricular, or organizational changes. Routinely gathering and summarizing such information produces better and more accessible information on whether the literacy program is providing an appropriate range of reading activities and whether the program is working to develop desired reading habits.

Using Checklists

Often, checklists reduce reading and writing to very simple lists of attributes. Although such checklists offer a shorthand for recording observations, the checks do not offer nearly as clear a picture as do "quickwrites" or "sticky-label notations" (discussed below). Of course, a checklist's value depends heavily on the nature of the items to be checked off. We see a potential role for checklists in organizing observational information; the use of checklists would follow the gathering of richer observational data. For instance, checklists could offer a quick way to record the book genres that a child has read. A form with a comprehensive list of the genres that children are expected to read (or to be able to write) could provide, at a glance, useful information for planning future lessons.

Managing Observational Records

How can teachers manage written records of classroom observations? How can such observations be organized so that they are useful for planning instruction and evaluating reading and writing development? We suggest a two-pronged approach.

First, each teacher would carry a clipboard at all times during the school day. On the clipboard would be two sorts of record-keeping devices: blank sheets of lined paper and a sheet of large self-stick labels (the sort you peel off and stick on large envelopes). The teacher would pay particular attention to gathering observational records on one focal child each day. The blank sheet of paper would have the child's name on it and might be used to record oral reading performance or to summarize responses to a brief interview or record a structured observation of on-task behavior. The file-folders labels would be used for recording information bits on the focal child and on other children across the day. The labels would be attached to individual children's record folders for later use. The teacher might place the full-page records in a child's folder or discard them after interpreting and summarizing the observations.

Second, at the end of the school day, the teacher would create a quickwrite summary based on the observational records of the day's focal child. This quickwrite should take no more than 6 to 10 minutes and could be organized around the following topics:

- Work the child was successful at
- Work the child had difficulty with
- Strategies the child needs to be taught
- Actions to take
- Actions other teachers can take

The teacher could compose this quickwrite summary and insert it in the focal child's folder or jot it in a three-ring notebook kept readily available for review during lesson planning. When this procedure is used, a quickwrite summary of each child is produced 8 to 10 times each year, as are sticky-label notations. This information is particularly useful for planning with support staff, collaborating with other teachers, and conferring with parents.

Observational records are incredibly useful sources of information for evaluating children's development across time (Power, 1996). They are far more useful than traditional gradebook entries for planning instruction or evaluating children's growth. A key to their importance is their permanence. Too often teachers jot notes on students' papers then lose those notes for planning when they return the papers to the students. The information collected during observations is not completely new to most teachers nor is the process of interpreting that information. What may be new is the gathering and storing of observations and later using those records to plan lessons or to evaluate children's development.

If the goal of evaluating children's work is to make sense of their development or lack of it, teachers need to look beyond the surface of an individual's performance, and they need to track performances across time. Proponents argue that this sort of "kid-watching" develops teachers' expertise and understanding of how children acquire reading and writing skills. This, in turn, results in higher-quality instruction and increased ownership of the outcomes of instruction. As teachers work to develop better classroom-based observation procedures to be incorporated into the assessment program, they accept more responsibility for what children learn from the lessons they teach.

Student Self-Evaluations   One unique aspect of the argument for instructionally useful assessment is the involvement of students in the evaluation process. We believe that developing students who are able to reflect on their own work should be a routine goal of evaluation. As children develop their understanding of reading and writing, they can become actively engaged in improving those processes. For instance, teachers can ask children to evaluate a story or a book rather than simply asking them questions about what they read. This is the kind of thinking about books that adults do—adults rarely interrogate each other about a book's content or about character names. Children might write or talk about their book selection and whether they are happy with it. Having children make an audiotape or videotape of themselves reading a book or story aloud, to take home to parents, to give to grandma, or to keep at school to be added to in later years is a powerful demonstration of improving proficiency, especially if the child prefaces the reading with a short comment explaining why he or she chose that particular text for taping.

The explanatory notes that children compose about a piece of writing—notes that describe how satisfied they are with the piece, how it came to be written, and so on—often offer wonderful insights into the composing process, and they can be attached to their writing. Self-evaluation does not merely ask children to grade their own work. It asks children to think and talk about their reading and writing in ways that have generally been absent from schools.

Interviews   There are two broad categories of interviews: structured and spontaneous. *Structured* interviews elicit the same information from each child. *Spontaneous* interviews are more free flowing and provide insights into children's thinking. As with other observation strategies, teachers need a system for recording at least the essence of the children's responses to the interview queries.

One way to get a sense of how students understand a school's literacy lessons is to interview them. While walking through your school, you might want to ask children the following sorts of questions:

Have you read any good books lately?

Tell me about the reading you are doing right now.

Who is your favorite author?

What sorts of books have you been reading lately?

Tell me how you chose this topic to write about.

Do you have any other pieces of your writing that I could read?

What do you like best about this piece of writing?

Johnston (1999) discusses asking children to describe themselves as readers and writers. In some classrooms children could only offer brief and rank-ordering comments such as "I'm pretty good. I'm in the Robins group." In other classrooms children provided different responses, such as "I like mysteries right now but I've been sort of stuck on them all year. I mean I have only read mystery books all year! I probably need to read some other stuff, too."

Similarly, some children seem unable to talk about their writing processes, or as one boy said, "We had to write about our summer so I just made something up." In another school, a different boy described his current writing project this way: "Well, I'm really interested in Native Americans. So I decided to write about the Navajo people. But when I started finding books and stuff, I thought, 'I can't write all this,' so I decided to write on Navajo homes. After I read a bunch of stuff, I found out that it was really the Hopis that built some of the most interesting dwellings so I decided to write about them instead. Actually, I ended up writing about one village called Walpi that was built on the top of a mesa." Both boys were in the same upper elementary grade, and both were considered good students by their teachers, but the interviews elicited quite different responses about the writing they had just completed.

Interviews can be useful because children often repeat what they hear from their teachers. If reading evaluation focuses on rank-ordering or on the number of books read or on test scores, children probably will use such criteria when they report. If length, penmanship, and spelling are the writing evaluation currencies, children's talk will focus on them. But when classroom evaluation of reading focuses more on selecting good books, summarizing and responding to those books, and sharing the books with others, the talk elicited is quite different. Likewise, when classroom evaluation of writing focuses on clearly communicating information when writing, on the uses of writing, and on the processes of planning, revising, editing, and so on, those are the sorts of things children mention (Johnston, 1998).

Interviewing children can provide extraordinarily useful information. But to be most useful for planning, modifying instruction, or evaluating programs, that information must be recorded, interpreted, and summarized. Children's responses do not have to be recorded verbatim, but observational notes should reflect or summarize the responses they give. Like other information, interview summaries can be attached to school records or placed in portfolios for later use.

Portfolios

Some schools have developed a portfolio process for organizing information on students' literacy development. So we describe four types of portfolios (even though our experience indicates that few pure examples of any of these types exist):

- *Best-works portfolios* (also called *showcase portfolios*) are collections of children's best work. Most often the children themselves select the works and explain why they included them. In some schools best-works portfolios reflect children's work over several years (or even a school career).

- *Process portfolios* contain several versions of a selected work. Such a portfolio might hold early drafts of a paper or poem to show how the piece developed over time. These portfolios, too, are usually organized by the children themselves.

- *Progress portfolios* are often managed by teachers. They hold collections of work intended to illustrate children's development over time. Often teachers include their observational records, notes, and checklists and use the collection for instructional planning and end-of-year evaluations.

- *Accountability portfolios* are relative newcomers, and many teachers view them with skepticism. The impetus for accountability portfolios seems to have come from the actions of several states (e.g., Vermont and Kentucky) that are attempting to shift statewide assessment to more authentic procedures. These portfolios usually contain items of student work mandated by a state education agency. The mandated items usually include some best works as well as samples of required work. The purpose of these portfolios is to evaluate the quality of instruction.

Much of the interest in portfolio approaches reflects the strong evidence that assessment practices drive instruction. As long as tests primarily measure student progress in meeting low-level literacy demands, classroom programs will focus more on that teaching than on developing higher-order literacy. Thus, persistent efforts have been made to shift assessment away from traditional practices. There is little doubt that the statewide high-stakes testing has had an impact on instruction—in our view a largely negative impact.

Likewise, good evidence shows that portfolio use can have a dramatic effect on instruction. Vermont's adoption of portfolio assessment for literacy and math had a substantial intended impact on the instructional practices and activities that routinely occur in classrooms (Koretz, Stecher, Klein, & McCaffrey, 1994). Similarly, Kentucky's adoption of a writing portfolio for school accountability produced substantially improved writing instruction and outcomes (Wolf, Borko, Elliott, & McIver, 2000). In fact, establishing a portfolio evaluation process may be the best way to stimulate professional conversation about a school's goals and needed curriculum shifts. When teachers have to decide what items will go into portfolios, when they must decide on the criteria for evaluating those items, and when they share students' work in an attempt to establish consistent scoring of work, they will find it enormously difficult to avoid engaging in professional talk about goals, curriculum, and outcomes.

Developing a Portfolio Plan

In most cases, a school portfolio plan will include more than one type of portfolio. What might a school portfolio plan look like? The public elementary schools in South Brunswick Township in New Jersey created a portfolio process that seems manageable in terms of time and paperwork and provides a rich compendium of information on each child's early literacy development (Educational Testing Service, 1991). Each portfolio includes the following:

- Self-portraits that children create at the beginning and end of each year.
- An interview protocol, completed each September, that includes questions on favorite pastimes, reading at home, and responses to school.
- A questionnaire that asks parents for assistance and information on their child and attempts to foster collaboration.
- Concepts about Print (CAP), Marie Clay's assessment of understanding of the conventions of print and books. The CAP is given at the beginning and end of kindergarten (and at later points to children experiencing difficulty).
- The Word Awareness Writing Activity at the end of kindergarten and in first grade.
- Unedited writing samples. These may include a teacher translation if sound-spelling, handwriting, or other problems make them difficult for others to understand.
- Running records of three reading samples collected near the beginning, middle, and end of the year. Each sample includes a comment on which strategies children used.
- Three records of a child's retelling of a story.
- A log recording titles of the books the child read that year.

The teachers also use a single numerical scale to rate all the work in a portfolio (ratings ranging from 1 to 4 indicate more- or less-developed literacy). The scale focuses on the development of strategies for making sense of print and characterizes a child level of development at the beginning and end of each year. This scoring allows quick comparison of the development of groups and subgroups of children in the district (e.g., contrasting development in different schools, contrasting development of boys and girls). This portfolio process functions primarily as an accountability tool for literacy learning. A student-organized portfolio would bring another dimension to this evaluation effort.

DeFina (1992) presents practical information on introducing portfolios in schools. He suggests several steps that need to be planned:

1. *Explain and educate.* Portfolios are not often well understood by anyone except those professionals who have long used them (e.g., artists, journalists, photographers, architects). Before jumping on a portfolio bandwagon, take time to help everyone develop a richer understanding of what portfolios can be and how they might improve the educational process.

2. *Decide how to and when.* Phase in portfolio evaluation over a period of time. Start small. Move slowly. Begin by implementing portfolio evaluation where it best fits into the current system (often, writing portfolios are a good first bet).

3. *Demonstrate and decide.* Students, as well as teachers (and parents), need demonstrations of how portfolios might be put together. It might be good to begin with diversity and work for more commonality of included works. Display portfolios at the school entrance and at faculty meetings and parent nights.

Maybe we should consider something beyond children's test performance when asking about the quality of school systems. What does the following ranking of the literateness of U.S. cities suggest about the schools in those cities? About the state curriculum and assessment frameworks?

Top 10 Most Literate Cities	Bottom 10 Least Literate Cities
Minneapolis, MN	El Paso, TX
Seattle, WA	Hialeah, FL
Pittsburgh, PA	Corpus Christi, TX
Madison, WI	Santa Anna, CA
Cincinnati, OH	San Antonio, TX
Washington, DC	Anaheim, CA
Denver, CO	Long Beach, CA
Boston, MA	Arlington, TX
Portland, OR	Fresno, CA
San Francisco, CA	Garland, TX

For the full report on methodology and complete ranking, see www.uww.edu/nga/cities.

4. *Establish the role of portfolios in grading.* Because portfolios are designed to show development and aimed at showcasing individuals' work, whether portfolios will be used in assigning grades needs to be determined.

5. *Rethink the classroom environment.* Classrooms must have some place to store portfolios—a location where children can access them easily. Likewise, an area for reviewing portfolios is very useful since the contents usually take more space than a single student desktop provides. Do classrooms have portfolio display tables?

6. *Organize.* For portfolios to work, they need to be integrated into the classroom schedule. Children will need time to conference with the teacher on the portfolio's contents. They also need time to select, review, and comment on the contents. Teachers also need time to jot notes and summaries to be included.

Involving parents in the portfolio process is important. For instance, while waiting their turn at parent–teacher conference nights, parents might review their child's portfolio and write comments to be included in the portfolio file. Interviews with parents or checklists that parents complete can also be added to portfolios. The portfolio can be a powerful discussion starter with parents and a good basis for a parent–teacher conference.

Grades and Report Cards

Every day, in every classroom, children engage in reading and writing activities that provide teachers with abundant opportunities to evaluate development. Ideally, a teacher's evaluation of student work would assist students in understanding what additional learning or demonstrations of learning were needed to improve the performance being evaluated. Likewise, evaluations would inform parents and other teachers about what strategies students had acquired and indicate what strategies remained undeveloped. What sense can a student, a parent, or another teacher make of some of the traditional evaluation messages? What does "88" mean on a comprehension assessment done after a second-grade student has been involved in a guided reading of a basal story? What does a grade of B– mean on an assignment to compose a persuasive essay in fifth grade? What sense can anyone make of a smiley face or "Good Job!!!" written at the top of an assignment?

The research on grading is clear on at least one issue: There is little evidence that grading practices provide reliable estimates of student learning (Hargis, 2003; Stiggins, Frisbie, & Griswold, 1989). The lack of any clear and consistent school policy on grading practices may be the most important reason. Consequently, teachers develop their own policies, and these vary widely from teacher to teacher. Even when teachers do not give letter or number grades and use some other scale (e.g., needs improvement, satisfactory, mastery of objective), there is little evidence that teachers teaching similar material at the same grade level evaluate the same things in the same way.

Report card grading policies vary by the weight teachers give to

- Effort
- Timeliness
- Test scores
- Extra-credit efforts

- Creativeness
- Compliance
- Neatness
- Homework

- Makeup work
- Participation
- Attentiveness
- Demeanor

Not every teacher, for instance, records the grades given homework assignments. Some factor in estimates of students' effort; others do not. Some offer students opportunities to retake tests or to redo assignments; other do not. Perhaps more important, all teachers at the same grade level do not create the same assignments or even teach the same content. Thus, a grade for an individual assignment means whatever the teacher wants it to mean, as does a report card grade. Because grades are rarely tied to any common content or standard, they rarely indicate what students know about a subject or what strategies they have developed. Prominent evaluation specialist Gene Glass argues that grades are "essentially arbitrary" and points out that there is no good way to make meaningful distinctions between a C+ and a B– (Willis, 1993).

Current grading practices seem to rest on the assumption that grades have a motivational effect—that students will work harder to achieve better grades. But effort is not often a particularly salient influence on grading, so extra effort does not necessarily improve a child's grades. Too often classroom evaluations simply rank-order children—much as norm-referenced test reports do. Some children receive good grades or positive comments, and others receive lower grades and few positive comments. This situation is especially troubling for struggling learners—children most likely to receive a steady stream of lower grades and less positive comments. Even when these children are developing improved reading and writing strategies, their performances are usually ranked behind the performances of their peers who do not find learning to read and write difficult. Motivation research (Wigfield, 1997) suggests that success precedes motivation, not the other way around, and that traditional assessment practices are rarely motivating to the very students who need the most motivation.

Children who have difficulty learning to read find the words on spelling lists harder to learn than do skillful readers. So even with equivalent time and effort in studying, children who read less well can be expected to spell fewer words correctly than their peers who have no difficulty learning to read. The child who improves from 10 of 20 weekly words spelled correctly to 12 of 20 correct will rarely feel better than the child who shows no improvement but consistently gets 18 or 19 of 20 correct without studying. The child who learns to spell 5 new words but still gets only 12 of 20 correct will hardly be motivated by his grade, especially when the child who previously knew how to spell 18 or 19 of the words achieved 20 correct with no studying.

What are grading practices attempting to achieve? Are grades supposed to tell students what strategies they need to acquire? Is the purpose of grades to let children know where they stand, academically, among their peers? Or are grades an estimate of how much effort students put forth to complete the assigned work (Hargis, 2003)? It may be useful to interview students and ask them to explain what they think an assignment grade means or what a report card grade means. It may also be useful to interview parents and find out what they think grades mean and how they interpret low grades. Do grades clearly inform other teachers about what children have learned or what they need to be taught? Do grades help teachers make sense of children as learners? Why are grades given?

In giving grades, we try to reduce a variety of complex cognitive activities to a single letter, number, or rating. Some children do not put forth much effort to receive high grades, and other children put forth much effort yet receive low grades. Some children develop many new skills, strategies, and knowledges but still receive low grades while others learn few new skills but obtain better grades. How can teachers adequately communicate progress toward learning goals across a six- or eight-week period in a single mark or grade? If we want assessment practices to foster learning and enhance student motivation, grading and report cards must be substantially rethought.

Some teachers who adopted more instructionally useful assessment practices in their classrooms have told us of the difficulty they have when they must give a grade on a report card. If they grade primarily on effort, there are howls from predictable corners—from parents and from students who have always gotten good grades with little effort. If they grade on growth, the same is true. But if they base grades on an estimated rank-ordering, children who worked hard and even those who exhibited substantial development may receive low grades that undermine not only the mentoring relationship that has evolved but also continued effort toward further improvement.

A proposal to toss out report cards and grade entries in students' cumulative files is not likely to be met with wholehearted approval by the public. The general public is reluctant to give up the familiar and traditional report cards and grades that students carry home. Much of this reluctance may be due more to a lack of familiarity with alternatives than to any real satisfaction with report cards. Nonetheless, for whatever reason, the average citizen feels comfortable with traditional grades and report cards, despite their limitations. Thus, changing the current situation will require some work. What can be done?

An Alternative to Traditional Report Cards   Afflerbach (1993) outlines a procedure for rethinking report cards (it seems to apply equally as well to grading). He lists four assumptions about effective reporting of student progress to parents, and he poses several questions for discussion and resolution. Here are the assumptions:

- Representatives from all groups who read, write, or rely on report cards should be involved in changing current practices.
- Reports should provide useful information about reading and writing development for other teachers, parents, and students.
- Flexibility that allows different teachers to communicate their knowledge of children's development must be designed into reporting procedures.
- Reports must be manageable for teachers and for parents or students who read them.

Improved communication of children's literacy development is a worthwhile goal but one that cannot always be achieved without much discussion. Creating a team to study, discuss, and propose changes in current procedures is the first step in a long process. The team will consist of teachers from different grade levels, parents, administrators, and, possibly, a representative from the school board (some schools might also include students). Here are the questions that Afflerbach poses for discussion:

- What is the purpose of the reading report card (and who is the audience)?
- What role does the report card play in communicating reading assessment?
- What are the responsibilities associated with the new report card?
- How can the school ensure that new report cards will be understood?

If the purpose of report cards (and grades) is simply to provide a rank-ordering of students, most schools will not have to revise much current practice. However, if the intended purpose of report cards is to inform parents about children's literacy development and to provide students with a larger sense of ownership of their development, then most current report cards will need drastic revisions.

Johnston (1992) asks whether all teachers need to use a uniform procedure for reporting to parents. We know of schools where all teachers do not use the same reporting system but can elect one of several formats for reporting progress to parents (traditional report card, individual narratives about each student, or parent conference). The uniformity of teacher reports to parents is not a given but rather an option to weigh.

Schools also need to consider whether the report card should be the primary means of communicating information to parents. Most schools organize parent–teacher conferences. Perhaps information on literacy development would be better communicated in this face-to-face setting. In some schools, students not only attend these conferences but also present their work to, and discuss it with, their parents and their teacher. Schools opting for teacher–parent or student-run conferences might rely far less on traditional report cards to provide parents with information (Austin, 1994).

The tradition of sending all students' report cards home simultaneously also needs to be reconsidered. If teachers are to compose narrative-style report cards for all students, it is almost essential that such report cards be released on a staggered basis. After perhaps four weeks of school the teacher might begin using quickwrite procedures described earlier in this chapter to create a narrative report that would be sent home with one student the following day. A student might stay after school and work with the teacher as the teacher writes the narrative. In such cases, a "best work" might be attached and become the focus of the evaluation sent home. If teachers wrote one narrative each day, Monday through Thursday, each child would receive a narrative report every six to seven weeks—or at least as frequently as most schools now release traditional report cards.

Acceptance of such radically revised procedures may not come easily, although parents report that the written comments on current report cards are the component they find most valuable. Teachers find the usual space for comments too small. But even if there were more space, teachers report, there would not be enough time to develop the written comments on traditional report cards issued simultaneously. In this context, narrative reports may seem especially daunting. In addition, not all teachers accept the premise that rank-ordering children is potentially damaging and not particularly motivating for students. Also, such drastic changes in assessment and reporting to parents would require teachers to know their students better and to know more about how children learn to read and write. The problem is not that altering reporting practices in this way will take enormous amounts of additional time—once learned, the procedures become part of the daily routine. The problem is that incorporating the observation and quickwrite procedures into the daily routine requires substantial changes in traditional teaching as well as in grading. But to create schools where all children are successful will require substantial new learning by teachers and substantial shifts in instructional practices. If instruction is to shift, assessment must also. In fact, shifts in assessment may offer the best way to foster shifts in instruction.

Summary

As Farr (1992) noted, "The assessment puzzle can be solved. The solution, however, is not as simple as identifying a nonexistent test that will do the whole job nor as arbitrary as eliminating most reading assessment" (p. 36). The norm-referenced achievement testing that has long dominated elementary reading assessment must be supplemented by more instructionally useful assessments of literacy development. The newer state-mandated performance-referenced assessments are a political reality, and perhaps the best we can expect is that those assessments will improve over time.

Different assessment practices better fit one purpose than another, but few of the traditional practices well serve the purposes of improving instruction, educating teachers, motivating students, and informing parents about how well literacy is being fostered. Although commercial norm-referenced tests and performance-referenced tests are being improved, such tests currently have limited potential to do anything other than inhibit change. Still, until alternatives are more fully developed and better known, tests of these sorts are likely to remain at the forefront of educational reform efforts—thus our call to begin to administer such tests anonymously. Anonymity would work to ensure that children are not harmed by unreliable assessment reports and would limit the current abuses of tests in many schools.

Robert Linn (2000), the noted test and measurement researcher, recently summarized his views on the current assessment mania.

> I am led to conclude that in most cases the instruments and technology have not been up to the demands that have been placed on them by high-stakes accountability. Assessment systems that are useful monitors lose much of dependability and credibility for that purpose when high stakes are attached to them. The unintended negative effects of high-stakes accountability uses often outweigh the intended positive effects. (p. 14)

The point is that it is hard to develop a single test that fulfills all the needs of policy makers, principals, parents, and teachers. We do not object to the premise that public schools and the teachers in them should be accountable for the academic growth they produce (or fail to). But accountability without authority is a worst-case scenario. To be told "You will achieve this result and you will do it this way with these materials on this timeline" creates a lose–lose situation for the teaching profession. Hold us accountable, but give us the authority and the resources to do what our professional judgment indicates must be done.

Professional Development: The Key to Change

R ecently, the local newspaper carried a story on a board of education meeting in a nearby school district. The board had added $5,000 to the existing $22,500 annual budget for professional development. A board member commented that such a sum would create "a world class in-service program." This $27,500 budget item represented less than one-tenth of 1 percent of the school district's $35.8 million total budget! Unfortunately, many school districts—in fact, most—allocate minuscule amounts for professional development activities and then puzzle over why change in schools is so slow. Suppose that school districts routinely followed the advice of the National Staff Development Council (Hirsh & Sparks, 1999) and invested 10 percent of the budget in professional development. In the district mentioned above, the professional development allocation would have been a little over $3.5 million.

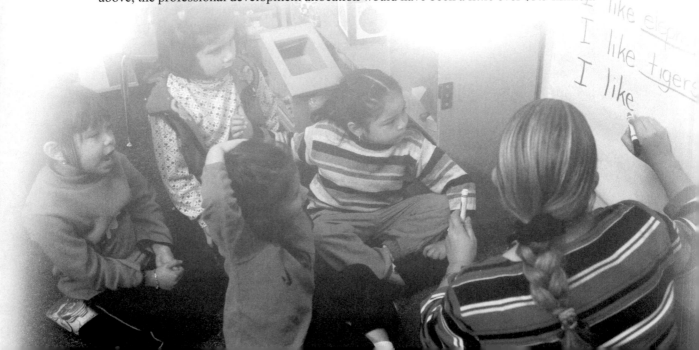

If that district had allocated even the 3 percent recommended by the National Commission on Teaching and America's Future (1997), over $1 million would have been allocated. If only 1 percent had been invested by that local school district, roughly $330,000 of additional funds would have been earmarked for professional development support.

In most school districts, roughly 80 percent of the annual operating budget is invested in salaries. Education *is* a people business. Schools do not improve unless a faculty improves. Elementary schools will change only when new strategies and new knowledge become incorporated into everyday practice. But we are hard-pressed to locate school districts that invest even 1 percent of the annual budget in supporting the professional development of district employees. We are not sure exactly why this is so, but we do have a few hypotheses.

First, too few people have viewed educational reform as primarily an issue of developing the expertise of teachers (Duffy & Hoffman, 1999). Most reform efforts to date have focused more on peripheral features of schooling—changing school schedules, mandating assessments, reorganizing student groupings, ordering different curriculum materials, investing in technology, attempting to involve parents—than on "core instructional" features (Elmore, Peterson, & McCarthy, 1996) such as how to design lessons that develop students' higher-order understanding, effective and efficient decoding skills, and independent self-monitoring strategies. The most common attempts to address these sorts of issues have involved purchasing new commercial curricular materials, but little investment was typically made in providing teachers with support in using those new curricular materials (Hoffman et al., 1998).

Second, much of the "in-service training" offered in schools has a rather dismal track record. Suffice it to say that little evidence supports continuing the traditional "one-shot" in-service training workshop. Given the limited effects of this popular format for teacher retraining, we are not surprised that few school district administrators see a need to invest more money in such workshops.

Third, most schools lack experience with activities that have a demonstrated record of fostering positive change. Even though research on professional development is still in its infancy, a number of basic findings can be used to enhance professional development efforts. Not surprisingly, however, much of this information has not found its way into many schools because of its relatively recent availability. One of our goals for this chapter is to introduce key findings reported in more detail by others (e.g., Fullan, 1991; Killion & Harrison, 1997; Little, 1993; Richardson, 1990; Taylor, Pearson, Peterson, & Rodriguez, 2005; Wolf et al., 2000).

Fourth, many believe that professional development is more an individual responsibility than a school responsibility. Linked to this belief is the notion that teachers who want to improve their professional practice will seek out appropriate activities on their own. Of course, it is true that teachers have a personal responsibility to engage in professional development throughout their careers. But, at the same time, school districts have a responsibility to support the professional development of their teachers. Professional development is a two-way street. Schools need to offer supportive frameworks to ensure that teachers have appropriate opportunities to engage in professional development activities. Teachers have the responsibility, at least, to take full advantage of the opportunities offered.

Fifth, in most schools no one carries much responsibility for fostering professional development among teachers and administrators. Principals often have some responsibility for professional development activities focused on classroom teachers, but someone else is responsible for reading teachers, special education teachers, paraprofessionals, food-service workers, librarians, and so on. Professional development activities are fragmented; there is no overall plan of action or schoolwide focus. When a school's professional development opportunities are best characterized as a series of separate, unconnected activities, there is little reason to expect that the efforts will produce any substantial change in educational practices or any great benefit to teachers or to the children they teach (Birman, Desimone, Porter, & Garet, 2000; Hirsh & Sparks, 1999; Joyce & Showers, 1988).

Creating schools where all children learn to read and write will require a broad, long, and well-planned effort. Before more money is sought to support the necessary professional development activities and opportunities for teachers and administrators, most schools would do well to rethink wholly the nature and purpose of professional development in relation to the needed changes. A good first step would be to examine the current school structure and organization with an eye toward identifying where professional development concerns might most profitably focus.

Looking at Your School

Research on schools suggests starting with a school inventory. No two schools are ever identical in staff quality, curriculum organization, teacher involvement, and so on. Rosenholtz (1989) identified three types of schools. She called them "moving," "in between," and "stuck." In *moving* schools, roughly 80 percent of the teachers viewed professional improvement as a lifelong endeavor. They felt they faced new challenges each year and noted various ways they had adapted and continued polishing their teaching repertoires. Teachers in moving schools tended to be collaborative and likely to seek out ideas from colleagues. They were likely to have reached a consensus about important goals and to seek out professional development opportunities. In interviews, they talked about how much they had yet to learn, and they noted questions that challenged them. In particular, they sought to improve their efforts to teach all children, especially children who found learning difficult. In many senses, moving schools were "self-improving systems."

At the opposite end of the Rosenholtz continuum are *stuck* schools. In them, few teachers saw professional development as an ongoing endeavor. Most felt they had "mastered" the necessary techniques by the end of their third year of teaching. Teachers in stuck schools saw little need to improve or to engage in any sort of extended professional development activities. School learning difficulties were felt to be primarily the fault of parents, not of ineffective instruction. Although these teachers might want a workshop on a new reading series, they generally were not interested in engaging in study of literacy learning so they might better understand their own teaching processes and their students' learning. Teachers in stuck schools felt they had little need for improved instructional repertoires and rarely were receptive to suggested professional development activities. The fact that the professional development activities offered to them rarely had any impact reinforced their belief that such activities were useless. As a result, fewer and fewer professional development activities were offered, and the instructional environment steadily declined in quality. Stuck schools often became increasingly dysfunctional and, over time, offered fewer opportunities for growth to either teachers or children. (In the middle of the Rosenholtz continuum are *in-between* schools, in which professional development was a priority, though not a high one.)

Even the worst-case stuck schools, however, have some faculty who would fit quite nicely with the faculty of moving schools. The trick in a stuck school is to build on that group of teachers, no matter how small, who are eager to engage in professional development and continued growth.

McLaughlin and Yee (1988) described key features of schools that seem similar to Rosenholtz's moving schools. They focused on teachers who thought of teaching as a career rather than as a job. Such teachers were found most often in schools that shared five characteristics. McLaughlin and Yee described these schools as

- *Resource-adequate* instead of resource-deprived. Teachers had at least the minimum curriculum materials and classroom resources needed to accomplish their goals.

- *Integrated* rather than segmented. Integrated schools had a unity of purpose, shared goals, and a shared sense of responsibility. Segmented schools, in contrast, had clear divisions within the faculty, an us-versus-them attitude about school administration, and little commitment to any common vision of what the school should or could be doing.

- *Collegiality* versus isolation from peers. Multiple collegial interactions created a school where colleagues were seen as a constant source of support and ideas for improving teaching. When teachers felt isolated in their own classrooms, they often failed to go beyond complaining about students and parents.

Most schools already have at least one "professional conversational community" or group of teachers who meet regularly but informally to talk with each other about instructional practice (Johnston et al., 1998). Such groups are found even in schools that seem to fit the stuck criteria, although the communities there often go to great lengths to mask their conversations from other peers. It is unlikely that any school can improve if large numbers of the staff are not involved in a professional conversational group. The key issue is developing, fostering, maintaining, and making the conversations more beneficial.

- *Problem-solving* orientation instead of problem hiding. In a problem-solving environment, teachers assumed a need for continued learning about teaching. They developed a stronger sense of group and were likely to reflect routinely on their own teaching. In problem-hiding schools, in contrast, teachers kept to themselves and rarely shared concerns or difficulties with their peers.

- *Investment centered* rather than payoff focused. When schools were investment centered, teachers were seen as resources rather than as problems. Through a variety of methods, investments were made in improving teaching, not just by rewarding the few who were deemed superior teachers. In investment-centered approaches, teachers were encouraged to take risks and to seek out resources for improvement.

Few schools have all of those features. Unfortunately, many teachers work in isolation in segmented schools in which problem hiding is more likely than problem solving. Administrators in such schools seem to to focus more on ferreting out "incompetent" teachers than on investing in teacher development. Most teachers do seem to have minimally adequate resources, thankfully, but teachers in schools serving the largest numbers of poor children are also those most likely to work in resource-deprived settings (Kozol, 1991).

A more recent study (Johnston et al., 1998) noted differences in district organizational plans that seemed to account for many of these differences. Schools in districts that emphasized top-down management through highly centralized decision making made little progress toward reform goals or toward improving student achievement in this longitudinal study. Schools in districts where decision making was more decentralized exhibited both greater instructional improvement and improved student achievement. Highly centralized district-level decision making seemed to create the worst of all worlds for change. When told how to teach, what to teach, for how many minutes, and in what manner,

It might be useful at this point to assess your school on the five characteristics sketched above. To do this, simply place a mark on the continuum to indicate the qualities of your school.

Resource adequate	⊢——————————⊣	Resource deprived
Integrated	⊢——————————⊣	Segmented
Collegial	⊢——————————⊣	Isolated
Problem solving	⊢——————————⊣	Problem hiding
Investment centered	⊢——————————⊣	Payoff focused

All but the first item are characteristics that cannot be developed by mandate or ensured by regulation and monitoring. What steps can be taken to improve the situation in your school?

teachers saw little reason to take much responsibility for the instruction. They did what they were told—end of discussion. The failures of children in those schools were ascribed to the failures of children to fit the program (or to the failure of their parents). The highly centralized schools were constantly imposing new "reforms" and new mandates, but things never got better for teachers or students.

Perhaps the most disturbing finding of this study (Johnston et al., 1998) was differences in the attitudes that administrators in the two types of district expressed concerning their teachers. Administrators in the districts with centralized decision making provided a quite negative description of their teachers (as lazy and not very skilled) as the rationale for centralized decisions. Administrators in the districts with decentralized decision making described their teachers more positively (as expert and hardworking). The researchers suggested that some districts seem to create less effective teachers and other districts nurture the development of teacher expertise.

A recent study followed undergraduates into their first years of teaching (Valencia, Place, Martin, & Grossman, in press). A key finding was the critical nature of the first workplace on shaping these new teachers' belief systems and instructional activities. Some of these teachers went to work in top-down districts where reading instruction was highly centralized and provided little opportunity to apply professional expertise ("just follow the manual"). Others went to work in environments where they were expected to work collaboratively with other teachers to create their own reading program while adhering to grade-level guidelines. After only two years, significant differences could be seen in both beliefs and instruction. Perhaps this is most easily illustrated by responses to queries about planning. The teachers in the highly controlled environment noted they didn't plan on weekends. "I just come in on Mondays and open the manual and go." Teachers working in the more collaborative and less controlling environment told how they spent many hours every weekend and in the evenings planning, locating resources, and discussing instructional difficulties with peers. The teachers in the top-down schools reported that struggling readers were someone else's responsibility whereas the teachers in the schools with few mandates noted the ways in which they were modifying instruction to better meet their students' needs. Someone once said that most schools get the teachers they create.

The creation of schools where all children learn to read and write will occur only with movement away from teacher isolation and problem hiding. Throughout this book, we have attempted to portray the resource-adequate classroom in an integrated environment focused on collegial problem solving. In this chapter, we attempt to build on these features and portray an investment-centered approach to creating schools that work better for all children. It is the classroom teachers working in any elementary school who will bear the brunt of the work ahead and also the brunt of responsibility for creating classroom environments that foster literacy in every child. Only by investing in classroom teachers can any school hope to become a school where all children learn to read and write. Remember this principle: A good school is but a collection of good classrooms.

The Future Does Not Have to Look Like the Past

Investing time, energy, and money to support the professional development of teachers makes good sense. Ongoing professional development is essential as schools restructure to meet society's expectations. Creating a school where all children acquire thoughtful literacy will go a long way toward meeting the new goals set for schools, but becoming a school where all children read and write thoughtfully will require teachers and administrators to develop new skills and strategies.

Inventory School-Sponsored Professional-Development Activities

To begin, consider "official" professional development opportunities in your school. What topics have been the focus of any recent traditional staff-development efforts? To complete the accompanying chart, you will need to locate information on the topics that have been the primary focus of professional development sessions that teachers have participated in. Check off the topics of sessions offered this year, last year, and two or three years ago. At this point, the inventory indicates only the breadth of topics covered (feel free to add additional boxes for other topics).

Focus	This Year	Last Year	2–3 Years Ago
Reading			
Writing			
Math			
Science			
Social studies			
Art/Drama			
Special education			
At-risk students			
Technology			
Drugs, alcohol, etc.			
Multiculturalism			
Instructional (e.g., activity-based)			
Organizational (e.g., ungraded)			

Once you have indicated the breadth of topics, highlight any topics that received a sustained focus across a two-to-three-year period (highlight those rows with checks in all three columns). Then circle all the checks for any topics in which the professional development opportunities involved actual classroom collaborations between teacher–participants (in each other's classrooms) or presenter–teacher collaborations in the teachers' classrooms (e.g., demonstration teaching, coaching). Finally, put an X on all the checks where the professional development opportunity was formally evaluated for changes in classroom practices or changes in student achievement (i.e., someone observed in classrooms to document changes and collected and analyzed achievement data from students of participating teachers).

The questions you want to try to answer from this activity were set out by Birman and her colleagues' (2000) study of effective professional development:

- What has been the content focus of professional development to date?
- What has been the duration, intensity, and coherence of those efforts?
- How often has an active learning component been included?
- Do we know the impact of the activities on classroom practice and student achievement?

Completing such an inventory is important for identifying long-term professional development projects, activities that actually involved going into classrooms, and activities that were evaluated for success in changing teaching practices or enhancing student achievement. Support will be easier to gain for future professional development efforts if a historical perspective is presented with a longer-term plan for supporting professional development and an evaluation component. The inventory is also a potential problem-solving activity. Gathering information on past efforts should improve understanding of which past efforts seemed most and least effective.

Inventory Personal
Professional Development Activities

The chart focuses primarily on "official" school-sponsored professional development activities—opportunities sanctioned and supported by the school, school district, or state education agency. Other sorts of professional development need to be considered as well, particularly personal ventures that are not school sponsored or funded, although a school might view them as beneficial and encourage participation.

It is time to recognize that teachers, on their own, engage in many activities that can foster professional development (e.g., undertaking personal professional reading,

We believe that every elementary school should have a professional library that includes recent books and professional magazines. As a starting point we suggest these books and magazines concerned primarily with children's literacy development. (See www.teachersread.net for other suggested books.)

Books	Magazines
Allington, R. L. (2006). *What really matters for struggling readers.* New York: Allyn & Bacon.	*The Reading Teacher*
Calkins, L. et al. (1998). *A teacher's guide to standardized reading tests.* Portsmouth, NH: Heinemann.	*Learning*
Cunningham, P. M., & Allington, R. L. (2003). *Classrooms that work.* New York: Allyn & Bacon.	*Booklinks*
Fountas, I. C., & Pinnell, G. S. (1999). *Matching books to readers.* Portsmouth, NH: Heinemann.	*Elementary School Journal*
Graves, D. (2001). *The energy to teach.* Portsmouth, NH: Heinemann.	*Teaching Exceptional Children*
Harvey, S., & Goudvis, A. (2000). *Strategies that work.* York, ME: Stenhouse.	*Instructor*
Johnston, P. H. (2004). *Choice words.* York, ME: Stenhouse.	*Educational Leadership*
Keene, E. L., & Zimmerman, S. (1997). *Mosaic of thought.* Portsmouth, NH: Heinemann.	*Language Arts*
	Education Digest

attending noncredit computer workshops at the local community college, guest lecturing in a college class). The chart focuses attention on the school-sponsored opportunities. Now you might simply list the various personal activities that teachers engage in to enhance their professional competence. We find that often school administrators are not aware of the personal ventures that teachers undertake. Administrators usually create only a short list that greatly underestimates the personal initiative of teachers—especially teachers in learning-enriched schools.

We mention this because our experience suggests that another characteristic of the moving school is institutional knowledge and recognition for teachers' personal professional development efforts. If personal professional reading were considered one useful strategy for continued professional growth, we would expect to find a large supply of current professional publications within easy reach of teachers in a school—not in the library or in the principal's office but on the bookshelf and in magazine racks in the faculty room. Back issues of magazines might be stored somewhere else, but recent issues would be at hand.

We will even go a step farther and suggest that if personal professional reading were valued we would see the following in schools:

- Subscriptions to professional journals for individual teachers
- Professional articles being routed to instructional staff
- Notes about new professional books included in a weekly or monthly memorandum
- "Teachers as reading professionals" groups discussing recent books
- Some time at each faculty meeting is set aside to discuss professional reading

Ideally, schools would also have a collection of classroom-focused videotapes that teachers might draw from. Recently, a number of such collections have been developed by several universities, publishing houses, and professional associations. Also, schools would provide encouragement and information about local professional groups such as affiliates of the International Reading Association, the National Council of Teachers of English, Phi Delta Kappa, and the Council for Exceptional Children. Schools interested in fostering continuing professional development would make that interest visible throughout the school.

Inventory Answer-Giving and Problem-Solving Opportunities

Another important question about recent professional development opportunities is the extent to which current activities might be classified as problem solving in their overall focus. This criterion is important because the most powerful evidence is that which teachers develop themselves. It is common to have a presenter intone "Research indicates. . ." and perhaps distribute a summary of relevant research. Many teachers and administrators, however, are hardly impressed by such efforts—unless the "research" supports their personal beliefs and personal experiences (Richardson, 1990). Examine school responses to these three research-based principles:

- Retention provides no benefit to children.
- Heterogeneous groups benefit all learners.
- Children need enormous amounts of easy reading to become proficient readers.

It is not difficult to find schools that are "aware" of these findings but where students are still retained and still grouped homogeneously for instruction, where classroom schedules and curriculum materials are organized so that most children spend little time actually reading, and where many children rarely read anything that is easy for them. Often, explanations of these practices invoke "practical knowledge" derived from experience: "Don't tell me retention doesn't work, just look at Jalen Jones!"

The best way to alter teacher beliefs is to engage teachers in problem solving through gathering local data on the question. Retention effects, for instance, can be examined by gathering information on 10 to 20 children who have been retained and comparing their school progress with that of low-achieving students who were not retained (or by studying their performance later in school). Alternatively, examining the records of children who drop out of the local high school will often highlight the substantial overrepresentation of children who were retained (McGill-Franzen, Ward, Goatley, & Machado, 2002).

Likewise, collecting information on the relative difficulty of texts read by higher- and lower-achieving readers will often highlight that some children have few high-success reading opportunities. Examining the time allocated for actual reading and writing during the school day may suggest that less time is spent than expected. Gathering local data is a useful activity, if only as a status check. Gathering descriptive information provides all teachers with better understanding of the variation in local practice and provides some information to complement the research summarized in professional journals.

Such problem-solving activity is useful because it offers teachers an opportunity to reflect on both intended and unintended effects of educational practice. Gathering even descriptive information on teaching practices and student outcomes also provides a basis for discussion and reflection. Teachers do not make decisions mindlessly, but teachers do justify decisions based on past and prevailing practice—practical knowledge gained from experience and from their own sense of what works for them in their classrooms. Unfortunately, what works for teachers does not always work for kids. Likewise, long-standing practices, or traditions, are not always the most effective practices. But if teachers are to consider changing current practice, more than an "expert" intoning "Research says . . ." will be required.

Who Participated in What?

As a final step, return to the chart we presented earlier. How many of the school-sponsored activities involved nearly all classroom teachers, regardless of their grade-level teaching assignment? How often were first-grade and fifth-grade teachers offered the same sessions? Did this occur in many instances, even though the professional concerns of teachers of 6-year-olds and 11-year-olds are generally quite different?

Now note the number of workshops that were offered for only relatively inexperienced teachers (one to three years' experience). What about workshops for only teachers with more than 20 years' experience, or for teachers with no previous professional-development activity in process approaches to writing, or for teachers with a broad background in children's literature? Most professional development programs fail to distinguish among even the broadest differences in teachers. This one-size-fits-all approach undermines the potential that many professional-development activities offer.

How much professional development activity was scheduled during the regular workday or work year? How many of the activities were "voluntary" and scheduled after a long school day, on weekends, or during summer vacation? Although many sorts of professional development need to occur during the normal workday, teachers also need longer blocks of time to puzzle through new ideas together, and they need time to do this when they are fresh and relaxed.

Where to Go from Here?

Completing a fairly comprehensive inventory of recent professional development support in a school is a useful starting point for rethinking future professional development efforts. Well-designed professional development support will be the key for helping stuck and in-between schools become moving schools. An array of activities are available, and deciding what professional development support to provide is the next step.

The Role of Outside "Experts"

If the one-shot workshop approach has little effect on teacher change, is there any useful role that outside experts, or consultants, can profitably play in professional development? We think there is (but then we both do consulting work with schools). But outside consultants play only a small role in any effective professional development plan targeted to change substantially the educational practices of a school. Nonetheless, outside consultants may be useful in any of the following roles:

- *Conversation starter.* Often an outside consultant can be very effective in getting needed discussion started. For instance, a consultant's strong presentation on why inclusionary and collaborative educational models are essential if all children are to learn to read and write can serve as the initiating event for discussions about restructuring the traditional segregated pull-out models for addressing the needs of struggling readers and writers. Many teachers, both classroom and pull-out teachers, are quite satisfied with the traditional segregated model. Most have no extended experiences with any other instructional plan. Hearing a rationale for change, learning about the evidence indicating that traditional models do not serve most children well, and having alternatives sketched may prod some teachers into conversations about changing local practice. In some cases, the consultant at the initiating event functions a bit like a lightning rod—attracting the heat that the issue may at first generate.

- *Surveyor of the larger landscape.* Outside consultants typically visit a number of schools each year and observe and discuss local practices at each site. Thus, they usually have a broader view of prevailing practice than do educators who have worked for many years in the same school. One sad fact is that most educators have rather provincial knowledge, usually limited to knowledge of their own school or school system. Consultants draw on an array of school experiences that provide a richer vision of the possibilities for improving school practice. In addition many consultants provide access to targeted resources such as specific professional books, videos, and websites that address issues of concern. Consultants usually are not more creative than school personnel, but because of the breadth of their experience they are able to provide many more examples of educational practices to draw from.

- *Content expert.* No one can be an expert on all things. If improving reading and language arts instruction is an important priority, obtaining the services of a consultant with expertise in that area makes sense. Often, consultants offer an odd combination of a breadth of experience on a narrow range of topics. For example, we think of ourselves primarily as "reading experts," and most often when we work with schools we focus on the reading and language arts curriculum and instruction. Neither of us has much to offer for improving the math program in a school or for modifying art, drama, theater, or music (except that we think each can and should be better integrated into the reading and language arts curriculum). Similarly, consultants who view themselves as cooperative learning experts or as classroom management experts may not have much expertise in teaching reading and language arts.

Most consultants will know very little about the school they visit. They know a lot about their specialty, and they have wide-ranging school experiences. What consultants will be able to accomplish will depend in part on whether they are able to work with a school long enough to become familiar with the current program, the professional staff, and the current classroom environments.

- *Evaluator.* Often, the notion of evaluation is narrowly conceived in education. Many consultants who do not consider themselves evaluation experts can, nevertheless, be very useful as independent evaluators of change projects. Having a set of naive eyes and ears around can be useful (*naive* here means not expert on local practice). A consultant can often ask the right questions quite naively.

For instance, one school had moved to trade books as the sole curriculum material for reading instruction, and teachers and administrators were quite proud about having "thrown out the basal." After visiting classrooms at the site, a consultant asked a number of questions that teachers found difficult to answer about observed local practices. The consultant questioned the mindless response journal activities observed, the limited range of genres found on the core-books list, the preponderance of story-map worksheets that occupied children, the limited representation of minorities on the core-books lists, and the presence of hundreds of chapter question dittos included in the locally developed curriculum packets. The consultant not only raised questions about these issues but also pointed to several articles and books that addressed these concerns. Ultimately, the consultant was able to assist in enhancing the breadth of the core-books lists and expand the time available for children to actually read and write each day. The consultant never completed a traditional evaluation report (although a two-page site report summary was developed), but the role the consultant played was that of an outside expert evaluator.

Consultants can provide useful feedback, or evaluation, but that role seems currently underdeveloped and underused. Asking consultants to complete a single-page site report, even consultants providing only a single session, offers the potential for gathering an outsider's perspective on the school and the school staff.

● *Partner in change.* Consultants can become partners in promoting change. Most, however, do not, because of the substantial time it takes to foster real change. To become a partner in change will almost always require at least a one-year commitment to work in the school and with the teachers, and often the time frame is even longer (although intensity of involvement should lessen across time).

Regardless of the role an external consultant is selected to fill, schools can enhance the usefulness of a consultant by providing that person with better information than is usually available. Consultants can only act on the information they have. With little information there will be little tailoring of the sessions to the school's needs. When schools provide information about the curriculum's special-program organization, previous initiatives in staff development, and the primary issue needing to be addressed, consultants can produce far more useful workshops. As consultants, we find having dinner (or breakfast) with school staff members useful before beginning the workday at the school. We also find that having time, while at the school, to visit classrooms and talk with teachers and administrators is enormously useful. More schools need to try to arrange consultant schedules to include such activities.

Alternative Professional-Development Opportunities

As noted earlier most professional-development activity continues to be traditional workshop sessions, although the use of alternative formats is occurring. Limited experiences with alternatives was the main theme of a national study of professional development among literacy professionals (Commeyras & DeGroff, 1998). Given the research now available on the impact of alternative opportunities, we hope that their use expands dramatically in the near future.

For Membership Information

International Reading Association, P. O. Box 8139, Newark, DE 19712-8139 (302-731-1600 or www.reading.org)

National Council of Teachers of English, 1111 West Kenyon Road, Urbana, IL 61801-1096 (217-328-3870 or www.ncte.org)

Association for Supervision and Curriculum Development, 1250 North Pitt Street, Alexandria, VA 22314-1453 (703-549-9110 or www.ascd.org)

National Staff Development Council, 5995 Fairfield Road, Oxford, OH 45056 (513-523-6029 or www.nsdc.org)

Little (1993) describes a number of alternatives to the traditional workshop-by-an-expert approach to professional development. Each of the following deserves full consideration as a potential course of action for sustained teacher development:

- *Teacher collaboratives/networks.* Typically such efforts are subject-matter specific. The Philadelphia Alliance for Teaching the Humanities in Schools (PATHS) is one example. In this case, teachers work with the various humanities collections and their curators and archivists in Philadelphia. PATHS involves teachers in original research, in "pure" intellectual activities divorced from everyday classroom practicalities, and in summer institutes held at the sites where the collections are stored. Unfortunately, few teachers report participating in such collaboratives (Birman et al., 2000).

- *Subject-matter associations.* Active involvement in professional organizations, such as the International Reading Association, the National Council of Teachers of English, and the Association for Supervision and Curriculum Development, can have substantive effects on professional development. Teachers become part of a larger professional community that extends far beyond their classrooms and broadens their perspectives on teaching and learning. Even teachers who assume no leadership roles in these organizations but read the newsletters and journals and attend state, regional, or national conferences benefit.

Unfortunately, Commeyras and DeGroff (1998) report that only one in five elementary classroom teachers holds membership in such organizations (compared to over half of all high school teachers). Since nearly two-thirds of elementary teachers reported that their teaching improved as a result of professional reading, it seems in the best interests of schools to encourage professional association membership and reading of the professional journals that membership brings. We recommend that school districts offer to pay membership fees for teachers. This small investment (usually $50 or less) would seem to offer high potential for developing expertise and improving practice.

- *School/university partnerships.* A number of large-scale partnerships have emerged over the past few years, but this alternative is still limited in scope. However, many classroom teachers have become involved on a lesser scale through the student-teaching function. As colleges and universities attempt to restructure preservice teacher education, larger roles, including in many cases adjunct faculty status, are developing for classroom teachers who provide field-based experience.

To these alternatives we would add several more:

- *Teachers as Readers (TAR) groups.* The primary activity involves teachers or administrators agreeing to read and meet monthly to discuss their reading. The Teachers as Readers effort typically involves a segment of the faculty at individual schools. It was developed as a strategy for enhancing classroom teachers' expertise in children's literature. Teachers read a wealth of children's books and discussed them with each other. Sometimes the goal was enhanced general familiarity with children's books. At other times a specific goal—such as enhancing awareness of culturally relevant children's books—was set. We have worked with TAR groups reading children's books focused on rural poverty in an attempt to enhance our own expertise about the available books and to explore our own beliefs about poor rural children and their families. Some TAR groups read adult literature to explore diversity in the United States.

We have also worked with TAR groups reading a single professional text with the goal of enhancing personal professional expertise. One group read Cunningham's *Phonics They Use* (2000), tried various instructional routines, and discussed their successes and problems. Another group of primary-grade teachers read Duthie's *True Stories* (1996) in an attempt to refine their uses of nonfiction in their classrooms. Other TAR groups read several books on a single topic over the course of a year or more as a way to develop expertise and reflect on various authors' perspectives on the topic.

The most successful TAR groups in our experience are voluntary but with book costs covered by the school. They begin, typically, with a problem or question. Recommendations for professional books on the problem are sought out and briefly reviewed. One or several books are selected by consensus of the group of interested teachers. Books are ordered, and a schedule for reading and discussion is agreed upon. When the discussion session opens, TAR participants use something akin to Keene and Zimmerman's (1997) discussion framework by relating, individually,

- Text to self (What of me did I see in the book? What have I done differently?)
- Text to text (What links do I see to other things I've read?)
- Text to world (What sense do the ideas make in our school/community?)

TAR discussion sessions are exactly that—discussion sessions. Each teacher relates his or her responses to the book and discusses these with other TAR participants. Reflecting on one's own responses and on the responses of others is the goal, not achieving a consensus about precisely what to change or do.

Administrators as Readers (AAR) groups usually bring together administrators from several schools or perhaps several districts who meet regularly to discuss books they have agreed to read. An AAR group in Ohio read this book and met to discuss its "usability." Each participant reported on shifts in school practices that were underway, shifts stimulated by the book. At the AAR session, additional ideas were generated and visits to each other's schools were planned.

Administrators might participate in TAR groups, but their presence sometimes has a "quieting" effect on teacher participants. Also, many topics that administrators might want to read about and discuss with other administrators would be of less interest to classroom teachers (designing more effective professional development, for instance). However, AAR groups have the same general goal as TAR groups: to heighten professional expertise (rather than developing action plans).

In some schools a summer-readers projects is a variation on the TAR concept. In one school, this project offered teachers the opportunity to earn extra salary during the summer months while reading and discussing children's books. The primary goal was to develop substantially greater teacher expertise in children's literature as the school moved to a literature-based reading and language arts curriculum. Teachers read hundreds of children's books over a period of a few weeks and discussed many of these books with colleagues. In other schools, teachers have met during the summer to read and discuss professional texts related to current issues or problems they encounter in their classrooms.

● *Telecommunication/computer support.* Many commercial online services (e.g., America Online, Earthlink) offer educational mail rings and online conferences that link teachers and administrators across the nation. On the day we wrote this chapter we could participate in hundreds of mail rings, including (1) discussing how to stop violence in schools (including experiences with and resources for peer mediation), (2) conversing online with children's author Patricia MacKissack, (3) discussing how inclusionary education is working, (4) discussing construction of portfolios for reading and writing, (5) receiving technical support for solving a problem with a CD-ROM curriculum package, and (6) discussing Lois Lowrey's book *The Giver* with an online TAR group.

A Few Useful Websites

These websites provide information to help you find other websites targeted to specific topics, issues, or curriculum areas.

Teachers Read, at www.teachersread.net

Federal Resources for Educational Excellence (FREE), at www.ed.gov/free

Classroom Connect, at www.corporateclassroom.com

The Global Schoolhouse, at www.globalschoolnet.org/GSH/

Kathy Schrock's Guide for Educators, at http://school.discovery.com/schrockguide/

Instructor Magazine, at www.teacher.scholastic.com/products/instructor

The federal government and many state agencies now provide online access to enormous databases with information about teaching, learning, curriculum, and so on. Not only can information be located, but articles and reports can be read on the screen or printed for distribution. Nearly every elementary school already has everything needed to hook an office or classroom computer to other sites around the nation and the world. The monthly school access fee is low or nonexistent. It is not the expense that is keeping schools off the information highway. Nevertheless, only a third of elementary teachers report using online resources (Commeyras & DeGroff, 1998).

Teachers who do use online resources are more likely to offer a focus on higher-order understanding, and a relationship between the use of online resources and positive instructional change has been documented (Becker & Ravitz, 1999). Sadly, only on relatively rare occasions have we found access to such resources readily available to elementary teachers. Few provide Internet access in the staff room. Few have technical support and training available on site. We expect that use of the Internet as a source of professional development will increase, particularly as content providers target teachers as a market. Already several firms and any number of universities have professional development activities available in Web-based formats (Kahn, 1999).

Resources for Guidelines on Teacher Inquiry/Research

Sweeney, D. (2003). *Learning along the way.* York, ME: Stenhouse.

Donoahue, Z., Van Tassell, M., & Patterson, L. (1996). *Research in the classroom.* Newark, DE: International Reading Association.

Lyons, C., & Pinnell, G. S. (2001). *Systems for change in literacy education: A guide to professional development.* Portsmouth, NH: Heinemann.

- *Teacher inquiry/teacher research.* There has been much interest in teacher research as a model for professional development. Some of this interest has been stimulated by the concern that classroom teachers do not view traditional research as particularly salient. Having teachers research their own practices in their schools seemed one way to enhance the salience of inquiry into practice. In addition, teacher inquiry/research has been viewed as central to fostering reflection on personal practice. Regardless of the underlying factors, the number of professional books and conference sessions devoted to teacher inquiry/research is growing at a tremendous rate. Only 25 percent of elementary teachers report being familiar with teacher inquiry/research, but 75 percent indicated an interest in learning more. Thus it seems that schools should be supporting teacher inquiry/research.

- *Data-gathering groups.* Related to teacher inquiry/research but different in key features, particularly ownership of the inquiry, data-gathering groups are another source of school-based research. The "cadres" established in Accelerated Schools (Levin, 1987) are one example of such a group. Cadres are groups of teachers (and parents or other community members) who set a particular question as their group focus. If the issue of flunking low-achieving students were selected for study, the cadre would search out external evidence and gather data about the effects of local practice (Allington & McGill-Franzen, 1995). Once the data are gathered, cadre members discuss the evidence and prepare a brief summary statement of findings to share with the larger faculty group. In some respects these data-gathering groups function a bit like traditional teacher committees. The important shift, however, is reflected in the name. The shift is to the collection of data, both external and local, on the question under study.

- *Personalized professional growth plans.* Personalized plans for professional growth are becoming more popular in schools, but we see relatively few formal arrangements for personalized professional growth in most schools we visit. Nonetheless, the potential of such plans seems substantial, especially from a career-cycle perspective.

The Gloversville, New York, schools created a professional growth plan that largely replaces the traditional teacher-evaluation process for tenured teachers. Instead, teachers and their building administrator together construct professional growth contracts focused on mutually agreed-upon professional goals. Once the goals are set (goals such as enhanced understanding of theme-based, literature-based reading instruction or organization of multi-age classrooms), teachers research at least two articles or books on the topic and locate a conference or institute on the topic that they might attend. They then meet with other teachers on their instructional teams (grade-level teams at the elementary school level) to discuss their professional improvement plan and how it relates to the team's planning responsibilities. Also, teachers prepare a professional-growth portfolio that contains a minimum of 10 items (a personally written professional article, lesson plans, photos, student work, video of a lesson, etc.). This portfolio is shared with the team and the school administrator at the end of each school year.

Photos of the classroom instructional environment might be included in a professional portfolio or annual report. This shared writing chart represents part of one teacher's work on a water theme in her primary class.

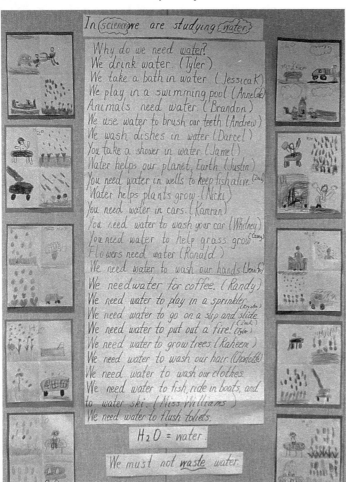

- *Annual reports.* This strategy is a variation of the annual report format that many colleges and universities use as an end-of-year faculty report. A simple outline that requests information on professional development activities during the past school year provides a forum for reporting personal professional development activity (noncredit workshops, association memberships, Teachers as Readers participation, personal professional reading, etc.) and reinforces the focus on the expectation of continued professional development.

- *Professional portfolio.* Similar in some respects to the annual report, teacher-developed professional portfolios foster reflection on professional practice. A teacher's professional portfolio might include such evidence of personal professional growth as a journal of responses to books and articles read, videotaped records of lessons, samples of personally developed curriculum plans or documents, and student portfolios with annotations explaining the significance of each included piece of student work. The question to be asked of a professional portfolio is, How do the included documents demonstrate professional development and personal reflection on professional practice?

- *Videotapes/DVDs.* Over the past five years, there has been explosive growth in the availability of potentially useful educational videos. Because most teachers, like everyone else, own videotape or DVD players, creating a library of video recordings focused on professional development topics makes sense. Today, some video products allow teachers to see an innovation in use in other classrooms, to observe an important educational summit, to view a television special on an educational topic, or to evaluate a presentation by an educational authority. Some video products will be best viewed at home, alone. Others will be good conversation starters for faculty meetings. But it isn't just the professionally produced video products that can be useful. As part of a teacher inquiry/research project, teachers have filmed their own classroom instruction and then later reflected (alone or with trusted colleagues) on the video record. Some teachers report being surprised after watching themselves on video. There is so much going on in a classroom that few teachers have time to reflect on what they are doing while they are teaching. The video record provides a source for stimulated recall of a lesson—every movement and utterance is up for review.

Among a number of videotape distributors are several good sources to begin establishing an educational video library. The Association for Supervision and Curriculum Development (www.ascd.org) offers an array of titles including "Involving Parents in Education," "Shared Decision Making," and "Schools of Quality" and also offers an audiocassette subscription to its primary professional magazine, *Educational Leadership.* Several commercial firms—Canter Associates (www.canter.net), Pearson Lesson Lab (www.lessonlab.com/professional development/reading-literacy/overview.cfm), The Video Journal (www.schoolimprovement.com), and Stenhouse Publishers (www.stenhouse.com)—offer videotapes on a variety of topics, including reading instruction.

- *Fifth-year sabbatical option.* Barth (1990) suggests offering teachers the option of receiving four-fifths of their pay for five years, with the fifth year free of teaching responsibilities. During the fifth year teachers might take courses to earn additional credentials. Alternatively, they might use that year to read professionally, to visit other schools, or to brush up on a hobby. Because the teacher would be working for reduced salary, schools would exert little control over the activities the teacher might select during the sabbatical year. This no-cost option would provide time for professional renewal and development.

- *Automatic leave policy.* Barth also recommends that schools automatically accept any teacher's request for an unpaid leave of absence, noting that teachers only request such leaves when personal or professional demands or opportunities create the necessary conditions. Whether the request comes from stressful conditions, unexpected opportunities, or simply a desire to reflect on one's career choice makes little difference. It does not make sense to force teachers to work when leave has been requested.

We often see some combination of these professional development activities in schools. We can recall only a few instances where TAR groups weren't also stimulating teacher inquiry/research or Internet searching for information relevant to the topic of the book being read. Teacher inquiry/research typically involves some professional reading as does data gathering. Likewise professional portfolio development may involve teacher inquiry/research, professional reading, video making, attending professional meetings, and so on. Our goal is to broaden perspectives on possible professional development activities and encourage support for some of the powerful activities that too often are ignored when professional development plans are created.

Professional Development across the Career

When teaching is viewed as a career, as opposed to a job, teachers are more likely to be viewed as developing professionals than as employees. Each teacher selected for employment is more likely than not to spend his or her professional career in the same school district. In most schools the teachers represent a range of teaching experience. A key question that needs to be asked is whether teachers dramatically improve their practice over time. We must ask whether current professional development efforts are moving each teacher forward toward ever-expanding expertise and expert practice.

Leithwood (1990) sketches the development of teachers' instructional expertise using the following stages:

- *Developing survival skills.* Beginning teachers arrive with less than fully developed knowledge of classroom management, limited knowledge and skill in using a variety of instructional models, poorly developed self-reflection on teaching, and limited knowledge for evaluating student performance. Most beginning teachers, for instance, know little about the actual teaching of reading or writing, and many tend to be familiar with but a single instructional model for such lessons.

- *Becoming competent in the basic skills of teaching.* Over the first few years of teaching, teachers either develop basic teaching skills or they leave teaching. This development includes learning more effective classroom management, using several teaching models, and habitually using certain teaching models with certain subjects. Teachers become more comfortable with one approach for teaching reading and writing, usually the prevailing instructional model found in the school. But teaching follows certain routines, and evaluation is still focused on learning problems, not teaching adaptations.

- *Expanding instructional flexibility.* After a few years of teaching, classroom management is largely automatic. Often, teachers now become aware of alternative instructional models for teaching reading and writing, and they begin to consider expanding their repertoire of instructional skills. Evaluation options also expand, and assessment strategies move closer to intended purposes. We have seen many experienced teachers adding trade books and process writing to their instruction, developing thematic approaches to integrate reading and writing activities, and experimenting with instructionally useful assessments such as portfolios.

● *Acquiring instructional expertise.* As teachers continue to develop professionally, classroom management disappears as a concern. Developing teachers create a fairly broad repertoire of instructional strategies that they feel comfortable with and can deploy depending on the instructional setting and situation. They elect certain teaching models depending on the students and the goals of the intended lesson. Teachers evaluate students using an array of techniques, and they use the evaluations to modify instruction.

● *Contributing to colleagues' instructional expertise.* At this stage, teachers display a breadth of competence. They are reflective about their own practice and able to assist other teachers in developing instructional expertise. These teachers have the potential to be powerful mentors. They have developed their instructional expertise and a reflective stance about their teaching. As mentors, they understand that less experienced teachers cannot develop new strategies without extended opportunities to try out new ideas while receiving supportive assistance.

● *Participating in a broad array of decisions at all levels of the educational system.* At this final stage the teacher exercises positive leadership for school improvement. The teacher has a breadth of experiences and broad understandings of how educational institutions work and how the current educational program in her or his school came to be.

Of course, there can be no single process of development that all teachers move through and no fixed time line for general professional development. Additionally, new evidence suggests that school and district contexts can powerfully shape or restrain teacher development.

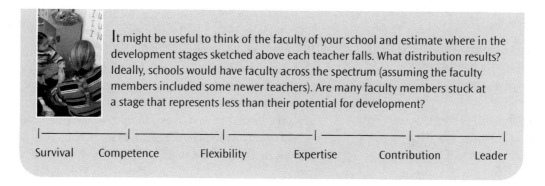

It might be useful to think of the faculty of your school and estimate where in the development stages sketched above each teacher falls. What distribution results? Ideally, schools would have faculty across the spectrum (assuming the faculty members included some newer teachers). Are many faculty members stuck at a stage that represents less than their potential for development?

|——————|—————|—————|—————|—————|—————|

Survival   Competence   Flexibility   Expertise   Contribution   Leader

There is evidence that some teachers seem to get stuck after becoming basically competent at instructional delivery. But even stuck teachers change, although the changes are surface-level changes—a little more writing but still formulaic writing that is graded and corrected in red pen, not a transformed writing activity that shifts the focus from neatness and spelling to constructing effective messages. In these classrooms, we might see children's literature used but taught one chapter per week with isolated vocabulary activities, chapter questions, and so on. In other words, new material is simply adapted for use with familiar routines (Hoffman et al., 1998).

An Action Plan for Professional Development

If we want to create schools where all children acquire reading and writing proficiency, it is the teachers and administrators who will change the instructional practices that occur in schools. Unfortunately, most people find change upsetting and difficult—two reasons why few schools (or companies) change much or fast. However, if education is to maintain public confidence, change must come to the educational system and that change will have to begin in elementary schools.

Throughout this book we propose changes that we feel are necessary. Many readers are overwhelmed by the sheer size and complexity of the changes needed at their schools. But change can be managed (somewhat). Change processes can be made more or less comfortable. Change can inspire people or it can simply wear them out. We would like to suggest several principles for attempting to change the instructional practices in any school.

In *The Right to Learn,* Linda Darling-Hammond (1997) summarizes the research on the most effective professional-development activities and notes three critical features to be concerned with:

- Professional development must center on the critical activities of teaching and learning.
- Investigations of personal and local practice must predominate.
- Substantial and sustained professional conversation about these investigations must take place.

(1) *Involve teachers in planning and gathering local data.* Teachers must be involved in planning change, and gathering local data is a good first step. Much of the useful data is already available but has not been organized in useful ways. Given the sheer quantity of testing, for instance, we might expect that all teachers in a building could quickly answer the question, What proportion of fifth graders (or fourth or sixth) have developed reading and writing abilities sufficient for success in middle school? But in many districts, virtually no one at an elementary school can answer that question. Part of the problem is that hardly anyone at the elementary school knows anything about reading and writing demands

in middle school—an odd situation in an educational "system." Often hardly anyone can answer any of these questions either:

- What proportion of children are identified as having a disability? Is that number comparable to the national average? How many children have been declassified each year for the past three years? Is that number comparable to other schools'?

- How many children are retained in this school each year? Are certain grades or teachers more likely to retain children than others? What is the long-term effect of retaining children in this school?

- How many books does each fourth grader read during any calendar year? How many are read as part of the school curriculum plan? How do the numbers compare to other schools'? To community expectations? How many books did children read over the summer? Did patterns of summer reading vary by which teacher a child had? By family SES? By reading ability?

- What is the most common sort of homework assignment that students are given? Do all teachers assign homework? Do teachers here assign more or less than teachers in most other schools? What do parents think?

- How much of their time do children actually spend reading and writing in this school each day? Are we satisfied with that amount? If parents were aware of this amount, would they be satisfied? Are there any substantial variations from one classroom to another?

- Does the pool of struggling readers get larger or smaller with each ensuing year of schooling? (In effective schools, the pool shrinks.)

- What genres (e.g., mystery, historical fiction, fantasy, biography) of reading and writing will all students be familiar with by the end of fifth grade? How many books of each genre will every fifth grader have read?

None of those questions is trivial, but in most schools no one has anything but a "best guess." We strongly believe in beginning with a good look at local data because such information is unfamiliar in most schools today. Such a procedure also establishes the "inquiring mind" mind-set necessary for a problem-solving course of change. Be aware, however, that local data collection can go on interminably and raise more questions and issues than can possibly be addressed right off. We mention this because at some sites the sheer magnitude of the problems identified by local data gathering has undermined the motivation to initiate change. So, after initial local data collection, we suggest the establishing of some priorities.

2 *Decide what you need more of and less of.* We have found the more/less strategy useful for beginning to think about change in instructional practice. Its basic premise is to identify some instructional practices that should be increased and some that should be minimized. For example:

- More opportunity to read during the school day, which can be accomplished if children spend less time on worksheets
- More reading outside school and less low-level homework
- More integration of writing with reading activities and less isolated writing that is separate from reading
- More collaboration among special teachers and classroom teachers and less planning in isolation
- More reading of "comfortable" books and stories and less reading in too-difficult texts
- Longer blocks of uninterrupted classroom instructional time and less fragmentation of the school day
- Larger numbers of books in classrooms and fewer skill and drill materials
- More decoding lessons drawn from reading and writing activities and fewer decoding lessons in isolation
- More instructionally useful classroom conversations and less interrogation

Those more/less statements represent only a few of the themes in this book yet are applicable to many schools. The idea behind this strategy is to make changes fairly concrete and easily measured. Too often in schools where children's literacy achievement is less than optimal, the objective is too broadly conceived as "increasing reading achievement." This objective gives teachers almost no direction for needed changes. When the focus is on changes that have a demonstrated relationship to achievement, the change process becomes easier to manage. In the examples provided above, individual classroom teachers can gather data on their own instructional practices as evidence that change is occurring.

(3) *Identify teachers who want to improve.* Roland Barth (1990) identified three types of teachers usually found in schools: (1) resisting teachers who generally rejected scrutiny and counsel from others and seemed to resist reflecting on their own practice; (2) teachers who rethought their own practice but did not generally welcome outside scrutiny or others visiting in their classroom (this was the largest group); and (3) teachers who actively pursued self-examination and exemplified most conceptualizations of the reflective teacher. The third type of teachers literally threw open their classroom doors to all comers, sought peer feedback, and were eager to engage in professional discussion of classroom practice.

In an ideal world, we would arrange schools so that teachers in the first group were encouraged and supported in their shift to membership in the second group and, ultimately, in the third group. Barth notes, however, that the competitive and evaluative pressures in most schools force shifts in the opposite direction—teachers move toward increasing isolation. What works to reverse this flow? Barth found that listening, really listening, to teachers' complaints, concerns, and suggestions made an enormous difference. Small encouragements to teachers to pursue the initiatives they raised seemed to rekindle sparks that had nearly died out.

Building on Barth's recommendations, we suggest indentifying teachers who are doing more of the things you like to see in the school and encourage and support those teachers. Find teachers who would like to change but have been at least temporarily defeated by a system of mandates and negative reinforcement. Encourage them to take risks. Help teachers find others to talk with and problem-solve with. Provide support more often than you criticize. Get into classrooms and help. Administer reading inventories alongside teachers who feel they have few appropriate books for many of their students. Then find appropriate books for their classrooms. Even a few books will help.

Publicize the more/less items widely, and be quick to praise any evidence of progress. Put the items in the weekly parent newsletter, and feature classrooms that have made shifts in the desired direction. Target single more/less items for a single-month focus for the whole school. Step in and try to make change more likely to happen. If increasing the amount of reading is on the list, consider a whole day "read-in" during which children read self-selected books and magazines all day. Open the library, bring out every classroom set of books you can find, invite teachers, children, and parents to donate old beanbag chairs and other soft, squishy places for reading. Set up discussion areas and book commercials where kids can find new books to read. One possible result is that kids actually will read all day. When this happens, many teachers experience dramatic shifts in their beliefs about students' reading interest and abilities and about the power of self-selected reading. Not every day should be like this, but some days certainly should.

4 *Look long.* Too often the search is for a quick fix. Changes to "dramatically improve reading scores this year" will more likely result in some manipulation of the assessment process than in beneficial changes in instructional practices. Changing instructional practice is a slow business. Teaching is a complex activity, and changing well-established instructional routines takes time and energy. Change is not amenable to simple mandates. Change occurs after teachers acquire new knowledge and experiment with using that knowledge in their own classrooms.

For instance, using a theme-based curriculum requires substantially more expertise about children's literature than most teachers have today. But simply providing professional development opportunities to increase expertise with children's literature is insufficient to implement theme-based instruction. Teachers need to acquire a repertoire of instructional practices that were less necessary in basal reader curriculum because the instuctor's manuals provided many suggestions for structuring the lessons.

As another example, consider learning to collaborate effectively with other teachers. Mandating collaboration does not work well because collaboration is a complex activity. Specialist teachers often have to acquire greater expertise in classroom instruction and the core curriculum before they can begin to plan collaboratively. Special education teachers, for instance, often have little working knowledge of classroom instruction and little familiarity with classroom core-curriculum materials. Even when teachers develop such knowledge, the problem of planning with the classroom teacher an instructional intervention for a student with learning disability remains. The complexity of change increases if the goal is not only collaborative planning but also inclusive education, and if the two teachers are expected to co-teach the child with special needs, as current federal regulations require.

The basic point is that change is hard and takes time. Fullan (1991) suggests that any substantial change will take 10 years of change activity. Unfortunately, few schools plan change at all, and those that do rarely extend planning beyond a single year. Our experiences have been more similar to Fullan's than different. We have seen dramatic changes in segments of schools in shorter time periods, but his 10-year estimate for change across an elementary school seems appropriate (see also Levin, 1987, or Walp & Walmsley, 1995, for other examples).

We suggest that combining the more/less and the look-long strategies will produce what many teachers see as a workable overall plan for educational change. But continuing local data gathering is also important because it provides real evidence that changes in teaching practices are taking place.

(5) *Focus on one classroom, one lesson at a time.* Remember that schools are collections of individual classrooms and change comes one classroom at a time. Also, classroom instruction is one lesson after another. But learning to do one lesson well seems to produce improvements in others lessons too.

Much has been written about the need for "systemic" change, and we agree that such change is critical. But *systemic* change is not *systemwide* change. Systemic change does not require everyone within the system to change in the same ways and change simultaneously. Systemic change typically involves changes in things that teachers have little control over and changes that are intended to free teachers to teach as well as they might. Needed systemic changes include the restructuring of how fiscal, curricular, and organizational issues are addressed.

Any *systemwide* improvement needs to start in the classroom. Improvement in one classroom, and then in other classrooms, takes time and is the result of the teachers changing a lesson and improving on prior practices. That improvement is professional development at its finest. A focus on individual classrooms and individual lessons keeps matters in perspective. If we considered all that needs to be changed and all the people who would need to change to restructure a school wholly, the task would seem overwhelming. Enormous tasks often undermine initiative—they seem too large to undertake. Individual classrooms, and lessons in those classrooms, seem much more manageable, especially when we begin by working with teachers interested in change.

One feature of The Learning Network (TLN) schools is their focus on improving classroom instruction. At Montview Elementary School in Aurora, Colorado, the TLN

The Lesson Study Process

In *The Teaching Gap,* Stigler and Hiebert (1999) suggest that the lesson study procedure used in Japanese schools has much to recommend it as a professional development activity. Here are the eight steps of the process:

1. *Defining the problem.* The problem might be enhancing student motivation for reading, for example.

2. *Planning the lesson.* Group effort begins with looking at articles and research to develop an idea to be tested. This step can take several months.

3. *Teaching the lesson.* One teacher teaches, but all group members participate in planning, engage in a dress rehearsal, and on the day of the lesson come to observe. Sometimes the lesson is videotaped.

4. *Evaluating the lesson and reflecting on its effect.* This step is usually done after school right after the lesson has been taught for the first time. The teacher who taught the lesson speaks first, sketching how she or he felt the lesson worked, noting any major problems. Other teachers then offer critiques. The focus is on the group-designed lesson, not on the teacher.

5. *Lesson revision.* Teachers in the group make revisions based on the critiques.

6. *Teaching the revised lesson.* The lesson is presented to a different class, and again the lesson is observed, often by the whole faculty as well as by the group that designed it.

7. *Evaluating and reflecting again.* The whole faculty may participate and sometimes an outside expert as well. The teacher who taught the lesson speaks first; observers then critique and suggest revisions.

8. *Sharing the results after the lesson gains group approval.* This sharing with a wide audience of other teachers may be accomplished in a written article, which is read by the whole faculty and the principal and might be forwarded to the state educational agency or university faculty members. These reports are unique because they link theories with examples.

Stigler and Hiebert point out that few teachers in the United States are experienced in such a process. Although American teachers often collaborate, the typical collaboration is on almost everything but the improvement of lessons. Nonetheless, the lesson study process seems to have much to recommend it.

process has been in place for several years (Hirsh & Sparks, 1999). Student achievement in the school serving a multi-ethnic lower-income neighborhood has risen steadily and now matches that of schools serving few lower-income children. Each teacher works with a "coach" to set goals for enhancing classroom lessons. Each week, after observing a lesson, the two meet and discuss the lesson and how it reflected improvement and which features might be further modified. This interaction resembles the lesson study process that Stigler and Hiebert (1999) discuss as a central characteristic of Japanese schools.

6 *Think commitment, not control.* Today education is undergoing upheaval as legislators and other policy makers rethink how to support the educational process. Two themes for "fixing" the problems of schools are central to these efforts. The first theme could be called implementing control strategies, or educational reform by mandate from afar. How far depends on whether the control-oriented policy making occurs at the federal, state, district, or school level. But in each case someone decides that something needs to be taught, for so many minutes, in a particular way, using particular curriculum materials. Policy makers of this bent believe that teachers and administrators must be told, literally forced, to do certain things.

The other theme emphasizes personal and professional commitment to doing what must be done to improve education. Central to this theme is recognition that the centralized control strategies so popular in the last 50 years have not achieved the desired ends. Increasingly stringent state and federal regulation has not resulted in substantially higher achievement for struggling readers and may have worked to limit educational opportunities for them. Similarly, school district administrators have begun to realize that increasing the number of central office mandates has not improved the quality of instruction, nor has it resulted in reliable improvement in student achievement. Very simply, many are coming to realize that neither excellence nor equity can be mandated from afar.

An alternative to control strategies are policies intended to enhance teachers' commitment to education, to their teaching, and to their students (Rowan, 1990). Thus, site-based management and shared decision making have been introduced in schools. Even the charter school legislation in some states allows teachers to take control of their schools. Turning more control over to teachers, it is argued, will result in greater investment in teaching and in improved instructional practice. Many teachers, however, remain skeptical about these shifts—for good reason. In too many places, shared decision making and site-based management have been implemented in name only. In these schools, teachers still have little or no authority over budget issues, curriculum issues, or scheduling, all central to effective classroom instruction. Instead, they are charged with making only trivial decisions, and even these, at times, have been countermanded by district officials.

For instance, in one school we worked with, teachers were unhappy with the standard report card process. After a year of meetings and research and compromise, they produced a proposal for a different procedure for reporting to parents. After several months, the proposal was rejected because it was not compatible with the district's computerized record-keeping system. No alternative was offered. No compromise. No suggestion was offered for altering the computerized record system. Such responses from district officials kill teachers' willingness to further involve themselves in the change process.

The value of shared decision making has been well documented in settings other than schools. In schools, it is intended to foster increased commitment to improving education on the part of the very people who are most central to instructional practice—classroom teachers. Shared decision making is not simply a means to absolve school and district administrators of responsibility; it shifts their role from plant foreman to team facilitator. Principals and district officials remain important players, but they become more service oriented under site-based and team decision models. Their responsibilities shift from enforcing compliance with mandates, rules, and regulations established by others to facilitating efforts toward improved local practice.

Finding Time for Professional Development

We conclude this chapter with a focus on one of the true dilemmas of school reform—finding time for professional development. Some have suggested that schools resist scheduling professional time at the end of the school day because teachers are tired after a long day of work and because after-school efforts provide only short blocks of time for professional development activities. A better idea, say these professional development proponents, would be to free teachers for half or whole school days to pursue professional development. Others respond that such a plan would disadvantage students, who would lose their regular teacher to professional development days. Better to schedule development for the summer months in their view. Summer efforts, however, do not allow teachers to experiment immediately with new ideas in their classrooms. Summer efforts also are often more expensive and more difficult to schedule, say proponents of school-day professional development activities. So when should professional development occur?

In our view professional development needs to be thought of as a perpetual part of every school day. Professional development should occur before school, after school, during the school day, during summers, and during professional leaves. Professional development activity should continue with appropriate adaptations throughout teachers' careers. Perhaps one primary difficulty of past professional development efforts has been an emphasis on trying to select the one best model, the one best schedule, the one best topic, and so on. This thinking leads to compartmentalized notions of what constitutes a professional development activity.

Consider the array of activities described in this chapter. Some, such as a Teachers as Readers group, seem better suited for after-school time slots than do others. Observing in another teacher's classroom, however, obviously fits best into the regular school-day schedule. Summer might be the best time to schedule an intensive session for teachers to familiarize themselves with an array of new children's books and integrate these books into existing thematic units.

Finding time for professional development will always be problematic, given other demands on educators. Still, most teachers are in front of students for only 4 or 5½ hours each day. This leaves from 3 to 4 hours of time for other activities each day (given an 8-hour school workday). But in most schools few if any attempts are made to capture these hours for professional development. In many schools teachers are expected to be in the building an hour before the students arrive and stay at least an hour after students are dismissed. There are 2 hours right off the bat that could be scheduled for various professional development activities! Add to this a 30-to-50-minute planning period each day.

With some rescheduling, we could have 2 or 3 hours every day for professional development. For instance, if teachers were required to arrive only 15 minutes before the children, we could add 45 minutes to the one hour at the end of the day. If some of the "specials" were moved into a flextime model, we could capture 30 to 50 minutes of planning time at the end of the day for some teachers (perhaps for all, if the flextime "specials" were rotated among grades). This would provide 2 to 3 hours of potential professional time every day. Suddenly school time would be available for TAR, teacher inquiry/research, Internet searches, and other professional growth activities.

Even without such restructuring we have found that when professional conversation is viewed as important, schools seem to find or create time for teachers to converse with one another. Some schools use morning team meetings, others block-scheduled team time during the day, and others an after-school collaboration period. For instance, at the Woodworth Elementary School in Leslie, Michigan, a "Lunch and Learn" (L&L) professional development program was developed. The L&L effort focused on watching professional videos linked to effective teaching of reading, writing, and spelling. Attendance was optional, but the district provided free lunches to staff members who participated. Although only about 30 minutes a day were available for watching and discussing the videos, the groups typically managed to complete the watching and discussion of one video each week. Costs were minimal. Some videos were purchased; others were borrowed from a countywide educational consortium.

The point is that many schools have found time for professional conversations and other staff-development activity. But to find the time requires that someone goes looking for it.

Other schools create time for professional development. At the Bellevue Elementary School in the St. Louis, Missouri, area, the staff has extended each school day by 10 minutes to gain a half-day each month for extra professional development activity. In other schools we have visited, similar plans have created early release times for students on Fridays and late arrival time at 11:30 for students on Wednesdays so that teachers could work together. At Alexander Elementary in Tampa, Florida, voluntary after-school meetings were scheduled on Mondays. On any given Monday, over half of the staff was in attendance. Videos were watched and discussed and professional articles were read and discussed. On Wednesdays, teachers new to the building were invited to attend sessions designed to support their induction into the Alexander professional community through peer assistance and collaborative discussion of policies and practices (Cantrell, Lang, & Mathews, 1999). In another school, an hour-early release of students and teachers each Friday created a monthly Saturday professional half-day for teachers.

We have never visited a moving school where everyone worked in isolation and professional conversation was largely absent. We believe that all schools could become moving schools; but for that to happen, many schools will need to begin to enhance professional development opportunities as of tomorrow.

Summary

The last 10 years have been challenging times in American education, and the next 10 promise to extend the challenge. Classroom teachers have been asked to (1) teach higher-order literacy skills and strategies, (2) implement process-based approaches to writing, (3) teach math as problem solving, (4) reduce reliance on homogeneous groupings, (5) include children with disabilities in the classroom social and instructional milieu, (6) help children develop technological proficiency, (7) integrate the curriculum, (8) use more instructionally useful assessment strategies, (9) work collaboratively with special teachers, and (10) become involved in shared decision making. These 10 items only partially represent the new expertise and the new roles classroom teachers have been expected to acquire. Yet, often, support for developing the needed expertise and for practicing the new roles has been in short supply (Johnston et al., 1998; Taylor et al., 2005). To achieve the necessary changes, teachers need support—both collegial and administrative.

In schools with at least minimally adequate resources, instructional improvement is largely a people-improvement undertaking. Schools improve only as fast as the instructional practice of teachers improves. Teaching well is a lifelong learning process that requires career professionals willingly engaging in self-improving development activities. Many schools currently do too little to either foster or support such lifelong learning. Teachers need to be viewed as substantial resources, and providing professional-growth opportunities for the teaching staff must be recognized as a long-term investment in maintaining high-quality instruction.

To create schools where all children learn to read and write, schools must become sites where teachers more often work collegially in a problem-solving framework focused on improving instructional practice. For too long educational policy and reform initiatives have largely ignored supporting classroom teachers. For too long schools have failed to foster collegiality and professional conversation. It is time to alter the situation and begin to reconsider how to create schools where all teachers learn and all acquire new instructional strategies continuously across their careers. Supporting teacher professional growth is a first step toward creating schools where all children become readers and writers (Hyde, 1992).

Family Involvement

Once again, the role families might play in educating their children has been thrust into the spotlight by national policy statements and the media. With the much ballyhooed America 2000 came the first national education goal: All children will start school ready to learn. This goal, and the particular wording of it, created much discussion. What child was not "ready to learn"? What did "ready to learn" mean? Some asked whether it might not be more appropriate to set as the goal "American schools will be ready for all learners." The net effect of placing school readiness as the first national education goal was to lift concern about families and children during the preschool years high on the national agenda. Political

candidates and education bureaucrats began intoning that "Parents are the child's first teachers." There were calls from high places to "Turn off the TV and read with your children." Thus, the bully pulpit of public office berated parents for not doing more. At the same time, however, scant attention was paid to shifts in the characteristics of the American family and the American workforce (Allington & McGill-Franzen, 1996; Berliner, 2005).

Several surveys of educators have identified the lack of readiness for school as a primary problem confronting schools. Thus, calls for more and better publicly funded preschool programs have been common (though full funding still is not) as have calls for expanding parent–family training efforts. In addition to the attention families attracted in discussions of the first national educational goal were other shifts in policy and practice that brought discussions of family roles and responsibilities to the forefront. One shift was an increasing amount of homework that elementary school children were assigned as a result of a call for more homework in *A Nation at Risk* (National Commission on Excellence in Education, 1983). Elementary schools implemented homework policies, in some cases even for kindergarten, and with homework came increased expectations of families in supporting and monitoring homework completion. As noted in a *Newsweek* (Begley, March 30, 1998) magazine cover story, there was, and is yet today, little evidence that increasing homework in the elementary grades has any positive effect on student achievement (at the high school level there is some such evidence). Nonetheless, although homework was uncommon for elementary students 30 years ago, today it is a common, if often unfortunate, experience for children.

Thus, two shifts in national education policy have increased the attention paid to the role families might play. But what is the responsibility of families? Only a short time ago that responsibility was basically seen as providing a healthy, happy, and well-behaved child for the school to educate. If families met these responsibilities and ensured regular school attendance, most teachers felt lucky. When did it become the family's responsibility to supervise daily worksheet completion sent home as first-grade homework? When did it become the family's responsibility to take a fourth-grade child to the public library to locate information on Chile for a written report assigned as an out-of-school activity? When did it become common to assign families the responsibility for developing initial literacy so that a child would meet a school's kindergarten entrance standard?

The point that needs to be made is that schools in the United States have recently been raising expected levels of family involvement in educating their children. This is true even though some schools had little success in getting all families to meet the previously lower levels of involvement. It is undeniable that families are important in the education of children. But families send their children to school to be taught, and many families have historically viewed that as the end of their responsibility. In fact,

In the 1993 *American Teacher Survey* by Metropolitan Life, 69 percent of the teachers rated federal support for developing programs to help disadvantaged families work with their children to prepare them better for school as the highest priority for funding. Three-quarters of all elementary teachers and 82 percent of inner-city teachers rated it as the highest-priority item. In a study of school principals (Allington et al., 1997), the majority indicated a distinct need for expanding preschool and family support programs. Oddly, not one of these principals indicated any need to strengthen his or her school's capacity to better address the needs of low-experience children!

Lareau (1989) found that many families viewed schooling as the school's job—not theirs. These families resented homework. They saw it as an attempt by the school to shift the workload to families. Many felt that if the child did not get the work done in school, either the teacher had not done a very good job of teaching or the child should be kept after school to complete the work under a teacher's supervision.

Many working-class families saw schoolwork as fitting only into the school day. Work not done in school today could be done there tomorrow. This view revealed an interesting parallel to the parents' work lives. These blue-collar parents did not bring work home. They left the job at the time clock. Their view of schooling was similar. The gap between the views of teachers and the views of families in working-class communities was enormous. In middle-class, white-collar professional communities, families more often took a different view. These families often asked for more homework for their children. This request seemed to parallel their work lives. The adults in these families often brought work home to do in the evenings or on weekends. They viewed homework as normal. Their complaints about homework focused on the low quality of much of the work assigned and the lack of careful evaluation of homework by teachers.

American educators are expecting more family involvement with their children's schooling today than they did only a few years ago. At the same time, larger numbers of children from families living in poverty are filling our schools, more children are living with a single parent, and more children are living with two parents, each working at full-time jobs. Very simply, schools are raising the demands on families as parental resources are shrinking. Simultaneously, families are raising their expectations for schools with calls for more early education programs, more after-school programs, and higher levels of support for students.

All of this is, of course, what makes an educator's life today so exciting. But solutions must be developed because schools cannot be effective without the confidence and support of the families of the children they teach. This chapter develops plans for reaching out to families, involving families, and supporting families. Families are the ultimate consumers of schooling because they choose to have the children stay or leave, particularly now that NCLB requires parent-choice programs that allow transfers from failing schools. However, families differ considerably in their knowledge of schools and the liberty they have to choose alternatives for their children.

Reaching Out to Families

Too often educators wait for families to contact them. They send home notices for parent–teacher conferences and, perhaps, PTA meetings, but too often they make no personal contact with families until some real problem exists. It seems better to think about ways to ensure that every family hears from the child's teacher personally before problems arise. For instance, Palestis (1993) describes the family outreach program in the Mine Hill, New Jersey, schools as part of the school district's obligation to the community. All Mine Hill teachers are trained in family involvement using *Parents on Your Side: A Comprehensive Family Involvement Program for Teachers* (Canter & Canter, 1990). In addition, teachers send NCR two-way communication forms home. The form has spaces for a teacher message and a reply (or question) from home, while providing both parties with a copy to keep. Each child has a Friday Folder that contains all graded assignments, homework, tests scheduled for the next week, and a family–teacher two-way communication form that either party can use to initiate a conversation. When families enter an elementary school in the Mine Hill district, they find a family center in the lobby with family education materials, including pamphlets, magazine articles, videotapes, and so on, that they can borrow. Also, teachers are given time to contact families with Happy Calls during two periods each week. These calls are simply to comment on progress and good deeds of children. This effort reflects the strong commitment the school district has made to keeping families informed—the first step in reaching out to families.

Many schools produce a monthly or even weekly newsletter for families. Researchers from Johns Hopkins University studied what information in school newsletters families actually read. Not surprisingly, families liked articles by and about children the best. They liked articles on classroom activities, social events, school programs, and recipes, too. Families reported that their children also read the newsletter, particularly articles about and by children. When student names appeared in the articles, families were more likely to read those aloud to their children (Herrick & Epstein, 1991).

Print is not the only medium for reaching out to families. Radio and television offer other possibilities for brief public-service messages. Creating one such ad each month, especially for radio, does not involve enormous effort. In large metropolitan areas, the messages to families might be addressed to all families in the district but still feature a single school, or even classroom, project. The message needs to communicate: "We are your schools. These are your children." The ads can offer sources for more information or invitations to visit schools generally or a particular school.

In larger metropolitan areas, cable television service is common. Each cable television system is required to provide public access channels. These channels can also provide a vehicle for reaching out to families. Schools need to worry less about producing slick-looking programs and more about putting children and schools on the screen in activities such as school plays, concerts, performances, guest readers, visiting authors, science fairs, and art exhibits. Families will tune in when the channel features children and their performances, products, displays, and productions.

Much of this outreach can be integrated into the reading and language arts curriculum. Newsletter production, not just the writing of articles, provides real-world experiences for children in composing, editing, and publishing. In addition to building oral language, the radio and television productions might involve scripting, editing, and captioning activities.

A different form of outreach is the consumer satisfaction survey. Schools might be well served to survey families on a regular basis, asking for their evaluation of school programs, staff, and productivity. This could be as simple as a short paper–pencil survey that is distributed at the end of the school year. Questions might take the form of a Likert-like scale and address issues of perceived instructional effectiveness, responsiveness to family concerns, fairness to students, and utility of special programs. There might also be a section asking for problems that need to be addressed and other concerns or praise for the school's efforts.

A survey such as this should provide a postage-paid mailer for returning the survey, although in some schools a simple drop box by the entrance might work just as well. We would suggest such a survey every year. The results work to identify family concerns that may need to be addressed if gaining family support is the goal.

Involving Families

Reaching out to families is a necessary first step, but it is only the first step. The ultimate goal is increasing the quality and amount of family involvement with children's education. Before working to improve family involvement, schools must clarify precisely what they want families more involved in. The importance of clarifying the meaning of family involvement became clear during the implementation of a requirement to "involve" families in schools to garner additional funding through the Arizona At-Risk Pilot Project (Vandegrift & Greene, 1992). Although family involvement was mandated, it was never defined. Various strategies were developed by participating schools, including workshops, parenting classes, newsletters, home visits, advisory committees, and social events. But teacher surveys after the first year of implementation suggested that family involvement had not increased. The common complaint was that the school offered a variety of new activities but families largely stayed home anyway.

In analyzing the activities and the teacher evaluations, the program evaluators were able to describe two dimensions of family involvement that seemed part of the definition. First was the notion of *supportiveness.* Families support their children and are understanding and reassuring. These families care immensely about their children, their well-being, and their education. Second was the notion of *active participation,* families making visible attempts to show their supportiveness. Visible, in this case, meant visible to teachers and, most commonly, involved volunteering at school, attending school functions, and initiating communication with teachers. Unfortunately, this definition of family involvement requires high levels of commitment and participation. It also requires that families have

- Free time from work
- Child care for other children
- Transportation to the school
- Clothing they felt comfortable appearing in school wearing
- Money to pay for all of the above

Some families are lucky enough to have such resources, but many poor and working-class families do not. Consider that the majority of the working poor are single women with children. These parents work the longest hours for the smallest paycheck. These are the parents with the smallest discretionary incomes, often lacking small amounts of money for bus fares or babysitters. They are also the parents least likely to have child care readily available and affordable. They are the parents most likely to be working between 3:00 in the afternoon and 9:00 in the evening, the time schools schedule most family activities. These parents are often supportive parents but not parents who are actively participating in school events.

In developing a broader framework for considering family involvement, Vandegrift and Greene (1992) suggest that there are four basic types of families, as illustrated in Figure 9.1. The families everyone wants to see are those that are both supportive of their children and actively participating in school activities. These families not only support their children but also reach out to the school by visiting, calling, and volunteering.

+ + Family *supports* child and is *actively involved* in schools	**+ −** Family *supports* child but is *not active* in schools
− + Family is *unsupportive* of child but *active* in schools	**− −** Family is *unsupportive* and *not active* in schools

Figure 9.1 ● Family-Involvement Categories

A second type of family is supportive of children but does not actively participate in school events. Adults in these families may have bad memories about their own schooling, they may be embarrassed by their lack of education or their children's difficulties at school, or they may simply feel inadequate in school settings. These families may also lack transportation or child care. They might have work schedules that conflict with school events. Some of these families will be limited by *all* of these factors. However, absence from school events does not indicate a lack of family support for the children. These families may help with homework and provide the safe, nurturing home that is essential. They may actively discuss school work and read newsletters or watch cable television productions of school events. They may be more than happy to use a school voice-mail system for communicating with teachers (even when they are unlikely to respond in writing). These families might welcome videos or DVDs on parenting that can be viewed in the home. Thus, these families can be involved and their involvement enhanced even without attending school functions.

A third group of families—we hope a small group—includes families that participate in school activities but are not supportive of their children. These families show up for everything, but observing their behavior with their child makes one shudder. These families ignore or abuse their children but still put on the appropriate front at school. These are the families that complain to teachers about their "stupid kid" and who harangue and belittle the child in front of peers and teachers.

The last group of families—we hope small as well—includes those who are not supportive of their children and do not participate in school activities. Sometimes the families' own problems take precedence over children's education and development. The stress that low-income families feel, the inadequacy that eats away at them, may undermine many of the supportive feelings parents typically feel about their children. An alcohol or drug addiction may also create such dependencies that normal human functioning is almost impossible.

The last two groups of families present schools with the most difficult problems. In most cases, schools will need to work with other agencies to address the difficulties faced by children in these homes. However, when parent support and involvement are unlikely, schools must redouble their efforts to support the children. This may mean developing peer tutoring or pairing children with adult volunteers. It may mean involving children in an after-school or Saturday-school homework support class. It may mean providing breakfast and snacks. Some children may need another adult in the school assigned as their advocate. Schools cannot penalize children for the families they have. Instead, schools must develop ways to support children if family support and involvement are in short supply.

When the broader view of family involvement is considered, it is easier to develop different strategies to reach different families. Family involvement begins with reaching out to families, not waiting for families to come. Unlike the cornfield baseball diamond in the movie *Field of Dreams,* simply creating family nights and parent events at school does not ensure that they will come. Reaching out to families is the first step in building family involvement because informed families view the school and its staff as caring immensely about their children. A second step is actually listening to families. An annual survey of family concerns is a good start in this regard. Too often, schools create family-involvement efforts with no input from families.

If increased family involvement is needed in your school, a good starting point is asking yourself what your school offers that makes it an attractive place for families to visit. Some schools have coffee and a parent lounge. Families are made to feel welcome, and schools encourage family members to stay around once they enter the building. Some schools create parent-advisory breakfast groups that meet weekly on an open-invitation basis. These before-school or early school-day affairs offer child care, conversations rather than lectures, and an opportunity for families to be heard. Some schools schedule regular family–school discussion sessions open to any family member who has questions, ideas, or praise for current efforts. Other schools have created community advisory boards with church leaders, business persons, families, and civic leaders. These boards also meet regularly to discuss the school, the programs, the children, and the community.

The Arizona At-Risk Pilot project concluded that the most successful family-involvement projects began when families had personal contact with someone from the school community (even other families) and high levels of active parent participation were not required, at least initially. Something as simple as receiving a Happy Call from the principal or teacher can provide much of the needed impetus to increase involvement.

Taking Inventory of Family Involvement

As in most other areas, a school might begin by inventorying current school resources, attitudes, and policies concerning family involvement. Are families, for instance, really welcome at the school, or do current policies work to restrict family presence and involvement in the building? In one school we visited, family members had to complete an application at least one week in advance of any classroom visit or activity involvement and then wait for written school approval to be granted. In contrast, a nearby school encouraged family members to drop in at any time, and the school administrator offered a brief but continuing orientation session to provide community visitors with basic operating procedures and ideas for different types of educational involvement. Near a coffeepot by the school's entrance a small gaggle of parents could be found at almost any time of day, usually talking quietly about their children and school programs. Some schools do even more to welcome families and community members into schools, but all schools need to ask whether families and community members are actually welcomed in the building.

Next, you might evaluate the number of positive personal school–family contacts that have occurred over the last month—especially the number of such contacts with the

In Chapter 3 we discussed the power of high-quality classrooms in overcoming home effects on learning, summarizing the work of Catherine Snow and her colleagues. But Snow and friends also noted a difference between teachers in high-quality classrooms and those in other classrooms. The difference was found in family involvement. Families were far more likely to participate in school events and communicate with the teachers in the high-quality classrooms. Effective teachers made many more personal parent contacts than did other teachers. They called families, wrote notes, and met with families before and after school. Perhaps families were more involved because these teachers were more successful with their children than other teachers. It is clear that teachers can involve families, but with many families the contacts must be initiated by the teacher, the contacts must be positive and personal, and the teacher must be persistent.

least-involved families. Ask whether the school–family contacts have been largely negative messages about children and whether even these have been bureaucratized messages sent on form letters. If the overwhelming majority of contacts between school staff and families in the past month have not been of the positive, personal variety, you have found the obvious starting point for increasing family involvement.

Next, look at the events offered for families. Has there been an array of levels of possible involvement offered over the past few months? Have school-based activities and events been scheduled at the families' convenience? Have families been offered clear, consistent, and achievable ideas for involvement in their children's education?

As a final information-gathering step, you may want to ask family members to evaluate school and teacher efforts in communicating with them and involving them in the educational process. The evaluation might be in telephone survey form, which asks for ratings on features such as whether the school

- Is a good place to send children
- Treats all children fairly
- Frequently contacts families with good news
- Makes families feel welcome
- Makes it easy for families to get information

In addition to a survey, schools might also conduct a series of focus-group sessions with adults from the community, parents, and, perhaps, older adolescents who attended the elementary school. Usually, focus groups respond to series of topics, and a record of the discussion that represents the various points of view expressed is kept. Focus groups often work best if they are organized and run by someone other than those being evaluated, in this case school staff members. Schools might have community members run the sessions and keep a record of the discussion flow, but the groups set the general topics to be discussed. Well-organized focus groups can provide a rich source of evaluative information to schools.

If schools are to foster family involvement, it will be important to gather information on existing efforts and on parent, family, and community satisfaction with those efforts. As new efforts are implemented, it is important to monitor the effects. As with most other areas of school operation, routinely gathering information on program outcomes, including evaluations from participants, provides a better basis for decisions about continuing the effort or changes that might be necessary.

Supporting Families

Schools must complement families in educating children. Some families need more support than others to become more involved in their children's education. When children come from families in which intergenerational illiteracy is evident, it seems obvious that schools cannot expect those families to provide much home support for children's literacy development. The scope and seriousness of intergenerational poverty and illiteracy has resulted in the recent focus on family literacy efforts by social and educational agencies. The National Center for Family Literacy (www.famlit.org/familyliteracyservices/index.cfm) defines comprehensive family literacy programs as comprised of four components:

- Basic literacy instruction for families
- Preschool and literacy education for young children
- Family education and support activities
- Regular parent and child activities

Such family literacy programs take many shapes. Services are delivered at school sites, at community sites, or in homes. Some are characterized by intensive short-term intervention efforts and others by less intensive long-term programs. Usually, though, the planning of these programs has to assume the need for long-term support if for no other reason than it took generations to create the family that exists today and it will take time to alter the current situation.

Family literacy programs are potentially powerful support programs. However, these programs, like most family support efforts, cost money to develop and maintain. But Head Start, Even Start, Title 1, special education, and other state and federal funding support are available for such efforts. In addition, funds through foundations and through social service and employment agencies of state and local governments can often be located to support such efforts.

Nearly any comprehensive family support program that one might design will require some substantial interagency collaboration. Comprehensive family support usually involves working with the social services community, the health community, and, often, agencies involved with employment and training. In most communities, these agencies and their services are neither well coordinated nor available at a single site. Is it possible to move health and social services into the school site? If not, can they be located near the

One simple and inexpensive strategy for gathering parental satisfaction information is a postcard sent home with each student that asks parents to rate their general satisfaction with the school their child attends. This could be a prepaid postcard requiring only a moment or two to complete and then dropped in the mail. Make parent identification optional. We might structure the postcard like Figure 9.2.

school? Failing all else, can families find out at the school, for instance, exactly where they need to go and whom they need to see to get eyeglasses for their child? Can they find out about GED classes with free child care at the school? Can they participate in adult basic literacy training at the school?

Interagency coordination of services and collaborative efforts present many bureaucratic obstacles to overcome, but the first obstacle is lack of school awareness of support services available to families and precisely how families access those services. In some schools, no one even knows where the Head Start program is offered, much less how to enroll children. In other schools, the Head Start program and the kindergarten and primary teachers use a common curriculum framework and common method of reporting children's development to families. In some schools, no one has ever considered applying for an Even Start family education project because the focus is on preschool-age children and their parents. In other schools, an Even Start effort links preschool and adult-

---

Dear Parent,

Tell us how we are doing. How well do you feel that _____ school is meeting your child's educational needs? Circle the number below that best shows your feelings.

1	2	3	4
My child's needs are not being met.	Only some of my child's needs are being met.	Most of my child's needs are being met.	I am very happy with the way my child's needs are being met.

Comments: _____

_____

_____

_____

_____

Figure 9.2 ● Sample Parent Survey Postcard

education programs to family involvement in school programs. In some schools, no one is aware that federal Title 1 programs must have a family-involvement component and that Title 1 funds can be spent supporting most of the activities described in this chapter. In other schools, Title 1 Parent Advisory Council members work actively on shared-decision-making teams and regularly sponsor family educational support activities. In some schools, virtually no effort goes into complying with the parent involvement mandated by the Individuals with Disabilities Education Act (IDEA). In other schools, parents are actively involved in developing the IEP, and the school can draw from this pool of child advocates to work with families to discern what educational options might most benefit children with disabilities.

It is never easy to establish comprehensive family support programs, but an increasing interest in interagency collaboration in federal and state agencies may offer new opportunities for developing and funding such efforts.

School-Linked Services: An Integrated Approach to Children and Families

Imagine that the mother of a first-grade student walks her son to school and brings his baby sister along. While she delivers her son for another day of classes at the school, the young mother stops in to see the school nurse to have her daughter's temperature checked and a throat culture taken. Then she moves to the satellite Women, Infants, and Children (WIC) office to be recertified for continued participation before dropping her daughter off at the on-site day care room. Next, she spends two and one-half hours in an adult education program where she works on improving her reading and writing skills. The focus of her literacy-development activities, however, is children's books and family stories rather than the more traditional skills workbook. That afternoon, after having lunch in the day care room with her daughter, she works in her son's classroom as a paid assistant, practicing her reading skills by introducing little books to small groups of children. This paid internship is part of a planned educational program that will lead to a Child Development Associate (CDA) certificate jointly planned and funded by the state Department of Social Services, the Department of Labor, Head Start, and Title 1.

Such a scenario could occur today but usually does not. Instead, the young mother would have to schedule and visit three, four, or five different agencies at just as many sites to accomplish the same activities (Bruner, 1991). The scenario described above is one example of what might be accomplished with school-linked services. School-linked service models are analogous to the modern superstores in that they attempt to offer "one-stop shopping" sites for a wide array of children's services. School-linked services is a radical idea in an era when more than 100 federal categorical programs provide educational and other services to school children. But the current fragmentation, duplication, and lack of communication hardly serves children well. The basic idea behind school-based services is to restructure the delivery of most social, educational, and health programs targeted for children and their families so that a coherent, continuous, and supportive effort with an emphasis on preventive intervention can be offered.

What might school-linked services programs look like? The New Beginnings effort at Hamilton Elementary School, located in one of the poorest and most ethnically diverse neighborhoods in San Diego, targets broad services to all families who live in the school attendance area (Payzant, 1994). The collaborative effort involves the city, the city schools, the county, the community college, the housing commission, the medical school, and the health center. A space crunch, common in most elementary schools, resulted in locating the New Beginnings School-Linked Services (SLS) effort in a modular building that was transported to the school site. All new entrants to the school report to the SLS site, where they are enrolled in school and scheduled for any social or health services they are eligible for. Through a shared resourcing agreement, a nurse practitioner is available on-site and a pediatrician is available part-time. A case-management approach, in which one professional manages all interactions and services provided to a family (as opposed to a series of such staff from each agency working with the family), is viewed as a primary key to preventing children from falling through the cracks in the health, educational, and social services networks. A common eligibility form has been designed to simplify applications to several educational, health, and social service programs. Teachers at Hamilton have been involved in planning and implementing the project and now are working with the New Beginnings staff members rather than simply referring children to various agencies. Families are more involved in school and are more frequently attending parenting education classes. Although the New Beginnings project has occasionally stumbled while breaking new ground, the effort serves as a model that other schools might emulate.

Some state and federal agencies have encouraged developing more comprehensive school-linked services, and several demonstration programs exist around the country. Several lessons have already been learned from these efforts (General Accounting Office, 1993):

- Leadership from the top is necessary. Commitment from a school superintendent and the Board of Education with commitments from state agency heads work to ensure success. When a principal, program director, or department head attempts to create the collaborative links without top-level support, much more effort seems necessary and success is less likely.
- Leaders selected to head the effort must have a talent for coalition building. Even after initial stages of planning are complete, successful efforts need ongoing nurturing of the original coalition members and efforts to expand membership of that coalition.

- Model programs vary as a result of different constituencies with differing needs. No single model can work everywhere. All models do not have to incorporate all possible other services and agencies. Create a program based on local needs and resources and local commitments.

- School staff need to be involved from the get-go. Teachers, especially, are central to the success of school-linked services because they are the members of the coalition who have the most regular and sustained contact with the children. Thus, teachers are, literally, the eyes and ears (and noses) of any school-linked services effort. Do not delay teacher involvement—have teachers active on the initiation team. School-linked services does not mean teachers have more to do. In fact, now teachers often have less to do, but more children often receive desperately needed services and support.

- Plans must be made for offering school-linked services during periods when the school is not operating. Most other state and federal agencies for children and families work on 12-month schedules and many work 7 days a week (health and law enforcement, for example).

- School-linked services should not interrupt children's academic work during the school day. Before-school and after-school services, Saturday service provision, and vacation services are all needed to achieve this. However, these efforts are also often more convenient for families. Do not fall into the trap of designing school-linked services to operate only, or even primarily, during normal school hours.

- School-linked services are neither simple to create nor a panacea that will solve all the problems educators face in working with children from families in trouble. Nonetheless, it seems that almost everyone agrees that it is time to rework the archaic and convoluted system of services that now exists in most communities. Schools seem a logical location for services targeted to serving the needs of children. School-linked services is an idea whose time has come.

Planning for Family Involvement

At this point, it may be useful to begin developing a three-year plan for increasing family involvement. The initial step is planning to improve a school's outreach efforts. What is currently being done and what else is needed? A second step is to evaluate current parental involvement using some scheme similar to the four parent group schemes presented earlier. What is the current nature of family involvement? What areas should be targeted for immediate attention? What resources seem needed? Perhaps most important, school staff must be asked whether they are committed to increasing real family involvement in the school. Are you ready and willing to involve families in activities that have the potential for giving families a voice in how the school works?

It may be useful to purchase Brenda Power's book and CD-ROM package, *Parent Power: Energizing Home–School Communications* (Heinemann at 1-800-793-2154 or www. heinemann.com). This useful package provides, in both English and Spanish, a variety of print documents: newsletter frames and articles, brochures, calendars of family support activities, press releases for media coverage, and much more.

James Voput's *More Than Bake Sales* provides a tested model for family involvement and comes with a video, *Parent Leadership: It Doesn't Happen Just Because You Say So,* which offers a close-up look at parent workshops and family literacy projects (both from www.stenhouse.com).

A variety of initial small steps might be taken to enhance family involvement in schools. A first step would be to enhance school-to-home communications. Ames and her colleagues (1993) studied how school–home communications influence parental involvement. They found substantial variation among teachers in the frequency of communication from school to home. Some teachers rarely contacted families, while others were characterized as high-communication teachers because home–school communications were a daily event. They found that high-communication teachers felt they were better able to meet the needs of difficult children and had more strategies for motivating and involving children in their schoolwork. Families of children in high-communication classrooms evaluated teachers as more effective, held stronger beliefs in their children's potential, and reported higher levels of involvement with their children's schoolwork. Children in the high-communication classrooms reported high levels of academic competence. School–home communications took the form of classroom newsletters, personal notes and telephone calls, review activities, and work folders that children regularly took home.

The focus of the most effective school–home communication was developing better understandings of classroom activities, curriculum, and plans; providing information on children's progress, accomplishments, and improvement; and offering information and direction on ways to help at home. Many low-communication teachers, in contrast, contacted families only when a child was in serious trouble (either academically or behaviorally). Ames and her colleagues (1993) commented that

> Teachers often contact parents to tell them that their child is having trouble and is not motivated, and then expect this information will stimulate the parents' assistance. Our initial findings suggest that such communications may not have the intended effect and may only discourage parents and make them feel less comfortable with the school and with their role as a helper. (p. 31)

A rich array of school–home communications fosters family involvement. But the most important communications must come from classroom teachers. When classroom teachers reach out and communicate regularly with families, especially about positive aspects of children's school experiences, families respond positively and increase their efforts to support their children.

A good beginning, then, is to establish improved communications from classrooms to homes. Perhaps as at the Mine Hill schools, a time should be set aside each week for each teacher to call families. Establishing a voice-mail system to facilitate telephone communications between teachers and families offers promising prospects. Assisting teachers in developing weekly classroom newsletters, perhaps attached to the weekly school newsletter, would enhance families' awareness of classroom activities. Developing clear guidelines on homework and creating homework help packets or weekly work folders for families might also be considered.

In another study teachers met and prepared monthly at-home-work packets for students at each grade level (Herrick & Epstein, 1991). These activities were developed by brainstorming current curricular topics that were to be covered during the month ahead. After selecting a single topic, the teachers developed games and activities that worked to develop the skills or strategies, and that families could do with their children. These were packaged in resealable sandwich bags and sent home with a simple set of directions for families. In some cases, teachers introduced the activity in classes so that children were familiar with the routines.

An evaluation of this procedure found that about two-thirds of the urban families used these packages with their children on at least several occasions and that the children from these homes had higher achievement at the end of the year. A key to the success of the packages was developing activities that were easy to do (e.g., nursery rhymes in kindergarten) and that families found useful. Rather than attempting to move families into hour-long nightly tutoring sessions, these teachers took a more modest approach.

The Parents as Reading Partners (PARP) program operates in several states and encourages a 15-minute daily parent–child reading time. Of course, children and their families need access to books to participate in this activity, and that presents a potential difficulty in many low-income families. Schools need to make appropriate books available if the PARP program is to be initiated. Some schools using this activity send small books home each night in those same resealable sandwich bags. Some rely more heavily on Reading Is Fundamental (1-800-RIF-READ or www.rif.org) to provide children with books for their homes. However, in most cases RIF cannot supply enough books for daily home reading.

Whenever take-home reading activities are assigned schools must (1) make it clear who is expected to read to whom and (2) ensure that if the child is to be reading to the parent that the book sent home is appropriately easy for the child to read. We suggest that children only take home books they have already read successfully in school if they are to do the reading.

A final caution about using PARP is in order. In some communities it has become competitive with classes striving for a banner or a pizza award and with some children being cast as pariahs because their families do not participate. The National Reading Panel

(2000) concluded that the evidence available indicated that reading incentive programs did not expand reading activity. Better readers still read the most and struggling readers continued to read little, if at all. In addition, when competitive pressure rises high enough, families cheat and indicate they read with children when they did not. Alfie Kohn's book (1999) *Punished by Rewards* provides a powerful indictment of reading incentives, and we are inclined to agree with much of his argument. As parents we admit that it seems impossible to actually read for 15 minutes each and every night all year long. Guidelines for PARP need to suggest but not require reading every night (maybe five of seven nights), and competitions should be avoided.

When encouraging families to read to their children at home, it is wise to be aware of Pat Edwards's cautions: Many adults do not know the routines of reading to children even if they read reasonably well themselves. Adults who grew up in homes where parent–child reading was not common have no background of life experiences to draw on when schools suggest they read to their children at home. Edwards (1989) and Jackie Munro (2001) both found enormous gaps between the read-aloud practices teachers expected and what the family members actually did. Thus, schools might present models of wonderful read-aloud performances at the opening of parent night or, perhaps, create a video product for parents to borrow that includes several read-aloud sessions.

Here are some of the books published in one classroom. Parent volunteers assemble the blank books with a dedication page at the beginning and an about-the-author page at the end. Children copy their revised/edited pieces into these books and then illustrate them. These child-authored books are popular reading choices during self-selected reading.

Christine Sylvester, who teaches at LaFollette Elementary School in Milwaukee, Wisconsin, uses classroom videotapes of lessons, field trips, guest readers, book sharing, and so on as a take-home activity. The tapes emphasize focusing on one or two children's involvement in a classroom lesson or activity. By setting the camera on a tripod and placing the microphone near the targeted children, she can capture voices and images while still teaching. She may have a child introduce or summarize the recorded event but often uses only the classroom video clip. Families can view the lesson with their child and discuss what is going on. The tape is sometimes used as a classroom learning activity as she replays it having the children comment on what they are doing and what else they might have done before sending it home. The tapes are an enormous hit with parents and children as well. The tapes seem to reduce the formality of the first teacher conferences and also open up opportunities for teacher and family communications.

Terri Austin uses student-run parent conferences in her classroom at Ft. Wainwright Elementary School in Fairbanks, Alaska. The basic idea is that students create portfolios of their work across the marking period and develop written rationales for the inclusion of each piece. The work is organized and stored in colorful three-ring binders. Students come to the parent conference and present the work and explain why it was selected. Other work they did across the period is photocopied for family members to take home with them. Family members, teacher, and student discuss the portfolio work, the other work samples, the effort, and the goals for improvement during the conference.

In Perrysburg, Ohio, pupils not only participate in the conferences, they lead the conversation. Steve Snyder, a sixth-grade teacher at Perrysburg's Woodland Elementary noted, "I feel I'm more honest because the student usually opens a can of worms I might not have opened" (Jacobson, 1999). Again, the strategy of involving students seems to have increased the interest and involvement of families.

Are You Ready for Authentic Family Involvement?

The nature of family involvement is changing as states mandate new relationships between communities and their school, between families, parents, community members, and educators. Many of the new roles are strikingly different from baking for a school bake sale or other traditional volunteer roles. For instance, the federal Title 1 program has long mandated parent involvement, but recent changes have dramatically strengthened the family-involvement component. The Title 1 regulations emphasize three components:

- Family involvement in the development of district and school policies and programs
- Building capacity for family involvement through increased support to families and the involvement of community organizations
- Jointly developed school–parent compacts detailing responsibilities and involvement

In other words, the Title 1 program has shifted from the "coffee and doughnuts" model of family involvement to one that requires parents and teachers to jointly produce a written parent-involvement policy for each building served by Title 1 funds.

This shift in Title 1 seems to mirror the recommendations made by Kuykendall (1992). She notes that while family members still play such traditional roles as tutors, volunteers, and neighborhood coordinators, they might also be involved as members of

- Staff selection committees
- Local school leadership teams
- School disciplinary teams
- School interior-design improvement teams
- School publicity teams
- Volunteer coordination teams
- Merit pay committees

Her listing includes assignments with real potential influence on school operations. These might be thought of as authentic family involvement because the roles concern the business of running schools. She argues that many families, especially minority and low-income families, respond far more positively to involvement that has real potential for changing schools. Historically, schools have often tried to keep families in "safe" involvement activities—activities in which families did what they were told and did not offer advice on what schools should do. Too often the communications to low-income families have had a condescending tone. Too rarely have teachers and administrators actually spent much time listening to low-income families, and even more rarely have these families felt their comments, ideas, and criticisms were taken seriously. School–home communications must become two-way communications with schools honoring the family members' voices.

Kuykendall notes that just getting information about schools, policies, practices, and procedures has often been difficult for low-income families. Too often these families have heard replies such as these:

> "We aren't allowed to give that information out."
> "That would take too much time."
> "It will cost you three dollars for each page."
> "We aren't required by law to do that."
> "We have a policy against that."
> "You will have to talk to someone downtown."
> "That's just the way we do it here."

Families are often refused outright any explanation of procedures, stonewalled, or discouraged from pursuing the matter. For instance, consider what happens when a parent requests his or her child be placed in or transferred out of a particular classroom or program.

Now, granted, it is less complicated to stonewall or to simply refuse to discuss the request than it is to listen and present the rationale for the existing placement. Perhaps attempts to shrug families off are so common because decisions in schools are, at times, rather quite arbitrary. But not attending to real parent concerns about issues and not addressing needed changes in policies and procedures work against families developing confidence in the school and work against building family involvement.

At this point, if increasing family involvement is still on the agenda (and it really has to be), it is probably time to bring in some parents to assist in the planning. Remember that families of preschool children should probably be included—those children are your future students. Remember that families of older and younger children need to be involved because the needs of these families are often different. Include families that are representative of the cultural, ethnic, language, and social class diversity of your school. For instance, if many families have not graduated from high school, several members of that group should be represented. If many families speak Spanish or any language other than English as their native language (or only language), they too need representation (even if this means finding a bilingual teacher or parent to translate). Families of children with disabilities need to be heard as well. Initially, give families chances to talk while the school staff listens and takes notes. Do not begin by outlining what can and cannot be done. Do not begin by responding to every idea with "We tried that once" or "We couldn't afford that." Instead, listen and list. Think of the time as the opportunity to brainstorm and to gather information.

Select specific topics, or work with family and community participants to select topics that will focus discussions. Topics such as homework, discipline, attendance, report cards, parent–teacher conferencing, and working in classrooms are all good starting points.

In the Accelerated Schools model (Levin, 1987), the school community creates cadres around issues. Membership includes teachers, parents, and community members. For instance, one group might examine scheduling in the school, perhaps looking at expanding the school's use or extending the school day. Another group might look at discipline procedures, another at testing, grading, and homework practices. No single group is expected to take on the job of addressing all issues. This model seems particularly useful because it prevents groups from becoming paralyzed by having too many issues to achieve any focus or real work toward resolution. After a brainstorming session or two (or three or four), it will be useful to consider forming smaller study groups to examine a smaller range of issues and develop some sense of options and opportunities to report back to the larger group.

For information on family involvement in schools, you may want to visit the following websites for newsletters, pamphlets, and other information (often free):

U.S. Department of Education, at www.ed.gov/parents/landing/jhtml

National Center for Family Literacy, at www.famlit.org

National Parent Teacher Association, at www.pta.org

In the school governance model developed by James Comer (1988), committees of equal numbers of parents and teachers make most decisions about school policies and practices. The general rule is that decisions are made by consensus, not by majority vote. This seems similar to the way a jury functions except that the committee can explore and refine the options until a consensus is achieved.

Families as the Public

A recent national poll indicated that only 25 percent of respondents rated schools nationally as good or excellent. However, twice that many (52 percent) rated their local schools as good or excellent. This oddity suggests that the contact that most citizens have with their schools leads them to believe their schools are doing a good job (parents of elementary school-age children tend to rate their schools even higher). For public education to prosper, it will need the support of the public. The families of the students in your school are the primary "reporters" on how your school is doing.

These families play a powerful public relations role in their conversations about your school with neighbors, relatives, priests, new home buyers, and even strangers they meet on airplanes or at the soccer field. Information about your school comes directly to them every day their child is in school. Their information about other schools is more likely to come from the media. Developing a good public relations program with the media is important but not as important as developing a good relationship with the families of your students.

Families as Resources

Too often we forget how much expertise exists in the families of the children who attend our schools and how much effort most parents make to help their children succeed in school. It is unfortunate, in our view, that much stereotypical thinking about certain types of families predominates in the educational field. There have been any number of studies illustrating how much time and effort lower-income families spend attempting to help their children in school (Compton-Lilly, 2000; Lareau, 1989; Moll & Greenberg, 1990; Taylor & Dorsey-Gaines, 1988). But families do differ in the sorts of support they can provide. Some families hire tutors when children struggle or enroll them in a Sylvan Learning Center (or one of the many competitors). Some parents buy special software programs or enroll their children in the Web-based tutoring programs now available (Web-based test preparation on the new state assessments is now a hot commodity). Some send their children to exploratory learning camps during the summer. But not all parents have the resources for such support.

Some parents take their children to the public library and help them locate resources for the school project. Some help their children organize their essays. Some even edit their children's work for them, thus ensuring a better grade. That better grade is awarded not because that child worked harder or had better developed writing skills but because she or he comes from a family with certain educational resources. But not all families have such resources. Some parents completed their schooling having never been required to write a research report or even an essay. Some left school never having actually read a book, much less been asked to discuss the primary motive of the book's central characters. Some parents left having never taken algebra or biology or composition. The children of these families are often more *school-dependent students.* Such students will need more support from the school than some other children simply because their families cannot provide the same sorts of educational support as others.

In a large national study (Grissmer, Kirby, Berends, & Williamson, 1994), parent educational levels were the best predictor of school success. Parents with higher levels of educational attainment seem to be able to provide qualitatively different types of support for their children's learning. The fact that high-education families typically have higher family incomes than families with lower-education attainment means that more funds are available to invest in educational supports of every type. That does not mean that lower-income families do not care about the education of their children. It does not mean that they do not work with their children on homework and projects. But some children have families that can offer more and different sorts of instructional support.

As Rogers (2003) and Purcell-Gates (1995) showed, lower-income families bring lots of efforts to bear in helping their children in school. These families often have unrecognized strengths when it comes to solving real-world literacy tasks, but few school literacy lessons relate much to real-world literacy demands (think about how much of the classroom reading is storybook reading followed by questions). Moll and Greenberg (1990) take this a step further when they talk of families as "funds of knowledge," although knowledge often not much valued in school. Their work with teachers in a lower-income minority community resulted in bringing some of those funds of family knowledge into the school. A unit on homes, for instance, focused for weeks on how homes are built and featured interviews with parents about the homes they lived in (when built? type of construction? materials?) and parents with special knowledge (electrician, carpenter, landscaper, real estate agent) coming to the classroom to share their expertise. In this unit, the community was integrated into the

Summarizing the results of their study of Latino family literacy, Paratore, Gigliana, and Krol-Sinclair (1999) concluded: "Our evidence suggests that despite sometimes limited English proficiency, low levels of formal education, and few economic resources, when parents were provided opportunities to learn from and collaborate with their children's teachers, all of them were willing and able to do so, and most did so consistently and effectively. Yet, in a few cases, their children still failed [at school]. Our challenge as teachers is to look beyond family issues to find productive paths to success for Latino children." (p. 112)

Bullies and bullying may not seem like a family issue but it is. Ahmed and Braithewaite (2004) studied school and family variables for more than 600 students ages 9–12. They note that:

- Bullies tend to come from families with more authoritarian child-rearing practices.
- Parents often engage in stigmatizing shaming behaviors with these children.
- Bullies tend to have few friends.
- They experience higher levels of hassles with schoolwork.
- They are less engaged in the school community.
- They express strong dissatisfaction with school.

However, these researchers concluded that "What school staff do in response to bullying appears to be as important as what students do in a bullying situation" (p. 37). In other words, school variables were more important than family variables for identifying who would be a bully and who would be a victim. They found that both bullies and victims appear to share social adjustment problems that extend across the domains of family and school. Both bullies and their victims dislike school, report having family problems, and see few constraints on bullying in the school setting.

Victims are more likely to be unpopular and members of a rejected group. They report being lonely at school, having few friends, being unhappy at school, and having trouble with schoolwork. They reported that school staff seemed uninterested and unresponsive to bullying.

classroom. Many of the family members involved were not well educated, but they were indeed experts with expertise to share.

All families have talents. All could be resources in educating all children. When we limit the discussions of family involvement to questions about what *they* aren't doing, we dramatically restrict the likelihood of engaging families in the most productive ways.

Summary

No school can be truly effective without parent support and involvement. As society changes, schools must also change and so too the relationship between families and schools. The American family has changed enormously in the past 35 years—more single-parent households, more mothers in the workforce full-time, more working poor families. In many respects American families today may have fewer resources for school involvement than was previously the case. Teachers notice these changes. But there is no reason to set expectations for involvement that many families cannot meet. Schools must neither penalize nor reward children for the families they have.

Nonetheless, many schools could make substantial improvements in the parent outreach, involvement, and support programs they offer (or should be offering). The first step is simply improving communication between the school and families. That involves enhancing efforts to let families know what is going on at the school through telephone calls, newsletters, videos, and television and radio productions. Because classroom teachers are the most important members of the school staff, they must be involved in any attempt to improve communication. Some schools are using e-mail, voice-mail systems, or classroom videos, for instance, to create new methods for teachers and families to communicate with each other. Other schools are moving school fairs, pageants, plays, and parent conferences to Saturdays or Sundays.

At the same time, there is a definite shift to new forms of family involvement as state and federal agencies mandate family participation on advisory boards, councils, and governing bodies. This form of participation was often not what schools had in mind when they sought to increase family involvement, but family and parental involvement in governance is increasingly common. Authentic involvement in running a school can create more complicated administrative situations and require new roles and skills for principals and teachers. But this sort of involvement seems to have the potential for revitalizing the relationship between schools and families. Central to shared decision making is the quality of information gathered about program outcomes, including satisfaction of families with the efforts of the school.

Finally, the idea of creating interagency family support services and family literacy programs especially is generating much activity. The goal is to create an intensive and long-term effort to break the cycle of intergenerational illiteracy and poverty that entraps too many families today. In these situations, schools operate within a consortium of social, health, and employment training agencies to foster parent support efforts.

Most schools can substantially improve their efforts at involving families in the education of their children. But as society changes in the United States, schools must also change. School programs must complement family efforts and must extend support to children whose families are unable or unwilling to provide the support needed to become readers and writers.

chapter 10

Schools That Work
for All Children

The preceding chapters offer a general framework for reconsidering the schools we have. The ideas and issues presented in this chapter fit within that framework but are more often site-specific. That some schools have 5 percent of their children identified as children with disabilities and other schools have 30 percent so identified suggests substantial differences in these schools. Some schools routinely educate 85 to 95 percent of students with disabilities wholly in the regular classroom, and other schools educate few of those students in that setting. Likewise, some schools enroll many immigrant children and others few. Some

schools have a linguistically and ethnically diverse student population, and others are much more homogeneous in this regard. Some schools have many children from families served by one or more public health or social service agencies, while other schools have few children whose families receive any such services.

This diversity necessities a flexible approach to restructuring. It means that different schools will face different challenges and have access to different resources. We firmly believe, however, that our framework will improve schools for *all* children. Our focus in this chapter on only some groups of children is meant to point to specific ideas and issues that may need to be incorporated into our general framework.

What Is Special Education?

Two landmark civil rights acts forever altered the educational experiences of individuals with disabilities in the United States. The first, the Education of All Handicapped Children Act of 1975 (PL 94-142), now known as the Individuals with Disabilities Education Act (IDEA), entitles pupils with disabilities to a "free appropriate" public school education in the "least restrictive environment." The second, the Americans with Disabilities Act of 1990 (ADA), an even stronger civil rights statement, assures citizens with disabilities full participation in nearly all segments of U.S. society. These two legislative acts create a strong legal entitlement for educating pupils with disabilities in their neighborhood schools with placement in regular classrooms that provide special services and necessary adaptations in furniture, equipment, and curriculum.

Although the U.S. Department of Education has taken a strong stance supporting inclusive education, the courts and the U.S. Office of Civil Rights have been even more forceful in asserting the rights of pupils with disabilities to an inclusive education in a neighborhood school. Currently, the way schools include or exclude pupils with disabilities from the mainstream education process widely varies. In some states, few pupils with disabilities are educated outside their neighborhood schools or in segregated classroom settings. In other states, most pupils with disabilities are educated away from neighborhood schools and in separate classrooms for all or part of the day. If there is any single predictable trend in the education of struggling learners and pupils with disabilities, it is the continuing press to adapt classrooms to better serve all children (Goodlad & Lovitt, 1993).

Inclusion and Collaboration

The Regular Education Initiative, which launched inclusive education, began when Madeline Will (1986), then undersecretary of education, wrote that the burgeoning enrollments in special education were alarming and, perhaps, indicated that regular education programs were reneging on their responsibility to educate all children. Others noted the extensive fragmentation of school experiences that many low-achieving students, including students with disabilities, encountered as they moved from the classroom program to a special program and back (Allington & McGill-Franzen, 1989). Will called for closer collaboration between regular education and special education staff and for renewed efforts to adapt regular education programs to the needs of children who varied, often minimally, from normal achievement or behavior.

Rising special education enrollments seemed linked, however, to increasing accountability pressures placed on schools rather than to any real increase in the numbers of children who were, indeed, handicapped in the traditional sense. For instance, in New York state, the numbers of young children identified as pupils with disabilities significantly increased as the stakes attached to statewide testing rose. Once school performance became public record and was published annually in local papers, more and more children were identified as handicapped before the administration of the first statewide assessment in third grade. The reason seemed clear. At that time, scores of children identified as handicapped were excluded from these reports. In fact, in six schools reporting substantially improved achievement on the statewide assessments, the rise in scores was almost wholly attributable to increased numbers of low-achieving children identified as handicapped and excluded from testing. Some school administrators admitted using the classification process to improve reported achievement (McGill-Franzen & Allington, 1992). Then, the IDEA of 1997 required the inclusion of pupils with disabilities on all district, state, and federal assessments of academic achievement. It also required that the academic progress of pupils with disabilities be measured against their attainment of the new state academic standards (McGill-Franzen & Goatley, 2001). The NCLB Act of 2001 goes further, requiring that schools demonstrate that their regular and special education instructional efforts produce evidence of comparable academic growth for pupils with disabilities.

The evidence available suggests that not only does inclusive and collaborative education work to produce improved academic performances of pupils with disabilities (with no negative effects on peers), but better social relations between pupils with disabilities and other children also result (Allington & McGill-Franzen, 1996; Epps & Tindal, 1987; Gelzheiser, Meyers, & Pruzek, 1992). But creating a school where all children are educated together is not necessarily an easy task, especially when accountability standards offer little recognition of the extraordinary efforts needed to educate some children. When public displays of a school's student performance are posted or published in the local paper, it is not surprising that teachers become less willing to voluntarily accept low-achieving children as their responsibility.

Achieving inclusion may be easier than achieving collaborative teaching. For a long time both classroom and special education teachers have simply done their own thing. It was a rare school district that set achieving the regular education curriculum goals as the standard for special education students, but that is now the mandated benchmark. The most common curriculum was a watered-down version of the regular curriculum, emphasizing isolated skills development and, often, nonacademic skills and self-esteem. Special education teachers were often unfamiliar with the regular curriculum and rarely used regular curriculum materials. Few special education programs set goals for "declassifying" students. Few special education teachers expected accelerated learning and a return to the regular classroom with no need for additional assistance. As one administrator put it, "Special education is for a lifetime."

This scenario is changing, however, as a result of the U.S. Supreme Court ruling in *Shannon Carter v. Florence County* (McGill-Franzen, 1994). Shannon had been diagnosed as having a learning disability with an attention deficit disorder, resulting in substantial underachievement. At issue in this case was whether Shannon's parents could be reimbursed for enrolling her in a private, non-special-education school when dissatisfied with the individualized educational plan (IEP) developed by the public school district. That IEP called for Shannon to achieve only four months' academic growth each school year in reading and math. The Court held in favor of the family, noting that Congress intended students with disabilities to benefit academically from the special education services to be provided, and the IEP was "inappropriate" because it held no benefit for Shannon, who would only continue to fall farther behind her peers given the IEP goals established. Justice Sandra Day O'Connor, writing for the majority, noted that:

> Public educational authorities who want to avoid reimbursing parents for private education of a disabled child can do one of two things: give the child a free appropriate education in a public setting, or place the child in an appropriate private setting.
> This is the Individuals with Disabilities Education Act's mandate, and school officials who conform to it need not worry.

Although the legal issue of focus was whether parents could unilaterally reject an IEP, enroll the child in a private school of their choice, and then be reimbursed for the costs of a non-special-education private school, the opinion of the Court seems to redefine an "appropriate" education for students with disabilities. "Appropriate" special education services are to accelerate learning so that pupils with disabilities will have their achievement normalized as Shannon did while at the private school. In fact, in weighing the decision, the Court decision emphasized the academic benefits Shannon received from the private school placement. The Shannon Carter case stimulated the return of all pupils with disabilities to public accountability rolls.

One problem not fully resolved concerns the appropriateness of various test "accommodations" for pupils with disabilities. The National Academy of Education report (Heubert & Hauser, 1999), *High Stakes,* devoted a complete chapter to this topic. The researchers recommended a variety of test accommodations including breaking assessment sessions into smaller segments, large-print versions, and use of adaptive technologies where possible. But they also advised that no accommodation that fundamentally alters the nature of the assessment be allowed. The example they offered of an inappropriate accommodation was reading a reading achievement test aloud to a pupil with learning disability. Such an "accommodation" would render test results meaningless and violate the intent of Congress that parents of pupils with disabilities and the public should be presented information on the current standing of pupils with disabilities in relation to state academic standards. However, they noted that reading math story problems to the same student would not violate the intent—to assess mathematical reasoning and problem solving.

As a result of these shifts in federal special education policies, the "appropriateness" of educational programs provided for pupils with disabilities is now evaluated against evidence of accelerated achievement. The expectation that achievement gaps will be closed is quite explicit along with targeting a date when achievement will be normalized.

But special education programs cannot achieve such results alone. The only strategy for developing programs that accelerate the learning of pupils with disabilities is one in which classroom teachers play a central role. Shifting judgments about the adequacy of

The most recent reauthorization of the IDEA calls for a new procedure in the identification of pupils with disabilities. This procedure is basically a prereferral process called "responsiveness to intervention (RTI)." While final regulations are being drafted as this chapter is written, the basic features of RTI are as follows.

- Prior to identification as a pupil with a disability, schools would provide a targeted and intensive instructional intervention for a student exhibiting academic difficulties for at least one academic year (e.g., reading specialist and classroom teacher work together to modify classroom instruction and the reading specialist provides targeted reading instruction in after-school program).

- Some portion of the federal funds targeted to special education services would be used to fund the intervention (current draft regulations set 15 percent as the portion).

- The key question to be addressed is whether the student has a disability or is just instructionally needy. If providing, say, adapted classroom reading instruction and an added daily very small-group reading lesson accelerates reading development, then the disability would be ruled out. However, if after such additional support reading development still lags far behind, the student might be considered as having a disability.

There are any number of unanswered questions about RTI at this point. But the compelling evidence that intensive intervention efforts (e.g., Reading Recovery, First Steps, etc.) can substantially reduce the size of the pool of students who struggle with reading and are then identified as pupils with disabilities has led policy makers to insist that schools first initiate an intensive and expert general education intervention before assigning students to a disability category.

efforts to educate students with disabilities from analyzing inputs (e.g., smaller classes, individualized lessons, specially certified teachers) to evaluating outcomes (e.g., academic gains, as measured by AYP), is identical to the shift that has occurred in the federal Title 1 remedial program. Where does a school begin to address this shift in focus?

The CSE

As a first step, schools will have to examine the current function of the Committee of Special Education (CSE)—the federally mandated interdisciplinary group that renders decisions about identification, placement, and IEP appropriateness. The intention behind the interdisciplinarity in the CSE was to ensure that a variety of views were heard. The required inclusion of the child's classroom teacher on the team was intended to provide a clearer view of what was needed for this child to be well educated in the regular education classroom. The special education teacher was to offer expertise on how the curriculum and classroom instruction might be adapted to meet the needs of such children better. The school psychologist was to provide expertise in the areas of psychological needs and interventions appropriate for the child and, perhaps, for various psychometric assessments. Other members (e.g., classroom teachers, reading specialists, speech and language therapists) were to provide specialized expertise that created a balanced team for considering how best to adapt regular education to meet the needs of children experiencing learning difficulty.

However, in too many cases, the CSE has served primarily to certify that a child has a disability after referral by a teacher and to verify that placement in the special class with the lowest enrollments is appropriate. Almost every study of how the CSE functions points to this scenario (e.g., Mehan, Hartweck, & Meihls, 1986; Rogers, 2003). Too often the CSE simply rubber-stamps the recommendations of the teacher, the psychologist, or the CSE chair (often an administrator). There is little evidence that most CSE deliberations thoughtfully analyze the current classroom placement (e.g., observe in the classroom as required and note current curricular and instructional modifications and their appropriateness) and recommend substantive adaptations of the existing classroom instructional program, though this is obviously intended in the language of the IDEA regulations.

How can it be demonstrated that a child cannot benefit from adaptations to the current classroom program if no adaptations are recommended, implemented, and evaluated? Yet the language of the law indicates that only after adaptations have been implemented and then documented to show no benefit can the child be considered for a more restrictive educational setting (e.g., 45 minutes of daily resource-room instruction). The IDEA also indicates that a school must document that a child who has been referred has received reading instruction based on scientific research. If the school cannot document the availability of research-based reading instruction, then no finding of a reading or learning disability is allowed. In many schools, the child's classroom teacher has not attended the CSE meeting and has not participated in discussions of how the classroom instruction might be modified. This lack of participation undermines the likelihood of adaptations occurring and the full collaborative involvement of the classroom teacher in implementing any special educational interventions.

The IEP

Once a child is identified as having a disability, an IEP be must developed. Again, in most schools, classroom teachers have, historically, had little involvement in this phase of the process of designing an appropriate educational intervention. The IDEA regulations are quite clear that the child's classroom teacher, the child's parents, and the special education personnel will create the IEP collaboratively. One reason for this mandate is that when schools routinely left developing the IEP to special education personnel, many classroom teachers felt a reduced sense of professional responsibility for educating the pupils with disabilities assigned to their classrooms. Likewise, when CSE meetings are not scheduled at the convenience of parents, it is not surprising that parent involvement is less than satisfactory—thus the requirement that IEP meetings must be scheduled at a time convenient for the parents (after school, evenings, Saturdays).

An IEP does not have to be a narrowly focused skills-driven document with a multitude of small behavioral goals. Two decades ago, Hasselriis (1982) noted that nothing in the regulations suggested breaking learning into detailed lists of skills to be mastered. He offered the following IEP goals developed for a child identified as having learning disability.

Annual Goals

She will branch into at least two additional areas of interest in her reading.

Her retellings will contain personal associations appropriate to the text.

The student will perceive herself as a reader and will voluntarily read a variety of books.

Short-Term Objectives

She will participate in daily sustained silent reading.

Retelling will be incorporated into content class reading assignments.

She will start a journal for personal writing and add to it daily for 10 minutes.

She will be asked to produce written retellings of readings and class discussions in content classes.

Each of these goals and objectives is measurable, and each is curriculum focused. But such goals are rarely found on an IEP even today.

Perhaps in most cases classroom teachers should develop the IEP. They are the professionals most familiar with the child's educational development and with the core curriculum, and pupils with disabilities usually spend more time with regular education teachers than with special education teachers even after classification. If the classroom teacher drafted the IEP and then revised it with special education personnel and parents, the nature of IEPs might change dramatically. So, too, might the level of professional responsibility held by the classroom teacher.

Improving Educational Programs for Pupils with Disabilities

For educational programs for pupils with disabilities to improve, several things must occur:

- Regular education personnel must become collaboratively involved in identification, instructional adaptation, IEP development, and the monitoring of the learning progress.
- Special education personnel must become collaboratively involved with regular education personnel and develop a close familiarity with regular education curriculum goals and materials.
- The educational focus for pupils with disabilities must become success on achieving state academic standards in the regular classroom.
- Special education must be viewed as a short-term intervention in most cases, and some near-term end point must be identified when a student will no longer need special education support.
- Special education programs cannot be administered from afar. Each school must have the flexibility to design appropriate interventions without much regard for past practices or some standard program.
- Accountability for academic acceleration of the academic growth of students with disabilities must be implemented.

Children and Special Education Services

Three categories of special education classifications account for about two of every three children identified as pupils with disabilities: learning disability, attention deficit disorder with or without hyperactivity, and behavior disordered/emotionally impaired. Because these classifications are so prevalent and because so little evidence exists to support current educational interventions as providing any substantial academic benefit, we discuss each of these classifications in some detail.

Learning Disability

It has been 30-plus years since learning disability (LD) became a recognized (and reimbursable) handicapping condition. Today over half of all children receiving special education services are pupils identified as persons with learning disability. Spear-Swerling and Sternberg (1996) provide a readable and comprehensive treatment of the development of the LD field and the issues to be confronted. Suffice it to say that even today there exists little evidence that children identified as having learning disability differ cognitively from other low-achieving students. The former are usually children experiencing difficulty in learning, especially in learning to read and write. They are usually children from low-income families. They often exhibit some difficulties in social skills or aggressive behaviors. They often exhibit difficulties in language-learning areas. But LD is a socially constructed belief system, not a demonstrated cognitive/neurological disorder or deficit. Identification of learning disability depends on the beliefs of the school personnel, not on a particular array of behaviors or test results. The child with LD in one school is the child with attention deficit disorder in another, the slow learner in another, the emotionally disturbed child in another, the remedial reader in another, and the language-impaired child in yet another school (Allington, 2002b).

This is not meant to deny that some children experience substantial difficulties with literacy learning. Instead, it is meant to point out simply that the label of learning disability does little to address the instructional problems some children present. There is good evidence that children identified as having learning disability benefit most from larger amounts of higher-quality literacy instruction than is usually needed by other children to succeed (Foorman & Torgeson, 2001). There is no good evidence that children with learning disability benefit from specific curricular approaches often touted as the solution to their problems. Some children simply need more and better instruction, and children with LD are among those children. Vellutino and his colleagues (1996) provided dramatic evidence that only 1 to 2 percent of students proved resistant to intensive remediation. He provided individual tutoring or very small-group intensive remediation to all K–2 students who needed it, regardless of the reason (e.g., absences due to illness, inadequate classroom instruction, difficulty learning). His tutoring was generally modeled after the lesson design offered in Reading Recovery sessions (Clay, 1991) and offered lots of reading and writing combined with explicit skills and strategies instruction. At the end of second grade, roughly 1 percent of all children met the achievement criteria for identification as children with LD, far fewer than the roughly 5 to 10 percent of students so identified in most schools.

Mathes and her colleagues (Mathes, Denton, Fletcher, Anthony, Francis, & Schat-schneider, 2005) contrasted effects of two quite different early interventions. One was a direct instruction intervention with scripted lessons and a sequential organization of decoding lessons. The other provided no scripted guidance and offered no sequential organization of decoding; it instead relied on the tutors to organize lessons based on student responses. Intervention lessons were offered to groups of three low-achieving readers daily. The interventions were delivered by certified special education or reading teachers who selected which intervention model they would teach.

The results indicated both interventions were comparably effective with both reducing the proportion of kids performing below the 30th percentile to roughly 1 percent of the total population. Both had comparable impacts on achievement as measured by effect sizes. Small differences did appear with the direct-instruction students demonstrating better word attack, while the responsive intervention students had better fluency performances. But there were no differences on broad measures of reading achievement. No child characteristics were found to interact with intervention type. In other words, both early intervention models worked to accelerate the reading achievement of struggling readers. This raises the question of whether we debate the specifics too much while ignoring the generalized finding that intensive, expert early intervention is a critical component in schools where all children become readers and writers.

These researchers noted that many of the children they served found learning to read difficult. But these children were not "disabled" in any medical, physiological, or neurological sense. They just needed more intensive and more expert instruction than most children. We agree with the researchers' assessment. The danger in identifying such children as "disabled" is that expectations have often been lowered, curriculum was watered down, and the intensive intervention needed was not offered.

In addition, the current fragmented curriculum that many students with learning disability receive produces disastrous results, which seem to stem from the fact that these children benefit most from a consistent and coherent curricular approach to teaching them to read and write. Very simply, LD might be thought of as "cognitive confusion" about literacy learning. Programs that present children with LD with multiple curriculum emphases and changing curriculum demands cannot be expected to produce "cognitive clarity" and successful literacy acquisition. But many schools continue to buy and use an alternative curriculum approach in a pull-out program with these students. Unfortunately, such decisions reflect nothing that we have learned about teaching struggling readers, including students with learning disability, to read.

The exemplary teacher studies (Allington & Johnston, 2002; Pressley et al., 2001; Taylor et al., 2000) suggest that the best hope for children with LD is a strong classroom literacy program taught by an expert classroom teacher who is provided adequate support in adapting instruction in a highly personalized fashion. Currently, children with learning disability are among those students most likely to drop out of school and most likely to enter adulthood with low levels of literacy and limited employment skills. Obviously, the programs now in place too often fail to provide substantial academic benefit to those students.

ADD and ADHD

More recently, the number of children (most often boys) identified as exhibiting attention deficit disorders (ADD) or attention deficits with hyperactivity disorders (ADHD) has dramatically increased. Often, the ADD or ADHD classification is linked to identifying a child as having learning disability, although this is not necessary (Snow et al., 1998). The most common treatments for ADD and ADHD, unfortunately, seem to rely heavily on the use of stimulant medications such as Ritalin, prescribed for at least half a million children (according to some estimates the number is nearer a million) (Coles, 1987). One is tempted to recall a similar period in the 1970s when hyperactivity was a common diagnosis. However, the landmark report by Schrag and Divoky (1975) seemed to quell the surge in administering pharmaceutical stimulant drugs common at that time. Today, children are again being identified as "immature," "antsy," "inattentive," "hyper," and so on, and many are again being administered stimulant drugs as a primary treatment. Thus, it would seem important to summarize what is currently known about ADD and ADHD and the effectiveness of the drug treatments.

Unfortunately, ADD/ADHD is still in the eye of the beholder. The criteria include items that describe nearly every child at some time:

- Fidgets with hands or squirms in seat, has difficulty waiting turns

- Blurts out answers

- Has difficulty playing quietly
- Has difficulty sustaining attention to tasks
- Interrupts or intrudes on others
- Loses things necessary for tasks at school
- Fails to finish chores
- Does not seem to listen

In school, such behaviors often follow from difficulty meeting the demands of the work presented or from a less-than-keen interest in the more passive activities common to classroom learning.

Swanson (1993) and Purdie, Hattie, and Carroll (2002) summarize the research on the effects of stimulant medication on children identified as exhibiting an attention deficit. Their analysis demonstrated that such drugs are more effective in influencing behavior than in enhancing learning. One can reasonably expect a temporary improvement in behavior, especially in impulsivity and overactivity, and a decrease in aggressive behavior and negative social interactions. At the same time, the researchers note that no significant improvements in reading skills, athletic skills, or positive social skills should be expected nor should long-term improvement in academic achievement be expected.

It seems obvious that ADD/ADHD is a "transactional disorder," a difficulty some children exhibit interacting with their social world. While exhibiting no intellectual deficiencies, these children are more active, more socially abusive, and more often disliked by peers and harder for adults to love. Many of these children do not "outgrow" the behavioral style that sets them apart. As adults they are more likely to change jobs frequently, have legal difficulties, especially involving substance abuse, and experience problems with long-term relationships. But this is not true for all such children. About half the children identified as exhibiting ADD/ADHD seem to function quite well as adults (Henker & Whalen, 1989).

Obviously, children vary in their level of physical activity and social skills, they differ in literacy development, and they differ in their interest in school-related learning. Some parents worry about children on the passive end of the scale, though few teachers seem to show great concern about the shy "bookworms" who would rather stay inside and read

"Given the potency of these drugs, they should not be given before more benign methods are attempted. But, given their effectiveness and relative safety, in combination with the intractability of ADHD, stimulants should not be rejected out of hand. To detect side effects and to demonstrate continued efficacy, comprehensive monitoring must be done throughout the course of the treatment, not only during the initial dosage adjustment phase, and drug holidays are often advisable. And, finally, given their limitations, stimulants should rarely, if ever, be used exclusively. Pills cannot teach the skills most hyperactive children lack" (Whalen & Henker, 1992, p. 341).

than go out and engage in physically active play. In school, it is the child at the other end of the activity spectrum who draws attention. Children who are very active, are often inattentive, and have difficulty with peer relationships are a cause for concern. But before such children are labeled and subjected to drug therapies, an honest judgment must be made as to who is most likely to benefit from such a course of action. The research offers little promise of long-term academic or social benefits to the child who is labeled and medicated.

Some evidence shows that nondrug therapies, such as cognitive-behavioral approaches, work to reduce inappropriate behaviors and enhance academic performance (Reid & Borkowski, 1987). In some cases, such methods have been used with medication with good results. Similarly, drug therapies combined with a 10-step parent-training program have demonstrated positive effects on social and academic performances (Anastopoulos, DuPaul, & Barkley, 1992). The 10-step program focuses on developing a more supportive home environment that emphasizes a consistent approach to behavior management and social development.

The widespread use of pharmacological treatments may be related to educator naivete about what the research has demonstrated. In a survey of both classroom and special education teachers, Snider, Busch, and Arrowood (2003) found that teachers did not know much about the research on ADHD and/or stimulant medications. All teachers believed medications improved school performance but special educators were more positive. Using the NIH Consensus Statement on the diagnosis and treatment of ADHD as a base, the researchers asked a number of questions. They found 90 percent of teachers believed that ADHD was brain dysfunction/neurological in source although research doesn't support that view. In addition, 94 percent thought medication improved academic achievement although research does not confirm this either. Over half of the respondents knew of none of the important documented side effects (e.g., tics, insomnia, stunted growth, drug abuse) of stimulant medications.

As with most other issues of importance, school communities should examine the long-term effects of current policies concerning children identified as exhibiting ADD/ADHD. Where do most referrals for ADD/ADHD come from? Do most children receiving medication benefit academically? For those children with normal intellectual capacities, academic success would seem a reasonable expectation if drug therapies are intended to address academic learning. Do these children graduate from high school and become productive citizens in the community?

There will always be children who are more active, distractible, and bothersome than others. The central question is, What sort of responses to such children might schools consider? For instance, would regular opportunities to engage in large-muscle movement activities stem some of the activity problems (as recess periods have been reduced or eliminated, have more children been identified as having ADD)? Can classroom teachers develop more effective routines for engaging all children in their work (do classrooms have sufficient collections of books that low-achieving children can read and want to read)? Can cognitive control strategies be developed in children having difficulty staying on-task or interacting with peers (making rules and routines explicit seems to assist some children; allowing greater flexibility in rules and routines assists others)? Decisions to employ stimulant medications with difficult children cannot become routine. Using such medications on active children seems to benefit adults (parents and teachers) more than it benefits children.

Behavioral/Emotional Disorders

Probably no child produces problems with so few workable solutions as the seriously misbehaving child. Most schools have but a single strategy for dealing with children who are aggressively misbehaving—sending the child away. In some cases, the child goes to another school or to a self-contained classroom with other misbehaving children. Few schools have an effective intervention plan for altering the child's behavior and returning the child to the classroom with substantial improvement in ability to control emotions and behavior. This is not to condone the aggressive, belligerent, and potentially dangerous behavioral displays that some children exhibit. But it is necessary to ask how current programs benefit the child exhibiting the misbehavior. We see the need for developing a school strategy for working more effectively with such children and their families in an attempt to improve behavior and socialization. Removing such children from the regular classroom or from the school solves the school's problem but rarely addresses the child's problems in any useful way.

We suggest that school personnel first take stock of current resources for addressing the issue of the seriously disruptive student. Who has the responsibility for evaluating the situation and implementing any sort of intervention? In our work in schools, we have found that in too many cases no one is charged with such responsibilities. Instead, many different staff members are seen as potentially responsible. For instance, classroom teachers are

Video Workshop, sponsored by the National Association of Elementary School Principals, produces *Episodes in Discipline: Strategies That Work* (video), 3 Regent Street, Suite 306, Livingston, NJ 07039 (201-992-9081 or www.naesp.org).

told to "bear with it" or to attempt to implement a reward/punishment scheme—to develop clear rules about behavioral expectations. Rarely, however, have teachers had much training with designing and implementing such classroom approaches. Principals often find unruly students sitting in the outer office, waiting for some form of punishment or using the area as a cooling-off site. But for seriously disruptive students, the wait in the outer office can turn that location into a maelstrom (although one principal told us that keeping a journal on hand and having students write about the incident that resulted in their being sent to the office had a wonderfully calming effect).

In some schools, the special education teacher is asked to serve as a resource, either in the classroom or by working with the child outside the regular classroom. In other schools, a guidance counselor or a social worker or a school psychologist is asked to intervene, but these staff members do not necessarily have the time, skills, or training to implement any sort of effective intervention. For instance, simply scheduling the seriously disruptive student into a small group-support session for 30 minutes a week is unlikely to provide an effective resolution. The more recent addition, an in-school suspension room, also removes the child from the classroom but typically offers little in the way of an effective plan for resolving behavioral difficulties.

Generally, the seriously disruptive child is no stranger to punishment. These children often come from homes where they have been punished quite severely though often inconsistently for misbehavior. They are also likely to receive many more commands from parents than other children, often with no explanation. Employing control-oriented approaches to behavioral problems, approaches that emphasize imposing external standards, has not worked nearly as well as approaches emphasizing internally derived standards (Becker, 1992). These children do not respond positively to escalating penalties and harsher behavioral standards and punishments. Instead, they simply grow angrier and more disruptive.

Schools might consider a variety of approaches in better addressing the problems that seriously disruptive students create. For instance, at Boys Town, where many such children are enrolled, a long-term staff development project has focused on helping teachers develop more effective routines and responses to such students. One strategy is to help staff learn to break the cycle of aggression–counteraggression by developing responses such as lowering the voice (instead of raising it), shifting to less confrontational postures, and using third-party observers in the classroom to identify teacher responses that generally create increased negative reactions by students. (Such students are likely to perceive sarcasm, criticism, shouting, and posturing as aggressive attacks and respond with increased aggression.) Other strategies include helping teachers learn to provide four positive comments for each corrective they issue, role-playing and rehearsing specific incidents and appropriate responses, providing meaningful rationales for behavioral routines (rather than dictums), and developing effective consequences for maintaining appropriate behavior (Dowd & Tierney, 1992).

Schools that work well for all children make a concerted effort to help children develop personal responsibility for their own actions. Children need to accept responsibility for their learning as well as for their behavior (often the two are related). At the same time, schools must accept the responsibility to help all children learn more effective self-monitoring strategies. We are of the opinion that simply ordering children around is not the preferred model for schooling. Thus, in addressing the issue of behavior problems, we offer summaries of three interventions that focus on developing students' competence.

Glasser's Control Theory　The work of William Glasser (1986, 1990) provides one of the most sensible and comprehensive treatments of behavior problems (including lesser problems such as motivation). He argues that all human behavior is an attempt to satisfy one of five basic needs: survival, love, power, fun, and freedom. He attempts to show that all of us control our own behavior and to show how coercive school power creates many of the difficulties often attributed to children. His characterizations of schools as holding fast to the "Boss–Teacher" model in an era of shared decision making is quite compelling.

Glasser's work is provocative in other respects as well. For instance, he counsels that calling parents of misbehaving children into the school is an admission that the school cannot handle its own problems. He suggests that students often benefit from being transferred out of classrooms where they have built up a negative reputation, because even after they have learned control strategies they find themselves in an "old" environment where they may be "discriminated" against because of past incidents. He emphasizes ignoring who was at fault and focusing on looking for solutions generated by the child. His approach involves students—in whole-class groups, cooperative teams, and individually—in social problem solving, curriculum problem solving, and outcomes assessment. His work in schools has earned him accolades from a wide range of educators, and his work has the good supporting documentation.

Dreikurs's Logical Consequences　Less well known and older, but still with substantial credentials, is the Logical Consequences model of Rudolf Dreikurs (Dreikurs, Grunwald, & Pepper, 1982). In this approach all behavior is again seen as purposeful. People behave in certain ways to gain attention, exercise power, exact revenge, or display an inadequacy. Dreikurs identified several subtypes of attention-getting behaviors and argued that, generally, children worked in a hierarchical sequence from gaining attention to displaying inadequacy. The approach rests on a democratic teaching style that provides reasonable guidance but emphasizes developing understanding that decisions are linked to responsibility. Children are involved in setting portions of the academic agenda as well as general routines and rules for classroom deportment. Like Glasser's Control Theory, Logical Consequences focuses on trying to understand why children behave the way they do and how to help children learn the consequences of their behavior. Evidence from schools adopting this approach indicates a reduced incidence of minor and major behavioral problems.

Two groups have developed and implemented conflict resolution programs in schools nationwide and continue to provide resources and training for other schools interested in adopting the process:

Educators for Social Responsibility, Resolving Conflict Creatively Program, 23 Garden Street, Cambridge, MA 02138 (www.esrnational.org)

Boys Town USA, at www.boystown.org

Conflict Resolution   Another effort that schools might consider is adopting one of several new approaches to conflict resolution. Because many behavioral displays result from personal conflicts between students, these approaches can stem much of the aggressive behavior found in many schools. Approaches to conflict resolution usually involve two sets of activities: training professional staff in conflict resolution strategies and training students to resolve conflicts through peer mediation. Both activities work to develop shared norms and strategies for dealing with conflicts (Johnson & Johnson, 1993).

School Violence   There seems to be a school violence report in the media nearly every week. Public concern about the topic is at an all-time high. Media coverage of homicides increased by 721 percent between 1992 and 1998 even though the actual homicide rate dropped by 20 percent (Hinds, 2000). The reality is that violence in schools has declined over the years and schools are just about the safest public environments available. Public Agenda, a nonprofit public opinion and research organization, recently produced an issues report on school violence. They note three approaches that might be taken to address the issue:

Choice 1. Promote a nonviolent culture. Reduce children's access to violent games, videos, movies, and television programs.

Choice 2. Provide more help to children at greater risk of violence. Create a system for identifying the few very troubled children and families, and fund appropriate interventions.

Choice 3. Provide greater moral discipline. Use child-centered child rearing methods at home and school but establish clear rules and consequences.

Almost directly in contrast to Control Theory and Logical Consequences is Canter's (1989) Assertive Discipline, a generally inflexible approach to discipline and behavior. His four steps—establishing rules, tracking misbehavior, using punishment, and implementing positive consequences—seem logical for an adult-centered setting. The approach is easy to use because it simplifies and standardizes traditional school rules. However, some evidence shows that discipline and behavior problems increase after the system is implemented. The rigidity of the system allows for little latitude in dealing with infractions and works against developing internal self-control strategies in children. In short, Assertive Discipline does little, if anything, to address the underlying cause of behavioral problems, and no research suggests it provides a solution to them (Render, Padilla, & Kvank, 1989). The approach seems to benefit educators more than it benefits children, for continued misbehavior leads to suspension, solving the problem the school is having. But suspension is unlikely to enhance either the behavioral controls or achievement of the suspended child.

Each approach has its advocates. Each has vociferous opponents. In the Public Agenda report (www.publicagenda.org) each approach is detailed with examples of the approach in action. None of the choices is simple.

The central question that must be asked is, How can this school more effectively solve the problems of students who exhibit serious and continued misbehavior, students who seem prone to reacting violently to perceived injustices? Segregating these children into special classes or special schools offers few benefits to anyone. For schools, segregation is incredibly expensive while being largely ineffective both behaviorally and academically. For a segregated child, this approach typically leads neither to improved self-control nor to improved academic achievement. The child simply grows up to be an angry, illiterate adult who can do real damage (or society can support the person in prison for the rest of his or her life, another expensive outcome).

There are no easy answers here, but it does seem that schools need better programs than what now usually exist. Perhaps it is time to think about short-term segregation with intensive intervention and a scheduled return to a regular classroom (though we believe Glasser is correct in suggesting a return to a different classroom). All children benefit from learning to take greater control over their actions. But as in most other areas of learning, some children need more and better support than others to achieve these goals.

Missing School and Moving Around

Some children miss more school and move from school to school far more frequently than do other children. In either situation, it is difficult to provide a high-quality education. But schools that work well for all children have processes and procedures for more effectively dealing with both problems.

Missing School

Teachers cannot teach children who are not in school. In some elementary schools, nearly one-third of the students are absent on any given day. Many schools have some children who have routinely been absent at least 20 days each year. Nationally, between 5 and 10 percent of Title 1 participants miss 20 or more days of school. Twenty days is a whole month of schooling. Across an elementary school career, 20 days of absence each year equals missing one full year of schooling. One-third of the children participating in any compensatory education program miss between 5 and 10 days of school each year (one to two weeks)—about twice as many absences as other children have.

How can schools increase attendance rates? At the Westmere Elementary School in Guilderland, New York, the principal developed what might be termed the "relentless" approach. First, when children did not show up for school, the school called the home to talk with a parent about the absence. The call might have come during the day, at dinnertime, or the following morning, but parents came to expect a call. The legal framework holds parents responsible for school attendance of children. Thus, the school had every right to expect children to be in attendance, and this was communicated to parents.

Still, some children were absent because they failed to get up on time and missed the bus. In this case, the principal got in his car and drove to pick them up, if necessary. If getting children up on time was a routine problem (perhaps a single parent worked late hours), the school purchased an alarm clock for the oldest child. Bus drivers were told to wait at least two minutes for some children, sounding the horn every 15 seconds. If that failed to increase attendance, then the family went on an early morning telephone list and could expect a call approximately 30 minutes before the bus was scheduled to arrive. If no one answered, the principal reported, he went to the home and banged on the door until someone got up, dressed the children, and put them in his car to go to school.

This "relentless" strategy worked to solve virtually all of the attendance problems the school experienced. The principal reported that implementing this approach beginning on the first day of school paid big dividends. After the first month, hardly any child missed a day of school for any reason other than illness. The principal remarked, "We can't teach children that aren't here. It shouldn't be our job to make sure kids come to school, but if we don't do it, who will?"

We have encountered other school administrators with almost identical attitudes and similar strategies. In one urban school, the principal organized neighborhood walkers into teams that got each other up and off to school. If one child was not ready when the team came by, then one team member (or a parent) stayed and waited for that child to get ready. In this case, team members called children in homes where rising on time for school was a problem. Team members knocked on doors to hurry tardy children up. In this school, the team approach worked well even though many families had no telephone.

Finally, in another urban school district, school and town officials collaborated to refer parents of children exhibiting attendance problems to the family court system under a child neglect provision. Since state law required school attendance, the courts held that ensuring attendance was a parental responsibility. After only a few months (and after a number of parents appeared in family court), attendance improved dramatically. However, such a strategy needs to have support in other segments of the community because taking parents to court does not often heighten those parents' satisfaction with the school. We do not recommend this strategy but mention it to illustrate some schools' seriousness about attendance.

Each school needs to take a hard look at current attendance patterns. If attendance is generally high (97-plus percent), a few children may still present attendance problems (often they are low-achieving students), and the school needs a strategy for dealing with them. However, if attendance drops much below 97 percent, the school needs to evaluate attendance issues more thoroughly and redesign efforts more broadly to ensure high daily attendance.

High-Mobility Families

"The United States has one of the highest mobility rates of all developed countries," according to the U.S. General Accounting Office (1994). The GAO report notes that low-income families move more often than higher-income families and that children who frequently move experience substantially higher rates of grade retention, low achievement, behavioral difficulties, and dropping out than similar children whose families do not move. One in six third graders has attended at least three elementary schools since the beginning of first grade. If these children were evenly distributed across all elementary schools, the average third-grade classroom would enroll four of these highly mobile children. But, of course, these children are not evenly distributed across schools.

Schools with many poor children, schools with substantial numbers of students from immigrant families, schools serving military installations, and schools enrolling children of migrant worker families are the schools where highly mobile children are concentrated. But all schools have some children who have attended many different schools, and all schools have children who depart before the year is completed and others who enroll some time after school commences. In fact, only 25 percent of all third graders have attended only one school, according to the GAO study. While highly mobile children are most at risk, any child who has changed elementary schools seems to be placed at more risk than a child who has never changed schools.

Most schools have no special programs or procedures for addressing the needs of students transferring in or out, according to the GAO study. Classroom teachers reported that, often, children simply appeared at the classroom door with a note indicating they were to be added to the class listing! Thus, with little, if any, warning, teachers were expected to integrate children into classroom routines and provide appropriate instruction. Records from previous schools often arrived days or weeks after the children and in too many cases never arrived. Even when schools received the records, teachers were not necessarily told

Homeless children present special problems for schools, but these problems are no greater than those faced by the children themselves. Although the total number of homeless children is not easily estimated, over 300,000 children spent some time in a state-certified shelter in New York City last year. The number of children who spent time in a noncertified shelter or with relatives or on the street or in an auto might double that number. The federal McKinney Homeless Assistance Act provides guidelines for educational rights of homeless children (and money to states to assist in meeting those guidelines). Perhaps the most important aspect of the federal act is the guarantee that homeless children can choose to attend school at either their last address or the address of their temporary home. The law does not require transportation for students to the school of their choice, but several legal rights organizations have set out to establish that right legally, arguing that denial of transportation for homeless children effectively eliminates the choice guaranteed under the federal act.

You can find many useful resources for supporting the education of homeless children at www.naehcy.org and www.serve.org/nche.

of their arrival. When teachers did examine the folders, they often found outdated or sparse information about academic performance and curricular placements.

Several steps might be taken to improve on the current situation. The first step would be to prepare a child-transfer card system that parents would present at the new school when enrolling their child. This transfer card would contain particularly relevant data on student curriculum placement and special-program participation. For instance, the card might include grade placement, reading level and curriculum materials currently used, writing levels and curriculum, math level and curriculum, and whether the child qualifies for free or reduced-price lunch, participates in Title 1 remediation or an ELL program, has been identified as having learning disability, or is involved in a behavioral improvement program.

In an ideal world, transfer cards could be standardized so that teachers have an efficient method of locating information about curricular placements and special-program participation. Developing a simple system for communicating important academic information to other educators is a first step. Ideally, the classroom teacher from the departing school would also write a short essay on the child that would accompany the transfer card and provide a telephone number so that the receiving teacher would be able to call and talk about the transferring child.

The second step would be to develop a procedure for supporting the classroom teacher attempting to get to know the entering child better. Often a single half-hour of released time to work individually with the transferring child would be sufficient to establish current reading and math levels and to gain insight into the child as a learner. Few schools seem to have any such procedure in place, so teachers try to find out about transferring children in a "catch as catch can" fashion.

The third step would be to consider how to support children who have transferred in. Again, most schools have no standard procedures, but classroom teachers have developed a number of supportive processes, such as appointing several children as "tour guides" to help the new student learn the geography and routines of the school. Several students are initially appointed to optimize the likelihood that a good social fit will be found. Other teachers have the student and several peers develop a brief "autobiography" that can be presented to the class and may feature family pictures and information about the child's previous school and region.

Ethnic, Linguistic, and Cultural Diversity

Today more than 40 percent of schoolchildren are minority-group members and 10 percent are designated limited English proficient. In most of the largest school districts in the United States, students from ethnic minority families represent a majority (Echevarria et al., 2004). It is difficult to find an elementary school that does not enroll children from a range of ethnic groups and children who come from homes where English is not the dominant language. Census data show that almost half the Spanish-speaking and Asian respondents indicated that English was not the primary language of the home. Schools have proportionally fewer teachers from ethnic minority groups than they have minority students. There is a dramatic shortage of teachers who are bilingual and almost no teachers who speak East Asian, Eastern European, or African languages (e.g., Hmong, Malay, Farsi, Polish, Croat, Swahili). The curriculum focus in most schools remains largely Eurocentric with little literature, history, or geography representative of the larger global community or even the rich diversity of U.S. society.

Schools must change to better meet the needs of increasingly diverse students. Schools need to become model communities that value the richness of different cultural traditions, promote bilingualism in all students, and integrate all members of society into a just community (Christian & Genesee, 1998). In this section we offer a preliminary exploration of some fundamental concerns and some opportunities that schools might elect to re-create themselves to achieve fuller participation by children from diverse families.

Children from Afar—Immigrants

The United States is a nation of immigrants. All but a very few citizens are products of immigration from somewhere else at some distant or near point in time. Immigration to the United States has always been quite high compared with immigration into other countries, and that remains the case today.

Immigrant children often provide many challenges for schools, usually problems associated with designing effective classroom instruction for children whose first language is not English and who do not speak or understand anything but the most basic English words. As refugees from nations torn with conflict arrive, schools face other problems as well. Often conflict has wholly disrupted schooling in those nations, in some cases for a long while. In other cases, the immigrant children are members of a persecuted class and were denied schooling even when it was available. Thus, schools are serving more children who have limited literacy in their first language.

For more information on best practices, and how-to classroom ideas, visit www. colorincolorado.org. You can sign up for a monthly newsletter focused on teaching ELLs.

These children may arrive here at age 10 or 11 having no previous school experience and no previous literacy instruction (Fu, 2003). In addition, many have experienced horrific traumatizing situations that few of us can, or care to, imagine. Combine this with little proficiency in English and the problems presented to schools become quite substantial.

Immigrant children and their families benefit from programs that develop understandings of schools and the schooling process in the United States. For instance, some parents may not understand the difference between textbooks assigned to a child for the school year and a library book that must be returned in two weeks. Likewise, everything from grading practices to volunteerism to grade levels to compulsory attendance may seem foreign. Of course, organizing sessions for parents (and older students) often means locating someone who can serve as a translator for the session (and for other school contacts as well). A good first step, then, is to think about providing introductory workshop sessions with a translator.

Barth (1990) describes an even more proactive initiative. An elementary school that enrolled mostly white, English-speaking students was informed in the spring that a number of Cambodian refugee children would be attending the school the following fall. The teachers, principal, and parents decided that it would be important for everyone in the school community to be familiar generally with Cambodian culture, language, and geography. Thus, that spring, "getting ready for the Cambodian children" became a broad-based theme of education at the school—in reading and language arts, social studies, art, music, and science. Everyone learned to say something in Cambodian. Classroom lessons focused on prejudice as well as on Cambodian culture and geography. In the end, when the Cambodian children and their families arrived to begin school in the fall, they found teachers and others (including custodians, teacher aides, cooks, bus drivers) who could greet them in their first language and classroom displays of Cambodian life, art, and history. They found an interpreter on-site to answer questions and explain general school policies. Few immigrant children have ever felt so welcomed to their new school.

Children Whose First Language Is Not English

Some children, many of them immigrants, enroll in school with little knowledge of English—these students are firmly monolingual. Others arrive with a firm control over their first language, which is not English, and some familiarity with English. Others arrive

Ethnic, Linguistic, and Cultural Diversity

266

and seem to be almost bilingual even if just beginning school. Finally, many children arrive at school speaking only English. We include this final group because they are the largest and because we often forget that they are one of two groups of monolingual children in the school. In a changing world economy where bilingualism is increasingly useful and important (which is why so many states have added study of foreign language to high school graduation criteria), it would seem that fostering bilingualism through dual language immersion programs for all children might easily be set as an educational goal.

Schools might think of children whose first language is not English as resources (since most schools in the United States are better equipped to teach these children English than to teach the monolingual English-only children to speak Cambodian, Cantonese, or Spanish). But such thinking seems generally uncommon (Christian & Genesee, 1998). We suppose that schools should be passionately fostering bilingualism and obviously not attempting to undermine first-language acquisition or ignoring literacy development in the first language. But how can that be done in an era when fewer than half of our nonnative English-speaking children participate in any sort of school-based native language instructional support?

Several federal educational programs, of course, might be used to provide services. Title 1, for instance must enroll second-language learners with low reading scores. Funds provided under the Bilingual Education Act (Title VII), the Emergency Immigrant Education Program, and the Transitional Program for Refugee Children are also available. But federal funding notwithstanding, many schools could create an improved instructional environment for children whose first language is not English. Not every program enhancement is expensive. In fact, some of the most powerful and promising activities, such as the earlier-noted school response to Cambodian immigrant children, are low-cost or no-cost efforts.

It seems that many Americans, educators included, assume that immigrant children are happy to have arrived in the United States. But immigrant children can be unhappy, lonely, and lost in the new world they have entered. Danling Fu (2003) includes several pieces written by Chinese immigrant children who were enrolled in the New York City public schools. These pieces speak to the real emotions often tied to immigration. "I miss China too much. I miss all my relatives, teachers, and friends. . . . There was so much to do in China: games, swimming, parks, oceans and bicycling. When we didn't have school, we ran all over the hills and fields, so much fun. Here we are locked in cage-like apartments and live like caged birds with bars on the windows, from which all you can see is other old buildings and their barred windows" (p. 4).

This small book provides a description of how one school worked hard to revise its instruction so that immigrant students were more successful. It is a wonderful example of "homegrown" reform.

Schoolwide Efforts   In one school, several bilingual dictionaries were developed cooperatively by English-speaking and non-English-speaking children (even monolingual English-only children worked on the project). This activity, of course, is useful only when children with limited English proficiency (or their parents) are literate in their first language. But the development of these dictionaries targeted vocabulary drawn from the core curriculum rather than simply using someone else's idea of a core-vocabulary word list. The dictionaries had sections for social studies, science, and math vocabulary, as well as a general vocabulary section where words common to the language arts curriculum were located. As one literate Asian mother commented, "This is such a good idea because now we can be so much more helpful at home." Copies of the dictionaries were kept on an office computer file so that they could be updated each year and even personalized for particular teachers. This effort cost virtually nothing because most of the work was done by children (and a few bilingual parents who proofed the final copies).

This school also used a "language buddies" system to support nonnative English-speakers. Each nonnative English-speaking child was paired with at least one language buddy, often an older student with more developed English-language proficiency. The school opened the school library and media center after school to provide a quiet but comfortable work space for the language buddies' activities. The older children often helped the younger children with homework or with reading and writing assignments, especially if no one in the younger child's family had yet developed those skills. Whenever possible, children with the same first language were placed in the same classroom (easier in this school with a mostly multiage classroom organization) so that the children could support each other's learning.

Finally, children with a non-English-language proficiency served as tutors for English-only children who were interested in learning a second language themselves. In other words, a voluntary after-school program was developed where children might learn the rudiments of Lao, Swahili, Polish, American Sign Language, or Spanish. The "staff" were the students with proficiency in the languages being taught and, sometimes, parents, community members, or staff members who spoke those languages.

Many favorite big books are available in both English and Spanish. Here, a young man leads the class in a rereading of the Spanish-language edition of Mrs. Wishy Washy *(Wright Group).*

Ethnic, Linguistic, and Cultural Diversity

Another important issue is the supply of foreign-language children's books available in classroom or school libraries (and foreign-language software as well). Children literate in their native language need to continue their reading in that language, too. In fact, the report of the National Academy of Education has found that developing and refining literacy skills in any language provides substantial benefits for English-language literacy acquisition (Snow, Burns, & Griffin, 1998).

Native-language literature also gives children culturally relevant material, enhancing both interest and comprehension. Similarly, providing a supply of English-language children's literature that focuses on the countries and cultures of the nonnative English-speaking children holds promise for fostering the English-literacy development of those children and helping other students develop a better understanding of their classmates' cultures. Professional magazines such as *BookLinks* serve as terrific resources for locating books on ethnic groups, nations, or regions of the world (e.g., Caribbean literature).

Another source for such books and volunteer readers is the parents of the second-language learners. Walters and Gunderson (1985) describe a program that recruited parents to serve as volunteers to read books to children in their native languages. These parents are often more aware of second-language children's books than the school librarian. But it is not just parents who can serve as resources. Schools can tap others in the communities, for their expertise and to serve as guest readers. We can think of no reason not to include such adults in a guest reader program, reading books in their native languages. What better way to show respect for other cultures than this? Because fairy tales are often universal, guest readers might present another culture's version, in the native language, to English-speaking children and then "translate" or summarize the tale afterward.

Vasquez (1993) discusses a telecommunications-based option. The intervention is an after-school program for Latino children called *La Clase Magica*. The Spanish-speaking children in this project are involved in a computer-based role-playing activity in which they report their progress to the Wizard and attempt to gain information about solutions to problems encountered during the computer adventure. Students write letters and progress reports to students in other school sites also involved in the activity through a telecommunications network.

Other schools might consider using the Internet to link second-language children to other speakers (readers/writers) of their native language. This seems especially useful for children who have limited access to other children who share their native language. Such a system might replace the language buddy intervention when no appropriate language buddy is available. Locating an online partner would require posting a query to other users on the network, but the potential seems promising.

Classroom Links Such activities are wonderful, natural extensions of well-designed classroom interventions offered under the auspices of English language learner (ELL) education programs. They are almost essential in today's schools, where children of multiple foreign-language backgrounds are enrolled. In the most common situations, schools simply cannot provide native-language instruction for children from, say, 13 different language backgrounds. Many schools find providing support for even the most common native language—Spanish—difficult because of the limited supply of certified Spanish bilingual teachers. The problems of locating qualified teachers with proficiency in Lao, Cantonese, Farsi, or any of the other less common languages is enormous. Nonetheless, children who arrive at school speaking these languages and with little proficiency in English and with little possibility of home support for English acquisition need instructional support.

Yet this support must be linked to classroom instruction. There is too much evidence that a traditional "skill and drill" ELL curriculum is insufficient. Just as with remedial and special education, efforts supporting children acquiring English must be focused on children's progress through the core curriculum. Segregated interventions are less powerful than efforts linked to and offered in the regular classroom.

The most promising approach, in our view, is the Cognitive Academic Language Learning Approach (CALLA), a strategy-based intervention that targets high-priority content from the core grade-level curriculum in supporting learners acquiring English in the classroom (Chamot & O'Malley, 1994). CALLA develops from the premise that second-language learners are, like all language learners, most successful when the language-learning activity is meaningful and authentic. Unlike the most traditional approaches (e.g., audiolingual), natural language use involving central curriculum topics is emphasized rather than drill and practice on isolated sentences selected to emphasize certain grammatical structures. When ELL teachers use the CALLA intervention design, the focus is on supporting learning in the classroom while developing language proficiency.

Of course, classroom teachers are important to the success of children acquiring English-language proficiency. Implementing the CALLA design requires closer collaboration between classroom teachers and specialist teachers (when these specialists are available). But classroom teachers might routinely make other adaptations for children acquiring English as a second (or third) language, although many of the practices that benefit any child who finds learning to read difficult also produce real benefits (e.g., increased opportunities to read and write, expanded access to personalized instruction, enhanced family-involvement support).

The development of the Sheltered Instruction Observation Protocol (SIOP) provides one good alternative for enhancing English language acquisition and academic content learning for

"If ELL students are to catch up academically with their native English-speaking peers, their cognitive growth and mastery of academic content must continue while English is being learned. Thus, the teaching of English as a second language should be integrated with the teaching of other academic content. . . . All content teachers must recognize themselves also as teachers of language" (Cummins, 1994, p. 56).

Oral proficiency in a second language and literacy development should not be confused. Some children seem to develop oral facility while still having difficulties with written language. Others develop literacy ahead of oral-language proficiencies. It is important that teachers do not overemphasize, for instance, oral reading and pronunciation accuracy while undervaluing comprehension and understanding. Similarly, the traditional notion that children cannot read and write a second language until they can speak that language with facility has been thoroughly discredited. In fact, all children, including second-language learners, acquire more control over language through their experiences with reading and writing (Weber, 1991).

ELL students (Echevarria, Vogt, & Short, 2004; see p. 77 for additional information). The SIOP model offers educators a system for analyzing the adaptations in curricular materials and lessons to better meet the needs of ELL students. The theoretical base for SIOP reflects that of CALLA, that language acquisition is facilitated through meaningful use and interaction. It is through the study of core curricular content with modified instruction in English that academic goals are advanced. Given current federal accountability requirements (e.g., achieving AYP for ELL students) and the general lack of preparation most teachers have in adapting lessons for ELL students, the SIOP model works to extend teacher expertise as well as enhance student growth.

There are other common routines to use if fostering growth in English is our goal. Reading to children fosters vocabulary growth. This seems doubly true for children learning English (Elley & Mangubhai, 1983). The language of books is simply different from the language of talk and the language of television (two other primary sources of language exposure). Thus, the classroom framework that we offer throughout this book, with an emphasis on reading several texts daily, provides more support than many traditional classroom environments. Similarly, the useful role of big books, language experience stories, predictable texts, careful strategy instruction, and repeated readings of little books are all important aspects of providing enhanced classroom support for children acquiring English as a second language (Rigg, 1989).

Finally, traditional educational assessments have not served second-language learners well. Traditional assessments of learners acquiring English proficiency typically underestimate potential for learning—Cummins (1994) calculated an average three-year underestimation. The suggestions offered earlier for valuing more authentic measures of literacy development hold true here, too.

Adapting classroom lessons is made easier when teachers have better knowledge of children's literacy development in their first language, when they have a variety of appropriate materials, and when they have considerate support from specialist teachers. In too many schools, classroom teachers have too little support. Nearly all schools can enhance the existing educational support for learners acquiring English proficiency. As greater numbers of ELL children enter schools, it is imperative that adaptations be made. As illustrated here, many useful efforts can be implemented with little added cost and modest effort.

Children from Ethnic, Cultural, and Religious Minority Groups

The children attending our schools represent the diversity of our society, but too often our curriculum fails to mirror that diversity. Much diversity can be found among native-born children whose first language is English. Asian Americans, African Americans, Native Americans, Pacific Islanders, and many children of Latino descent are from families with a longer history in this country than, say, many Irish American families. We would have schools celebrate diversity by examining community histories and family histories. It is in these local histories that diversity can be treated most naturally (McGill-Franzen & Rogers, 2000).

Family stories, oral histories of community members, local history projects, and collaborations with state and local history societies all offer enormous potential for helping all children understand the unique contributions of diverse community members (Moll & Greenberg, 1990). But the second benefit is that teachers become more sensitive to the funds of knowledge that all communities possess. Much interest in such projects can be stimulated by well-stocked collections of children's books that represent diverse authorship, characters, settings, and eras as well as genres. In fact, for many children, literature may offer the only opportunity to acquire understandings of other cultures and the experiences of members of ethnic minority groups.

Imagine including stories of Mormons, Muslims, and Mennonites with the usual stories about Methodists (or other mainstream religions). Imagine stories developing the experiences of Korean Americans, Russian Jewish immigrants, and Navajo children in our society today. Imagine planning social studies curricula focused on the experiences of children during different historical eras and emphasizing the diversity of childhoods in North America across the past three centuries. Imagine fifth graders who could construct a reasonably accurate diary entry for children from different geographical regions with membership in various ethnic or religious groups at various points in North American history (a diary entry describing a day in the life of an African American slave child in Virginia in 1850, a midwestern Methodist farmer boy in that same era, a New England blue-blooded daughter in 1900, or a Japanese American daughter in San Francisco in 1945).

We emphasize the importance of stocking schools (and curriculum) with books representing the diversity of the United States because the best evidence available suggests that the collections in few schools are even minimally adequate in this regard. Without a planned approach, school

Shirley Brice Heath has written a powerful book recounting cultural differences in three communities and describing how schools responded in ways that fostered learning. Her book *Ways with Words* (1983) is a classic text on language use in the classroom and communities.

Katherine Au's *Multicultural Issues and Literacy Achievement* (2005) provides a readable source for rethinking traditional school reading programs.

collections develop into collections of books that represent only a narrow slice of experience. In fact, one strength of basal reader anthologies is their inclusion of a much broader array of peoples and their stories than is commonly found in school-developed core-books literature curricula. Sad to say, but basal anthologies better represent the diversity in our society than do most school book collections.

Providing children with access to stories representing the diversity of U.S. society is seen as one way to foster tolerance through increased awareness of the contributions and experiences of diverse members of our society, to reduce prejudice, and to improve achievement of minority students. Providing access, however, may be the easiest part of creating schools that celebrate diversity and actually achieve the goals noted above. More difficult is achieving balanced portrayals of different groups. For instance, many are wary of creating a "victims" curriculum in which the focus is primarily on the trials and tribulations of various ethnic minorities rather than on their contributions. Likewise, many are wary of "heroes" approaches that primarily focus on the outstanding achievements of selected successful minorities without developing an understanding of the struggles many minority groups have faced.

Religious tolerance is another potentially heated issue. How can schools foster an understanding of Hinduism or Islam without fostering concern from Hindus, Muslims, and Christians, for instance, about the accuracy and value of the information? Yet it is difficult to understand cultures without developing some sense of the role that religion plays and some sense of beliefs central to the dominant religion.

Finally, how do schools foster appreciation for diversity without developing stereotypical views in students? Navajo culture and Iroquois culture were quite different. The experiences of free African Americans in the North were different from the experiences of enslaved African Americans in the South (and different from the experiences of northern white Americans). The members of the various Asian and Indo-Asian cultures who have immigrated to the United States in the last century also represent enormous diversity themselves. Similarly, the experiences of Cuban immigrants and the experiences of Mexican immigrants and Latinos moving stateside from Puerto Rico are quite diverse. Somehow, the exploration of diversity must foster appreciation for diversity within ethnic, cultural, and religious groups. One recommended strategy is to plan to use several works about each cultural group—works that collectively present both positive and negative aspects of minority experiences.

Ladson-Billings (1994) in her book *The Dreamkeepers: Successful Teachers of African-American Children* argues the need for culturally relevant instruction. If children do not see themselves in the curriculum materials, how can they see the curriculum as relevant to their lives? Diversity is now a fact of life. The sooner schools create curriculum that reflect it, the sooner schools will serve all children well.

James Banks, director of the Center for Multicultural Education at the University of Washington, argues that emphasizing broad conceptual themes such as "immigration," "racism," "intercultural interaction," and "folktales" is one useful strategy for incorporating the experiences of diverse groups of people into a school's curriculum. These themes can be studied for a full year and, across that period, the experiences of various groups contrasted and compared.

In her book *Other People's Children: Cultural Conflict in the Classroom* (The Free Press, 1995), Lisa Delpit notes, "I have found that if I want to learn how best to teach children who may be different from me, then I must seek the advice of adults—teachers and parents—who are from the same culture as my students."

There seem to be several broad principles for framing education that fosters understanding of, and respect for, diversity (Education Research Service, 1991). One principle is to develop a pro-student philosophy. Do teachers see minority students as potential lawyers, teachers, and brokers? Are cultural differences viewed as limitations or as useful resources? For example: Is fluency in Spanish seen as a limiting factor or as a bonus? Is familiarity with Hopi customs and religious rituals seen as interfering with learning or as a rich background to foster learning?

A second principle is that no one method is best for teaching any student or group of students. Children are individuals—every child is unique. We worry that stereotypical

Resources

- *Multicultural Education* includes a 40-minute videotape of successful school projects, the book *Teaching with a Multicultural Perspective,* and a facilitator's handbook. Contact: Association for Supervision and Curriculum Development, 1250 North Pitt Street, Alexandria, VA 22314-1453 (703-549-9110 or www.ascd.org).

- *Americans All* offers comparative historical materials for both teachers and students on six major ethnic groups across U.S. history. Contact: People of America Foundation, 5760 Sunnyside Ave., Beltsville, MD 20705 (301-982-5622 or www.americansall.com).

- *World of Difference,* a project of the Anti-Defamation League, is designed to address prejudice and discrimination. Curriculum resources and teacher training are available, as well as a catalog of multicultural resources. Contact: World of Difference Institute, 823 United Nations Plaza, New York, NY 10017 (212-885-7811 or www.adl.org).

- *Rating Instructional Conversations: A Guide* offers clear guidelines for observing classroom talk with an eye on the quality of the conversations, especially as related to diverse student populations. Many other reports and products are also available. Contact: National Center for Research on Cultural Diversity and Second Language Learning, Center for Applied Linguistics, 1118 22nd Street, N.W., Washington, DC 20037 (202-362-7070 or www.cal.org).

- *Anti-Bias Curriculum: Tools for Empowering Young Children* offers a rich array of classroom activities. Contact: National Association for the Education of Young Children, Washington, DC (1-800-424-2460 or www.naeyc.org).

notions about how best to teach x kinds of students will undermine learning generally. We are wary of "learning-styles" authorities who argue for particular instruction patterns for different ethnic groups. We are wary because each child is unique. We admit that traditional classroom organization and interactional patterns often do not provide a good fit between some children's experiences before school and after enrolling. We encourage modifying classroom organization in ways that produce a better match between cultural patterns and teaching activities (e.g., cooperative learning is seen as a better fit with many minority cultures than traditional competitive organization structures). But in much of this book we argue for a shift away from traditional organizational patterns to better meet the needs of all students.

A third principle is to keep everyone's attention focused on the goals of educating for diversity. Return regularly to the three goals set earlier: (1) fostering tolerance through increased awareness of the contributions and experiences of diverse members of our society, (2) reducing prejudice, and (3) enhancing minority-student achievement. No matter what changes are implemented, unless you can point to progress toward each of these goals, the changes will be fruitless.

Summary

Let us reiterate a critical point: This book is intended to offer school administrators, supervisors, and teachers useful information on creating schools that achieve literacy with all children. In this chapter, we focus on specific groups of children often placed at risk in the schools we have. These children present special challenges for educators who are concerned about the academic progress of all children. Nonetheless, we argue that the information and ideas offered in our first nine chapters provide a broad framework for rethinking the nature of schools with an eye on enhancing the learning of all students but especially students at risk of school failure. Enhancing school and family relations works to benefit English-language learners as much as others. Creating a high-quality professional-development plan can work to benefit immigrant students as well as students with learning disability or ADD. Increasing children's access to books and to opportunities to read and write benefits minority students, poor students, learners acquiring English, students with disabilities, and others (Guthrie & Humenick, 2004). Experiencing the diversity of U.S. society in classroom literature and curriculum collections benefits all students, for all will likely spend their adult lives in an increasingly diverse nation.

Nonetheless, some students do present special difficulties. But schools simply cannot keep adding new programs and new staff in an attempt to deal with every student presenting a special problem. In short, schools must work to foster change in classrooms by developing teachers' capacity to more effectively educate all children.

A Tour through a School:
What to Look For

In this chapter, we take you on a visit to a school where many children arrive at risk for school failure but all become readers and writers. In this school we bring together many of the components that we describe in the previous chapters. We have not seen a school with all these components in place, but we have seen various combinations of them in many schools. We intend this school to be "ideal," to help you develop your vision of what a school might look like after many years of hard work when commitment, caring, and determination are present. The school tour is based on examples from Cunningham and Allington's *Classrooms That Work: They Can All Read and Write* (2007), in which you can find more detail about the classroom instruction.

Before School Starts

We arrive at Becoming School, Anywhere, U.S.A., around 7:15 in the morning. Although school doesn't officially start until 8:30, some children have already been dropped off and other children are walking toward the school. The school administrator greets the children as they walk through the door, calling each by name and sharing a quick conversation with some of them. Teachers are arriving on-site to begin grade-level team meetings held daily from 7:30 to 8:15. The school office staff is on the telephone reminding several families that children should be up, dressed, and about ready to leave for the bus stop. As the year wears on, fewer of these calls are needed.

Most children head directly to the cafeteria, where a nutritious breakfast awaits them. As they enter, a teacher's aide sits at a small table collecting permission slips from fourth and fifth graders who plan to go on the Saturday field trip to the state museum and collecting the grocery store receipts from any parent or child who contributes them for the store-sponsored school incentives program. At another table a parent volunteer is distributing RIF books to first graders.

Once fed, the children go in a variety of directions. At the exit they find large-print copies of important announcements. Some head for the gym or playground, where they shoot baskets or play on the swings and slides. Some of the younger children head for the kindergarten room, where they take part in a story circle as community paraprofessionals read to small groups of children and have them sing songs and repeat common nursery rhymes. Other children head to the media center, where they look at books and magazines, work on projects, or do their homework. Several children are at work on the computers. Other children are exploring a DVD about pyramids. Some children are met by the reading teacher, the LD teacher, or the ELL teacher. These teachers work on a flextime schedule and provide services before school to almost one-quarter of their caseload. Several children head for the music room, where they put in their practice time on their musical instruments. A few children who aren't feeling well go to the school clinic, which is staffed each morning by a community health nurse practitioner. Still other children head for the guidance room, where a community–school counselor helps them develop conflict resolution skills to resolve some problems they are having.

As eight o'clock approaches, activity at the school picks up. Buses are scheduled to arrive by 8:00 so that children who need breakfast can eat and be in their classrooms before 8:30. Teachers have completed their team meetings and are in their classrooms greeting children at 8:15. As children enter the classrooms, they take their cards from the attendance board and place them in the appropriate lunch option slot so that instructional time is not wasted taking attendance and figuring out lunch. Shortly after 8:30 a paraprofessional makes his rounds to record attendance and lunch counts. By noting the cards remaining on the attendance board and the number of cards at each lunch option, this assistant can do the attendance and lunch counts for the entire school with little or no interruption for teachers. Latecomers know they must track down this assistant and report their presence and lunch choices.

At 8:15, some other important people—surrogate lap readers—also arrive in classrooms. Becoming Elementary School has a parent support and involvement program, including sessions on the importance of reading to children and how to read to a young child. Each Friday, prekindergartners, kindergartners, and first graders take home a numbered packet containing six carefully selected books that parents/caretakers are requested to read to their child. Children return the packet on Thursday and are given a different packet the next day. On Thursday, the lunch/attendance aide returns to the prekindergarten, kindergarten, and first-grade classrooms and picks up the tray of returned packets. He then assigns each child a different numbered packet for the following week and returns the tray with the new packets and reminder notes to be clipped to children who forgot to return the packet on Thursday. On Friday morning, as he makes his attendance/lunch rounds, he collects the late-returned packets and returns with the new packets, which the children take home that afternoon.

How time is spent is a critical factor in how well children learn to read and write. If each teacher spends 10 minutes of allocated instructional time each day getting attendance and lunch figured out, that is 1,800 minutes annually—30 hours, one entire week—of lost instructional time. Multiply that times six years of elementary school and you have 30 days or six weeks of school allocated to attendance taking and lunch counts! Administrators can work to have routine duties handled efficiently by someone other than the teacher.

With these book-distribution procedures in place and the how-to-read-to-your-child video training, most parents do read most of the books to their children most weeks. But, most is not all. Some parents did not come for the training. Others just can't (or don't) find the time. Still others can't read—or they can read in their first language but not in English. Convinced that regular lap-reading is a critical component in children's early reading success, Becoming School has a Plan B for children whose parents do not read the books to them. (With little children, it isn't hard to find out which parents did and which didn't. Just ask them. They'll tell you.)

All children whose parents/caretakers do not read the books to them are assigned surrogate lap readers. Many of the surrogate lap readers are parents who drop their own children off at school and then are willing to donate 10 to 15 minutes of their time each day to lap-read with another child. Each morning at 8:15, they go to their surrogate child's classroom (or to the cafeteria if their child is a latecomer or breakfast eater), gather the child up, and read from the packet of books (which for these children stays in the classroom instead of being sent home). In addition to the volunteer "drop-in-while-you-drop-off" parents, other school personnel read to certain children.

Becoming School has a child advocate program. Children whose parents do not come for parent conferences, IEP meetings, and so on, are assigned a school employee—another classroom teacher, specialist teacher, paraprofessional, custodian, or secretary—who will be that child's advocate. This person fills in for the parent at conferences, and so on,

These before-school options indicate that the community is committed to providing children with nutritional and health services they need along with opportunities to do homework, work on projects, practice musical instruments, and so on, if they don't have these opportunities at home. The nurse practitioner, the counselor, and several of the specialist teachers begin and end their day earlier than other staff members (some specialists begin later and depart later to work with other children in after-school programs). The other activities are supervised by volunteers or paraprofessionals.

and touches base with the child regularly. When the child in need of an advocate is also a child in need of a surrogate lap reader, the advocate fills this role, too, if possible. (Classroom teacher, administrator, and secretary advocates can usually not be surrogate lap readers at 8:15 because they are needed at their posts, but others—paraprofessionals, specialist teachers, custodians, and so on—usually can.)

At 8:30, the instructional day begins, and as we peek into classrooms on our way to the prekindergarten and kindergarten classes where we will start our tour, we notice that instruction has actually begun in the classrooms.

Visiting in the 4- and 5-Year-Olds' Classrooms

We begin our classroom visits in the 4-year-olds' classes (prekindergartens). As we enter, the children are gathered at various centers and engaged in the exploratory activity that is the work of 4-year-olds. Children work with sand and water, build with blocks and Legos, work with a variety of art materials, put puzzles together, and engage in activities in the dramatic play center, which this month is set up as a grocery store. (The area has numerous cereal boxes and other packages found in grocery stores. Signs telling what is on sale and how much items cost and shopping lists are provided for children to follow.) They also write messages and notes to each other (most of which only the writer can read) in the writing center and read (or have a grandparent volunteer read to them) a variety of things—big books, little books, magazines, signs—in the reading center.

During center time, the teacher circulates, greeting children and helping them to get the day off to a good start. As always, she has her file-folder labels on a clipboard, and when she notices accomplishments, problems, or other things that she wants to remember, she records them by putting the child's initials, the date, and her comment on one of the labels. At the end of the day, she will stick them to each child's anecdotal record folder. Today, she jots notes about a child "reading" a little book in the library corner to a stuffed animal, noting that his voice sounds like a reading voice and that he is doing a good job of telling a story that matches the pictures. She notes that another child is drawing at the writing table and "reads" her drawing to the teacher. Another child has created strings of letters and "reads" her "writing." These notes describe the different levels of conceptual

Many children have had 1,000 or more hours of "informal" literacy encounters before coming to school. From these encounters, they develop critical understandings about reading and writing and "I can" attitudes toward their inevitable inclusion into the literate community.

1. They know that when you read or write there is some story or information that you are trying to understand or communicate.

2. They know that reading and writing are two important things that people who are bigger than they are can do and that because they want to be big, they must learn to do it, too.

3. They know from the overwhelming adult approval and pleasure at their fledgling attempts at pretend reading, reading some signs and labels, and writing that they are succeeding at mastering this mysterious code.

Our major literacy goal in classrooms for 4-year-olds should be to simulate the reading and writing encounters many children have had, which lead them to develop these critical understandings and attitudes. It is important to remember that children who have had few print, story, and book experiences need a rich supply of these experiences and a pre-K program is a good place to provide them. Thinking of these children as "inexperienced" creates a different view of instructional needs than thinking of them as "developmentally delayed," "language impaired," "slow," "unready," or any of the other labels commonly given to children who enter school inexperienced in literacy activities. The critical nature of providing these children with a print-rich, story-rich, book-rich classroom becomes clear when we take this view.

development each child exhibits about writing. She will use these notes in developing her small-group writing lessons.

The teacher tries to talk with each child during the morning center time and spends a few extra minutes with the children she has identified as being most "at risk." She engages children whose English acquisition has lagged behind peers (because English is not their first language or because they have had few real conversations with adults) in some conversation about what they are doing at the center. She points to things in the pictures they have painted or to their block construction, and she fosters their talk with her about what they are doing. She asks about the little books they are "reading" and the writing they produce. Because these conversations are one-on-one and related to something they are actually doing, the children are more willing to talk than they are in a small-group or whole-class setting. She also notices that children talk with each other more during center time. In fact, knowing that listening and speaking are major language goals, she encourages this child–child talk as she visits the centers and engages the children in conversations. She

Reading and writing are language. They are integrally connected with listening and speaking. Classrooms in which many children become fluent readers and writers are classrooms in which listening and talking are important, encouraged activities. Silence is not golden!

gets them to talk to her and to one another about what they are doing. Later, during both story circle times, she will read and reread favorite big books and encourage children to chime in and read along with her as she points to the words.

Although we could stay in the 4-year-olds' classes all day, we must move on if we are to visit classrooms at all grade levels. As we enter the kindergartens, children there are also in center-based activities that look very much like the centers we saw in the 4-year-olds' classes. In addition to the reading and writing that you would expect to find in the reading corner and at the writing table, literacy activities are apparent in other centers. This month, the dramatic play center has become a restaurant. The children ordering food are "reading" the menus and the waiters/waitresses are "writing down" their orders. In another area, road signs are an important part of the play as children construct a village with blocks.

The teacher circulates through the centers, talking, observing, and making notes on her clipboard file-folder labels. As she stops in the writing center, she is once more reminded that all children can write if she accepts whatever writing they do. She picks up a paper that is clearly a list in "scribble writing." "Read to me what you wrote," she asks. The child proceeds to point to each scribble and tell her that these are foods he likes to eat and reads the foods. The teacher notes on the child's label that he can read his scribbles and seems to have top–bottom and left–right orientation but few specific letters yet. Another child has made a drawing of himself and his pet and has labeled the drawing with his name and his pet's name. One child is writing sentences that have many correctly spelled words in them and other words clearly readable from his sound spelling. Yet another child is listing dangerous ("DAGRS" to him) animals, copying the words from the newspaper animal board, the animals listed down the side of the data chart, and a book on large animals he picked up from the bookshelf next to the writing center.

When the teacher goes to the rocking chair and sits down, the children realize that center time is over. They quickly clean up what they have been working on and come to sit on the floor. As the teacher waits for everyone to come, she leads the children in some of their favorite songs, chants, and fingerplays. When the whole group assembles, she picks up her newspaper and says, "I found something last night to add to our animal board."

She then shows them a picture of a baby tiger born at the zoo and reads them the beginning part of the accompanying article. After a brief discussion, she cuts the picture and article from the newspaper and adds it to a board already full of information/pictures/words about animals. Several other children have brought animal pictures/articles they have found, and as they tell about each one—where they found it, who read it to them,

. . . . ●

281

and so on—it, too, is added to the collage. The teacher then takes some index cards and writes labels on them—*pit bull, zoo, python, Siamese cat*—stretching and segmenting the sounds as she writes, reads each aloud, and attaches these labels next to the pictures/articles. This animal board bears little resemblance to the neat, bordered bulletin boards sometimes found in classrooms. It is cluttered with a motley collection of animal-related articles, pictures, and words that the teacher and children have been on the lookout for since they began their animal unit. It is clear from the responses of the children, however, that they are proud of "their" animal board and that they are learning that magazines and newspapers are a real-world source of information to which they have access.

Next, the teacher takes out a big book of *Brown Bear, Brown Bear, What Do You See?* by Bill Martin. It is clear from the responses of the children that they have read this book several times before. The teacher points to each word as the children read in chorus with her.

Before turning the page, she asks the children if they remember what the next animal is going to be. Most children know that the red bird is next. She turns the page, and the children are delighted to see that they are correct. Led by the teacher, who continues to point to the words, they all read together.

Once the book has been read and enjoyed again, the teacher passes out two or three words to each child. The words have been written on sentence strips and then cut so that the size of the strip each child is given matches the size of the word written on it. "Being the Words" is a favorite activity in this classroom. The children have been the words before to make the sentences in other predictable books and in chants and poems, but this is the first time they have gotten to be the words for *Brown Bear*. The children eagerly look at the word they are given and then up at the still-displayed *Brown Bear* book. Some children recognize some words—particularly the concrete ones. The child holding the word *bear* says, "Oh, boy! I get to be the bear!" Other children recognize the color words—*red, yellow,* and so on. Children who get commas, periods, and question marks clearly recognize these as punctuation marks used in sentences.

The teacher then opens the book back to the first page, and the children eagerly read the opening sentence in unison. As they read, they look at the words/punctuation marks they are holding to see whether they are any of the words in this sentence. Some children immediately recognize their words. Others need help from the teacher or from a child sitting near them. The children then come up next to

The two classrooms we have visited are print rich. In addition to lots of different kinds and sizes of books are boards such as the animal board that tie into the unit being studied and that have words as well as pictures. There are signs and cereal boxes and labels and lists. A variety of writing surfaces and implements are readily available for children to write with. (Worksheets are not often part of print-rich preschool and kindergarten classrooms.) Successful classrooms for struggling readers immerse children in language and in the variety of print we encounter in our everyday world.

the book and get themselves in order to make the sentences. Once the words are all in place, the children who aren't words in this sentence read the sentence as the teacher moves behind each child holding a card.

These children sit down, and the teacher displays the next page. The teacher points to the words as the children read. As they read, they look at their words to see whether they are any of these words. The children who are the words in this sentence get themselves in correct left–right sequence (with a little help from their friends), and the other children read the sentence.

The children continue to be the words for a few more pages. The next several pages are matched and sequenced much more quickly as the children begin to realize where their words come in the pattern. After making seven pages in the book, the teacher collects the word cards, assuring the children who are complaining about not getting to be a word yet that they will be the words for the other pages later in the week.

The teacher then leads the children in a quick "get the wiggles out" movement activity in which she has them move like the animals in the *Brown Bear* book. After this brief but essential break, the children settle down and the teacher picks up a marker and gets ready to write. She "thinks aloud" about what she might write, and the children watch eagerly, encouraging her to "draw something!" The teacher tries to model different levels of writing on different days. Some days, she writes a whole paragraph. Other days, she writes a sentence and then illustrates it. On some days, she draws a picture and labels it. On still other days, she writes a list. As she writes, she sound-spells some words, saying the words aloud very slowly and putting down some letters to represent the sounds. In this way, she demonstrates for the children the different levels of writing and shows them that all these ways of writing are accepted. On this day, she writes two sentences:

Mr. Hinkle will vzt us aftr lunch.
He will brng his pet trtl.

She doesn't read the words aloud as she writes them, except for saying the words very slowly when she is using sound-spelling to model this for the children. The children all watch very closely and try to read what she is writing. Many of them recognize the words *Mr., lunch,* and *pet.* She then draws a simple picture to illustrate this sentence and labels Mr. Hinkle and the turtle. The children are amazed to hear that Mr. Hinkle—who teaches fourth grade—has a pet turtle.

Snack time is next, and the teacher passes out raisins. The children look up at the "food board" and notice that the teacher has attached a picture from the raisin box to the space under the letter *r.* As they munch on their raisins and whatever else they might have brought for snack time, they review the other foods they have so far on their food board. So far, five letters have food pictures attached to them:

b—bananas   d—donuts   m—milk   j—juice   r—raisins

After snack time, some children go to their tables, others go to a corner of the room that contains all the predictable big books they have read this year, and others go to the reading corner, which has puppets and stuffed animals in addition to books. The observer would have trouble knowing which children were supposed to go where, but the children know exactly where to go. Each child can read in the reading corner one day and can read the big books on another day. On the other three days children read at their seats. This procedure has been in place for two weeks and is working quite well. Having all the children spread out in the room created problems because there weren't enough good "spreading-out places." This new arrangement seems to offer exactly the right balance of freedom and structure so that the children spend most of their time actually reading—or "pretend reading," if that is where they are!

The children reading at their tables find small bins of books there. The bins contain a variety of books and are rotated so that each table gets a different bin each day. One bin is

Reasonable and Observable Literacy Outcomes for Kindergartners

1. They "pretend read" favorite books and poems/songs/chants.

2. They write and can read what they wrote even if no one else can.

3. They "track print"—that is, show you what to read and point to the words using left–right and top–bottom conventions.

4. They know word jargon, can point to just one word, to the first word in the sentence, to just one letter, to the first letter in the word, to the longest word, and so on.

5. They recognize and can write some concrete words—their names, names of other children, and favorite words from books, poems, and chants.

6. They know when words rhyme, and they can make up rhymes.

7. They can name the letters and tell words that begin with the common initial sounds.

8. They are becoming adept at writing using sound-spelling.

9. They can listen to stories and informational books and retell the important information.

10. They see themselves as readers and writers and new members of the "literacy club."

filled with animal books—the topic they are studying in combined science/social studies units. Included in the bin are the two books children listened to at the listening center this morning. Many of these books are too hard for most of the children to read, but they love looking at the pictures and do find some animal names they recognize.

A second bin contains books gathered up for the last topic studied—families. The children enjoy looking at these books, most of which have been read to them, and many can read the predictable books.

Another bin of books contains "oldies but goodies," which the children want to read again and again. All children can make attempts at reading such favorites as *Go Dog Go* and *The Three Little Pigs.*

Another bin contains class books. These books, written during shared writing and illustrated by the children, are perennial favorites of the children. The first class book contains a photo and a few sentences about each child in the class. This is still one of the most popular books and is reread almost every day by someone. Currently they are writing and illustrating a class book about animals, which will be added to this bin when it is finished.

There are also two bins of library books. One bin contains those checked out from the public library, and the other those checked out from the school library. The teacher has arranged with both libraries to check out 20 to 30 books to keep in the classroom for a month. She chooses two or three children to go with her on a special trip to the public library every month to return the old books and pick out new ones for the public library bin. By the end of the year, all children will have made this special after-school trip. For many children, it is their first trip to the public library, and some children are amazed that they can get books, videos, and other goodies to take home "for free." At the end of the year, the whole class makes a trip to this library again, and most children get library cards. The monthly trips with two or three children to the public library and the library-card-getting field trip take extra time and effort, but introducing these children early to a free, unlimited source of reading material makes it worthwhile. When the children have read their own books for about 15 minutes, the teacher chooses several books or parts of books to read to them.

Visiting in the Primary Classrooms

The morning is moving on, and we must make it to the primary grades if we are going to see instruction in all segments of the Four Blocks instructional program (see Chapter 2). The 2¼ hours designated for reading/language arts in the primary classes is divided into four blocks of 30 to 40 minutes each: Guided Reading, Self-Selected Reading, Writing, and Working with Words. These four blocks represent the major approaches to literacy instruction.

The first class we enter has just finished their Working with Words block. Activities in this block are designed to help children learn to (1) recognize and spell automatically the high-frequency words that occur in almost everything we read and write and (2) look for patterns in words so that they can decode and spell less frequent words that they have not been taught. A Word Wall of high-frequency words written on construction paper of various colors catches our eye as soon as we enter. Five words are added to the Word Wall each week, and each day the children engage in a 5-minute clapping/chanting/writing activity to practice these important words.

Word Walls are one essential feature of classrooms where all children become readers and writers.

As we enter, the children are sorting words they have made in their Making Words lesson. From these words in the pocket chart, the teacher picks up *at* and says, "Who can come and hand me three words that rhyme with *at*?" A child hands her the words *sat, rat,* and *cat.* The teacher then has someone find the word that rhymes with *rot—cot* the word that rhymes with *oats—coats* and the word that rhymes with *coast—roast.* The children spell the rhyming words and decide that these words all have the same letters from the vowel on. The teacher reminds the children that words that have the same spelling pattern usually rhyme and that this is one way many good readers and writers read and spell words.

"What if I were writing and wanted to write *boats.* Which of the rhyming words we made today would help me?" The children decide that *boats* rhymes with *oats* and *coats* and would probably be spelled *b-o-a-t-s.*

"What if I were writing about foods I liked and wanted to spell *toast.* What rhyming words would help?" The children decide that *toast* rhymes with *roast* and *coast* and would probably be spelled *t-o-a-s-t.* Likewise, they decide how the rhyming words they have made would help them to spell *flat* and *shot* if they wanted to write these words.

Although the four blocks can be used in any order, the teacher in this classroom follows Working with Words with the Guided Reading block. On

There is no one best way to teach children to read and write. Each different approach has strengths, and some children have strong learning preferences for one approach over another. By using each of the four major approaches, we provide four roads to the goal of literacy for all and maximize the possibility that all children will arrive there.

The ability to decode and spell unfamiliar-in-print words is worthless if children don't use the strategies they know while reading and writing. If we emphasize common spelling patterns and help children use the patterns they sort for to spell a few other words, children will learn how to use familiar patterns to spell words they need in their writing. In teaching, we often get what we teach. Transfer needs to be taught!

some days they do a shared reading in a big book—the teacher reads the book first, and the children join in on subsequent rereadings. On other days the teacher supports the reading of the children in basal readers, literature collections, or trade books of which they have multiple copies. For today's lesson, the teacher chooses *The Carrot Seed* (1945), by Ruth Krauss. As often as possible, she tries to find things for the children to read that tie in to the science or social studies unit they are studying. *The Carrot Seed* is perfect for their current Seeds and Plants unit.

The teacher displays a copy of *The Carrot Seed* and points to the title. "What word do we see here that we just made in our Making Words lesson?" she asks. The children quickly identify the word *carrot*. The teacher then points to the word *seed* and asks the children to look at the picture on the cover of the book and think about what the boy is doing and what word the letters *s-e-e-d* might spell. The children realize that the boy is planting something, and using the picture clue and what they know about letters and sounds, they are able to figure out the word *seed* and read the title of the book, *The Carrot Seed.*

The teacher and the children then look at all the pictures in the book and talk about what is happening. The teacher makes sure to introduce orally key vocabulary as she talks about the pictures. Next, the teacher assigns reading partners who will read the story together, and she tells them that after they read the story, they will act it out. Cheers from the children let us visitors know that acting out the story is a popular activity in this classroom.

As the partners finish reading, the teacher hands them index cards, indicating the part they will play in the story reenactment. She then gathers the children around her, and they retell the story with emphasis on what the main characters would do. The child who had gotten the "seed" card would be put on the floor and lie there, motionless. The "carrot" would be pulled from the ground and wheeled away by the little boy. The mother and the father and the big brother and then everyone would shake their heads and say, "It won't come up!" The little boy would plant and sprinkle and pull weeds and finally proudly wheel the carrot away.

Space is cleared in the center for a "stage," and *The Carrot Seed* is acted out. This is a low-budget, off-off Broadway production that lacks props, costumes, and rehearsal, but no one seems to care. The children get into their roles, and the story is retold with the events occurring in the correct sequence. The only complaints are from those children who had to be part of the "everyone" but wanted starring roles. The teacher assures them that there are no little parts and that they will act it out again tomorrow and perhaps their luck will be better!

As we leave this classroom, the teacher begins her daily math/science time. On some days, she finds it impossible to integrate the two, so the class does only one or divides the hour between the two. Most days, however, the teacher finds that doing science and math together is a natural integration. Today, she hands out containers filled with various kinds of seeds. She then leads the children in a variety of counting, sorting, predicting, classifying, and weighing activities with the seeds. The children work in groups at their tables, sorting the seeds by putting the ones that are alike together, estimating and then counting to see how many of each type of seed they have, and graphing to show which seeds they have more and less of. The teacher gives out simple balance scales and has the children predict which seeds weigh the most and the least. They then weigh the different seeds and determine that it would take "more than they had" of the tiniest seeds to weigh as much as one of their largest seeds. The children are particularly amazed by how tiny carrot seeds are.

Next door in another primary classroom, the children are in the Writing block. This block always begins with the teacher writing something on the overhead as the children watch. They watch and listen as she thinks aloud about what to write.

"I always have so many things I want to write about on Mondays. I could write about going shopping this weekend and finding my car with a flat tire when I came out of the store. I could write about the funny movie I watched on TV. I could write a list of different kinds of seeds I ordered from the seed catalog this weekend." The teacher decides on a topic and begins to write. As she writes, she models for the class how she might sound-spell some words. She stops and says a word aloud slowly and writes down the letters she can hear. She also looks up at the Word Wall occasionally and says, "I can spell *many* because we just put it on our Word Wall" and "I will look at *some* on our Word Wall because *some* is not spelled the way you would think it should be."

The writing minilesson takes approximately 10 minutes, and the children are then dismissed from the big group to go to their own writing. Children are at various stages of the writing process. Five children are working at the art table, happily illustrating their books. When asked why they got to make books, they proudly explain that you had to write three pieces first. Then, you had to pick the best of the three and get a friend to be your editor—just like we do for the teacher at the overhead. Then, you go to the editing table and the teacher helps you edit it and you copy it in one of these books (holding up stapled, premade, half-sheet construction-paper-covered book).

Four children are at the editing table with the teacher, who is helping them do a final editing of their pieces. Four other children, two identified as having learning disability, work at another table

Integration can take many forms and is a key component in classrooms where time is used efficiently. Separating all the subject areas is a peculiarly American phenomenon. Primary classrooms in many other countries don't have separate time blocks, text books, and grades for separate subjects. Reading, writing, and math are skill subjects and need some content to make them real to children. That content can often be found in science and social studies curricula. Integration of two or more subject areas maximizes learning and time.

Sound-spelling is a powerful tool. It allows children to write ideas that go far beyond the words they can spell correctly. As children sound-spell, they are using whatever letter–sound knowledge they have. A child who represents *motorcycle* as *modrsikl* is not in danger of spelling *motorcycle* like this forever. There is the danger, however, that spelling *they* as *thay* may become practiced and thus more permanent because *they* is used so frequently in writing. Things that we do the same way over and over become automatic, which means we do them without any conscious attention. When we have a Word Wall of high-frequency words that the children practice daily and refer to while writing, most children become automatic at spelling correctly these highly frequent, often irregularly spelled words. (For a readable, sensible discussion of sound-spelling, see Anne McGill-Franzen's *Kindergarten Literacy,* 2006.)

with the LD teacher, who has just arrived in the room. She works with each of the four children in turn as they edit their pieces. A few pairs of children are helping each other edit before proceeding to the editing table. The other children are working away on their first drafts.

The classroom is a busy working place. At a signal from the teacher, the children once again gather on the floor, and the Monday children line up behind the Author's Chair. (All the children are designated by a day of the week, and on their day they get to share.) The first child reads two sentences of a new piece begun today. He calls on various children who tell him that they like the topic (dinosaurs) and give him ideas for what he might like to include. One child suggests a good dinosaur book for him to read. The second author reads a completed piece and calls on various children, who tell him they like the way he has stayed on the topic (his new baby sister) and ask questions ("Does she cry all night?"

"Is this the only sister you've got?"). The third and fourth children read unfinished pieces and get praise and suggestions. The final author proudly reads the book she has just "published" with technical assistance from the Title 1–funded paraprofessional who is assigned to the "publishing room" in the school and laminates the children's stories and binds them into books.

After the Writing block, this class of children goes to lunch, and we head next door to another primary classroom, where the children are just returning from lunch. Most of the children go to their places for some "quiet time." Seven children join the teacher at the back table to read some "fun" books. The teacher had formed this after-lunch bunch when she realized that many children were not fluently reading the books and stories she was using during the morning Guided Reading block. These children read with partners and, in this manner, are able to enjoy, discuss, and act out the stories. She knows from the observations she made and wrote on the file-folder labels that many children are not really at their instructional level in these materials. They depend on their partners to help them figure out many words. The teacher knows that they enjoy being included in the activities but need to read easier selections. To help them develop their reading fluency and learn to figure out unfamiliar words independently, she needed to provide them with some reading materials in which they could recognize almost all the words.

The teacher decided to use the 15 minutes after lunch to provide some easy reading to meet the needs of children for whom the material read during the Guided Reading block was really too hard. Further, she decided that she wanted some "good reading models" in the group that came to be called the After-Lunch Bunch. Each day, the children come in from lunch and look to see whether they are in the After-Lunch Bunch. Every child finds his or her name there at least once a week, but the children whose need for continued easy reading had instigated the formation of this group find their names three or four (but not five) days a week. By including all the children, but the still-struggling readers more often, the teacher is able to provide for the needs of the weaker readers without having the After-Lunch Bunch viewed as a "bottom group."

To grow in their reading ability, children must read materials in which they can recognize at least 97 to 100 percent of the words and understand most of what they are reading. Teachers need to be concerned about children experiencing high-success reading in classroom materials, and they need to find ways to provide high-success reading opportunities. Administrators need to work to ensure that support for multilevel classroom libraries and curriculum materials is at hand. (See Allington's *What Really Matters for Struggling Readers,* Allyn & Bacon, 2006, for an extended discussion of the research on high-success reading and practical advice on supporting teachers.)

Each day, the children find their names on the After-Lunch Bunch list and join the teacher and read something together. The teacher uses a variety of materials—stories from old basals, multiple copies of easy library books, and so on—but always chooses material in which the lowest-achieving readers can read almost all the words. Generally, she leads the children to talk about the book or story by looking at the pictures and talking about what is happening, then lets each child read it by himself or herself, and then leads a brief meaning-oriented discussion of the story. If there is time, she has the children read selected parts orally. Before the children start to read, she reminds them of the strategies they know for figuring out an unfamiliar word:

- Put your finger on the unknown word, and say all the letters.
- Use the letters and the picture clues.
- Try to pronounce the word by looking to see whether it has a spelling pattern or rhyme that you know.
- Keep your finger on the word, and read the other words in the sentence to see whether it makes sense.
- If it doesn't make sense, go back to the word and think what would make sense and have these letters.

The combination of easy reading in which they know most of the words and some reminders and support as they try to apply the strategies they are learning to unfamiliar words is helping the lowest-achieving children become independent readers. Having a few good readers in every After-Lunch Bunch provides models for expressive oral reading and discussion. The short After-Lunch Bunch sessions are generally enjoyable for all the children and for the teacher.

Using three reading groups has been our major attempt to address the various reading levels of children. The lack of success for this three-group system is evident when we realize that most children in the bottom groups never achieve grade-level reading and that most high-achieving readers can read way beyond the materials usually used in the top reading group. Children simply do not come in three convenient levels. Many teachers are now trying to organize their instruction to flexibly use whole-class, small-group, and cooperative group/partner arrangements. The After-Lunch Bunch extra reading time is only one example of how teachers use a variety of instructional groupings to meet the needs of their diverse children.

Becoming School arranged the schedules of the special-subject teachers—art, music, physical education—so that for one hour each week they took all the children at a particular grade level, thus providing a dependable hour of grade-level team-planning time each week. The support teachers (bilingual, remedial, special education, speech) who work with children at that grade level keep that hour free and join the classroom teachers to plan coordinated instruction.

Next on the schedule is the Self-Selected Reading block. The teacher has arranged books in several plastic bins and has put one bin on each of the five tables. The children eagerly read the books while the teacher walks around with labels on the clipboard, talking with children about their reading and asking them to read a page to her. She makes notes about what different children are reading and how well they are reading. She notes their use of phonics, their attempts to figure out unknown words, their fluency, their self-correction, and other reading behaviors. She also asks them what they like about the book they are reading and, sometimes, suggests another book they might like.

Next, the teacher reads a book to the students. Today, she reads an informational book with many pictures of seeds and the plants that grow from them. She also shows them a seed catalog that she has brought from home, quickly flipping through it and pausing briefly to show a page or two of the illustrations.

As we make our way to the intermediate wing, we notice all the second-grade teachers with a Title 1 reading teacher and a special education teacher huddled and busily planning in a second-grade teacher's classroom while the second graders participate in special classes (art, music, physical education, and library).

Visiting in the Intermediate Classrooms

We arrive in the intermediate wing and work around the lunch schedule of the different classes. As we enter one classroom, the teacher is reading aloud an article that appeared in the Sunday paper. The teacher begins each afternoon by reading from a variety of real-world sources. On Mondays, the teacher usually brings in the newspaper and shares some interesting tidbits with the children. Other days, the teacher reads from informational books, magazines, joke and riddle books, pamphlets, and so on. This teacher is determined to have his students see reading as an essential part of their real world.

We see a Big Word Board. The words displayed on this board are related to the unit topic for the week. This week's unit is on pollution, and the words on the Big Word Board are

pollution	environment	recycle	renewable
pollutants	environmental	conservation	combustion
resources	chemicals	fertilizers	pesticides

In addition to the unit-connected Big Word Board, on which the words change weekly, there is also a Word Wall of frequently misspelled words. The teacher began the Word Wall at the beginning of the year with words he knew many of the children would misspell. The first five words added to the wall were:

they	were	friend	from	said

As the year went on, he was alerted to words that many children were misspelling in their first-draft writing and added words the children evidently needed.

When children are writing, they are encouraged to use sound-spelling and whatever resources they have for spelling words—unless the words are on the Big Word Board or the Word Wall. The teacher insists that these words—which are so readily accessible—be spelled correctly, and students' eyes can be seen going to the Big Word Board or the Word Wall when they are writing.

Environment Pollution			
Where	**Causes**	**Possible Solutions**	**Our Area**
Air			
Water			
Soil			
Land			

This week, the topic being studied is pollution. The children watched a video that showed some of the most serious sources of pollution, and they began filling in some information on a data chart graphic organizer.

The video described some general pollution problems but was not specific to the geographic area in which the school is located. The teacher shares some newspaper articles from local sources, and more information—particularly in the last column, "Our Area"—is added to the data chart. The homework assignment was to interview two adults about pollution in the local area and determine what these adults think the most significant problems are. The students share what they found out through their interviews/research. Most talked with someone about the problem and were surprised to learn how high the level of concern is. Homework assignments like this engage children in meaningful communication with adults for real purposes. All children can be successful at this, and it increases their personal involvement and motivation for the topic under study.

Next, the teacher gives out a list of local businesses. Included on the list are stores and fast-food restaurants that the children go to regularly. He then teaches a supported writing lesson in which he demonstrates how to write a list of questions to ask to find out what, if anything, the business is doing about recycling. As the children watch, he writes his own list of questions to ask his brother, who works at a car dealership.

After writing his questions, he lets pairs of students decide who or what business they would interview and helps them construct a list of questions to ask. Getting answers to these questions will be another homework assignment.

As we enter the next classroom, the children are having their Everybody Read Time. They read from any book they choose. Many children have at their desk a book they are in the middle of reading. Other children choose a book from the bins of books that rotate each day to different tables. Each bin is filled with a variety of books, including books by minority authors, some high-interest, low-vocabulary books, and informational books with lots of pictures. Children are designated by days of the week, one-fifth of the class for each day. On Monday, the Monday people can read anywhere and anything in the room— newspapers, magazines, joke books, the newspaper board, and so on. On the other days, the Monday people stay at their seats and read. In this way, everyone gets a chance to "spread out" and read anything one day each week, but most of the class is seated quietly at their desks reading books, magazines, or other materials.

As the students in this classroom settle down to read, we go next door where a group is reading a basal reader selection about a family homesteading in Iowa. Some of the other students are reading self-selected books or social studies–related materials. Another small group is working with the Title 1 reading specialist teacher for their second reading lesson of the day. Before having students read the basal selection, the teacher began a Then and Now Chart, and the children brainstormed some of the differences they thought would exist in their lives if they were transported back to the prairie of the 1800s. Those students then return to their desks to read the selection. Meanwhile, the teacher holds individual conferences with three of the students engaged in self-selected reading. At each conference they discuss the story. The students read a bit of text quietly so that the teacher can jot accuracy and fluency levels on their labels. When the other students finish reading the basal, they reconvene with the teacher and discuss what they read and complete the chart. The teacher has them vote on whether they would rather live "then" or "now." "Now" wins hands down!

In the next classroom, the teacher is beginning her Writing Block while being observed by a colleague. Each day, the teacher models how to think of topics and writes a short piece on the overhead. She tries to write a variety of pieces so that children see that writing can take many forms. She tells the children that she used to write a lot when she was their age—most of her writing was for herself, and she didn't let anyone else see it. They know that she used to keep a diary and write in it every night. Sometimes, she writes in her diary the way she did when she was their age. They think that it is hilarious when she writes like an intermediate-age child. She doesn't read aloud what she is writing, except when she is sound-spelling a word. Then, she says the word very slowly—exaggerating the sounds. The children are always eager to see "what she will write today."

Once the teacher finishes her piece, attention turns to the Editing Checklist:

> Discussion of what is read is a sharing of ideas and opinions. Discussion is what we engage in with a friend or an airplane seatmate whom we notice reading a book that we have just read. Teachers lead discussions, helping the children take turns and adding to their ideas when appropriate. Discussion is *not* questioning. Questioning is assessment, not instruction. If, after children read, teachers usually ask a lot of questions, children focus their attention on remembering. If, after children read, teachers usually engage them in discussion, children focus their attention on understanding and deciding what they think. Questioning fosters remembering. Discussion fosters comprehension.

Our Editing Checklist
- There is a title.
- Every sentence makes sense.
- Every sentence begins with a capital and ends with a punctuation mark.
- People and place names have capital letters.
- Words that might be misspelled are circled.
- The writing stays on the topic.
- Things people say have commas and quotes (She shouted, "Help!").

As each editing convention the children have learned is mentioned, the class reads the teacher's piece and helps the teacher fix what they think needs fixing. She circles the words she sound-spelled so that she will remember to check these in a dictionary or get some help with them if she

> For years, we taught language conventions (e.g., punctuation, capitalization) from a language book and had children practice these skills on worksheets. Transfer from these isolated activities to children's writing was often minimal. When the language conventions are integrated into the teacher's writing demonstrations, children learn to read the teacher's writing, their own writing, and each other's writing as editors do. By developing their editing skills children learn to produce good, readable pieces.

publishes this piece. The children decide that her piece stayed on the topic well but that some additional capital letters and punctuation marks are needed.

After this writing minilesson, the colleague returns to her own classroom. The teacher takes the children who are publishing a piece this week to the back table, and the other children pursue their own writing. Some children begin new pieces. Others continue writing on an already-begun piece. Some children look in books to get ideas and to find words they want to spell. The Word Wall and Big Word Board are also looked at as children need spelling help. They can be heard saying words very slowly and listening for the sounds they want to represent as they sound-spell some words just as their teacher did.

Every day at 2:10, the teacher reads to the class from a chapter book, choosing works of high interest to children at this age but varying genres so that the children are exposed to a variety of types of literature. When selecting books, the teacher also incorporates books that provide an introduction to this multicultural society we have created. This week she is reading *Get On Out of Here, Philip Hall* (Greene, 1981). When she finishes each book, there are always many children who want to read it for themselves. She asks those who want it to put their names on little slips of paper. She then pulls one slip (without looking) and hands the book to that lucky child. The other slips are then pulled and used—in the order pulled—to make a waiting list, just as at the library. The children perceive this procedure as fair, and there are always waiting lists for the chapter books the teacher has read aloud. Even children who could not have read the book by themselves can often read and enjoy it after they have listened to it read aloud. Whenever possible, the teacher tries to read aloud a book by an author who has written similar books or a book that is one of several in a series. Children on the waiting list for the book read are often delighted to get a similar book to read in the meantime.

These four books by Russell Freedman were read by fifth-grade students as they studied both the author's style as well as writing about history.

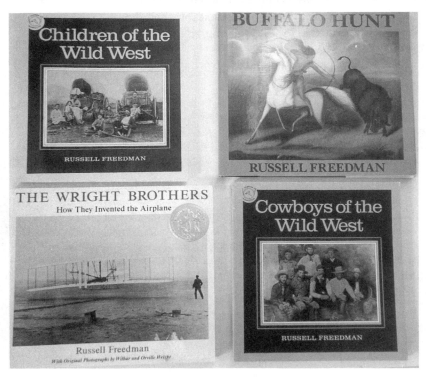

Given all that there is to accomplish, intermediate teachers usually can't do everything every day in the same way that primary teachers can. In addition, intermediate-age children need larger blocks of time to pursue reading, writing, and research. Not everything can happen every day, but all the important components should happen regularly. Here are time-allocation guidelines that a teacher of struggling intermediate-grade readers might follow:

Every Day (No Matter What)

1. Teacher reads to the class from a chapter book.
2. Teacher reads something to the class from a newspaper, magazine, riddle book, joke book, book of poetry, or other "real-world" source.
3. Children choose something they can read accurately, fluently, and with comprehension from a large and varied selection to read for 30 minutes.
4. Children read about the topics they are studying in science, social studies, math, and language arts.
5. Children do a Word Wall activity with high-frequency, commonly misspelled words and/or with topic-related big words.

Two or Three Times a Week

1. Children participate in Guided Reading/Thinking activity.
2. Children participate in Guided Writing/Thinking activity.
3. Teacher models topic selection and writing a short piece.
4. Children write for 30 minutes on a topic of their own choice.
5. Children work with words—looking for patterns, learning how to chunk and decode big words, and so on.

Once a Week

1. All children share something they have written.
2. All children share something they have read.
3. One-third of the class revises, edits, and publishes a piece of writing.
4. Children read to their little buddies.
5. Children do research related to topic.

How Classrooms Must Change   The intermediate classroom in which struggling readers become eager, achieving readers and writers is not a traditional classroom. Traditional classrooms must change—and the needed changes are fairly radical. One thing that must change is the way grades are determined. Grades must be based on effort and not on some notion of grade level and the tests in the teacher's manuals. This is difficult for everyone to accept because there is a need to maintain some kind of standard. But no one works if they know that they will fail anyway.

The curriculum materials must change. We cannot expect struggling readers to learn to read, or to learn social studies and science from books they cannot read! All children need to have books they can read in their desks and in their hands every day all day long.

The schedule must change. In some intermediate classrooms, time is allocated to a dozen different subjects every day. Even the language arts are broken down into reading, writing, spelling, language, handwriting, and study skills. Then there is math, science, social studies, physical education, music, art, foreign language, and computers. Instruction becomes small, isolated segments when separate subjects are presented this way. This choppy, fragmented scheduling is antithetical to understanding how people learn. We learn as we work with information, applying what we are learning to solve problems and achieve goals. In classrooms in which intermediate-age children are transformed from struggling to achieving, teachers do whatever is within their power to help children make connections. They take whatever time is allocated and create a schedule that allows for as much integrated learning as possible. But the necessary changes in schedule are easier for teachers to accomplish in schools where minimizing fragmentation of the curriculum and the daily schedule has become a schoolwide goal.

The final needed change relates to how the teacher and children work with one another. The intermediate classroom that succeeds will not be one where the teacher teaches the whole class all the time, nor can it be one where children are assigned to static reading groups based on achievement levels. Intermediate-grade children span a range of reading and writing proficiency, and instruction that treats them all the same or that arbitrarily divides them into three groups cannot meet their various needs. The intermediate classroom in which many struggling readers are learning and growing more literate is one where various flexible learning arrangements are used. Children read, write, edit, and research with partners and in small groups. Teachers who succeed with older struggling readers spend a great deal of time early in the year role-playing and modeling cooperative ventures and make a "working together" atmosphere a top priority in their classrooms. They have a "We're all in this together" and a "United we stand, divided we fall!" attitude, and they work with children to help them learn how to work with one another.

The next class we visit is getting ready for the students' regular Tuesday afternoon visit with their kindergarten buddies. Every Monday, after lunch, some kindergartners bring some favorite books from the kindergarten. A sticky note is attached to each book with the name of the kindergarten child who would like to have that book read to him or her tomorrow. The books are quickly distributed to the "big buddies," who then practice reading that book in preparation for tomorrow's reading. Some children record their reading to hear how they sound. The children eagerly read the books, which include such classics as *Are You My Mother?*, *The Little Red Hen,* and *The Snowy Day.* The teacher sits with one boy who is a very hesitant reader and who needs her help to successfully read this book tomorrow. She leads him to look through the pictures, predicting what will happen, and so on, in the way she wants him to with his "little buddy" tomorrow. As they look at the pictures, she supplies words and phrases needed so that he can successfully read the book. They then read and enjoy the book together. She praises him for his reading and reminds him to take the book home and practice reading it aloud. Finally she tells him to read it with her once more as soon as he arrives at school tomorrow. All this support is provided so that he will be able to read fluently to his "little buddy," with expression and enthusiasm.

After School

It is now 3:00 and the school day ends. As we make our way to the media center, we pass the classroom of the teacher we observed modeling the writing process with a colleague observing. They are busy reviewing the lesson and discussing possible changes the observer will make when she teaches that lesson tomorrow. In another classroom the teacher is busily attaching the Monday children's anecdotal comment labels to each child's folders. She then puts a clean sheet of labels on her clipboard. She puts the initials of each Tuesday child on several labels so she will remember to take note of their progress and problems tomorrow. On several other labels she puts the initials of other children and a few words— "solves math problems?"; "using self-correction strategies?"; "using strategies taught for figuring out unknown words?"; "really reading during Self-Selected Reading?"—that will remind her tomorrow to observe some problem areas she was concerned about for particular children. She then sits at her desk and completes her quickwrite summary for the focal child of the day. The quickwrite is composed on the iMac computer in her classroom, printed, and stored on the hard drive and in the child's evaluation folder. This allows easy access to both copies, and the computer version can be edited and used in the six-week summary report to parents.

As the school day officially ends, some children head home, and other children head for their afternoon enrichment/remediation classes. A variety of activities and "clubs" meet on different afternoons. Some special teachers begin and end their day an hour after the classroom teachers do, and they, with paraprofessionals, parent volunteers, and community organizations, run an extended-day program until 5:30. Today several classroom teachers and other staff members meet after school to discuss ideas for improving strategy instruction they found in the book *What Really Matters for Struggling Readers* (Allington, 2006). Several teachers have read Pressley's (2002) *Reading Instruction That Works* and note complementary features of these two texts. One notes that Pressley spends more pages on phonemic awareness than Allington does and wonders why. Another teacher, who read the preface to the Allington book, notes that he recommended Cunningham's *Phonics They Use* (2004) for readers interested in phonological skills and basic decoding lessons. The discussion then turns to various speculations about how much Allington, Pressley, and Cunningham actually agree about reading instruction. But we have to leave before they reach any sort of consensus.

We settle down to meet with the administrator and other staff members. Having seen it in action, we know that it is possible to have such a total school effort to promote the literacy development of all children, but we have a million questions about schoolwide issues that go beyond reading and writing and about where to start.

Summary

A school tour can be a useful vehicle for better capturing the possibilities for reorganizing elementary schools. But tours of different schools reveal the differences that emerge as a result of differences in students, communities, and professional staff. Our school tour was meant not to reflect a one-best-way vision of what elementary schools might be but rather to attempt simply to portray a school that reflects some of our basic themes.

At this time, you may find it useful to take a tour of your own school. Think about the key themes presented in this book. Take notes as you walk or talk quietly into a small tape recorder. What do you see as you tour? Are classrooms rich with print? Are children actively reading and writing? Are they eager and engaged readers and writers? Do you see teachers reading to children? Do you see teachers demonstrating the thinking processes used in reading and writing? Are children developing editing skills? Is instructional time being well used? Are parents involved in classroom support activities? Do you notice any professional conversations about instructional practice?

After the tour, sit and compose a quickwrite on what you observed. Spend no more than 5 to 10 minutes. But save your summary. Later it will prove useful for noticing changes that are occurring. A single walking tour can provide much information, but repeated tours, with longer stays in various locations and chats with a variety of people (including little people), provide even better information. The key questions are: What do you want to see more of? What do you want to see less of in this school?

Getting Started

Schools that work are collections of classrooms that work. The starting point for creating schools that work is the classroom. To develop a school where all children become readers and writers, we must begin by developing a school where every classroom teacher becomes more expert in teaching children to read and write. Creating a school where teachers are continually developing their expertise means developing a professional learning community. This requires a sort of leadership that often seems in short supply, according to school superintendents and researchers (see the special series on this topic in *Education Week* at www.edweek.org).

School change is driven by individual change; as enough individuals change, schools also change. The popular literature on school change is peppered with phrases

"It is much easier to nail down what an effective school is than to struggle with a broader definition of *good school* . . . maybe that's why policy makers avoid trying" (Sergiovanni, 2000, pp. 93–94).

like "systemic reform," "whole school designs," and "comprehensive school reform." But a decade of such reform efforts by federal, state, and local education agencies illustrates a central problem: All mandates are ultimately translated and acted on by individual principals and teachers (McGill-Franzen, 2000). And no matter how you read the research available, the evidence that mandated master planning produces substantive positive effects on teaching or learning is incredibly slim given the money spent and energy sapped by such efforts (Allington & Nowak, 2004; Berends et al., 2002; Herman & Stringfield, 1997). We would be happy to report that such efforts worked, if they did. But given what we have learned about teachers and teaching over the years, we believe that it makes no sense to think that mandates will improve instruction in the classroom. Teachers teach *what* they know and *who* they are (we are paraphrasing and combining the assertions of Linda Darling-Hammond and Susan Ohanian).

In our final chapter we review some recent findings about how to create schools where all children become readers and writers. We begin by discussing the importance of school culture because schools differ in the dominant beliefs and attitudes of the professional staff about the need for change (the need for professional learning). Then we review the basis for our emphasis on developing a professional learning community and the leadership style necessary for creating such schools. We close with recommendations for getting the change process started.

School Culture and Teacher Ownership

A culture is usually thought of as a group of people with a shared belief system and common rituals, practices, and customs. As we have trekked through schools across the United States over the past 30 years, we have been struck by how different school cultures can be. Differences in the beliefs of teachers and administrators seem to account for differences in responses to children who find learning to read difficult (Allington et al., 1997). In some schools many of these children are retained in grade owing to professional beliefs that with time will come the maturity essential for learning. In other schools, such children participate in an intensive, early intervention program designed to accelerate literacy development, because of professional beliefs that learning difficulties are not a problem of immaturity but a problem of limited experiences—an instructional problem. Other schools may classify these same children as having learning disability, provide services for them through a special education program, and actually not expect them ever to attain literacy competence, because they believe these children have impaired cognitive processes that preclude normal literacy development. Finally, some schools don't do much to or for these children because of the dominant belief that one-third or more of the children will always remain behind their peers in literacy development (in these schools, belief in the prophetic power of the bell-shaped curve is strong). In all these schools, different professional beliefs shape the rituals and practices that affect children.

The research on teaching indicates that professional beliefs drive educational decisions about how school personnel will respond to children experiencing difficulty in school. In fact, once we identify the belief system of a school, we can relatively easily predict the responses the school has created. Teachers' beliefs can also be shaped by their school's culture. When new teachers, especially inexperienced teachers, arrive at a school, they adopt the prevailing belief system and join the dominant culture (Valencia et al., in press). The culture of schools must often change to create schools that work better for all children. How teachers and students think about and value learning and how they go about the day-to-day routines and rituals determine how schools work. For instance, in some schools, teachers work collaboratively and watch each other teach, talk, and puzzle through instructional problems together, while in other schools teachers are congenial but are rarely collegial (Barth, 1990). There is a difference between being friendly and being professionally supportive and helpful. Some school cultures support collegiality, and others support congenial isolationism.

Timar (1994) discusses the federally funded Title 1 program, which provides monies to support the education of disadvantaged children:

> The program developed its own culture, one that favored uniformity and procedural regularity over innovation, experimentation, and the exercise of professional judgment. Schools could be sanctioned for not following the rules, but they could not legally be sanctioned for failing to teach students. (p. 53)

The Cultures of Learning

Schools that work emphasize student learning. They focus on fostering collaboration and developing student independence. They focus less on identifying academic winners and losers and more on helping all children achieve high levels of academic proficiency. They still consider achievement test scores (which are expected to show continuing growth), but they weigh other evidence of learning as well. These schools do not define learning solely by test scores, but test scores play a useful role. Here, other evidence of learning is routinely gathered and considered when student academic development is reviewed (Wolf et al., 2000). For instance, the school might collect and organize annual data on student reading habits outside of school, on library usage, on independent projects, and on service activities of children. In addition, student work might be collected and organized into developmental portfolios so that teachers can more easily judge qualitative improvements in student work across time. Reports of student progress focus less on ranking the child with peers and more on motivation for learning and acquiring more complex strategies and understandings.

A school's culture affects how students perceive learning. When learning is seen as primarily a matter of "ability," student effort is undermined. When we make much of rank-ordering children by achievement, we undermine student effort. We actually create schools where no one works very hard. Students who start school "ahead" remain ahead, and those who start "behind" remain behind even if both groups work hard. When you work hard but still remain behind, there is little motivation to continue to work hard. When you don't have to work very hard to stay ahead of the pack, there is little incentive to work hard. In competitive-emphasis school cultures, students often see each other (and themselves) as either winners or losers, and in most cases only the "winners" care to continue playing the game, though even they don't often play very hard (Pressley, 2006).

In addition, competitive cultures foster teacher competition, which creates resistance to collaboration. In one school we visited, the administrator proudly announced that he rank-ordered teachers each year based on their students' standardized test performances and posted the results in the teachers' lounge. In another school system, the superintendent told us that he released to the local newspaper the ranked-ordered performance of students on state exams for each teacher and had warned teachers, "You can't hide. Every parent and taxpayer will know who is doing their job." In these schools, teachers narrowed their curriculum focus and worked simply to produce high scores on the standardized tests. No teacher wanted to be "saddled" with low-achieving students, and teachers admitted pushing to retain or classify these students as having a disability. Teachers also worked in isolation, keeping "good ideas" to themselves in an attempt to gain an advantage over their colleagues. Neither school had good test results. Worse yet, neither school produced real readers and writers.

School Cultures and Goals

Ames and Ames (1994) describe two types of broad educational goals: ability goals and task goals. Ability goals focus on one student's demonstration of achievement compared to other students' demonstrations. Task goals focus on student improvement compared to past performance or some standard. When schools emphasize *ability* goals, most students seek to avoid challenging tasks and avoid working cooperatively because the goal is to achieve the highest ranking possible. In schools where *task* goals reflect the school culture, students are more likely to take on challenging tasks and more likely to work hard at improving because the goal is not outstripping classmates but learning a skill, a strategy, or content (Guthrie & Humenick, 2004).

When task goals are emphasized, teachers tend to think and talk differently about students. Rather than describe students in rank-order terms ("Jimmy is one of my slowest students"), teachers are more likely to discuss what students are learning and accomplishing ("Jimmy is working on developing clearer summaries of the materials he reads"). When task goals are emphasized, teachers often anguish over giving required grades because, traditionally, grades have been the school's official rank-ordering of students among their peers. But when low-achieving students work hard, make good progress, and still rank below many of their peers, the traditional ability–goal orientation of school report cards forces teachers to assign average or lower grades to students who have been working hard and developing new understandings and skills. This creates a situation that is unlikely to motivate continued effort by these students (Johnston, 2004).

At this point, it should be clear that teachers develop or maintain particular beliefs as a result of participating in a particular school culture. When a school district mandates rank-order comparisons of students on report cards or fosters rank-ordering of teachers on students' standardized test scores, it is not surprising to find (1) little teacher collaboration, (2) little student cooperation, (3) a focus on low-level learning tasks such as those found on traditional achievement tests, (4) low motivation for schoolwork among lower-achieving students, and (5) an avoidance of academic risk taking by all involved. In schools where the culture emphasizes rank-ordering teachers or children, it is difficult to foster thoughtful literacy, real academic work, collaborative teaching and learning, instructional experimentation, and shared decision making (Johnston et al., 1998).

> Linda McNeil (2000) notes that reform efforts in one urban district produced an unintended outcome. "They tried to teacher-proof the curriculum . . . By doing so, they have made schools exceedingly comfortable for mediocre teachers who like teaching routine lessons according to a standard sequence and format . . . They made being a Texas public school teacher exceedingly uncomfortable for those who knew their subjects well, who teach in ways that engage their students, who want their teaching to reflect their own continued learning" (p. 187).

Changing School Culture

Rowan (1990) discusses two broad strategies that have been suggested for improving schools: control strategies and commitment strategies. *Control* strategies call for an elaborate system of rules, regulations, and mandates designed to standardize the instruction offered in schools and thereby improve student achievement. Some mandates point to the use of particular instructional materials, other mandates focus on the amount of time to be spent teaching different subjects, and others on the skills to be mastered at each grade level and link them to student promotion policies. Many policies foster a competitive atmosphere by publicly rank-ordering schools on achievement and rewarding some schools (Blue Ribbon schools, for example) and penalizing others (a state's "deficient schools" or "F" school listings). Some school districts have gone further, issuing mandates for the number of instructional groups, the pacing of schedules for completing curriculum units, and daily homework assignments. Rowan and others (e.g., McNeil, 2000; Murphy, 1998) conclude that accumulated evidence indicates that control strategies can work to change teacher behavior, but the most common changes identified seemed not to be changes that actually benefited students or enhanced higher-order learning. Thus, after two decades of relatively futile attempts to improve schools through increased control strategies, we think it is time to experiment with commitment strategies.

Michael Fullan notes that "systems have a good track record for keeping things the way they are. Systems don't have a good track record for changing things. Individuals have that track record. It's individuals, working, first of all, despite the system, and, secondly, connecting with other kindred spirits, that will begin to develop the critical mass that changes the system." (From Fullan's address at the 1994 meeting of the Association for Supervision and Curriculum Development in Chicago.)

Commitment strategies call for reducing bureaucratization while fostering professional independence and decision making. The goal is to increase educator involvement in the instructional process. Proponents of commitment strategies (e.g., Allington, 2002a; Fullan & Hargreaves, 1996; Harwayne, 1999) argue that teachers take more professional responsibility for educating children when they have ownership of the instructional plan and decision making occurs on the "shop floor." Motivation to improve is higher when the improvements are locally defined and locally monitored, teacher by teacher, day by day. The evidence on the effects of commitment strategies is well developed and suggests that they enhance teacher collegiality and collaboration, which can have a positive impact on the instructional process and student learning (Combs, Miser, & Whitaker, 1998; Leithwood & Jantzi, 1999; Wolf et al., 2000). Commitment strategies require an accountability-with-autonomy model of leadership.

Accountability with Autonomy

In a study of shared decision making—a primary accountability-with-autonomy model—in two schools that enrolled large numbers of at-risk children (between 75 and 95 percent of children received free- or reduced-price lunches), Ames and Ames (1994) found that providing a four-day focus session for instructional leadership teams (selected teachers and the principal) fostered an initial team building. The sessions were organized around student achievement, instructional process information, and school climate data gathered before the sessions began. Each team was given standardized test data that had been disaggregated to show how well different groups of students were performing (boys versus girls, economically advantaged versus disadvantaged, and breakdowns by ethnicity). Teams were also provided with data from measures of the degree of experimentation that teachers felt were encouraged, the quality of instructional support, the teachers' satisfaction with the curriculum, the presumed potential of students, and so on. Teams were guided through a process of examining these data and were asked to identify school strengths and weaknesses and to translate these findings into specific goals and action plans.

Teams were also introduced to a framework for analyzing instructional aspects of the school programs. This framework focused on the tasks that children were assigned, common student groupings for instruction, the amount of time that was allocated for various instructional activities, common evaluation activities used to assess students and teachers, and an inventory of how teachers and students were offered recognition. Finally, teams were asked to develop a plan to share the results of their analyses with their schools' faculty and enlist the cooperation of all teachers in implementing changes they had identified as needed.

Shared decision making in these schools worked more smoothly and resulted in earlier and greater improvements in instructional processes. Collegial and collaborative efforts among faculty improved, and the goals set for students rose. In short, Ames and Ames (1994) provide good evidence that shared decision making can foster shifts in school culture and lead to improved educational processes.

Fullan and Hargreaves (1996), Harwayne (1999), and Herzog (1997) describe different accountability-with-autonomy models. In each case the emphasis is more on individual reflection on instructional problems, although this reflection and analysis are usually done with others. In all three cases, a climate of trust must first be created; experimentation is encouraged; mistakes, lessons gone bad, are expected; and support for puzzling through instructional problems is readily available from other teachers and from administrators or teacher–leaders. Stigler and Hiebert (1999) offer the collegial "lesson study" as another framework for initiating an accountability-with-autonomy process that improves teaching and learning. But no matter what model is selected, the focus must remain on improving instructional practices.

Implementing an accountability-with-autonomy model is not easy because it involves a substantial "reculturing" in most schools. A shifting of traditional beliefs, not only about teaching and learning but also about the roles and responsibilities of nearly everyone involved, is necessary. We know more about the difficulties of implementing shared decision making at this point than about the difficulties of implementing other models (Holloway, 2000).

Early efforts toward shared decision making often go offtrack, and as a result the process loses its focus on instructional efforts (Cohen & Spillane, 1992). One reason for emphasizing school data is to keep attention focused on instructional improvement. Without the data, the deliberations become bogged down in discussions and debates about trivial elements of the schooling process. Implementing shared decision making requires a new sort of work, but the potential it holds for improving the process of education is enormous.

Even when school teams have substantial authority, two issues—access to information and power status—almost always seem problematic. The problem of information access is often simply a matter of personnel having little experience or awareness of school cultures other than their own. Most teachers have limited experiences because they have taught in only one school district and often at only one grade level in a single school building. Most administrators have relatively limited experiences as well. They do not have experiences in schools quite different from their own to draw from when contemplating change. Without access to alternatives to the way things "have always been done," there is little experimentation and the danger of mutual reinforcement of poorly informed decisions increases (Fullan & Hargreaves, 1996).

Taylor, Pearson, Peterson, and Rodriguez (2005) report on one of largest and most intensive studies of professional development in reading. They studied the implementation of a research-based reading reform model. Their findings are similar in many respects to those of other researchers: A classroom emphasis on meaning, engagement, and higher-order tasks produced results superior to classrooms focused on skills development and lower-order tasks in the high-poverty schools they studied. Even a focus on low-level comprehension skills (as opposed to higher-order discussion and questions) had a negative effect on reading achievement. Explaining this, the authors note, "high amounts of mechanistic practice on comprehension skills are taking time away from other important comprehension activities such as higher level talk about texts and use of comprehension strategies during reading" (p. 57).

In the schools earning the highest ratings for reform effort, student scores improved substantially over the 2-year period, while schools rated as exhibiting low-reform effort actually had student reading performance decline over that same period. Not surprisingly, teachers in the higher-effort schools changed their instructional practices more than teachers in the low-effort schools. They changed by adding more of the powerful instructional practices and reducing the use of those practices not associated with research-based reading instruction.

The researchers noted that the teachers in the improving schools were more likely to engage with a substantive study topic for at least 3 or 4 months and meet at least monthly to share the study group findings (e.g., multiple readings and discussions on comprehension strategy lessons or discussion-based comprehension lessons). These were more collegial schools where the faculty focus was on sharing, collaborating, and improving reading instruction. This was accomplished, in large part, by an effective internal leadership team that was typically led by a teacher leader who was very knowledgeable about classroom reading assessment and instruction and was respected by the teachers.

 Roland Barth (1990) comments on the traditional authoritarian school administration: "An inevitable consequence of this patriarchal model of leadership—aside from a certain amount of order and productivity—is the creation of a dependent relationship between principal and teacher" (p. 133). The dependent relationship fosters teachers who never explore alternatives and rarely reflect on their practice or the outcomes of their practice. Instead, they just "do what they're told" and leave it at that. In such situations it is unlikely that schools will improve much because teachers become dependent on being told precisely and specifically what they should be doing. No school administrator ever has time to observe, diagnose, intervene, demonstrate, and educate every teacher in the building. Unless teachers develop greater independence, our schools will remain largely as they are today.

Low-reform-effort schools have been previously reported in the research on school change. Generally, these schools have been labeled as low-commitment or low-capacity schools. In other words, these are schools where no one has accepted the challenge of change or where no one has the expertise to foster improved reading instruction. In some cases, these may be schools where everyone is so busy following an often incoherent set of multiple mandates that time to actually engage in the work of developing teacher expertise seems unavailable. In other cases, these schools have a "quick fix" mentality believing that a new packaged program or the addition of an after-school program will somehow solve the problem of teacher inexpertness. In the end, as Taylor and colleagues once again remind us, it is developing teacher expertise that really matters.

The changing nature of power and authority in accountability-with-autonomy models is another area that is often problematic. In other words, school administrators and teachers (parents, too, in some cases) have to unlearn one set of power and communication relationships and then relearn (or create) new processes and procedures. Shifting to collaborative models of leadership has proved difficult for many school administrators.

Jazz Combo as the Metaphor for School Leadership

There seems to be a need for a new metaphor to describe school administrators' roles. Perhaps replacing the metaphor of the school administrator as manager, CEO, orchestra conductor, or architect with the metaphor of the school administrator as leader of a jazz combo would be appropriate (Smith & Ellet, 2000). Most traditional metaphors for principals have the administrator "in front" rather than "alongside" teachers. The leader of a jazz combo has more responsibilities than other members of the group, but the "authority" the leader has is largely assigned by the other members. And when it comes to the work of the combo—the playing—the leader's task is not to direct the other musicians but to foster their working together.

The problem with "on top" or "in front" is that such language implies that organizations improve when workers "follow" a leader. But school administrators move on. Reliance on a charismatic visionary to "lead" the school along the path to sustained improvement is not realistic. For sustained change to occur, teachers must be supported "in constructing their own knowledge and skills in harmony with others" (Smith & Ellet, 2000, p. 7). The needed shift is from thinking about developing a school leader to working to develop leadership capacity within schools.

In accountability-with-autonomy models, a school administrator's authority derives less from an organizational hierarchy and more from teachers' assignment of authority to the school-administrator position. One strategy that seems particularly useful is for the school administrator to observe and

A new Web-based interactive course, *Effective Leadership*, is being offered by the Association for Supervision and Curriculum Development. More information can be found at www.ascd.org in the Professional Development Online area.

Changing School Culture

monitor continually the effects of the changes being implemented. In one school we know, the principal observes for inconsistencies with the team or individually developed instructional plan. If higher-order learning is the established goal, a teacher using worksheets would be asked to explain how that assignment fit into the overall philosophy of the school. In another school, the principal and the teachers gather student assessment data and teacher-developed summaries of learning progress. These are presented monthly to the school team and serve as a basis for continuing discussion of whether the elected change is accomplishing the intended goal. Another principal reports that her job is primarily to nudge folks in particular directions:

> My job as a leader is to stay at the cutting edge of things in education and to make sure teachers see things, hear them, and talk about them. People come to you with ideas and you can help them. . . . Sometimes you can best help by offering a creative alternative, keeping the person moving in a positive direction. . . . My teachers laugh at me because I'm always making them an offer they can't refuse—but if I do, I try to make it really a better idea. (Cushman, 1992, p. 8)

Administrators Might Teach

In Rochester, New York, one change produced by the move to shared decision making was school administrators being assigned to teach for part of every day. Under the plan, administrators taught one to two hours daily, in a subject area of their choice. Some school administrators became co-teachers in classrooms. Others worked with a particular group of children before, during, or after school. A few took over a classroom to free up a teacher who then took on some of the leadership tasks in the building. Still others rotated through the building, serving as a sort of substitute teacher, so that teachers could visit each other's classrooms. Involving administrators in the practice of teaching was seen as useful for several reasons:

- The experience allowed administrators to talk with some greater sense of practice in team sessions.
- Such participation reduced the us/them nature of discussions in team sessions.
- Such participation communicated the high value placed on teaching.
- Teaching provided administrators with the "classroom" view of problems.

Evaluation of Administrators and Teams by Teachers

One final aspect of the shift to an accountability-with-autonomy model of leadership is having teachers evaluate administrators. Perhaps first suggested in the joint proposal developed by the National Education Association and the National Association of Secondary School Principals, and now used in the Principals' Executive Program, the process offers teachers regular anonymous opportunities to give administrators feedback on their leadership. We think giving administrators regular feedback on perceived performance—feedback from teachers, parents, and, perhaps, community members—is a good idea. Without a feedback loop, it is difficult to know how adequate one's performance is.

In an article entitled "The Contemporary Principal," Checkley (2000) offers a composite advertisement for a principal's position. It reads as follows:

Wanted: An Exceptional School Leader

Must know how to implement change that helps ensure the academic success of all students. Must be an instructional leader and have the ability to promote teacher growth. Must be dedicated to creating a shared vision of an outstanding school through collaboration with faculty, parents, and community members. Must have strong interpersonal skills, excellent communication skills.

How to Begin

Creating schools where all children become readers and writers will not be a simple task. Our society is demanding higher academic performance from students—all students. The combination of a changing economy and a changing society works to up the ante for schools. Today, schools are expected to teach a more diverse group of children and to raise the performance level of all students to standards historically held for only a few.

So how to begin? In the remainder of this chapter we offer a brief guide for initiating change in your school. The focus is on developing the capacity, the expertise, of every teacher to provide higher-quality reading and writing instruction. Remember our earlier paraphrase of Fullan and Hargreaves (1996): One or two exemplary classrooms in a building are examples of individual initiative, but a school with many exemplary classrooms is the result of leadership.

If Not You, Who?

The creation of a school that works better for all children starts with you. Waiting for the state education agency or the district superintendent to develop the appropriate plan, allocate the needed money, schedule the necessary professional development, and so on, will ensure that next year your school will look pretty much as it does this year and as it has looked for the last few years. Schools that work for all children are not the product of a state-mandated school improvement plan or the result of a federal program grant or a plan developed and mandated by district office personnel. Schools are changed by the people who work in them. Others outside the school can help the change process along, but those people do not do the changing that needs to be done.

To change a school, we need to foster commitment, expertise, and conversation. Without productive and extended conversation about prevailing practices and outcomes, it will be nearly impossible to change school programs and educational outcomes. We believe that this book provides a number of issues to address and a variety of strategies for beginning to address those issues through professional conversations. If you do not initiate the conversations, who will?

If Not Here, Where?

You may not think your school is a good candidate for engaging in this process of change. Other schools have a more adventurous and expert faculty, a more experienced administrator, greater faculty commitment, better community support, fewer problem students, more

"Unfortunately, we don't have the kind of money that it would take to do that." We hear this excuse far too often in schools where much needs to be done. We say *excuse* because we have never seen an American school where the issue was lack of money rather than a problem with how money was allocated. Let us give you an example.

In a southern urban school district there was an underperforming school that served mostly minority children from low-income families. When the new principal arrived, the school library was bare bones and classroom libraries barely existed. But as the new principal explained to us, "Lots of money was being spent supporting teaching activities that research has shown are largely ineffective." So she set about making effective teaching easier. First to go were the multiple copy machines and the bottomless supply of copy paper. One copy machine remained. Each teacher was provided with two reams of copy paper (1,000 sheets) for the year (or roughly one copy per child per week). When that supply was exhausted, teachers who wanted to copy worksheets had to go to Kinko's and pay for the copies themselves. That saved the school about $8,000. Then went the consumable workbooks and test preparation booklets. No more spelling book, reading workbook, math workbook, or language arts workbook. And no more of those test practice workbooks! That saved about $50 per student or roughly $27,000. Then a few paraprofessional lines disappeared but the salaries and fringe benefit funds were retained. Another $30,000.

Now with that $65,000 the principal provided classroom teachers with $500 gift cards from a local bookstore. Teachers were to begin the process of buying books for their classroom libraries. Single copies. Some informational titles linked to the core curriculum. Some favorite books of children (e.g., *Captain Underpants*). Some classic children's literature. Teachers were able to purchase approximately 100 books that first year. The bookstore not only provided a nice discount to the school but also sent a monthly printout of who had bought what.

Now $53,000 remained. After allocating $25,000 to the school library, there was still $25,000 left to begin to build two book rooms filled with bins of multilevel books and $3,000 to buy professional texts for Teachers as Readers groups. And that was just in the first year! By the fourth year, children had what we would consider easy access to an array of interesting books. One of the missing pillars of scientifically based reading instruction. But there was also more reading, more discussion, and more collaborating occurring in classrooms (and in the staff room). More of the missing pillars. And teachers were more expert about, and more confident in, providing reading instruction that met the needs of all children. The fifth year led to recognition as a Title 1 School of Distinction.

It's rarely about the money. It is almost always about local leadership capacity to recognize what matters and finding where funds are being wasted on materials and resources that no theory or empirical evidence supports.

space, and so on. But no school that needs changing is ever the perfect place to initiate change. If change does not begin in your school, where will it begin?

It may be that other schools seem to be in a sorrier state and more in need of change. It may be that other schools seem to have better resources to support change. But the school you work in is the school you can change. Listen to what Madeline Cartwright (1993), principal of the James G. Blaine Elementary School in Philadelphia, said:

> Don't talk about systems, or cities, or other schools. Say, I'm going to make *this* school a better place for teachers, I'm going to make *this* school a better place for parents, I'm going to make *this* school a better place for children. Say, I'm going to sweep up that one block. Not all the blocks in Philadelphia. Not all the blocks in America. This one block. That's what we did at Blaine.

If Not Now, When?

There never seems to be a good time to initiate change. It always seems as though the schedule this year is already full, the money needed is not readily available, school personnel will need to be better prepared, student achievement is not really so bad, and everything is basically under control. We have never worked with a school that took up the challenge of change because it was a "slow" year and initiating substantial change would keep the faculty busy. There never will be a better time to begin than right now, while the ideas and arguments presented in this book are still fresh in your mind.

Beginning the process of creating a school where all children become readers and writers does not mean that tomorrow everything will be topsy-turvy. Beginning the process is the most important step, but it is only the first step. Beginning to change, according to Sergiovanni (1991), starts with taking stock of the current situation.

Take Stock

In workshops we often ask school administrators to identify three aspects of their schools that they would nominate for national excellence recognition (we also ask teachers to identify three things about their classrooms that they would like to present at a conference). Every school (and classroom) should have some feature that deserves recognition. It might be student attendance records, ease of access to the physical plant, a print-rich kindergarten program, a parent-run after-school technology program, a locally developed literature-based science theme, a video-based portfolio system, the professional-development strand, a performing arts effort, or almost any other aspect of the school or schooling process.

Many school administrators (and teachers) find it difficult to complete this assignment. But when we ask for a list of three school problems, they have difficulty limiting the list to three items! Nonetheless, we pursue the listing of exemplary practices because every school has its strong points (though it seems we do not reflect on them nearly enough).

What are the most positive aspects of the current school culture (remember that culture encompasses beliefs and practices)? What are the high points, the aspects of the school that could withstand scrutiny? What are the assets of the school? Every school has some model families, model classrooms, model teachers, model students. We begin the change process by identifying the assets that can be drawn on to initiate and support change.

Taking stock also involves an honest status report about current school culture and student outcomes. We have offered a number of data-gathering procedures for taking stock. One powerful focus for this phase is to examine the school experiences of a single cohort of children (who entered kindergarten together) and to identify how the school responded to the risks these children faced. How many children who arrived for kindergarten at risk of school failure have had that risk ameliorated and are now active, achieving students? How many students who arrived at risk are still at risk or are experiencing school failure?

Another way of considering the current school culture is to identify how many children in a cohort are truly well prepared for middle school after their six- or seven-year stay in the elementary schools. Are all children ready to go to middle school, and are they equipped academically to function with the independence generally considered appropriate for early adolescents? Do any children seem ill equipped for the demands of middle school? If we examined kindergarten entrance records of a cohort about to go off to middle school, could we identify the children most likely to be deemed unready for the transition? Has the school reduced the risks for at-risk children? Are fewer children at risk as they head for middle school than when they began school?

If we were to examine these students' achievement records by gender, ethnicity, and family socioeconomic status, would we find a pattern of performance differentiation? Would those records show that poor children were just as likely to be ready for middle school as their more advantaged peers? Would we find that more boys had been retained or more often identified as having LD than girls? Does the reading achievement of minority students equal that of other students? Has the school achieved the goal of educating well all children, regardless of their gender, ethnicity, or family status or income?

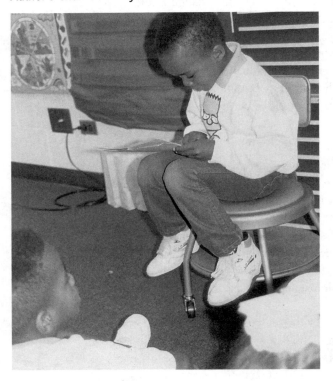

Will we reduce the risk for children as they progress through our schools? Will this young man in the Author's Chair be ready for middle school?

What aspects of your school would you nominate for a state or national recognition program? What about your school would you like featured on a local television program? What would you like to share with other educators and with the public? List three aspects of your school that you would nominate.

1. _____

2. _____

3. _____

Focus on the adults and the work environment. What are the real strengths of the faculty? Remember that good schools are collections of good classrooms. Every school has some superb teachers. Every school has teachers willing to take a risk, to experiment, to change. Every school we have worked in has had teachers chafing under the current system and eager for change. Every school we have worked in has had teachers who knew precisely what change was needed to make the school work better for all children. These teachers might not have had a comprehensive plan, but they could identify practices that needed to be altered to better serve children at risk.

What sorts of professional conversations and collaborations now occur in your school? Every school has some. Be ready to build on these as you locate them. How could those collaborations and conversations be extended to others and, perhaps, into the arena of public conversation?

Set the Stage for Change

A central question, then, is, How do we build on the existing strengths of the school? How can teachers who are eager to change be encouraged to take that step? How can we extend and foster professional collaboration and conversation? We believe that a good first step is to encourage more diversity in educational practice within the school. McNeil (2000) points to evidence that prescriptive mandates are more popular with less-effective teachers than with more-effective teachers. Perhaps this is true because following a mandate minimizes personal accountability for outcomes. Barth (1990) notes that tightly prescribed instructional practices that constrain instructional diversity in a school also work to constrain reflection and discussion of educational practices. When teachers pursue different strategies for meeting the needs of children, there is a basis for professional discussion of practice. When everyone simply follows a mandated plan, there is little reason to talk. When school administrators attempt to monitor closely compliance with mandated instructional practices, teachers rarely speak openly about their concerns or the weaknesses of the mandated system.

Sergiovanni (1991) notes that the supervisory function of school administrators has three potential purposes:

- *Quality control.* Basic monitoring of school functions through visiting classrooms; talking with teachers, students, and parents; reviewing curriculum plans, materials, and lessons.
- *Professional development.* Working to understand what teachers need to teach and what they need to learn to grow and develop professionally.
- *Teacher motivation.* Nurturing motivation and commitment to teaching as a career, to the school, and to students.

He offers the 80/20 rule for school administrators: When more than 20 percent of supervisory time and money is spent on evaluating for quality control or less than 80 percent of supervisory time and money is spent on professional improvement and enhancing both expertise and motivation, the quality of schooling suffers.

One first step in creating a school that works better for all children is to foster diversity in classrooms. It is important to remember that it is not only children who differ but also teachers. There can never be one best way to serve the needs of all children and no one best practice that all teachers can use effectively. Don't forget to shine a light on the diversity in instruction. There will be few conversations and little teacher learning if instructional diversity is kept a private matter.

Share Instructional Practices

Celebrate the diversity that emerges, and work to ensure that teachers develop greater shared knowledge of the instructional diversity across the school. Barth (1990) tells of holding faculty meetings in individual classrooms rather than in the library or in some other common location. At the beginning of each meeting he asked the classroom teacher to take 5 minutes to provide a tour of the classroom and the instructional program, emphasizing any components that she or he considered especially successful or unique. This process required teachers to reflect on their teaching and identify the practices they most wanted to share with colleagues. Over time, of course, this strategy fostered much sharing of knowledge of instructional practices, and it fostered conversation and collaboration.

Alvarado (2000) argues that teachers' visits to other classrooms in their own school and to classrooms in other schools are the one "absolutely necessary" strategy for fostering teacher development and instructional change. Such visits should be targeted specifically to some effective instructional activity that the observed teacher is using. Alvarado notes, for instance, that Teacher X should visit Teacher Y's classroom because Teacher Y is using a Word Wall in a way that promotes the sort of skill and strategy learning that

Teacher X is working hard to improve. Generic classroom visits are largely ineffective, though just as expensive as targeted visits. Alvarado also advises that teachers make these classroom visits in groups of two or more, so there is someone to talk to about what was observed. After the initial visit it is important that Teacher Y then visit Teacher X's classroom to offer support and coaching on implementing and using Word Walls effectively. Finally, Teacher X and Teacher Y share their experiences with using Word Walls with the other faculty in their building. Teacher X's classroom may then become one of the classrooms that other teachers interested in using Word Walls visit.

The first step in breaking down the mutual invisibility that occurs in schools where teachers work largely in isolation from one another is to create settings where diversity is welcomed and where awareness of instructional practices is fostered. A final step in this process is recognizing teacher learning as well as experimentation. "What have you learned from this? About this? As a result of this?" are all good queries that foster reflective discussion of practices.

We think that recognizing and celebrating diversity is critical. Fostering the development of greater shared knowledge about instructional problems and practices is a fundamental feature of celebrating instructional diversity.

One planned feature of The Learning Network schools is a weekly, voluntary meeting in which instructional problems are presented and discussed. At Montview Elementary in Aurora, Colorado, we observed one strategy for developing such meetings as productive experiences. A large sheet of butcher paper was posted in the staff room. Teachers simply put instructional problems they wanted to address on the sheet throughout the week. At the faculty meeting, the posted problems were reviewed quickly by the teachers running the meeting, and one or two were selected to focus on. Sometimes the teacher posting a problem was asked to elaborate on the problem before the faculty split into work groups to discuss the problems. School administrators joined these groups. Each work group then engaged in conversations concerning the problems posed. Each team worked to develop a response to the problem. Some teams located useful resources, and others offered experienced observations on the problem. Some problems required a reconsideration of schedules or resources. But each 60-to-90 minute meeting solved core instructional problems. Each fostered not only professional conversation but professional collaboration on implementing the proposed solution.

The teachers were willing to publicly post instructional problems because at their school the following statements were true:

- Teaching is perceived as problem finding and solving.
- Instructional diversity is encouraged.
- Trust has been developed.
- Postings lead to productive conversation and collaborative support.

Look Long, Start Easy

Often, goal statements, or mission statements, are seen as the initial step in the change process. We disagree. In our experience, the typical goal-setting process results in a broad, vague, and pleasant-sounding statement that suggests nothing in particular except that the school hopes to do better. Instead of engaging in what can become an extended process of developing a high-minded statement, we suggest that the first steps are

- Fostering shared knowledge of instructional practices to stimulate
- Professional conversations about those practices as a strategy for
- Developing professional expertise and risk taking that leads to
- More evidence-based instructional practices being used by more teachers, which results in
- Improved levels of academic performance in larger numbers of students.

Our advice to schools has long been "look long, start easy." The look-long advice is meant to convey the notion that change takes time. It seems useful to think about the school three years from now rather than the school tomorrow. What would you like to see happening more often three years hence? What would you like to see happening less frequently? Everything cannot change at once, so pick the important changes. Because every school is unique—with a particular staff, a particular set of students, particular parents, particular resources, and so on—there is no one change that everyone can start with. But opening up a dialogue among the school staff is critical, and that is often the first goal we set.

The start-easy advice simply means go with the easiest changes first. As we have repeatedly noted, good schools are collections of good classrooms. Which classroom teachers are the most likely to be willing to experiment? Which grade levels will be most likely to share ideas during grade-level team meetings? Which teachers will open up their classrooms to other teacher–observers? Which teachers would agree to observe others? Every school we have ever worked in had teachers who wanted change and were willing to work for change. Those are the teachers we advise beginning with.

It is a delicate balancing act, however. School administrators cannot just offer public recognition for these teachers and wish everyone else would become more like them! In fact, applauding these teachers' work may backfire as other teachers feel the sting of not being included in the rank-ordering of the "best" teachers. Instead, school administrators must convey to the change-agent teachers that their efforts are appreciated and that further experimentation will be supported.

The most useful strategy we know for communicating the message about these classes is to focus broadly on the results. The focus cannot be confined to standardized test scores because, first, those scores are available only once a year in most schools and, second, test scores have a very narrow focus. Instead, we encourage focusing on student performances in writing, in reading literature, in science or social studies. For instance, create an area in the foyer for students to display their work—not only the work of one or two of the "best" students but also a display of the work of a whole class. Imagine a display of the essays that every child in a fourth-grade classroom wrote after completing an oral history project, or a video of a class production of a play students developed from a piece of literature, or detailed site maps of different plots of land around the school with every plant indicated by genus and species (and maybe even indications of the insects and animal life observed on the plots), or a display of writing or reading portfolios for a whole class for the fall semester. In other words, put the experimentation on display.

What things would you like to see more frequently in your school? Less frequently? Perhaps an increase in writing activity during the school day? What would you reduce or eliminate to create the space needed for more writing activity? Perhaps less low-level seatwork? Maybe fewer whole-class interrogation sessions after a reading assignment? Would others in your school agree with your lists? Creating more of/less of lists often provides a clearer focus for planning and evaluation.

Expect Resistance and Skepticism

Whenever schools attempt to change, to move forward, we can expect to find teachers who, at best, are skeptics and, at worst, actively resist and work to undermine change. So what to do with these teachers? First, realize that skepticism is a normal response. For many years, schools in the United States have been under attack by a variety of reformers. We have seen open schools, open-space schools, nongraded schools, promotion standards, authentic assessments, phonics, basals, whole language, manipulative math, and hands-on science rise and fall in popularity just in the course of our careers. Many teachers also have seen all this change trumpeted, attended all the training workshops, worked to implement the new ideas, only to see all of it washed away in the next rush to reform. So why not be skeptical?

The only solution we know for skeptical colleagues is demonstrating an idea's workability and even modestly improved results. Most of the skeptics we have encountered—and that is a fairly substantial number—ask only to be left to their own devices, at least for now. If we implement change around them and if that change produces good results, most skeptics become curious, then conversational, and finally experimental. Our goal has been to entice skeptics into the change process. We neither ignore them nor attempt to convert them aggressively, but we do try to get them to watch what is going on. We try to engage them in professional conversations.

We think that touting reforms too soon, too loudly, and too aggressively can actually lessen the likelihood the change will ever succeed. Too often reformers have trumpeted one quick fix after another, from one state commissioner of education to another, from one superintendent to another, or from one principal to another. But there are no quick fixes to the difficulties that beset education today. In fact, many of the difficulties we face are the result of attempted quick fixes. Thus, we argue for a slower pace of implementation. We argue for trying things on a small scale before jumping in wholeheartedly. We argue for letting reforms stand on their results and for modesty in our claims.

Madeline Cartwright (1993), the principal of Blaine Elementary School in Philadelphia, offers her advice:

People would say, "Aw, your so-called solutions are simple." Yes they are. If the child has no clean clothes, you get him clean clothes. . . . If you know parents have to go to work in the morning, why wait until 8:45 to open school doors? Open the school at 7:30, and if you haven't got your own people there to watch the kids, find others. . . . Someone must do these things for the children. If a child's hungry, someone must feed him. If he's dirty, someone must wash him. If his clothes need laundering, someone must clean them. . . . We had children for whom no family or agency was taking care of such needs. So we did it. . . . The age we live in demands that we extend such efforts. We speak of how we want to help children, but then we allow ourselves to be tangled in bureaucratic nonsense and help never reaches those who need it. (p. 153)

In addition to adding a washer and a dryer to the school-equipment inventory, Ms. Cartwright provided every child with a personalized book bag, set up a fund from which any child could get money for field trips or school supplies, organized parents as school helpers, and began a myriad of other "commonsense" initiatives!

A Parting Word

We have avoided creating a name or an acronym for our school-change efforts. There is something particularly attractive (and particularly American) about a five-step process or a three-point plan. But in our combined 50-plus years of experience in elementary schools, we have uncovered a few truths.

- First, creating schools that work for all children takes time, energy, and leadership.
- Second, no two schools are ever alike, so each school must develop its own plan on its own schedule.
- Third, every school can improve itself, but not every school does.
- Fourth, honestly and openly examining how change benefits children is the surest way to create better schools.
- Fifth, and finally, good schools are collections of good teachers, and creating schools where all children become readers and writers is simply a matter of figuring out how to support teachers in their efforts to develop the expertise needed to foster the reading and writing proficiencies of every student.

Five years from now the people most likely to still be coming to your school each day are the teachers who work there now. The children enrolled now will be gone; many of the parents who stop in as they drop off their children will no longer be dropping children off. Investing in developing teachers' instructional expertise and capacity for collaborative problem solving will continue to pay benefits for a very long time.

references

Achilles, C. M. (1999). *Let's put kids first, finally: Getting class size right.* Thousand Oaks, CA: Corwin Press.

Adams, M. J. (1990). *Beginning to read: Thinking and learning about print.* Cambridge: MIT Press.

Afflerbach, P. (1993). Report cards and reading. *The Reading Teacher, 46,* 458–465.

Ahmed, E., & Braithewaite, V. (2004). Bullying and victimization: Cause for concern for both families and schools. *Social Psychology of Education, 7,* 35–54.

Allington, R. L. (1983). The reading instruction provided readers of differing abilities. *Elementary School Journal, 83,* 548–559.

Allington, R. L. (1991). The legacy of "slow it down and make it more concrete." In J. Zutell & S. McCormick (Eds.), *Learner factors/teacher factors: Issues in literacy research and instruction* (pp. 19–30). Chicago: National Reading Conference.

Allington, R. L. (1993). *Regulatory and fiscal influences upon the organization of literature-based reading programs.* Paper presented at the annual meeting of the American Educational Research Association, Atlanta.

Allington, R. L. (1994). What's special about special programs for children who find learning to read difficult? *Journal of Reading Behavior, 26,* 1–21.

Allington, R. L. (1999). Crafting state educational policy: The slippery role of educational research and researchers. *Journal of Literacy Research, 31,* 457–482.

Allington, R. L. (2002a). *Big brother and the national reading curriculum: How ideology trumped evidence.* Portsmouth, NH: Heinemann.

Allington, R. L. (2002b). Research on reading/learning disability interventions. In A. E. Farstrup & S. J. Samuels, (Eds.), *What research says about reading instruction* (3rd ed., pp. 261–290). Newark, DE: International Reading Association.

Allington, R. L. (2004). Setting the record straight. *Educational Leadership, 61*(6), 22–25.

Allington, R. L. (2005, May/June). The other five pillars of effective reading instruction. *Reading Today, 22,* 3.

Allington, R. L. (2006). *What really matters for struggling readers: Designing research-based interventions.* Boston: Allyn & Bacon.

Allington, R. L., & Broikou, K. (1988). Development of shared knowledge: A new role for classroom and specialist teachers. *The Reading Teacher, 41,* 806–811.

Allington, R. L., & Guice, S. (1997). Literature curriculum: Issues of definition and control. In J. Flood, S. B. Heath, & D. Lapp (Eds.), *Handbook of research on teaching literacy through the communicative and visual arts* (pp. 727–734). New York: Macmillan.

Allington, R. L., & Johnston, P. (2002). *Reading to learn: Lessons from exemplary fourth-grade classrooms.* New York: Guilford.

Allington, R. L., & McGill-Franzen, A. (1989). School response to reading failure: Chapter 1 and special education students in grades 2, 4, & 8. *Elementary School Journal, 89,* 529–542.

Allington, R. L., & McGill-Franzen, A. (1992). Unintended effects of educational reform in New York State. *Educational Policy, 6,* 397–414.

Allington, R. L., & McGill-Franzen, A. (1993). Placing children at risk: Schools respond to reading problems. In R. Donmeyer & R. Kos (Eds.), *At-risk students: Portraits, policies, programs, and practices* (pp. 197–218). Albany, NY: State University of New York Press.

Allington, R. L., & McGill-Franzen, A. (1995). Flunking: Throwing good money after bad. In R. L. Allington & S. A. Walmsley (Eds.), *No quick fix: Rethinking literacy programs in America's elementary schools* (pp. 45–60). New York: Teachers College Press.

Allington, R. L., & McGill-Franzen, A. (1996). Individual planning. In M. Wang & M. Reynolds (Eds.), *Handbook of special and remedial education* (pp. 5–35). New York: Pergamon.

Allington, R. L., & McGill-Franzen, A. M. (2003). The impact of summer loss on the reading achievement gap. *Phi Delta Kappan, 85*(1), 68–75.

Allington, R. L., McGill-Franzen, A., & Schick, R. (1997). How administrators understand learning difficulties: A qualitative analysis. *Remedial and Special Education, 18,* 223–232.

Allington, R. L., & Nowak, R. (2004). "Proven programs" and other unscientific ideas. In C. C. Block, D. Lapp, E. J. Cooper, J. Flood, N. Roser, & J. V. Tinajero (Eds.), *Teaching all the children: Strategies for developing literacy in an urban setting* (pp. 93–102). New York: Guilford.

Allington, R. L., & Walmsley, S. A. (Eds.). (1995). *No quick fix: Rethinking literacy programs in America's elementary schools.* New York: Teachers College Press.

Allington, R. L., & Woodside-Jiron, H. (1998). Decodable texts in beginning reading: Are mandates based on research? *ERS Spectrum, 16,* 3–11.

Allington, R. L., & Woodside-Jiron, H. (1999). The politics of literacy teaching: How "research" shaped educational policy. *Educational Researcher, 28*(8), 4–13.

Alvarado, A. (2000). Improving the essence of teaching. *Education Update, 42*(3), 8.

American Library Association. (1998). *Information power: Building partnerships for learning.* Chicago: Author.

Ames, R., & Ames, C. (1994). Creating a mastery-oriented schoolwide culture: A team leadership perspective. In M. Sashkin & H. Walberg (Eds.), *Educational leadership and school culture.* Berkeley, CA: McCutchan.

Ames, C., with Khoju, M., & Watkins, T. (1993, March). *Parents and schools: The impact of school-to-home communications on parents' beliefs and perceptions* (Report No. 15). Baltimore: Johns Hopkins University, Center on Families, Communities, Schools, and Children's Learning.

Anastopoulos, A. D., DuPaul, G. J., & Barkley, R. A. (1992). Stimulant medication and parent training therapies for attention deficit-hyperactivity disorder. In S. E. Shaywitz & B. A. Shaywitz (Eds.), *Attention deficit disorder comes of age.* Austin, TX: Pro-Ed Publications.

Anderson, L. W., & Pellicier, L. O. (1990). Synthesis of research on compensatory and remedial education. *Educational Leadership, 48,* 10–16.

Anderson, R. C., & Pearson, P. D. (1984). A schema-theoretic view of basic processes in reading comprehension. In P. D. Pearson (Ed.), *Handbook of reading research* (pp. 255–291). White Plains, NY: Longman.

Applebee, A. N. (1991). Literature: Whose heritage? In E. Hiebert (Ed.), *Literacy for a diverse society: Perspective, practices, and policies* (pp. 228–236). New York: Teachers College Press.

Au, K. (2005). *Multicultural issues and literacy achievement.* Mahwah, NJ: Lawrence Erlbaum.

Austin, T. (1994). *Changing the view: Student-led parent conferences.* Portsmouth, NH: Heinemann.

Backus, D. (2000). I'm always posing questions. *Journal of Staff Development, 21,* 24–25.

Bafumo, M. E. (1998). The roots of learning. *Educational Leadership, 55,* 66–69.

Barth, R. (1990). *Improving schools from within: Teachers, parents, and principals can make the difference.* San Francisco: Jossey-Bass.

Barton, P. E., & Coley, R. J. (1994). *Testing in America's schools.* Princeton, NJ: Educational Testing Service.

Bean, R. M. (2004). *The reading specialist: Leadership in the classroom, school, and community.* New York: Guilford.

Bean, R. M., Swan, A. L., & Knaub, R. (2003). Reading specialists in schools with exemplary reading programs: Functional, versatile, and prepared. *Reading Teacher, 56*(5), 446–455.

Beck, I. L., & McKeown, M. G. (1993). Why textbooks can baffle students and how to help. *Learning: A newsletter from the National Research Center on Student Learning, 1,* 2–4.

Becker, H. J., & Ravitz, J. (1999). The influence of computer and Internet use on teachers' pedagogical practices and perceptions. *Journal of Research on Computing in Education, 31,* 356–384.

Becker, J. (1992). Power corrupts. *Child and Youth Care Forum, 21,* 71–73.

Begley, S. (1998, March 30). Homework doesn't help. *Newsweek,* 12–18.

Berends, M., Bodilly, S., & Kirby, S. (2002). Looking back over a decade of whole-school reform: The experience of New American Schools. *Phi Delta Kappan, 84*(2), 168–175.

Berliner, D. C. (2005, August 2). Our impoverished view of educational reform. *Teachers College Record.* ID number:12106. Retrieved October 31, 2005, from www.tcrecord.org

Birman, B. (1988). How to improve a successful program. *American Educator, 12,* 22–29.

Birman, B. F., Desimone, L., Porter, A. C., & Garet, M. (2000). Designing professional development that works. *Educational Leadership, 57,* 28–32.

Blue, E. V. (2003). Investigating the effectiveness of an integrated learning system on early emergent readers. *Reading Research Quarterly, 38*(2), 172–207.

Bond, G. L., & Dykstra, R. (1967). The cooperative research program in first-grade reading instruction. *Reading Research Quarterly, 2,* 5–142.

Boyer, E. L. (1995). *The Basic School: A community for learning.* Princeton, NJ: Carnegie Foundation for the Advancement of Teaching.

Bracey, G. W. (2002). *The war against America's public schools: Privatizing schools, commercializing education.* Boston: Allyn & Bacon.

Bracey, G. W. (2003). *On the death of childhood and the destruction of public schools.* Portsmouth, NH: Heinemann.

Brown, K. J., Morris, D., & Fields, M. (2005). Intervention after grade 1: Serving increased number of struggling readers effectively. *Journal of Literacy Research, 37*(1), 61–94.

Bruner, C. (1991). *Thinking collaboratively: Ten questions and answers to help policy makers improve children's services.* Washington, DC: Education and Human Services Consortium.

Buly, M. R., & Valencia, S. W. (2002). Below the bar: Profiles of students who fail state reading assessments. *Educational Evaluation and Policy Analysis, 24*(3), 219–239.

California State Department of Education. (1987). *English-language arts framework for California public schools, K–12.* Sacramento, CA: Author.

Cameron, C. E., Connor, C. M., & Morrison, F. (2005). Effects of variation in teacher organization on classroom functioning. *Journal of School Psychology, 43*, 61–85.

Canter, L. (1989). Assertive discipline: More than names on the board and marbles in the jar. *Phi Delta Kappan, 71*, 57–61.

Canter, L., & Canter, M. (1990). *Parents on your side: A comprehensive family involvement program for teachers.* Seal Beach, CA: Canter Associates.

Carlisle, J. F., Schilling, S. G., Scott, S. E., & Zeng, J. (2004). *Do fluency measures predict reading achievement? Results from the 2002–2003 school year in Michigan's Reading First schools.* (No. Technical report #1). Ann Arbor, MI: University of Michigan.

Cartwright, M. (1993). *For the children: Lessons from a visionary principal.* New York: Doubleday.

Chamot, A. U., & O'Malley, J. M. (1994). *The CALLA handbook: How to implement the cognitive academic language learning approach.* Reading, MA: Addison-Wesley.

Checkley, K. (2000). The contemporary principal: New skills for a new age. *Education Update, 42*(3), 1–8.

Christian, D., & Genesee, F. (1998). Two-way immersion. *Talking Leaves, 2*(2), 7.

Clay, M. M. (1990). The Reading Recovery programme, 1984–88: Coverage, outcomes and Education Board district figures. *New Zealand Journal of Educational Studies, 25*, 61–70.

Clay, M. M. (1991). Reading Recovery Surprises. In D. Deford, C. Lyons, & G. S. Pinnell (Eds.), *Bridges to literacy: Learning from reading recovery* (pp. 55–75). Portsmouth, NH: Heinemann.

Clay, M. M. (1993). *Observation survey of early literacy achievement.* Portsmouth, NH: Heinemann.

Cohen, D. K., & Spillane, J. P. (1992). Policy and practice: The relations between governance and instruction. In G. Grant (Ed.), *Review of research in education* (Vol. 18, pp. 3–49). Washington, DC: American Educational Research Association.

Coles, G. (1987). *The learning mystique: A critical look at learning disabilities.* New York: Pantheon.

Coley, R., & Goertz, M. (1990). *Educational standards in the 50 states: 1990* (Research Report No. 90–15). Princeton, NJ: Educational Testing Service.

Combs, A. W., Miser, A. B., & Whitaker, K. S. (1998). *On becoming a school leader: A person-centered challenge.* Alexandria, VA: Association for Supervision and Curriculum Development.

Comer, J. P. (1988). Educating poor minority children. *Scientific American, 259*, 42–48.

Comer, J. P., Haynes, N., Joyner, E., & Ben Avie, M. (1996). *Rallying the whole village: The Comer process for reforming education.* New York: Teachers College Press.

Commeyras, M., & DeGroff, L. (1998). Literacy professional's perspectives on professional development and pedagogy: A national survey. *Reading Research Quarterly, 33*, 434–473.

Compton-Lilly, C. (2000). "Staying on children": Challenging stereotypes about urban parents. *Language Arts, 77*, 420–427.

Cooley, W. (1993). The difficulty of the educational task: Implications for comparing student achievement in states, school districts, and schools. *ERS Spectrum, 11*, 27–31.

Cooper, H., Nye, B., Charlton, K., Lindsay, J., & Greathouse, S. (1996). The effects of summer vacation on achievement test scores: A narrative and meta-analytic review. *Review of Educational Research, 66*, 227–268.

Cuban, L. (1990). Reforming again, again, and again. *Educational Researcher, 19*, 3–13.

Cummins, J. (1994). The acquisition of English as a second language. In K. Spangenberg-Urbschat & R. Pritchard (Eds.), *Kids come in all languages: Reading instruction for ESL students* (pp. 36–63). Newark, DE: International Reading Association.

Cunningham, J. W., Erickson, K. A., Spadorcia, S. A., Koppenhaver, D. A., Cunningham, P. M., Yoder, D. E., & McKenna, M. C. (1999). Assessing decoding from an onset-rime perspective. *Journal of Literacy Research, 31*, 391–414.

Cunningham, P. (1982). What would make workbooks worthwhile? In R. Anderson, J. Osborn, & R. Tierney (Eds.), *Learning to read in American schools: Basal readers and content texts* (pp. 113–120). Hillsdale, NJ: Lawrence Erlbaum Associates.

Cunningham, P. M. (2004). *Phonics they use* (4th ed.). Boston: Allyn & Bacon.

Cunningham, P. M., & Allington, R. L. (2007). *Classrooms that work: They can all read and write* (4th ed.). Boston: Allyn & Bacon.

Cunningham, P. M., & Cunningham, J. W. (2002). What we know about how to teach phonics. In A. Farstrup & S. J. Samuels (Eds.), *What research has to say about reading instruction* (3rd ed., pp. 87–109). Newark, DE: International Reading Association.

Cunningham, P. M., Hall, D. P., & Defee, M. (1991). Non-ability-grouped, multi-level instruction: A year in a first grade classroom. *Reading Teacher, 44,* 566–571.

Cushman, K. (1992, September). The essential school principal: A changing role in a changing school. *Horace: Newsletter of the Essential Schools, 9,* 1–8.

D'Agostino, J. V., & Murphy, J. A. (2004). A meta-analysis of Reading Recovery in United States schools. *Educational Evaluation and Policy Analysis, 26*(1), 23–38.

Daneman, M. (1991). Individual differences in reading skills. In R. Barr, M. L. Kamil, P. B. Mosenthal, & P. D. Pearson (Eds.), *Handbook of reading research.* (Vol. 2, pp. 512–538). White Plains, NY: Longman.

Darling-Hammond, L. (1997). *The right to learn: A blueprint for creating schools that work.* San Francisco: Jossey-Bass.

Darling-Hammond, L. (1999). *Teacher quality and student achievement: A review of state policy evidence.* Seattle: University of Washington, Center for Teaching Policy. Retrieved from www.ctpweb.org

Day, J. P. (2001). How I became an exemplary teacher (although I'm still learning just like anyone else). In M. Pressley, R. Allington, R. Wharton-McDonald, C. Block, & L. Morrow (Eds.), *Learning to read: Lessons from exemplary first-grade classrooms.* New York: Guilford.

DeFina, A. (1992). *Portfolio assessment: Getting started.* New York: Scholastic.

Delpit, L. (1995). *Other people's children: Cultural conflict in the classroom.* New York: Free Press.

Denham, C., & Lieberman, A. (Eds.). (1980). *Time to learn.* Washington, DC: National Institute of Education.

Denton, D. R. (2001). *Finding alternatives to failure: Can states end social promotion and reduce retention rates?* Atlanta: Southern Regional Education Board. Retrieved from www.sreb.org

Donahue, P. L., Voelkl, K. E., Campbell, J., & Mazzeo, J. (1999). *NAEP reading 1998: Reading report card for the nation and the states.* Washington, DC: U.S. Department of Education, Office of Educational Research and Improvement.

Donoahue, Z., Van Tassell, M., & Patterson, L. (1996). *Research in the classroom.* Newark, DE: International Reading Association.

Dowd, T., & Tierney, J. (1992). *Teaching social skills to youth.* Boys Town, NE: Boys Town Press.

Downing, J. E., Ryndak, D. L., & Clark, D. (2000). Paraeducators in inclusive classrooms: Their own perceptions. *Remedial and Special Education, 21*(3), 171–181.

Dreikurs, R., Grunwald, B. B., & Pepper, F. C. (1982). *Maintaining sanity in the classroom: Classroom management techniques.* New York: Harper & Row.

Duffy, G. G. (1993). Rethinking strategy instruction: Four teachers' development and their low achievers' understandings. *Elementary School Journal, 93,* 231–247.

Duffy, G. G. (1997). Powerful models or powerful teachers? An argument for teacher-as-entrepreneur. In S. Stahl & D. Hayes (Eds.), *Instructional models in reading* (pp. 351–365). Mahwah, NJ: Erlbaum.

Duffy, G. G. (2001). The case for direct explanation of strategies. In M. Pressley & K. C. Block (Eds.), *Comprehension instruction.* New York: Guilford.

Duffy, G. G. (2003). *Explaining reading: A resource for teaching concepts, skills, and strategies.* New York: Guilford.

Duffy, G. G., & Hoffman, J. V. (1999). In pursuit of an illusion: The search for a perfect method. *Reading Teacher, 53,* 10–16.

Duke, N. K. (2000). For the rich it's richer: Print experiences and environments offered to children in very low- and very high-socioeconomic status first grade classrooms. *Reading Research Quarterly, 37,* 441–478.

Duthie, C. (1996). *True stories: Nonfiction in the primary classroom.* York, ME: Stenhouse.

Echevarria, J., Vogt, M. E., & Short, D. (2004). *Making content comprehensible for English learners: The SIOP model.* New York: Pearson/Allyn & Bacon.

Edmonds, R. (1981). Making public schools effective. *Social Policy, 12,* 56–61.

Education Research Service. (1991). *Culturally sensitive instruction and student learning.* Arlington, VA: Author.

Educational Testing Service. (1991). *ETS Developments, 37,* 6–7.

Edwards, P. A. (1989). Supporting lower SES mothers' attempts to provide scaffolding for books. In J. B. Allen & J. Mason (Eds.), *Risk makers, risk takers, risk breakers: Reducing the risks for young literacy learners* (pp. 222–248). Portsmouth, NH: Heinemann.

Elley, W. B., & Mangubhai, F. (1983). The impact of reading on second language learning. *Reading Research Quarterly, 10,* 53–67.

Elmore, R. F., Peterson, P. L., & McCarthy, S. J. (1996). *Restructuring in the classroom: Teaching, learning, and school organization.* San Francisco: Jossey-Bass.

Entwisle, D. R., Alexander, K. L., & Olson, L. S. (1997). *Children, schools, and inequality.* Boulder, CO: Westview Press.

Epps, S., & Tindal, G. (1987). The effectiveness of differential programming in serving students with mild handicaps: Placement options and instructional programming. In M. Wang, M. Reynolds, & H. Walberg (Eds.), *Handbook of special education: Research and practice* (pp. 213–248). New York: Pergamon.

Epstein, D. (1998). *Failing boys: Issues in gender and achievement.* London: Open University Press.

Farr, R. (1992). Putting it all together: Solving the reading assessment puzzle. *Reading Teacher, 46,* 26–37.

Fielding, L. G., & Pearson, P. D. (1994). Reading comprehension: What works. *Educational Leadership, 51,* 63–68.

Fielding, L. G., Wilson, P. T., & Anderson, R. C. (1986). A new focus on free reading: The role of trade books in reading instruction. In T. E. Raphael (Ed.), *The contexts of school-based literacy* (pp. 149–160). New York: Random House.

Fischer, M. (1990). *Fiscal accountability in Milwaukee public elementary schools: Where does the money go?* Milwaukee: Wisconsin Policy Research Institute.

Fisher, C. W., & Berliner, D. C. (1985). *Perspectives on instructional time.* New York: Longman.

Foorman, B. R., & Torgeson, J. (2001). Critical elements of classroom and small-group instruction promote reading success in all children. *Learning Disabilities Research and Practice, 16,* 4.

Fountas, I. C., & Pinnell, G. S. (1999). *Matching books to readers: Using leveled books in guided reading, K–3.* Portsmouth, NH: Heinemann.

Fractor, J. S., Woodruff, M. C., Martinez, M. G., & Teale, W. H. (1993). Let's not miss opportunities to promote voluntary reading: Classroom libraries in the elementary school. *Reading Teacher, 46,* 476–484.

Fu, D. (2003). *An island of English: Teaching ESL in Chinatown.* Portsmouth, NH: Heinemann.

Fullan, M. (1991). *The new meaning of educational change.* New York: Teachers College Press.

Fullan, M., & Hargreaves, A. (1996). *What's worth fighting for in your school?* New York: Teachers College Press.

Gambrell, L., Wilson, R., & Gannt, W. (1981). Classroom observations of task-attending behaviors of good and poor readers. *Journal of Educational Research, 74,* 400–404.

Gamoran, A. (1986). Instructional and institutional effect of ability grouping. *Sociology of Education, 59,* 185–198.

Gardner, H. (1993). *Multiple intelligences: The theory in practice.* New York: Basic Books.

Gelzheiser, L. M., Meyers, J., & Pruzek, R. M. (1992). Effects of pull-in and pull-out approaches to reading instruction for special education and remedial reading students. *Journal of Educational and Psychological Consultation, 3,* 133–149.

General Accounting Office. (1994). *Elementary school children: Many change schools frequently, harming their education* (Report 94-45). Washington, DC: Health, Education, and Human Services Division.

George, P. S. (1988). *What's the truth about tracking and ability grouping really?* Gainesville, FL: Teacher Education Resources.

Gerber, S. B., Finn, J. D., Achilles, C. M., & Boyd-Zaharias, J. (2001). Teacher aides and students' academic achievement. *Educational Evaluation and Policy Analysis, 23*(2), 123–143.

Glasser, W. (1986). *Control theory in the classroom.* New York: HarperCollins.

Glasser, W. (1990). *The quality school: Managing students without coercion.* New York: HarperCollins.

Goodlad, J. I., & Lovitt, T. C. (Eds.). (1993). *Integrating general and special education.* New York: Merrill.

Goswami, U., & Bryant, P. (1990). *Phonological skills and learning to read.* East Sussex, UK: Erlbaum.

Greene, B. (1981). *Get on out of here, Philip Hall.* New York: Dial Press.

Grissmer, D. W., Kirby, S. N., Berends, M., & Williamson, S. (1994). *Student achievement and the changing American family.* Santa Monica, CA: RAND, Institute on Education and Training.

Guice, S., Allington, R. L., Johnston, P., Baker, K., & Michelson, N. (1996). Access?: Books, children, and literature-based curriculum in schools. *The New Advocate, 9,* 197–207.

Guthrie, J. T. (2002). Preparing students for high-stakes test taking in reading. In A. Farstrup and S. J. Samuels, (Eds.), *What research has to say about reading instruction* (pp. 370–391). Newark, DE: International Reading Association.

Guthrie, J. T. (2004). Teaching for literacy engagement. *Journal of Literacy Research, 36*(1), 1–28.

Guthrie, J. T., & Anderson, E. (1999). Engagement in reading: Processes of motivated, strategic, knowledgeable, social readers. In J. T. Guthrie & D. Alvermann (Eds.), *Engaged reading: Processes, practices, and policy implications* (pp. 17–45). New York: Teachers College.

Guthrie, J. T., & Humenick, N. M. (2004). Motivating students to read: Evidence for classroom practices that increase motivation and achievement. In P. McCardle & V. Chhabra (Eds.), *The voice of evidence in reading research* (pp. 329–354). Baltimore: Paul Brookes Publishing.

Haladyna, T. H., Nolan, S. B., & Haas, N. S. (1991). Raising standardized achievement test scores and the origins of test score pollution. *Educational Researcher, 20,* 2–7.

Hall, D., Prevatte, C., & Cunningham, P. (1995). Eliminating ability grouping and reducing failure in the primary grades. In R. L. Allington & S. A. Walmsley (Eds.), *No quick fix: Rethinking literacy programs in America's elementary schools.* New York: Teachers College Press.

Hammill, D., & Swanson, L. (in press). The NRP's analysis of phonics instruction: Another point of view. *Elementary School Journal.*

Hargis, C. H. (2003). *Grades and grading practices: Obstacles to improving education and to helping at-risk students.* Springfield, IL: Charles C. Thomas.

Harp, L. (1993, March 17). Study details how districts, schools divvy up money. *Education Week, 22,* 1, 21.

Harvey, S., & Goudvis, A. (2000). *Strategies that work: Teaching comprehension to enhance understanding.* York, ME: Stenhouse.

Harwayne, S. (1999). *Going public: Priorities and practice at the Manhattan New School.* Portsmouth, NH: Heinemann.

Hasselriis, P. (1982). IEPs and a whole language model of language arts. *Topics in Learning and Learning Disabilities, 14,* 17–21.

Heath, S. B. (1983). *Ways with words.* New York: Cambridge University Press.

Henker, B., & Whalen, C. K. (1989). Hyperactivity and attention deficits. *American Psychologist, 78,* 216–223.

Herman, R., & Stringfield, S. (1997). *Ten promising programs for educating all children: Evidence of impact.* Arlington, VA: Educational Research Service.

Herrick, S. C., & Epstein, J. L. (1991). *Improving school and family partnerships in urban elementary schools: Reading activity packets and newsletters.* Baltimore: Johns Hopkins University, Center for Disadvantaged Students.

Herzog, M. (Ed.). (1997). *Inside Learning Network schools.* Katonah, NY: Richard C. Owen.

Heubert, J. P., & Hauser, R. M. (1999). *High stakes: Testing for tracking, promotion and graduation.* Washington, DC: National Academy Press.

Hiebert, E. H. (1999). Text matters in learning to read. *Reading Teacher, 52,* 552–556.

Hiebert, E. H., & Taylor, B. (1994). *Getting reading right from the start: Effective early literacy interventions.* Boston: Allyn & Bacon.

Hillocks, G. (2002). *The testing trap: How state writing assessments control learning.* New York: Teachers College Press.

Hinds, M. D. (2000). Violent kids: Can we solve the problem? *Social Education, 64,* 225–231.

Hirsh, S., & Sparks, D. (1999, November). Helping teachers grow: What your school board should know about standards-based professional development. *American School Board Journal, 43,* 37–40.

Hodgkinson, H. (1993). American education: The good, the bad, and the task. *Phi Delta Kappan, 74,* 619–623.

Hoffman, J. V., McCarthy, S. J., Elliott, B., Bayles, D., Price, D., Ferree, A., & Abbott, J. (1998). The literature-based basals in first-grade classrooms: Savior, Satan, or same-old, same-old? *Reading Research Quarterly, 33,* 168–197.

Hoffman, J. V., Roser, N. L., & Battle, J. (1993). Reading aloud in classrooms: From the modal to a model. *Reading Teacher, 46,* 496–503.

Holloway, J. H. (2000). The promise and pitfalls of site-based management. *Educational Leadership, 57*(7), 81–82.

Hopfenberg, W. S., & Levin, H. M. (1993). *The accelerated schools: Resource guide.* San Francisco: Jossey-Bass.

Hyde, A. A. (1992). Developing a willingness to change. In W. T. Pink & A. A. Hyde (Eds.), *Effective staff development for school change* (pp. 171–190). Norwood, NJ: Ablex.

Jachym, N., Allington, R. L., & Broikou, K. A. (1989). Estimating the cost of seatwork. *Reading Teacher, 43,* 30–37.

Jacobson, L. (1999, August/September). Three's company: Kids prove they have a role at the parent–teacher conference. *Teacher Magazine, 23.*

Jimerson, S. R., & Kaufman, A. M. (2003). Reading, writing, and retention: A primer on grade retention. *Reading Teacher, 56*(7), 622–635.

Johnson, D., & Johnson, D. (1993). *Teaching students to be peacemakers.* Edina, MN: Interaction Books.

Johnston, F. R., Invernizzi, M., & Juel, C. (1998). *Book buddies: Guidelines for volunteer tutors of emergent and early readers.* New York: Guilford.

Johnston, P. A. (2005). Literacy assessment and the future. *Reading Teacher, 58*(7), 684–686.

Johnston, P. H. (1992). Nontechnical assessment. *Reading Teacher, 46,* 60–62.

Johnston, P. H. (1998). The consequences of the use of standardized tests. In S. Murphy (Ed.), *Fragile evidence: A critique of reading assessments* (pp. 89–101). Mahwah, NJ: Erlbaum.

Johnston, P. H. (1999). Unpacking literate achievement. In J. Gaffney & B. Askew (Eds.), *Stirring the waters: A tribute to Marie Clay* (pp. 27–46). Portsmouth, NH: Heinemann.

Johnston, P. H. (2000). *Running records.* York, ME: Stenhouse.

Johnston, P. H. (2004). *Choice words: How our language affects children's learning.* York, ME: Stenhouse.

Johnston, P. H., & Allington, R. L. (1991). Remediation. In R. Barr, M. L. Kamil, P. Mosenthal, & P. D. Pearson (Eds.), *Handbook of Reading Research* (Vol. 2, pp. 984–1012). New York: Longman.

Johnston, P. H., Allington, R. L., & Afflerbach, P. (1985). The congruence of classroom and remedial reading instruction. *Elementary School Journal, 85,* 465–478.

Johnston, P., Allington, R. L., Guice, S., & Brooks, G. W. (1998). Small change: A multi-level study of the implementation of literature-based instruction. *Peabody Journal of Education, 73,* 81–103.

Joyce, B., & Showers, B. (2002). *Student achievement through staff development* (3rd ed.). Alexandria, VA: Association for Curriculum Supervision and Development.

Juel, C., Biancarosa, G., Coker, D., & Deffes, R. (2003). Walking with Rosie: A cautionary tale of early reading instruction. *Educational Leadership, 60*(7), 12–18.

Kahn, B. H. (1999). *Web-based instruction.* Englewood Cliffs, NJ: Educational Technology.

Keene, E. O. (2002). From good to memorable: Characteristics of highly effective comprehension teaching. In C. C. Block, L. Gambrell, & M. Pressley (Eds.), *Improving comprehension instruction: Rethinking research, theory, and classroom practice* (pp. 80–105). San Francisco: Jossey Bass.

Keene, E. O., & Zimmerman, S. (1997). *Mosaic of thought: Teaching comprehension in a reader's workshop.* Portsmouth, NH: Heinemann.

Killion, J., & Harrison, C. (1997). The multiple roles of staff developers. *Journal of Staff Development, 18,* 34–44.

Kim, J. (2004). Summer reading and the ethnic achievement gap. *Journal of Education of Students at Risk, 9*(2), 169–189.

Knapp, M. S. (1995). *Teaching for meaning in high-poverty classrooms.* New York: Teachers College Press.

Knight, S., & Stallings, J. (1995). Implementing the Accelerated School model in an urban elementary school. In R. L. Allington & S. A. Walmsley (Eds.), *No quick fix: Rethinking literacy programs in America's elementary schools* (pp. 236–252). New York: Teachers College Press.

Kohn, A. (1999). *Punished by rewards: The trouble with gold stars, incentive plans, A's, praise, and other incentives.* Boston: Houghton Mifflin.

Koretz, D., Stecher, B., Klein, S., & McCaffrey, D. (1994). The Vermont portfolio assessment program: Findings and implications. *Educational Measurement, 13,* 5–16.

Kozol, J. (1991). *Savage inequalities: Children in America's schools.* New York: Crown.

Krauss, Ruth. (1945). *The carrot seed.* New York: Harper.

Kuhs, T. M., Johnson, R. C., Agruso, S. A., & Monrad, D. M. (2001). *Put to the test: Tools and techniques for classroom assessment.* Portsmouth, NH: Heinemann.

Kuykendall, C. (1992). *From rage to hope: Strategies for reclaiming black and Hispanic students.* Bloomington, IN: National Educational Service.

Ladson-Billings, G. (1994). *The dreamkeepers: Successful teachers of African-American children.* San Francisco: Jossey-Bass.

Lamme, L. (1976). Are reading habits and abilities related? *Reading Teacher, 30,* 21–27.

Langer, J. A., & Allington, R. L. (1992). Curriculum research in writing and reading. In P. W. Jackson (Ed.), *Handbook of research on curriculum* (pp. 687–725). New York: Macmillan.

Lareau, A. (1989). *Home advantage: Social class and parental intervention in elementary education.* Philadelphia: Falmer.

Leinhardt, G., Zigmond, N., & Cooley, W. (1981). Reading instruction and its effects. *American Educational Research Journal, 18,* 343–361.

Leithwood, K. A. (1990). The principal's role in teacher development. In B. Joyce (Ed.), *Changing school culture through staff development* (pp. 71–88). Alexandria, VA: Association for Supervision and Curriculum Development.

Leithwood, K., & Jantzi, D. (1999). Transformational school leadership effects: A replication. *School Effectiveness and School Improvement, 10,* 451–479.

LeTendre, M. J. (1991). The continuing evolution of a federal role in compensatory education. *Educational Evaluation and Policy Analysis, 13,* 328–344.

Levin, H. M. (1987). Accelerated Schools for disadvantaged students. *Educational Leadership, 44,* 19–21.

Linn, R. L. (2000). Assessments and accountability. *Educational Researcher, 29*(2), 4–16.

Little, J. W. (1993). Teachers' professional development in a climate of educational reform. *Educational Evaluation and Policy Analysis, 15,* 129–151.

Lloyd-Jones, R. (1977). Primary trait scoring. In C. R. Cooper & L. Odell (Eds.), *Evaluating writing.* Urbana, IL: National Council of Teachers of English.

Lyon, G. R. (1996). Learning disabilities. *The Future of Children, 6*(1), 54–76.

Mace, A. (1997). Organizing the instructional resource room. In M. Herzog (Ed.), *Inside Learning Network schools* (pp. 275–288). Katonah, NY: Richard C. Owen.

Mathes, P. G., Denton, C. A., Fletcher, J. M., Anthony, J. L., Francis, D. J., & Schatschneider, C. (2005). The effects of theoretically different instruction and student characteristics on the skills of struggling readers. *Reading Research Quarterly, 40*(2), 148–182.

McGill-Franzen, A. (1987). Failure to learn to read: Formulating a policy problem. *Reading Research Quarterly, 22*(3), 475–490.

McGill-Franzen, A. (1992). Early literacy: What does "developmentally appropriate" mean? *Reading Teacher, 46,* 56–58.

McGill-Franzen, A. (1993). "I could read the words!": Selecting good books for inexperienced readers. *Reading Teacher, 46,* 424–426.

McGill-Franzen, A. (1994). Compensatory and special education: Is there accountability for learning and belief in children's potential? In E. H. Hiebert & B. M. Taylor (Eds.), *Getting reading right from the start: Effective early literacy interventions.* Boston: Allyn & Bacon.

McGill-Franzen, A. (2000). Policy and instruction: What is the relationship? In R. Barr, M. Kamil, P. Mosenthal, & P. D. Pearson (Eds.), *Handbook of reading research* (Vol. 3, pp. 891–908). Mahwah, NJ: Erlbaum.

McGill-Franzen, A. (2005). In the press to scale up, what is at risk? *Reading Research Quarterly, 40*(3), 8–12.

McGill-Franzen, A. (2006). *Kindergarten literacy.* New York: Scholastic.

McGill-Franzen, A., & Allington, R. L. (1992). Flunk 'em or get them classified: The contamination of primary grade accountability data. *Educational Researcher, 21,* 19–22.

McGill-Franzen, A., & Allington, R. L. (1993, December 13). What are they to read? Not all kids, Mr. Riley, have easy access to books. *Education Week,* 26.

McGill-Franzen, A., Allington, R. L., Yokoi, L., & Brooks, G. (1999). Putting books in the room seems necessary but not sufficient. *Journal of Educational Research, 93,* 67–74.

McGill-Franzen, A., & Goatley, V. (2001). Title I and special education: Support for children who struggle to learn to read. In S. Neuman & D. Dickinson (Eds.), *Handbook of early literacy research* (pp. 471–483). New York: Guilford.

McGill-Franzen, A. M., Lanford, C., & Adams, E. (2002). Learning to be literate: A comparison of five urban early childhood programs. *Journal of Educational Psychology, 94*(3), 443–464.

McGill-Franzen, A., & Rogers, R. (2000). Transforming family knowledge to academic curriculum. Paper submitted for publication.

McGill-Franzen, A., Ward, N., Goatley, V., & Machado, V. (2002). Teachers' use of new standards, frameworks, and assessments: Local cases of NYS elementary grade teachers. *Reading Research and Instruction, 41*(2), 127–148.

McGill-Franzen, A., Zmach, C., Solic, K., & Love-Zeig, J. (in press). The confluence of two policy mandates: Core reading programs and 3rd grade retention. *Elementary School Journal.*

McLaughlin, M. W., & Yee, S. M. (1988). School as a place to have a career. In A. Lieberman (Ed.), *Building a professional culture in schools* (pp. 23–44). New York: Teachers College Press.

McNeil, L. M. (2000). *Contradictions of school reform: Educational costs of standardized testing.* New York: Routledge.

McQuillan, J. (1998). *The literacy crisis: False claims, real solutions.* Portsmouth, NH: Heinemann.

Mehan, H., Hartweck, A., & Meihls, J. L. (1986). *Handicapping the handicapped.* Stanford, CA: Stanford University Press.

Meisels, S. J. (1993). Doing harm by doing good: Iatrogenic effects of early childhood enrollment and promotion policies. *Early Childhood Research Quarterly, 7,* 155–174.

Mergendoller, J., Bellsimo, Y., & Horan, C. (1990). *Kindergarten holding out: The role of school characteristics, family background, and parental perceptions.* Novato, CA: Beryl Buck Institute for Education.

Michelson, N. (1993). *Wanderers: Selecting books for independent reading.* Paper presented at the National Reading Conference, Charleston, SC.

Millsap, M. A., Moss, M., & Gamse, B. (1993). *Chapter 1 implementation study: Final report.* Washington, DC: U.S. Department of Education, Office of Policy and Planning.

Moll, L. B., & Greenberg, J. C. (1990). Creating zones of possibilities: Combining social contexts for instruction. In L. C. Moll (Ed.), *Vygotsky and education: Instructional implications and applications of sociohistorical psychology* (pp. 319–348). New York: Cambridge University Press.

Morphett, M., & Washburne, C. (1931). When should children begin to read? *Elementary School Journal, 31,* 496–503.

Morrow, L. M. (1991). Promoting voluntary reading. In J. Flood, J. Jensen, D. Lapp, & J. Squire (Eds.), *Handbook of research on teaching the English language arts* (pp. 681–690). New York: Macmillan.

Munro, J. K. (2001). *Responses to a take-home reading program.* Unpublshed dissertation, University of Albany, SUNY.

Murphy, S. (1998). *Fragile evidence: A critique of reading assessments.* Mahwah, NJ: Erlbaum.

National Association for the Education of Young Children. (1998). *Learning to read and write: Developmentally appropriate practices for young children.* Washington, DC: Author.

National Center for Educational Statistics. (2004). *Who teaches reading in public elementary schools? The assignments and educational preparation of reading teachers.* Washington, DC: U.S. Department of Education, Institute of Education Sciences.

National Commission on Excellence in Education. (1983). *A nation at risk.* Washington, DC: Author.

National Commission on Teaching and America's Future. (1997). *Doing what matters most: Investing in quality teaching.* New York: Author.

National Education Commission on Time and Learning. (2000). *Prisoners of time: Too much to teach, not enough time to teach it.* Portland, ME: Stenhouse.

National Reading Panel. (2000). *Teaching children to read: An evidence-based assessment of the scientific research literature on reading and its implications for reading instruction.* Retrieved June 16, 2000, from www.nationalreadingpanel.org

Neuman, S., & Celano, D. (2001). Access to print in low-income and middle-income communities. *Reading Research Quarterly, 36,* 8–26.

Nicholson, T., & Tan, A. (1999). Proficient word identification for comprehension. In G. B. Thompson & T. Nicholson (Eds.), *Learning to read: Beyond phonics and whole language* (pp. 150–173). New York: Teachers College Press.

Nye, B., Konstantopoulos, S., & Hedges, L. (2004). How large are teacher effects? *Educational Evaluation and Policy Analysis, 26,* 237–257.

Olson, L. (1998, April 15). An 'A' or 'D': State rankings differ widely. *Education Week,* 1, 18.

Palestis, E. (1993). Prize-winning family involvement in New Jersey. *Education Digest, 58,* 14–17.

Paratore, J. H., Gigliana, M., & Krol-Sinclair (1999). *What should we expect from family literacy?* Newark, DE: International Reading Association.

Paterson, K. (1998). *The spying heart.* New York: Lodestar Books.

Payzant, T. W. (1994). Comprehensive school services in San Diego. In C. E. Finn & H. Walberg (Eds.), *Radical education reforms.* Berkeley, CA: McCutchan.

Pearson, P. D. (1993). Teaching and learning to read: A research perspective. *Language Arts, 70,* 502–511.

Perie, M., Grigg, W. S., & Donahue, P. L. (2005). *The nation's report card* (No. 2006–451). Washington, DC: National Center for Educational Statistics. Retrieved from http://nces.ed.gov/nationsreportcard/pdf/main2005/2006451.pdf

Popham, J. (2001). *The truth about testing: An educator's call to action.* Alexandria, VA: Association for Supervision and Curriculum Development.

Power, B. M. (1996). *Taking note: Improving your observational notetaking.* York, ME: Stenhouse.

Pressley, M. (2002). Improving comprehension instruction: A path for the future. In C. C. Block, L. Gambrell, & M. Pressley (Eds.), *Improving comprehension instruction: Rethinking research, theory, and classroom practice* (pp. 385–399). San Francisco: Jossey-Bass.

Pressley, M. (2003). A few things reading educators should know about instructional experiments. *Reading Teacher, 57*(1), 64–71.

Pressley, M. (2006). *Reading instruction that works: The case for balanced teaching* (3rd ed.). New York: Guilford.

Pressley, M., Allington, R. L., Wharton-McDonald, R., Collins-Block, C., & Morrow, L. (2001). *Learning to read: Lessons from exemplary first-grade classrooms.* New York: Guilford.

Pressley, M., Hilden, K., & Shankland, R. (2005). *An evaluation of end-of-grade 3 Dynamic Indicators of Basic Early Literacy Skills (DIBELS): Speed reading without comprehension, predicting little.* East Lansing, MI: Literacy Achievement Research Center, Michigan State University.

Pressley, M., Wood, E., & Woloshyn, V. E. (1992). Encouraging mindful use of prior knowledge: Attempting to construct explanatory answers facilitates learning. *Educational Psychologist, 27,* 91–109.

Puma, M. J., Karweit, N., et al. (1997). *Prospects: Final report on student outcomes.* Washington, DC: U.S. Department of Education, Office of Planning and Evaluation Services.

Purcell-Gates, V. (1995). *Other people's words: The cycle of low literacy.* Cambridge, MA: Harvard University Press.

Purdie, N., Hattie, J., & Carroll, A. (2002). A review of the research on interventions for attention deficit disorder: What works best? *Review of Educational Research, 72*(1), 61–99.

Reid, M. K., & Borkowski, J. G. (1987). Causal attributions of hyperactive children: Implications for teaching strategies and self-control. *Journal of Educational Psychology, 79,* 296–307.

Render, G. F., Padilla, J. M., & Kvank, H. M. (1989). Assertive discipline: A critical review and analysis. *Teachers College Record, 90,* 605–630.

Richardson, V. (1990). Significant and worthwhile change in teaching practice. *Educational Researcher, 19,* 10–18.

Rigg, P. (1989). Language experience approach: Reading naturally. In P. Rigg & V. G. Allen (Eds.), *When they don't all speak English: Integrating the ESL student into the regular classroom.* Urbana, IL: National Council of Teachers of English.

Rogers, R. (2003). *A critical discourse analysis of family literacy practices: Power in and out of print.* Mahwah, NJ: Lawrence Erlbaum Associates.

Rosenholtz, S. (1989). *Teachers' workplace: The social organization of schools.* New York: Longman.

Roth, J., Brooks-Dunn, J., Linver, M., & Hofferth, S. (2002). What happened during the school day? Time diaries from a national sample of elementary school teachers. *Teachers College Record.* Retrieved from www.tcrecord.org/Content.asp?Content ID=11018

Rouse, C. E., & Krueger, A. B. (2004). Putting computerized instruction to the test: A randomized evaluation of a "scientifically-based" reading program. *Economics of Education Review, 23*(4), 323–338.

Rowan, B. (1990). Commitment and control: Alternative strategies for the organizational design of schools. In C. B. Cazden (Ed.), *Review of research in education* (pp. 353–389). Washington, DC: American Educational Research Association.

Rowan, B., & Guthrie, L. F. (1989). The quality of Chapter I instruction: Results from a study of twenty-four schools. In R. E. Slavin, N. Karweit, & N. Madden (Eds.), *Effective programs for students at risk* (pp. 195–219). Boston: Allyn & Bacon.

Sanders, W. L. (1998, December). Value-added assessment. *School Administrator, 55,* 101–113.

Schmitt, M. C., Askew, B. J., et al. (2005). *Changing futures: The influence of Reading Recovery in the United States.* Worthington, OH: Reading Recovery Council of North America.

Schrag, P., & Divoky, D. (1975). *The myth of the hyperactive child.* New York: Pantheon.

Sergiovanni, T. J. (1991). *The principalship: A reflective practice perspective.* Boston: Allyn & Bacon.

Sergiovanni, T. J. (2000). *The life world of leadership: Creating culture, community, and personal meaning in our schools.* San Francisco: Jossey-Bass.

Sharpe, M. N., York, J. L., & Knight, J. (1994). Effects of inclusion on the academic performance of classmates without disabilities: A preliminary study. *Remedial and Special Education, 15,* 281–287.

Shepard, L. A., & Smith, M. L. (1989). *Flunking grades: Research and policies on retention.* Philadelphia: Falmer.

Shepard, L. A., & Smith, M. L. (1990). Synthesis of research on grade retention. *Educational Leadership, 47,* 84–88.

Sizer, T. (1988). *Horace's compromise: The dilemma of the American high school.* Boston: Houghton Mifflin.

Slavin, R. E., Madden, N. A., Dolan, I. J., & Wasik, B. A. (1996). *Every child, every school: Success for all.* Thousand Oaks, CA: Corwin.

Smith, C., Constantino, R., & Krashen, S. (1997). Differences in print environment: Children in Beverly Hills, Compton and Watts. *Emergency Librarian, 24*(4), 8–9.

Smith, L., & Ellett, R. (2000). *Reconceptualizing school leadership.* Paper presented at the American Educational Research Association, New Orleans.

Smith, M. L. (2004). *Political spectacle and the fate of American schools.* New York: Routledge/Falmer.

Smith, M. W., & Wilhelm, J. D. (2002). *Reading don't fix no Chevy's: Literacy in the lives of young men.* Portsmouth, NH: Heinemann.

Smith, R. C., & Lincoln, C. A. (1988). *America's shame, America's hope: Twelve million youth at risk.* (Report prepared for the Charles Stewart Mott Foundation.) Chapel Hill, NC: MDC.

Snider, V. E., Busch, T., et al. (2003). Teacher knowledge of stimulant medication and ADHD. *Remedial and Special Education, 24*(1), 46–56.

Snow, C., Barnes, W., Chandler, J., Goodman, I., & Hemphill, C. (1990). *Unfulfilled expectations: Home and school influences on literacy.* Cambridge: Harvard University Press.

Snow, C. E., Burns, M. S., & Griffin, P. (1998). *Preventing reading difficulties in young children: A report of the National Research Council.* Washington, DC: National Academy Press.

Spear-Swerling, L., & Sternberg, R. J. (1996). *Off track: When poor readers become "learning disabled."* Boulder, CO: Westview Press.

Spivey, N. N. (1996). *The constructivist metaphor: Reading, writing, and the making of meaning.* New York: Academic Press.

Stahl, S. A., Duffy-Hester, A., & Stahl, K. A. D. (1998). Everything you wanted to know about phonics (but were afraid to ask). *Reading Research Quarterly, 33,* 338–355.

Stanovich, K. E. (2000). *Progress in understanding reading: Scientific foundations and new frontiers.* New York: Guilford.

Stiggins, R. J., Frisbie, D. A., & Griswold, P. (1989). Inside high school grading practices: Building a research agenda. *Educational Measurement: Issues and Practice, 26,* 5–14.

Stigler, J. W., & Hiebert, J. (1999). *The teaching gap.* New York: Free Press.

Stipek, D. (2004). Teaching practices in kindergarten and first grade: Different strokes for different folks. *Early Childhood Research Quarterly, 19,* 548–568.

Stoddard, A. J. (1957). *Schools for tomorrow: An educator's blueprint.* New York: Fund for the Advancement of Education.

Strickland, D. S., & Walmsley, S. A. (1994). *School book clubs and literacy development: A descriptive study.* Albany, NY: National Research Center in Literature

Teaching and Learning. Retrieved from http://cela.albany.edu

Stullich, S., (2000, December). *What the research says about paraprofessionals.* Paper presented at the National Forum on Title I Paraprofessionals. U.S. Department of Education, Washington, DC.

Swanson, J. M. (1993). Effect of stimulant medication on children with attention deficit disorder: A review of reviews. *Exceptional Children, 60,* 154–162.

Taylor, B. M., Frye, B. J., & Maruyama, G. M. (1990). Time spent reading and reading growth. *American Educational Research Journal, 27*(2), 351–362.

Taylor, B. M., Pearson, P. D., Clark, K., & Walpole, S. (2000). Effective schools and accomplished teachers: Lessons about primary grade reading instruction in low-income schools. *Elementary School Journal, 101,* 121–165.

Taylor, B. M., Pearson, P. D., Peterson, D. S., & Rodriguez, M. C. (2003). Reading growth in high-poverty classrooms: The influences of teacher practices that encourage cognitive engagement in literacy learning. *Elementary School Journal, 104*(1), 4–28.

Taylor, B. M., Pearson, P. D., Peterson, D. S., & Rodriguez, M. C. (2005). The CIERA School Change Framework: An evidence-based approach to professional development and school reading improvement. *Reading Research Quarterly, 40*(1), 40–69.

Taylor, D., & Dorsey-Gaines, C. (1998). *Growing up literate: Learning from inner-city families.* Portsmouth, NH: Heinemann.

Tierney, R. J., & Shanahan, T. (1991). Research on the reading–writing relationship: Interactions, transactions, and outcomes. In R. Barr, M. L. Kamil, P. B. Mosenthal, & P. D. Pearson (Eds.), *Handbook of reading research* (Vol. 2, pp. 246–280). New York: Longman.

Timar, T. (1994). Federal education policy and practice: Building organizational capacity through Chapter 1. *Educational Evaluation and Policy Analysis, 16,* 51–66.

Tivnan, T., & Hemphill, L. (2005). Comparing four literacy reform models in high-poverty schools: Patterns of first-grade achievement. *Elementary School Journal, 105*(5), 419–441.

Toll, C. A. (2005). *The literacy coach's survival guide: Essential questions and practical answers.* Newark, DE: International Reading Association.

Valencia, S. W., Place, N. A., Martin, S. D., & Grossman, P. L. (in press). Curriculum materials for elementary reading: Shackles and scaffolds for beginning teachers. *Elementary School Journal.*

Valencia, S. W., & Wixson, K. K. (2001). Inside English/language arts standards: What's in a grade? *Reading Research Quarterly, 36*(2), 202–211.

Vandegrift, J. A., & Greene, A. L. (1992). Rethinking parent involvement. *Educational Leadership, 50,* 57–59.

Vasquez, O. A. (1993). A look at language as a resource: Lessons from La Clase Magica. In M. B. Arias & U. Casanova (Eds.), *Bilingual education: Politics, practice, and research.* Chicago: University of Chicago Press.

Veatch, J. (1959). *Individualizing your reading program.* New York: Putnam.

Vellutino, F. R., Sipay, E. R., Small, S. G., Pratt, A., Chen, R., & Denckla, M. B. (1996). Cognitive profiles of difficult-to-remediate and readily remediated poor readers: Early intervention as a vehicle for distinguishing between cognitive and experiential deficits as basic causes of specific reading disability. *Journal of Educational Pychology, 88,* 601–638.

Venezky, R. L. (1998). An alternate perspective on Success for All. In K. K. Wong (Ed.), *Advances in educational policy* (Vol. 4, pp. 145–165). Greenwich, CT: JAI Press.

Walp, T., & Walmsley, S. A. (1995). Scoring well on tests or becoming genuinely literate: Rethinking remediation in a small, rural school. In R. L. Allington & S. A. Walmsley (Eds.), *No quick fix: Rethinking literacy programs in America's elementary schools* (pp. 177–196). New York: Teachers College Press.

Walters, K., & Gunderson, L. (1985). The effects of parent volunteers reading first language (L1) books to ESL students. *Reading Teacher, 39,* 66–69.

Wasik, B. A. (1998). Volunteer tutoring programs in reading: A review. *Reading Research Quarterly, 33,* 266–293.

Weber, R. (1991). Linguistic diversity and reading in American society. In R. Barr, M. L. Kamil, P. B. Mosenthal, & P. D. Pearson (Eds.), *Handbook of reading research* (Vol. 2, pp. 97–119). New York: Longman.

Whalen, C. K., & Henker, B. (1992). Social impact of stimulant treatment for hyperactive children. In S. E. Shaywitz & B. A. Shaywitz (Eds.), *Attention deficit disorder comes of age.* Austin, TX: Pro-Ed Publications.

Wheelock, A. (1992). *Crossing tracks: How untracking can save America's schools.* New York: New Press.

White, T. G. (2005). Effects of systematic and strategic analogy-based phonics on grade 2 students' word reading and comprehension. *Reading Research Quarterly, 40*(2), 234–255.

Whitehurst, G. J., & Lonigan, C. J. (2001). Emergent literacy: Development from prereaders to readers. In S. Neuman & D. Dickinson (Eds.), *Handbook of early literacy research* (pp. 11–29). New York: Guilford.

Wigfield, A. (1997). Children's motivations for reading and reading engagement. In J. T. Guthrie & A. Wigfield (Eds.), *Reading engagement: Motivating readers through integrated instruction* (pp. 14–33). Newark, DE: International Reading Association.

Wilhelm, J. D. (2001). *Improving comprehension with think-aloud strategies.* New York: Scholastic.

Will, M. (1986). *Educating students with learning problems: A shared responsibility.* Washington, DC: U.S. Department of Education, Office of Special Education and Rehabilitation Services.

Willis, S. (1993, September). Are letter grades obsolete? *ASCD Update, 35,* 1, 8.

Winfield, L. F. (1991). Lessons from the field: Case studies of evolving schoolwide projects. *Educational Evaluation and Policy Analysis, 13,* 353–362.

Wolf, S. A., Borko, H., Elliott, R. L., McIver, M. C. (2000). "That dog won't hunt": Exemplary school change efforts within Kentucky reform. *American Educational Research Journal, 37,* 349–396.

name index

Photo Credits